THE HARVESTER RENAISSANCE LIBRARY
General Editor: Gāmini Salgādo,
University of Sussex

I:
THE VANITY OF DOGMATIZING:
THE THREE 'VERSIONS'

THE HARVESTER RENAISSANCE LIBRARY
General Editor: Gāmini Salgādo,
University of Sussex

This series is devoted to important texts primarily from the sixteenth and seventeenth centuries, which have been hitherto relatively inaccessible. In addition, some titles will be included which, although available in the secondhand and antiquarian market, are needed in modern, critical editions. Works of imaginative literature as well as those of historical, political and philosophical interest will be included.

A distinctive feature of each volume will be a substantial critical introduction by a scholar intimately acquainted with the work and its background, together with a comprehensive bibliography and note on the provenance of the texts reproduced. Each text will be reproduced by photolithography in its original size and from the fullest and most reliable edition available.

Books from The Harvester Press are produced to quality specifications, being printed on papers free from acid and wood, and supplied in durable library bindings.

The Harvester Renaissance Library: 1

The
Vanity of Dogmatizing:
(The Three 'Versions')

scepsis scientifica and Essay against confidence in philosophy.

by Joseph Glanvill

with a critical introduction
by STEPHEN MEDCALF, University of Sussex

The Harvester Press · Hove · Sussex · 1970

THE HARVESTER PRESS

42 Woodland Drive
Hove Sussex
BN3 6DL
England

'The Vanity of Dogmatizing' first
published in 1661 London
'Scepsis Scientifica' first
published in 1665 London
'Essays on Several Important Subjects
in Philosophy and Religion' first
published in 1676 London

This edition with full texts of 1661, 1665 and
part of 'Essays' 1676 first published in
1970 by The Harvester Press Hove as 'The
Vanity of Dogmatizing: The Three Versions'
'The Harvester Renaissance Library' number 1

Introduction and notes © Stephen Medcalf 1970

Printed in England by Stephen Austin and Sons
Limited Hertford Bound by Hunter & Foulis Ltd
Edinburgh

Design by Richard Moseley The
Restif Press Brighton

Library of Congress Catalog Card Number 78–121122
SBN 901759 90 2

Contents

Acknowledgements

The material of this introduction was partly accumulated while I was doing a research degree at Oxford: I should like to acknowledge the frequent help given me by my tutor, H. V. D. Dyson, and my supervisors, Dame Helen Gardner, Miss Iris Murdoch, and Miss Rosemary Syfret.

I must acknowledge three books whose contribution to my work is far greater than appears in the notes, since a great part of the primary material cited there was conveyed to me through them: Jackson Cope, *Joseph Glanvill, Anglican Apologist*, St. Louis: 1956; George Williamson, *The Senecan Amble*, London: 1951; and R. F. Jones *et al.*, *The Seventeenth Century*, Stanford: 1951. Finally, I should mention Cleanth Brooks and William K. Wimsatt, *Literary Criticism*, New York: 1957, which first drew my attention to the possibilities of studying Glanvill's re-writing of his *The Vanity of Dogmatizing* as a guide to the relation of figurative to non-figurative language.

My thanks—and those of my publishers—are due to those who lent the copies from which the texts have been reproduced: to Merton College, Oxford and its Librarian, Dr. Roger Highfield, and to The London Library and its Librarian, Stanley Gillam.

The following abbreviations have been used: V. for *The Vanity of Dogmatizing;* S. for *Scepsis Scientifica,* and E. for Essay *Against Confidence in Philosophy*.

Note on the text

All three works in this edition have been reproduced in their original size, and the two-colour title-page of *The Vanity of Dogmatizing* has been exactly reproduced. The three separate works have been reproduced from the following copies:

The Vanity of Dogmatizing, from the copy in The London Library (Shelf-mark: 45209) by permission of The Librarian.
Scepsis Scientifica, from the copy at Merton College, Oxford (Shelf-mark: 80. e. 11) by permission of The Librarian.
The Essay *Against Confidence in Philosophy,* from the copy of *Essays on Several Important Subjects in Philosophy and Religion* at Merton College, Oxford (Shelf-mark: A8/18) by permission of The Librarian. This copy belonged to F. H. Bradley.

Two of the works in this edition have previously been re-printed once. *The Vanity of Dogmatizing* was reprinted in facsimile, with a short bibliographical note by Moody E. Prior, New York: Facsimile Text Society, 1931. Series 3, volume 6. *Scepsis Scientifica* was reprinted, re-set, with a lengthy introductory essay on the life and works of Glanvill by John Owen, London: Kegan, Paul, Trench & Co., 1885. The *Essay Against Confidence in Philosophy* has never been reprinted.

References: *Vanity,* Wing G 834. *Scepsis,* Wing G 827. *Essay,* from Wing G 809.

The author

JOSEPH GLANVILL was born at Plymouth in 1636. He was educated at Exeter and Lincoln Colleges, Oxford, and was ordained in the Church of England in 1660. He wrote a number of books on religious and philosophical matters, of which the most famous are *The Vanity of Dogmatizing* (1661), and his empirical defence of the belief in witches, *Sadducismus Triumphatus* (1681). In 1664 he was elected to the Royal Society, of which he was an active member and defender. In 1666 he became Rector of Bath, where he died in 1680.

The editor

STEPHEN MEDCALF was born in Essex in 1936. He was educated at Chigwell School, and Merton College, Oxford, where he took a first in the Honours School of English Language and Literature after taking a second class in Honour Classical Moderations. He was awarded the Matthew Arnold Essay Prize in 1962, and in 1963 he took a B. Litt. for his work on Joseph Glanvill's re-writing of his *The Vanity of Dogmatizing*. During 1962–3 he was a schoolmaster at Malvern College, Worcestershire, since when he has been a Lecturer in English in the School of European Studies at the University of Sussex. He is now at work on a book about the literary criticism of the Bible.

Introduction

The Vanity of Dogmatizing (1661) was Joseph Glanvill's first book, published when he was twenty-five. Its language is rich in metaphor and neologism, its thought is effervescent: he was soon so dissatisfied with these characteristics as to give the book a light but pervasive revision and rename it *Scepsis Scientifica*, in 1665: and so dissatisfied with this in turn as to translate it radically into one of a collection of *Essays on Several important subjects in Philosophy and Religion*, "Against Confidence in Philosophy, and Matters of Speculation" in 1676. The last version, still recognisably the same book in structure and matter, is rendered wholly different by its spare and abstract diction: one can see in it the beginning of a style of thought and language which lasts into our own time, the classic style of English rational empiricism.

Two epochs and two extremes of the human mind overlap in the three books: roughly, the end of the scholastic era with the beginning of the scientific, and a metaphorical and figurative with an abstract non-figurative way of describing the world. (The two pairs do not, of course, necessarily coincide although there are reasons which we shall discuss later for seeing an affinity between them.) Glanvill himself has given us a symbol for the change in his story of the Scholar Gypsy: for it was in the *Vanity* that Matthew Arnold found the story, to him that of the departure of a man

". . . born in days when wits were fresh and clear,
   And life ran gaily as the sparkling Thames;
     Before this strange disease of modern life,
   With its sick hurry, its divided aims,
     Its heads o'ertax'd, its palsied hearts, was rife."

Arnold, to stress the contrast with modern life, tends to picture the scholar as on a vague, never-ending quasi-mystical quest, seeking a fugitive and gracious light and waiting for a spark from heaven, while in Glanvill's version he had a firm and practical aim, to experiment with the gypsies' art of "heightening the *Imagination* to that pitch, as to bind anothers" (V. p. 198). Yet Glanvill's style, overflowing with the marvel and wonder of the enterprise, contrives to shew this aim mingled with something of the magic Arnold recognised in it, the utility and the beauty of science pleasant and undivided.

Perhaps by 1665 Glanvill had heard what is now thought to be the true version of the story: for Francois Mercure van Helmont, who left the University of Leipzig to live with the gypsies, to learn, not as far as we know telepathy, but the language and customs of the gypsies, was inquiring after Glanvill's second book, *Lux Orientalis*, (1662) when he stayed in England in 1670 with Glanvill's preceptor, the Cambridge Platonist Henry More; an earlier connection seems not unlikely (1). At any rate, from *Scepsis Scientifica*, the story was removed. Glanvill would, no doubt, have been surprised, and with some justification, at the suggestion that when he did this he was not only destroying a little allegory of a new Fall of Man, but furthering some "strange disease of modern life" as well. For him, in the words of the *Vanity's* opening sentence, "Our misery is not of yesterday, but as antient as the first Criminal, and the ignorance we are involved in, almost coeval with the humane nature..." But, in spite of the pessimistic scepticism to which he here pretends, the wonder with which his style is imbued, as I have pointed out, makes one feel that he was not afflicted when he wrote the *Vanity* with the sceptical self-consciousness which Arnold diagnoses as our disease: but that it *was* that self-consciousness which led him to remove the story of the Oxford scholar and to make all the revisions of 1665 and 1676. Whatever be the truth about Arnold's diagnosis, it is my contention that we can better understand and conceivably correct the bases of our own thought by studying what happened to Glanvill between the *Vanity* and the *Essay*.

II *The Vanity of Dogmatizing*

Glanvill was born in 1636, the son of a merchant in Plymouth. Appropriately for this social class and place, he was brought up a strict Puritan. "In my first Education", he says, "I was continually instructed into a Religious and fast adherence to every thing that I was taught, and a dread of dissenting in the least Article. This Discipline I underwent in my younger days, and thought very strangely of those that believed any thing different from the Opinions of my Instructors" (2). Under the Commonwealth, in the same year, 1652, as John Locke went up to Christ Church and Thomas Traherne to Brasenose, he went up to Exeter College, to an Oxford whose enfranchising atmosphere Traherne describes: "Having been at the University, and received there the taste and tincture of another education, I saw that there were things in this world of which I never dreamed; glorious secrets, and glorious persons past imagination. There I saw that Logic, Ethics, Physics, Metaphysics, Geometry, Astronomy, Poesy, Medicine, Grammar, Music, Rhetoric, all kinds of Arts, Trades, and Mechanisms that adorned the world pertained to felicity; at least there I saw those things, which afterwards I knew to pertain unto it; and was delighted in it" (3).

The effect on Glanvill seems to have been primarily that he made the transition which has been familiar since in the Church of England, from fundamentalist to Broad Churchman: but he was also caught by a feeling for science not unlike Traherne's. Exeter College itself was at this time severely Puritan: and Glanvill lamented later, according to Anthony à Wood "that his friends did not first send him to Cambridge because, as he used to say, that new philosophy and the art of philosophising were there more than here in Oxon" (4). But neo-Platonism was certainly studied at this time in Oxford (as Traherne's lecture-notes show) and, though Glanvill is not known to have attended it, the Invisible College, forerunner of the Royal Society, was meeting regularly at Wadham. Somehow, either at Exeter or at Lincoln College, whither he migrated in 1656, or perhaps during a briefer time in London (he was for six months in 1658–9 chaplain there to Francis Rous, Provost of Eton and a Puritan of mystical tendency), Glanvill became an admirer of many new thinkers—of Pierre Charron (1541–1603) who united Greek scepticism about all knowledge with the theology of the negative way, of Francis Bacon (1561–1626), of Petrus Gassendi (1592–1655), the Frenchman who, beginning as a strong sceptic, later developed a kind of empiricist mitigated scepticism, of Descartes (1596–1650), of Henry More (1614–1687), of Sir Kenelm Digby (1603–1665), the scientist and magician, of John Wilkins (1614–1672), leader of the Invisible College, and of Sir Thomas Browne (1605–1682): writers making in Glanvill's interpretation of them, for a combination of scepticism and intoxication with the mystical, and all liberally drawn upon in the *Vanity,* with ebulliently generous acknowledgement (except for Wilkins, from whose *Discovery of a World in the Moone,* of 1638, probably come such matters as Glanvill's observations on there being more than one centre of gravity in the universe). In the Epistle Dedicatory of the *Vanity,* written from "*Cecill house in the Strand*" on March 1, 1660/1, he explains to the "Reverend my ever honored FRIEND, Mr. Joseph MYNARD, B.D." (apparently Joseph Maynard, like Glanvill a Devon man, Fellow and later Rector of Exeter) that the book is "a fortuitous, undesigned abortive", (Sig.A3ᵛ) and originated as a preface castigating Enthusiasm and vindicating Reason in matters of religion. The preface grew beyond all bounds, while the book itself—on the Soul's Immortality—was rendered unnecessary by the publication in April, 1659, of More's *The Immortality of the Soul.* The first draft of the *Vanity* must then date either from Glanvill's six months in London with Rous or from the earlier period at Lincoln. It was evidently the outgrowth of Glanvill's turning away, during the last years of the Commonwealth, from Puritanism towards a Platonist rationalism. His scepticism was thus a reaction from Puritanism in origin, although it had become a positive and total attitude to the universe.

The book is not, however, intellectually consistent. The pessimistic scepticism of the opening, describing a miserable ignorance consequent upon the Fall, "the curse of the Serpent is fallen upon *degenerated humanity*, that it should go on its belly, and lick the dust", (p. 12) is continually being superseded by the joyful wonder of "How are the Glories of the Field spun, and by what Pencil are they limn'd in their unaffected bravery?": (p. 44) and both the sad and the joyful scepticisms are contradicted by an awestruck admiration for the advances of seventeenth-century science "The last Ages have shewn us, what *Antiquity* never saw; no, not in a *Dream*" (p. 188). This kind of inconsistency is however native to the tradition of Renaissance scepticism on which Glanvill drew—we can find it in Erasmus, Montaigne, Charron, and Sir Thomas Browne alike: it derives perhaps from the combination of Greek philosophical scepticism with Christian humility before God. Glanvill is scarcely to be blamed for it: rather praised for the particular balance which he derives from his inconsistency, a balance of constantly hopeful inquiry and modest confession of incapacity, "that discreet modest aequipoize of Judgement, that becomes the sons of *Adam*" (p. 223). This poise we can very readily relate both to the mood of charity to the minds of other men and worship in face of the universe which he learnt from Browne, and to the enthusiasm for experimental and speculative science which he perhaps contributed himself. The influence of "ingenious Dr *Browne*" (p. 204) in style and temper is so pervasive in the *Vanity* that every page will offer examples. It is of course more difficult to shew that Glanvill learnt from nobody the trick of at once praising the scientific method for carrying us out of ignorance, and denying the conclusions of science themselves any claim to final truth.

Nevertheless, in spite of the (appropriate) difficulty of demonstration, there may be some originality in the appearance in a context imbued with admiration for the New Philosophy of the list of necessary deficiencies in science, which can be found under headings in the table of Contents, chapters XX–XXII: (1) We cannot know any thing to be the cause of another, but from its attending it; and this Way is not infallible . . . (2) There's no .demonstration but where the contrary is impossible. We can scarce conclude so of anything . . . (3) We cannot know any thing in Nature. without the knowledge of the first springs of natural motion, and these we are ignorant of . . . (4) Because of the mutual dependence and concatenation of Causes, we cannot know any one without knowing all . . . (5) All our Science comes in at our senses, their infallibility inquired into . . . (Sigs. S8r v).

The Greek Sceptic Sextus Empiricus provides in principle the critique of causation: "since aetiology as a whole deals with the non-apparent, it is unconfirmed by any agreed evidence derived from appearances" (5). But he was not a devotee, as Glanvill was, of a system of enquiry built up on the ascertaining of natural causation. Conversely, Francis Bacon and Thomas Browne, both acquainted with the new science, provide precedents in their critique of idols and discovery of vulgar errors, for looking at the causes of human ignorance: but their attacks are general, directed at an ancient frailty rather than at new science.

Glanvill may, however, have learnt something from Gassendi, who propounds a moderate scepticism in which empirical investigation interpreted by an atomic theory "accounts for our experience of sense-qualities, but does not tell us anything about the nature of things-in-themselves, except how they appear in relation to us" (6). Boyle was developing a similar position at the same time as Glanvill: he says in "A Proemial Essay . . . with some Considerations touching EXPERIMENTAL ESSAYS in general . . .", published in the same month as the *Vanity,* March 1661, ". . . I wish . . . that men, in the first place, would forbear to establish any theory, till they have consulted with (though not a fully competent number of experiments, such as may afford them all the phenomena to be explicated by that theory, yet) a considerable number of experiments, in proportion to the theory to be erected on them. And, in the next place, I would have such kind of superstructures looked upon only as temporary ones . . ." (7).

In 1673 again (after a period during which he and Glanvill corresponded) he said in his *Excellence of Theology* "That physical certainty which is pretended for the truths demonstrated by naturalists, is, even where it is rightfully claimed, but an inferior kind or degree of certainty, as moral certainty, also is . . ." (8).

On correspondence with the views of Locke in this area, I shall speak when we come to deal with the *Scepsis Scientifica*.

There is a possibility that in the following century, when the *Vanity* was still read (for Johnson at least admired it) (9), Hume may have learnt something from Glanvill's critique of causation. There is, indeed, nothing in Glanvill (who says merely that any particular cause is uncertain because we must deduce it from a concomitant) like Hume's reduction of the very notion of cause to "an object, followed by another, and where all the objects similar to the first are followed by objects similar to the second" (10). But some hint may have passed from one to the other.

The merits of the book were well summed up by Dr John Worthington, in a letter to Samuel Hartlib written a month after publication:

> "He is a young man, and abating some juvenile heat, there are good matters in his book. As one said of the parts of pregnant young men, we may guess what the wine will be; and it will taste better when broach'd some years hence" (11).

The two serious faults in the book perhaps arise from this "juvenile heat": the rather tiresome attack on Aristotelianism, a philosophy whose very terms Glanvill was simply not interested in understanding, and the astonishing ignorance of the real teaching of his most praised idol, Descartes. The Descartes Glanvill admires is the amateur natural philosopher of the vortices to whose work he had probably been introduced by Henry More. Of the originator of a scepticism which would lead to an indubitable truth from which a valid system of certainties might be again built up, he seems ignorant. Nor would this thirst for a certainty smacking of dogmatism have been congenial to him.

Indeed, in 1663, an English Roman Catholic called Thomas

White, in a Latin attack on the *Vanity, Sciri, sive sceptices et scepticorum a iure disputationis exclusio,* translated in 1665 as *Exclusion of Scepticks from all Title to Dispute,* pointed this out: "Sure I am, none more largely pretends Demonstration, than Des Cartes; so that, nothing is more unseemly than for his adorers to profess Scepticism" (12). It is presumably significant that the passages in praise of Descartes are somewhat toned down in the *Scepsis,* and that, as Jackson Cope points out: "In the entire remainder of Glanvill's work there are fewer references to Descartes and his philosophy, and those less ecstatic, than in this first book" (13).

These two faults, however, were natural enough to an enthusiastic young man all ardent for the new science in 1660, when Scholasticism was still a great enemy to be defeated, and Descartes the figurehead of novelty. They do not seriously mar the *Vanity.* Even Thomas White, an Aristotelian who claims that much certain knowledge can be obtained in the things mysterious to Glanvill by syllogistic reasoning, judges Glanvill, as Worthington had, gently. He says that he "with a great deal of wit and an unfordable stream of eloquence (which will ripen with his years) prosecutes what he . . . takes for a truth" (14).

III *Scepsis Scientifica* and John Locke

It was presumably the need to answer Thomas White which suggested to Glanvill the idea of reissuing the *Vanity* bound up with his reply *Scire/i tuum nihil est:* or, *The Author's Defense of the Vanity of Dogmatizing* and *A Letter to a Friend concerning Aristotle.* There was some delay in the publication caused by a violent fever which, as Henry More wrote to Lady Conway in late 1663, brought Glanvill "to the very brink of his hope of enlargement out of this earthly prison into the more open world of spirits" (15).

However, on 18 October 1664, the book was given its imprimatur. In it, *The Vanity of Dogmatizing* had become *Scepsis Scientifica;* and Glanvill in his prefatory *Address to the Royal Society* explains why. He had grown discontented with his youthful taste for "the *musick* and curiosity of *fine Metaphors* and *dancing periods*" and preferred *"manly sense*, flowing in a *natural* and *unaffected Eloquence"* (Sig. C4r). As he was now dedicating the book to the Royal Society, he was bound to say this, for this youthful style "possibly is not so suitable to the graver *Geniusses*, who have out-grown all *gayeties* of *style* and *youthful relishes"* (Sig.A2v): particularly as there can be little doubt that he hoped, having sent them the book, to be elected to the Society. And in fact, at the Royal Society meeting of 7 December 1664, "The Lord Brereton presented a book written by Joseph Glanvill, M.A., intitled *Scepsis Scientifica* dedicated to the Royal Society; the dedication of which was read. Mr. Glanvill, the author, was proposed candidate by Lord Brereton" (16).

The revision which Glanvill desired, he claims that he "was grown too *cold"* to care for doing: and underlines this by saying that the faults of the book might be more easily forgiven if it were left in the state given it by "an immaturity of *Age* and *Judgment"* (Sigs.(4r & v)).

Yet in fact the book is, though not radically, at least very thoroughly revised, both in style and matter. Very few pages are left completely unchanged, although the changes are not such as to justify detailed discussion. As I have already said, the eulogies of Descartes are a little toned down and the enthusiasm for Kenelm Digby tempered. Thus the eulogy on the pair of them, pp. 33—4 of the *Vanity,* is omitted, and Kenelm Digby's "sympathetic powder" is "with circumstances of good evidence asserted by" him (S.p. 125) rather than "for matter of fact put out of doubt" (V.p. 207). But some fantastic stories not asserted by anyone as eminent as Digby are simply omitted: Glanvill still accepts the idea of "sympathised" hands, but removes the story of how such a hand decayed when the owner of the hand to which it had been "sympathised" died (V.pp. 205—6). The whole story of the Scholar Gypsy is lost: and the long account of Adam's faculties at the beginning of the *Vanity* is heavily cut.

But these changes in matter, some of which we shall discuss later, betray an unease about the book's temper without materially altering it. This is likewise the effect of the stylistic alterations, which, though pervasive, are small, the greatest being a reduction of Latin coinages and conceits. Three years later, when Glanvill's *Plus Ultra* was in preparation, Oldenburg, the secretary of the Royal Society, still called him—in a letter to Boyle of 1 October 1667—"A florid writer, one of our royal collegiates, who intends some paralipomena relating to the history of our society" (17). 'Florid' is a usual term for the figurative style of Browne, or (in sermons) of Andrewes, to some extent a counterpart of metaphysical poetry. (Thus R. Parr in a *Life of James Usher* published in 1686 says that Usher in his time at Oxford in 1642 "quite put out of countenance that windy, affected sort of Oratory . . . called *floride* preaching, or strong lines" (18).)

At this stage in his life, then, it would seem that Glanvill had no notion of the possibility of radically changing his style; as in matter, so in style, he was concerned to make his book "graver", but without any strong notion how to do this. The radical revision was not to come until 1676.

Meanwhile, *Scepsis Scientifica* seems to have repeated the success of the *Vanity*. Besides its reception by the Royal Society, there is some ground for thinking it exercised an influence on John Locke. Locke read White's *Sciri* (he notes from it a description of Descartes as "vir acutissimus"—"Cartes . . . Vir. Acutiss. Albius Scept A 186") (19) which may suggest that he was likely to have read also the book it attacks, whether as *Vanity* or *Scepsis.*

There are a number of parallels in both word and matter between the *Scepsis* and Locke's *Essay Concerning Human Understanding* of 1689: most notably in Locke's treatment of the fourth deficiency of science in Glanvill's list, which I have already given. Glanvill observes that "to the *knowledge* of the most contemptible *effect* in nature, 'tis necessary to know the whole *Syntax* of Lawes, and their particular *circumstances,* and *modes* of action" (p. 159). Thus "we can have no true knowledge" in such matters "except

we comprehend all" (p. 156). Elsewhere in the *Scepsis* he says
". . . we cannot profound into the *hidden things* of Nature, nor
see the first springs and wheels that set the rest agoing. We view
but small pieces of the *Universal* Frame, and want *Phaenomena* to
make intire and secure *Hypotheses*" (p. 13). (This passage is
peculiar to the *Scepsis*.) And again:

> "But now our *senses* being scant and limited, and Nature's
> operations subtil and various; they must needs transcend, and
> out-run our Faculties. They are only Nature's grosser wayes
> of working, which are *sensible*; Her finer threads are out of
> the reach of our dull *Percipient*. Yea questionless she hath
> many hidden *Energies,* no wayes imitated in her obvious
> pieces . . ." (p. 51).

With this compare Locke's:

> "For how much the being and operation of particular sub-
> stances in this our globe depends on causes utterly beyond our
> view, is impossible for us to determine. We see and perceive
> some of the motions and grosser operations of things here
> about us; but whence the streams come that keep all these
> curious machines in motion and repair, how conveyed and
> modified, is beyond our notice and apprehension: and the great
> parts and wheels, as I may so say, of this stupendous structure
> of the universe, may, for aught we know, have such a
> connexion and dependence in their influences and operations
> one upon another, that perhaps things in this our mansion
> would put on quite another face, and cease to be what they
> are, if some one of the stars or great bodies incomprehensibly
> remote from us, should cease to be or move as it does" (20).

Another pair of passages parallel in word and thought, this time
on a more general wondering scepticism, are Glanvill's:

> "Nor is the composition of our *own Bodies* the only wonder,
> we are as much nonplust by the most contemptible *Worm*, and
> *Plant,* we tread on. How is a drop of Dew organiz'd into an

Insect? or, a lump of Clay into a more perfect *Animal*? How are the Glories of the Field spun, and by what Pencil are they limn'd in their unaffected bravery?" (S.p. 33).

and Locke's:

"There is not so contemptible a plant or animal, that does not confound the most enlarged understanding. Though the familiar use of things about us take off our wonder, yet it cures not our ignorance, When we come to examine the stones we tread on, or the iron we daily handle, we presently find we know not their make; and can give no reason of the different qualities we find in them" (21).

But the most important resemblance, although it is probably due to a common background rather than direct influence, is in their philosophies of perception. Glanvill asserts that all sensitive perception is derived from motion; that "what we term *heat* and *cold,* and other qualities, are not properly according to *Philosophical* rigour in the Bodies, their Efficients but are rather *Names* expressing our *Passions*": that in errors of the senses, it is not truly the senses that are at fault for "they give us the truth of their Sentiments": only the understanding errs in interpretation (S.pp. 65, 67).

Locke maintains that "simple ideas" (i.e. sensations) proceed from the texture of the object—from its primary qualities: that nevertheless, if taken for what they are, *appearances* answering to the powers that produce them, they cannot be false (22).

It is plain that Glanvill's philosophy is much in harmony with Locke's; in particular on the basic point of believing that there is an external universe which we do not and cannot see as it is—we see only a kind of picture of it, which so far as it consists of sensations is entirely reliable, but is apt to be distorted by the understanding. From this position proceeds Locke's formal doctrine of the distinction between "real essence", what a thing really is and "nominal essence", that which we think a thing is when we name it; and the doctrine which he asserts with a firmness which scarcely seems justified by his arguments that the "real essence" of things is unknowable.

- This is of extreme importance; for by examining the theory of language which Locke develops from the presuppositions shared by him with Glanvill, it is possible to see the grounds and pattern of the language which Glanvill wrote, when he gave *Scepsis Scientifica* the revision which he desired, but did not understand fully enough to carry through at first. Already, when his language and the sensibility embodied in it was baroque, figurative, and old-fashioned, his theory implicitly demanded something quite different.

For from the philosophy shared by Locke and Glanvill the picture theory of language naturally arises. Our ideas picture the universe, and words picture our ideas: the picturing however is not direct, but a matter of correspondence and symbolic relation. "We may not think," says Locke, "(as perhaps usually is done) that they are exactly the images and resemblances of something inherent in the subject; most of those of sensation being in the mind no more the likeness of something existing without us, than the names that stand for them are the likeness of our ideas, which yet upon hearing they are apt to excite in us" (23).

To this notion of a distanced, objectively mysterious world Locke adds the notion that the elements of our experience must be clear and distinct ideas.

> "It is not everyone, nor perhaps any one, who is so careful of his language, as to use no word till he views in his mind the precise determined idea which he resolves to make it the sign of" (24).

> "Names made at pleasure, neither alter the nature of things, nor make us understand them, but as they are signs of and stand for determined ideas" (25).

Now in this second sentence "determined" is the reading of the fourth edition. In the first three editions, Locke had had "clear and distinct" ideas: he explains the substitution in the introduction to the fourth edition: "Clear and distinct ideas are terms, which, though familiar and frequent in men's mouths, I have reason to think everyone who uses, does not perfectly understand" (26). That is, he objects to them as cant terms: in his first three editions he must have been using the phrase as that which Descartes had made a commonplace for the requirements of a true philosophy.

The consequences of this doctrine of the necessity of clear and distinct ideas for the theory of language we must defer for a page or two in order to show that Glanvill shared this additional doctrine in the years when he was completing the transformation of his prose style.

IV: Glanvill's *Essay* and Theories of Language

In 1676 Glanvill (now established as Rector of Bath and Fellow of the Royal Society) revised and published the major part of his life's work in one volume: seven *Essays on Several Important Subjects in Philosophy and Religion.* All the essays, which are described in his preface, are obsessively of the empiricist and religious school of thought associated with the Royal Society.

The revision of *Scepsis Scientifica* is what one would expect from this background. The credulities are removed (at least, what Glanvill's age considered credulities: alas, the prophecy of wireless "That Men should confer at very distant removes by an *extemporary* intercourse . . . without unwarrantable correspondence with the people of the Air" (S.p. 149) has gone, while the curious thrones of Memory on pp. 7−8 and the odd experiment on pp. 11−12 remain).   And an answerable style to this sober empiricism is at last achieved.

For what Glanvill would consider such an answerable style there are three important documents: Bishop Sprat's remarks on the demands placed by the Royal Society on language, in his *History of the Royal Society* of 1667: Glanvill's remarks on Sprat's style in that book, in his own *Plus Ultra* of 1668: and his views on sermon style in *An Essay concerning Preaching* of 1678.

On 7 December 1664, at the same meeting when Glanvill was

admitted a member, the Society voted a "committee for improving the English language" (27): and on 18 January 1665, "it was ordered, that Dr Wilkins meet the first time (at least) with the committee for improving the English tongue; and that particularly he intimate to them the way of proceeding in that committee, according to the way of the council, viz. chiefly to improve the philosophy of the language" (28). Dr Wilkins, whom we have already met as one of the influences on Glanvill's *Vanity,* had been thinking as far back as 1654 of what an ideal language would be like: a line of thought which issued in 1668 in his monumental *An Essay Towards a Real Character and a Philosophical Language.*

Whether this committee ever did anything, we do not know: perhaps no more than inspire Sprat's dictum, that the Society has "been most rigorous in . . . a constant Resolution, to reject all the amplifications, digressions, and swellings of style: to return back to the primitive purity, and shortness, when men deliver'd so many things, almost in an equal number of *words.* They have exacted from all their members, a close, naked, natural way of speaking; positive expressions; clear senses; a native easiness: bringing all things as near the Mathematical plainness, as they can: and preferring the language of Artizans, Countrymen, and Merchants, before that of Wits, or Scholars" (29).

The Society can scarcely have been as rigorous as Sprat claims: or they would never have accepted *Scepsis Scientifica.* Further, it is clear that at least three kinds of ideal are conflated here—a taste for the matter-of-fact language of practical life: a rhetorical model of easiness and informality: and a philosophical ideal. But the presence of the philosophical ideal is most important: for the assumption here that the world consists of a number of clearly separable things which can be described in "positive expressions; clear senses" in a language somewhat on the model of mathematics is reminiscent of Locke's picture theory of language with its "clear and distinct ideas", and adds to this notion the model of mathematics. This model is again reminiscent of Descartes, as we shall see later.

Glanvill's first reaction in 1668 to these ideals, in *Plus Ultra,* is as

we might expect from the preface to *Scepsis Scientifica* attentive
only to the rhetorical side of Sprat's *History*; he says that:

> "the *Style* of that Book hath all the *properties* that can
> recommend any thing to an *ingenious relish*: for 'tis *manly*, and
> yet *plain*;   *natural,* and yet not *careless* . . . Not rendered
> *intricate* by long *Parentheses,* nor *gaudy* by *flanting Metaphors*;
> not *tedious* by *wide fetches* and *circumferences* of *Speech,* nor
> *dark* by too much *curtness* of *Expression*:" (30)

The attention to the needs of the audience, and the stress on
fluency and familiarity seem a world away from Sprat.   And,
I think, there is no ground here for the kind of radical revision we
shall find in 1676.   All the same, working even in this passage we
can see an insistence on clearness of sense and a distrust of metaphor which have a natural place in the theories of Locke and
Descartes which we are approaching.

In contrast, Glanvill's doctrine of preaching ten years later has
a strong and probably conscious Cartesian flavour.   The preacher,
he says, must *"state* the *notion* of the truth, or duty you speak of.
This is exceeding necessary in order to the forming clear and
distinct conceptions in the minds of the hearers; for so much any
Man knows, as he distinctly understands, and no more . . ." (31)

Here again is Locke's cant term that goes back to Descartes.   With
the belief which it expresses goes a distrust of metaphors, except,
Glanvill allows, insofar as they can be applied in the form of
"lively colours" to hold the audience's attention.

Let us now return, first to Descartes and then to Locke, to see
the consequences of the belief in clear and distinct ideas.

V: Locke and Descartes on Language and the World

Let us first outline Descartes' philosophy, insofar as it may concern
us, and as it appears in the *Meditations,* the *Principles,* and the
Discourse on the Method of Rightly Conducting the Reason (32).
Its presuppositions are that we must begin the construction of our
philosophy from clear and distinct ideas (by which he means ideas
which strike the mind with the force of axioms: but I think the

phrase has latent in it a kind of logical atomism, in virtue of his "distinct"); and that we must develop from these in a way following the pattern of mathematics.

His philosophy has the following features of interest to us: that the world consists of "substances" (roughly equivalent here to "things" and "objects", though Descartes uses the word indiscriminately to denote particular objects such as individual *souls* and *bodies*, and general principles such as *mind* and *matter*); by "substances" he understands things which so exist that they need no other thing in order to exist, except God: (33)

that *mind* and *matter* (or, it must follow, mental and corporeal things) are such substances, whose respective essential characteristics arc thought and extension: (34)

that our sensations properly exist only within our minds, though some of them may represent things outside our minds: (35)

that what exists outside our minds, and outside any mind, has only such characteristics as are measurable (36).

Associated with these later points is that reorganisation in our notions of perception typified in the change of meaning of the words "object" and "objective". They connote today "thing as it exists, or would exist, were it not presented to consciousness": but in scholastic usage they connote "thing as presented to consciousness". For before Descartes' time the important point about material objects was felt to be that they could be presented and perceived: and medieval philosophy tends to consider that what we perceive of an object is a real aspect of it, the intelligible or sensible species. But since Descartes' time the general feeling has been that what we see of objects is a mere interpretation of what they really are. This is the central point of the present enquiry and I shall enlarge on it later as it appears in Glanvill's text.

A language, then, fit to describe such a universe will be likely to have some such characteristics as these:

First, it will bear some broad similarity to mathematics. It will, therefore, be clear: each word will be closely defined—either in terms of its referent or its use.

Next, it will have words of great generality and clarity, corresponding to *clear and distinct ideas* (words such as "substance-having-the-characteristic-extension", viz. *matter*). In this again it will resemble mathematics.

Thirdly, it will present a picture of the universe, corresponding to it in logical structure—of a universe conceived as composed of clear and distinct entities, corresponding to clear and distinct ideas.

Fourthly, it will sharply distinguish between mind and matter, and between subjective and objective.

Fifthly, it will avoid metaphor as a way of knowing and describing. For metaphor depends on the assumptions that the universe does not consist of *wholly* distinct entities, and cannot therefore be fully described in positive and distinct terms; that categories can be crossed: that one object may be seen in terms of another object. And these assumptions will not live in the extremely dissociated universe of Descartes.

The general reliability of this list of requirements for such a language is confirmed by an outline given us by Descartes himself in a letter to Mersenne, discussing proposals for a universal language (37).

This project appears to originate with Bacon, who had in mind the Chinese written system: from him stem a number of attempts, which would be created with the interests of merchants very much in mind, and would bear a close relation to the characteristics of existing languages. To this ideal, Descartes added the notion of making the universal language dependent on the "clear and simple ideas" of the true philosophy. His language, therefore, would be regulative, would readjust and correct the whole structure of thought. Similar was that projected by Wilkins and Ward, and actually brought to a conclusion by Wilkins, which we have already mentioned.

We do not need the request of the Royal Society that Wilkins meet with the committee for improving language to advise them, to see that this ideal of regulating language in conformity with some system analogous to mathematics with the aid of "clear and simple ideas" has been, in Sprat's *History,* applied to an existing language, English. That this further underlies Glanvill's stated views on style might be hard to prove: but it is clear that the whole range of Cartesian views on language may be called in to illustrate the views of anyone who like Glanvill accepts the crucial foundations of a picture theory of language working on an experience divisible into clear and distinct logical atoms.

Here once more we return to Locke, who, though as an empiricist he distrusts the idea of a classification of the universe, holds in common with the rationalist Descartes this doctrine, that the universe as we actually perceive and name it is composed of irreducible logical atoms: ideas. Mental activity is confined to arranging these *ideas.*

The consequences of this for theory of language may be seen in four passages:

First, in Locke's total denial of synaesthesia: for his celebrated story of the blind man who said that red must be like the sound of a trumpet is told without any notion that a sighted man might assent to such a similarity and as a reflection on the blind man's conceit (38). Now if simple ideas are so absolutely clear and distinct as this, it is clear that we can in no case describe one simple idea in terms of another, or obtain knowledge of what we have not experienced by means of metaphor.

Secondly, and in consequence, in his refusal to believe that mystical experience may be communicated:

". . . no man inspired by God can by any revelation communicate to others any new simple ideas, which they had not before from sensation or reflection. For whatsoever impressions he himself may have from the immediate hand of God, this revelation, if it be of new simple ideas, cannot be conveyed to another either by words or any other signs. Because, words, by their immediate operation on us, cause no other ideas but of their natural sounds: and it is by the custom of using them for signs, that they excite and revive in our minds latent ideas; but yet only such ideas as were there before. For words, seen or heard, recall to our thoughts those ideas only, which to us they have been wont to be signs of, but cannot introduce any perfectly new, and formerly unknown simple ideas. The same holds in all other signs; which cannot signify to us things of which we have before never had any idea at all" (39).

Thirdly, in a general hostility toward metaphor: it is only emotive and cannot be a way of knowing:

"Since wit and fancy find easier entertainment in the world, than dry truth and real knowledge, figurative speeches and allusion in language will hardly be admitted as an imperfection or abuse of it. I confess in discourses where we seek rather pleasure and delight than information and improvement, such ornaments as are borrowed from them can scarce pass for faults. But yet if we would speak of things as they are, we must allow that all the art of rhetorick, besides order and clearness, all the artificial and figurative application of words eloquence hath invented, are for nothing but to insinuate wrong ideas, move the passions and thereby mislead the judgment, and so indeed are perfect cheats: and therefore however laudable or allowable oratory may render them in harangues and popular addresses, they are certainly, in all discourses that pretend to inform or instruct, wholly to be avoided: and where truth and knowledge are concerned, cannot but be thought a great fault either of the language or person that makes use of them" (40).

Finally, we find these doctrines embodied in a programme—given incidentally during a discourse against syllogisms—of stylistic reform:

"Indeed syllogism is thought to be of necessary use, even to the lovers of truth, to show them the fallacies that are often concealed in florid, witty, or involved discourses. But that this is a mistake will appear, if we consider, that the reason why sometimes men, who sincerely aim at truth, are imposed upon by such loose, and as they are called rhetorical discourses, is, that their fancies being struck with some lively metaphorical representations, they neglect to observe, or do not easily perceive what are the *true* ideas, upon which the inference depends. Now to show such men the weakness of such an argumentation, there needs no more but to strip it of the superfluous ideas, which, blended and confounded with those on which the inference depends seem to show a connexion where there is none; or at least do hinder the discovery of the want of it; and then to lay the naked ideas, on which the force of the argumentation depends, in their due order, in which position the mind taking a view of them, sees what connexion they have, and so is able to judge of the inference without any need of a syllogism at all" (41).

This is precisely the programme which we shall find Glanvill following as he rewrote the *Essay*: stripping of metaphor and accentuation of logical connections in his at first florid and witty discourse. These ideas surely then were at least latent in his mind: and we may say, latent in the minds of all the creators of modern prose.

But the ideas seem to make a scarcely satisfactory picture of the universe. And we may ask what it would be like for Locke's theory not to be true, in order to find out what we lost from our language in the later seventeenth century.

The crux comes with the question: is the first state of knowledge to do with knowing a number of positive, radically distinct ideas (of whatever kind) or is it to do with knowing things as they resemble one another—with consciousness of metaphor? Locke and Descartes answered, that the first stages are "simple ideas" and "all the clear and simple notions that are in us": but Bacon adopted the latter view, with his *philosophia prima*:

"Is not the precept of a musician, to fall from a discord or harsh accord upon a concord or sweet accord, alike true in affection? . . . Is not the delight of the quavering upon a stop in music the same with the playing of light upon the water? . . . Neither are these only similitudes, as men of narrow observation may conceive them to be, but the same footsteps of nature, treading or printing upon several subjects or matters" (42).

Coleridge likewise implicitly takes the latter course in assimilating consciousness, not to Fancy, which is his equivalent of the Lockeian rearrangement of ideas, but to Imagination, which "dissolves, diffuses, dissipates, in order to re-create" (43). If the former opinion is true, relations between the things we know will be purely external, having nothing to do with their essential natures (Locke indeed says that relation is "not contained in the real existence of things, but something extraneous and super-induced") (44). If the latter is the correct view, things will partly or wholly be constituted—will be wholly or partly describable in terms of their relations with other things. The movement of Glanvill's revision is from the latter to the former view.

VI: Glanvill's removal of metaphor

Let me now give some examples of Glanvill's carrying out of Locke's programme. The removal of metaphor is pervasive, so much so as to convert what we may call a "symbolic" picture of the world into a "positive" one. In the *Vanity* he will say "is as dark as Ignorance itself" (p. 30), and in the *Essay* translate this symbol, this metaphor, by the positive "is altogether unintelligible" (p. 6)—giving the common term of the analogy instead of the analogy itself. Or again, in the *Vanity* he will describe an object in a phrase containing two kinds of things in both of which it participates: "aqueous Crystal" (p. 47) or "Aethereal Coal" (p. 78) and translate it into the positive word "Ice" (p. 11) or "Sun" (p. 20) in the *Essay*—destroying in Jackson Cope's phrase "the limitlessness of a resonant universe" (45).

A fuller example, in which we can see the full shift from *Vanity* through *Scepsis* to *Essay*, is:

"It's a great question with some what the *soul* is. And unlesse their phancies may have a sight and sensible palpation of that more clarified subsistence, they will prefer infidelity itself to an unimaginable Idea" (Vp. 18).

For the second sentence, the *Scepsis* has:

". . . most have been deceived in this *Speculation,* by seeking to grasp the *Soul* in their *Imaginations*; to which gross faculty, that purer essence is unpalpable: and we might as well expect to *taste* the *Sunbeams*" (Sp. 14).

There may seem little loss of metaphorical quality, in fact less than a speaker of today's English might imagine, since "grasp" is not cited by the *New English Dictionary* of mental activity until 1680. Nevertheless it seems just to say that one could more easily use "grasp" and be unaware of its not being a literal use, than one could use the double noun "sight and sensible palpation". If this is so, then there is a double loss: firstly, of awareness that the word used is figurative, causing some danger of one's supposing that one is describing this particular mental process literally (which, unless there is a definite act of a definite faculty actually corresponding to this description, will be a fabrication), and secondly, of the full non-figurative corporeal weight of the words "grasp" or "palpation" with their sensuous vividness, with a consequent loss of comprehension of whatever the figure was intended to convey.

In fact, the word is tending to receive what Donald Davie terms a "fiduciary use" (46), a meaning that one takes for granted without weighing or considering it.

The *Essay* carries the process further: ". . . Men would *form* some *Image* of the Soul in their *Fancies*, as they do in the contemplation of *corporeal* Objects" (p. 2).

Here Glanvill would seem to have made a radical attempt at removing the figurative element. But any understanding we have of his new phrase is still figurative. In fact, the thing described here, imagination, it would seem, can only be understood by means of a figure. And there is once more a danger of taking the new phrase literally as if "form some Image" gave a precise and positive description of what happens in imagination. It is not clear that it does give such a description. No such danger was present in using the evident figures of "grasping" and "palpation".

Moreover, the alteration from "have a sight and sensible palpation" and "grasp" to "form some Image" indicates a change from a notion of imagination as apprehensive, as directly grasping at its object, to a notion of imagination quite dissociated from its object and merely forming images of it.

The largest scale removal of a metaphor is of the account of unfallen Adam which begins the *Vanity*: "Our misery is not of yesterday, but as antient as the first Criminal . . ." (p. 1). Thus abruptly Glanvill opens: before demonstrating the thesis of his book—that we are, actually, now, in a state of extreme ignorance— he assumes it, and states the cause of our condition. Browne begins the *Vulgar Errors* and Burton the *Anatomy of Melancholy* in just the same way.

Glanvill goes on to describe in great detail what he presumes "the *Man* was", (p. 2) having the perfections of all animals, and able to perceive all that we now need scientific instruments for, by his natural faculties. In his preface he loses confidence a little, suggesting that his description could be interpreted in terms of the Fall's being an allegory of pre-existence, or literally, or "If all this satisfie not, I begg from the ingenious the favour of this consideration: That some grains must be allowed to a *rhetorical* display, which will not bear the rigour of a *critical severity*. But whether this mine *Hypothesis* stand or fall, my Discourse is not at all concerned" (Sig. B4vf.).

The point of this description lies in its being of an ideal state, a perfect state which is conceived by contrast with the real and imperfect state. The picture of unfallen man was there to provide background and depth for the picture of fallen man: we might say that it renders what would have been a positive picture of man's limitations into an open picture of man's imperfections—instead of "man can do only so much as *this*" we have "man falls short of doing so much as *that*."

When he wrote it, however, he did not think he was writing mere fantasy: he refers with some scorn to "the Hyperbolies that fond poetry bestowes upon its admired objects" (pp. 3–4). The case is, I think, that he wrote what was demanded by the contrast of real and ideal without bothering about the objective truth of his descriptions of the ideal. No doubt while he wrote he fully believed, in a sense, in the truth of his description: but it would be wrong to say he believed in its literal, objective and historical truth. It is a different kind of belief.

He is infected by some literalist doubts in the *Preface*: and these dominate the story in the *Scepsis*. There, he incorporates the material of the *Vanity's* preface, and omits all the detailed speculation about Adam's powers. And the entire opening paragraph, with its glories of unquestioned affirmation, is removed in favour of a piece of tentative logic. The new process is in intention quasi scientific: Glanvill in the *Scepsis* even has in mind an anthropological enquiry into "any hints of conjecture from the present." Again, the *Vanity* had "While man knew no sin, he was ignorant of nothing else, that it imported humanity to know", (p. 11) where the point of the sentence is a piece of metaphysical punning on "knowing sin" and "knowing fact" which would carry conviction only to a mind arguing by analogy. The *Scepsis* has "While Man was *innocent* he was likely *ignorant* of nothing, that imported him to know" (p. 4). The analogising pun has gone, together with the "else" that enforced it: the logical "likely" does the work of arguing instead. Here and throughout a forcible kind of poetry becomes a piece of weak prose logic.

The same effect, with the same myth can be seen in one sentence later in each book:

> "But how the purer Spirit is united to this clod, is a knot too hard for fallen Humanity to unty" (V.p. 3).

> "But how the purer Spirit is united to this *clod*, is a knot too hard for our degraded intellects to unty" (S.p. 15).

The *Vanity* portrayed the present situation mythically, in such a way as to make it open on an ideal past: the *Scepsis* tries to portray it literally and positively. It has abandoned the poignancy and depth together with the reference to an ideal: it gives a closed picture. And yet it has only submerged the ideal reference, submerged it so far that the glory it shed on the sentence has vanished, although "degraded" still depends for its meaning on implicit reference to an ideal state from which we are degraded.

In the *Essay*, Glanvill omits the whole passage on pre-fallen Adam: and the last sentence we quoted now ends "is beyond the reach of any of our faculties". The *Essay* achieves a positive world, of consummated literalism, in which the *Scepsis* failed. But the myth has gone, and with it the depth it imparted to the book, the light and shade of contrast, and the existential contrast of real and ideal. It had had its use in manipulating certain feelings otherwise hard to express, and suggesting an open picture of unlimited resonance. So in fact had all the symbols we describe: the small images which compose the structure of sentences are essentially similar to the great image which governed the book: and to all, I take it, it is possible to give a hypothetical faith in place of a positive credence. (In *Lux Orientalis 1662,* Glanvill's second book, the whole theme of the pre-existence of souls has the same status).

I would suggest, further, that the metaphor in all these sentences expresses a particular transaction between mind and its subject-matter—indeed the very one intimated by one of the metaphors—a "sensible palpation". Toland in his *Christianity not Mysterious* observes that the basic principle of evidence is *"the exact Conformity of our Ideas or Thoughts with their Objects or the Things we think upon."* (47). This precisely expresses the kind of picture-theory of thought and of language which supposes metaphor to be a deceit, rather than a way of handling the material of the universe: and it is perhaps clear now that another name for this picture-theory is the concept of objectivity, which I would define as the belief that we should try to be conscious of objects as they would be if we were not conscious of them.

VII: The Concept of objectivity

For the scholastic, as we have seen, perception consists in the mind's receiving through the agency of the senses, something about its objects which is essentially akin to mind—the sensible and intelligible species. This *species*, says Gilson, "is not one being and the object another, (but) the very object under the mode of species" and therefore "it is not the species of the object that is present in thought, but the object through its species" (48). Objects are thus essentially presentable to man's consciousness.

Consequently, in scholastic usage, *obiectum* means "thing presented to consciousness." But in the mid-seventeenth century it apparently became impossible to believe that objects were so presented. Hobbes is the first person to use the word in English with the sense of dissociated "external object"—in the opening paragraph of *Leviathan*.

"Concerning the Thoughts of man, I will consider them first *Singly* and afterwards in *Trayne*, or dependence upon one another. *Singly*, they are every one a *Representation* or *Appearence*, of some quality, or other Accident of a body without us, which is commonly called an *Object*. Which *Object* worketh on the Eyes, Eares, and other parts of man's body; and by diversity of working, produceth diversity of Appearences" (49).

This use seems to arise from the materialist disquisition on perception in which it is embedded. The adjective "objective" is cited from 1647 in the modern sense. But the use of *subject* in a corresponding sense, as perceiving self rather than thing-in-itself, dates from Rust's *A Discourse of Truth*, written before 1670 (when Rust died) but published by Glanvill in 1677. Rust is concerned to distinguish between truth "in the *Object* and in the *Subject*": it is not clear whether the use of subject in a new sense is simply correlative with Hobbes' insistence that one can only think of objects as existing on their own, and use the word only in that sense, or whether as the *New English Dictionary* suggests it is consequent on Descartes making the mind's consciousness of itself the starting point of enquiry, hence considered as the *subject* of all knowledge.

In either · case, Glanvill perhaps derived from this book his distinction in ΛΟΓΟΥ ΘΡΗΣΚΕΙΑ (1670), repeated in the *Essays*, between "*Reason* in the *Faculty*, which is the *Understanding*: and . . . *Reason* in the *Object*, which consists in those *Principles*, and *Conclusions* by which the *Understanding* is *informed*" (50).

From this source then, he may have learnt the new sense of object, which appears in the *Essay*. For while he always, in theory, despised the scholastic doctrine of "intentional species" it appears to me that in practice it fits his earlier sensibility better, as it certainly does his earlier language.

In *Vanity, Scepsis* and *Essay* alike he has the sentence (with minor modifications): "But how is it, and by what Art doth the soul read that such an image or stroke in matter . . . signifies such an object?" Here the use is indifferently scholastic or modern: *object* means "what the soul is presented with", though the doctrine is unscholastic. But a few sentences later we find in the *Vanity* and *Scepsis*:

> "An infant may hear the sounds, and see the motion of the lips; but hath no conception conveyed by them, not knowing what they are intended to signify. So our souls, though they might have perceived the motions and images themselves by simple sense; yet without some implicit inference it seems inconceivable, how by that means they should apprehend their *Archetypes*" (V.p. 30, S.p. 22).

The *Essay* has:

> ". . . an Infant hears the sounds, and sees the motion of the Lips, but hath no conception convey'd to him, for want of knowing the signification of them: such would be our case, not

withstanding all the motions and impressions made by external things, if the Soul had not some unknown way of learning by them the quality of the Objects" (E.p. 6).

In this second use, it is clear that the sense of *objects* is peculiarly modern—not "objects of the soul's study", but "external things, things in which there subsist qualities which the soul may guess at."

The contrast between the two phrases "apprehend their Archetypes" and "learning by them the quality of the Objects" is moreover very strong, and reminiscent once more of the distinction between "sensible palpation" and "form some Image". It is a little weakened by the *Essay's* also using the earlier phrase in another sentence where it is found inconceivable that the soul should "apprehend what they *signifie* . . ."; but weakened only very little. In contrast to "what they *signifie*" and to "the quality of the Objects", *Archetypes* suggests that what is perceived is the very object, and "apprehend" in the strongly metaphorical early style has a suggestion of "sensible palpation."

Object has been stripped of the connotation that it is something which is in some sense a constituent part of consciousness, and left only with its thinghood: the soul's consciousness can no longer grasp but only form images of things. And throughout Glanvill's rewriting, as a result, the experience of actual personal consciousness of things is excluded as far as possible. A certain sense of the facts is altogether gone.

VIII: Substantial quality in seventeenth century prose

Throughout the *Essay*, it is Glanvill's aim to write something like a scientifically rigorous report: take for example the passage which begins in the *Vanity*:

"If after a decoction of *hearbs* in a Winter night, we expose the liquor to the frigid air; we may observe in the morning under a crust of ice, the perfect appearence both in *figure* and *colour,* of the Plants that were taken from it . . ." (V.pp. 46–7).

In the *Essay* it becomes:

". . . after a decoction of Herbs in a frosty Night, the shape of
the Plants will appear under the Ice in the Morning . . ." (E.p.11).
The first description has all the air of a particular picturesque
incident: the latter of a general law.

- The result is clearly a loss of what we may call substantial
quality: of the vividness and detail which express the particularity,
thisness, inscape of a thing.   It is equally clearly a gain in
generality and objectivity, for which we want to avoid that sense
of grasping a particular fact immediately, as it were with our
hands, given by substantial quality.

This phenomenon is constant through the *Essay*: concrete
images are removed or toned down, picturesque words removed in
favour of immediately relevant ones, particular words give place to
generalised words, and richly connotative words to barer ones.

The whole complex tendency is a common one, if we compare
the early with the late seventeenth century. But there is one way
in which early seventeenth century style seems to contradict the
attribution to it of concreteness: for it is peculiarly rich in abstract
nouns.

However, I should like to suggest that these words which seem to
us abstract had for the younger Glanvill a greater substantial
quality. This is most evidently the case where the abstract noun
slips into a personification, as when the *Vanity* has "which
Philosophy allows not" (p. 37) and "by the blind hits of *Chance*"
(p. 42) where the *Essay* will substitute "and not to be allow'd to
be" (p. 7) and "by chance" (p. 10).

It is evident where the abstract noun facilitates any figure, as "is
as dark, as Ignorance itself" (V.p. 30) for which the *Essay* gives "is
altogether *unintelligible*" (p. 6): or again where an abstract noun
is used with a transitive verb in the *Vanity* ("There's no *Hypothesis*
yet extant can resolve us" (p. 48)) and an intransitive verb in the
Essay ("will still remain a question" (p. 12)).

But for the most part, the cause is a feeling easy to specify in
some cases but often elusive, that the nouns are doing more work

in their sentences than one would expect: "But I shall not stir in the waters, which have been already mudded by so many contentious enquiries" (V.p.˙19), "I shall not stir in the Waters that have been troubled with so much contention" (E.p. 3).

The tendency is common in the early seventeenth century. It is for ˙Glanvill's exemplar Browne that the nouns seem most pervasively to be doing this sort of work: but it appears in the plainest and most straightforward of literary styles (Bacon's for instance).

I believe this substantial quality of abstract nouns is the main reason why early seventeenth century prose seems always ready to step into metaphor, indeed to be radically metaphorical. In Glanvill it has two notable accompaniments which suggest that it is part of a consistent way of looking at the universe.

First, the "universe described in abstractions having substantial quality" is a living universe. The *Essay* removes the life with the substantial quality, putting for example "the effects of Destiny" (p. 24) for the more personal *"placits of destiny"* (V.p. 129): or removing entirely such phrases as "every being incessantly aspires to its own *perfection,* and is restless till it obtains it; as is the trembling *Needle,* till it find its *beloved North*" (V. p. 107).

Secondly, the air of openness which the universe of the *Vanity* wears is partly gained from the substantial quality of *nouns denoting things which limit our experience.*

The simplest case is one where the limit is not of the whole universe, but only the limit of sight—the *Vanity* says that "those that never travail'd without the *Horizon,* that first terminated their Infant aspects, will not be persuaded that the world hath any Country better than their own" (p. 226). The *Essay* will not speak of the limit in this substantial way: only of what the limit contains: "those that have always liv'd at home, and have never seen any other Country, are confidently persuaded that their *own* is the best" (p. 29). The *Vanity* speaks of the limit, and by implication of what lies beyond it: the *Essay* of the country within the limit. The former looks out to other countries, the latter resolutely in on one. The *Vanity* is open, the *Essay* positive.

In a number of passages, there is the same contrast in dealing with the limits of the whole world of facts: "This is a riddle, which must be left to the coming of *Elias*" (V.p. 20) and "beyond the conviction of any thing, but *Dooms-day*" (V.p. 126) where the *Essay* substitutes "is beyond the reach of any of our Faculties" (p. 4) and "beyond possibility of conviction" (p. 24). Again, in terms of space rather than time, compare ". . . if there be a repose naturally obtainable this side the *Stars,* there is no way we can more hopefully seek it in," (V.p. 228) and ". . . if there be any repose obtainable by the Methods of Reason, there is nothing so like to afford it, as *unconcernment* in doubtful Opinions" (E.p.31).

The mind ceases to reach out to the stars, and confines itself to this world: in fact, the advice is the same, only in one expression it has a background of infinity and in the other it is positive.

These features are again associated with substantial quality when we find the *Vanity* speaking of "brave Wits, that have gallantly attempted, and made Essays worthy Immortality", which nevertheless "have submitted to Fate, and are almost lost in Oblivion" (pp. 145–6), and the *Essay* speaking instead of "great Wits . . . that made noble Discoveries" of which "the most considerable . . . have perisht and are forgotten" (p. 28). As a direct result here of the symbolic substantial habit of mind there is in the *Vanity* a terminus in infinity for human action – Immortality – Fate – Oblivion. Actions open on infinity. In the *Essay* they are closed on themselves, positive–noble Discoveries–perisht–are forgotten. Both pictures convey the same facts: both in a sense have the same limits: but in the *Vanity* the limits are substantially conceived, and therefore can be overpassed. In the *Essay* they are no more than implied, they are mere negations, and cannot, so far as is said, be overpassed.

IX: Conclusion

It would seem, then, that Glanvill chose in the end to give a positive picture of his universe, one in which a kind of openness, livingness and substantial quality was not expressed. Substantial quality is the objective correlative for a sense of the facts as if we grasped them with the hands, in fact for "knowing what it is like for a thing to be true": the later Glanvill tends to omit this from his knowing, making "knowing a thing" consist altogether of "knowing what the thing is like" and "knowing that it is true." He tries to exclude the relation of the observer to the observed: that is he tries to write objective prose. He tries to exclude what Whitehead calls "perception in the mode of causal efficacy", which is vague, heavily loaded with emotion, and gives a sense of immediate contact, and accept only "perception in the mode of presentational immediacy", which is precise, emotionally negative and dissociated from feeling of contact (51). In this Glanvill is in a new sense a precursor of Hume: for according to Whitehead, Hume's philosophy isolated perception in the mode of presentational immediacy from perception in the full sense. Glanvill and the other creators of modern prose did for our sensibility what Hume did for philosophy: that is they created a tendency to deny the validity of man's feeling of relatedness directly perceived in the universe, and to reduce what man is conscious of to a series of atomic facts.

For all the losses, they made gains in accuracy and verifiability. It is not clear whether they could have made those gains without the exclusion of certain things from a claim to be described: mystical experience, for example. But a fuller attention to the function of imagery and metaphor in describing might have saved them. Imagery seems to correspond to *knowing what it is like for a thing to be true,* to grasping a thing. Sense perceptions require no imagery to grasp them, or one might say provide their own imagery. Imagery however enables one, by attributing substantial quality, to grasp abstractions, generalisations and acts of the mind. It is the appropriate mode of expression for that consciousness apprehensive and, in the old sense of the word, objective which the young Glanvill had. It provides also a kind of homage and worship for things, which a positive and objective prose cannot.

The world we live in probably both divides into facts, to suit the

positive picture, and goes out into mystery, to suit the figurative.
We have need of all possible styles of prose and poetry to describe
it: but, it seems, we have need to be on our guard in case, trusting
to ordinary language, we are in fact obeying presuppositions
imposed on it by dead philosophers.

It was gain, then, that Glanvill's new style was created: loss that
it destroyed an old style. C. S. Lewis observes that if you wanted
to write a style in which "every sentence would . . . smell of
Heaven" you would have to write a prose like Traherne's: but that
by modern canons you wouldn't be allowed to (52).

There is something in this. Traherne, although his style was pure
of the grotesqueries of Browne and the younger Glanvill, kept all
the advantages they had. He created also a sane and happy world-
picture: and it occurs to me that the origins of what is defective
in both the world-picture of modern science, and the seventeenth
century reform of prose style may be traced in his complaint in
the description, part of which I quoted earlier, about the education
which he shared with Glanvill at Oxford:

> "There I saw into the nature of the Sea, the Heavens, the
> Sun, the Moon and Stars, the Elements, Minerals and
> Vegetables. All which appeared like the King's Daughter, all
> glorious within; and those things which my nurses, and
> parents, should have talked of there were taught unto me.
>
> Nevertheless some things were defective too. There was
> never a tutor that did professly teach Felicity, though that be
> the mistress of all other sciences. Nor did any of us study
> these things but as *aliena,* which we ought to have studied as
> our own enjoyments. We studied to inform our knowledge,
> but knew not for what end we so studied. And for lack of
> aiming at a certain end we erred in the manner" (53).

The VANITY of

Dogmatizing:

OR
Confidence in Opinions.

Manifested in a

DISCOURSE

OF THE

Shortness and *Uncertainty*

OF OUR

KNOWLEDGE,

And its *CAUSES*;

With some

Reflexions on *Peripateticism*;

AND

An *Apology* for *PHILOSOPHY.*

By *JOS.* GLANVILL, M. A.

London, Printed by E. C. for *Henry Eversden* at the *Grey-Hound* in St. *Pauls-Church-Yard.* 1661.

TO THE
Reverend my ever honored
FRIEND,
M^r. *JOSEPH MINARD*, B. D.

SIR,

I Dare not approach so much knowledge, as you are owner of, but in the dreſs of an humble ignorance. The leſſer Sporades muſt vail their light in the preſence of the Monarch Luminary; and to appear before you, with any confidence of Science, were an unpardonable piece of Dogmatizing. Therefore whatever be thought of the Diſcourſe it ſelf, it cannot be cenſur'd in this application; And

A 2   though

though the Pedant may be angry with me, for ſhaking his indear'd Opinions; yet he cannot but approve of this appeal to one, whoſe very name would reduce a Sceptick. If you give your vote againſt Dogmatizing: 'tis time for the opinionative world, to lay down their proud pretenſions: and if ſuch known accompliſhments acknowledge ignorance; confidence will be out of countenance; and the Scioliſt will write on his moſt preſumed certainty; This is alſo vanity. Whatever in this Diſcourſe is leß conſonant to your ſeverer apprehenſions, I begge it may be the object of your charity, and candor. I betake my ſelf to the protection of your ingenuity, from the purſuits of your judicious cenſure. And were there not a benign warmth, as

well

Dedicatory.

well as light *attended you,* 'twere a *bold venture to come within your* **Beams.** *Could I divine wherein you differ from me;* I should be strongly *induced to note that with a* **Deleatur**; *and revenge the presumption, by differing from my present self.* If any thing *seem to you to favour too much of the* Pyrrhonian : *I hope you'l consider, that* Scepticism *is less reprehensible in enquiring years, and no crime in a* Juvenile *exercitation.* But I have *no design against* Science : *my indeavour is to promote it.* Confidence *in uncertainties, is the greatest enemy to what is certain; and were I a* Sceptick , *I'de plead for* Dogmatizing : *For the way to bring men to stick to* nothing , *is confidently to perswade them to swallow all things.*

The Treatise *in your* hands *is a*

A 3   *fortui=*

The Epistle

fortuitous, undesigned abortive; and
an æquivocal effect of a very diverse
intention: For having writ a Dif-
course, which formerly I let you know
of, of the Soul's Immortality: I
defign'd a preface to it, as a Corre-
ctive of Enthufiasm, in a Vindicati-
on of the ufe of Reafon in matters of
Religion: and my confiderations on
that Subject, which I thought a fheet
would have comprifed, grew fo voluminous, as to fill fourteen: which, being
too much for a Preface; I was ad-
vifed to print apart. And therefore reaffuming my Pen, to annex
fome Additional Inlargements to the
beginning; where I had been moft
curt and fparing: my thoughts ran
out into this Difcourfe, which now
beggs your Patronage: while the two
former were remanded into the obfcurity

rity of my private Papers : *The latter
being rendred lefs neceffary by his* Ma-
jefties *much defired , and feafonable
arrival ; and the former by the maturer
undertakings of the accomplifht* Dr. H.
More.

I have no Apologie *to make for my
lapfes, but what would need a new one.
To fay they are the* Errata's *of one that
hath not by fome years reach't his
fourth* Climacterical, *would excufe
indeed the poverty of my judgement, but
criminate the boldnefs of this* Addrefs.
*Nor can I avoid this latter imputation,
but by being more criminal: and to
fhun this refpectful prefumption , I
muft do violence to my gratitude. Since
therefore your* Obligations *have made
my fault, my duty; I hope the fame
goodnefs, that gave birth to my crime,
will remit it. Hereby you'l further in-*

The Epiſtle Dedicatory.

dear your other favours : and make me as much an admirer of your vertues, as I am a debtor to your civilities: which ſince I cannot do them right in an acknowledgement ; I'le acknowledge, by ſignifying that the greatneſs of them hath diſabled me from doing ſo : an impotence, which a little charity will render venial ; ſince it ſpeaks your ſelf its Author. Theſe your indearments will neceſſitate me to a ſelf-contradiction ; and I muſt profeſs my ſelf Dogmatical in this, that I am,

Cecill-houſe in the
Strand, March 1.
1660.

SIR,

Your moſt obliged

And

affectionate Servant

JOS. GLANVILL.

The Preface.

Reader,

TO complain in *print* of the multitude of *Books*, ſeems to me a ſelf-accuſing vanity, whileſt the querulous Reprehenders add to the cauſe of complaint, and tranſgreſs themſelves in that, which they ſeem to wiſh amended. 'Tis true, the births of the Preſs are numerous, nor is there leſs variety in the humors, and phancies of peruſers, and while the number of the one, exceeds not the diverſity of the other, ſome will not think that too much, which others judge ſuperfluous. The genius of
one

one approves, what another difre-
gardeth. And were nothing to pafs
the Prefs, but what were fuited to
the univerfal *gufto*; farewel *Typogra-*
phy. Were I to be Judge, and no o-
ther to be gratified, I think I fhould
filence whole *Libraries* of Authors,
and reduce the world of Books into
a fardle : whereas were another to
fit *Cenfor*, it may be all thofe I had
fpared, would be condemn'd to
darknefs, and obtain no exemption
from thofe ruines, and were all to be
fuppreft, which fome think unworthy light; no more would be left,
then were before *Mofes*, and *Trifme-*
giftus. Therefore, I feek no applaufe
from the difgrace of others, nor will
I Huckfter-like difcredit any mans
ware, to recommend mine own. I
am not angry that there are fo many
Books

Books already, (bating only the *A-nomalies* of impiety and irreligion) nor will I plead the necessity of publishing mine from *feigned* importunities. Those that are taken up with others, are at their liberty to avoid the divertisement of its perusal: and those, to whom 'tis not importunate will not expect an *apology* for its publication. What quarter the world will give it, is above my conjecture. If it be but indifferently dealt with, I am not disappointed. To *print*, is to run the gantlet, and to expose ones self to the tongue-*strapado*. If the more generous *spirits* favour me, let *pedants* do their worst: there's no smart in their censure, yea, their very *approbation* is a scandal.

For the *design* of this Discourse, the

the *Title* speaks it. It is levied againſt
Dogmatizing, and attempts upon a
daring Enemy, *Confidence in Opinions.* The *knowledge* I teach, is *ignorance* : and methinks the Theory of
our own natures, ſhould be enough
to learn it us. We came into the
world, and we know not how ; we
live in't in a ſelf-neſcience , and go
hence again and are as ignorant of
our receſs. We grow, we live, we
move at firſt in a *Microcoſm,* and can
give no more Scientifical account, of
the ſtate of our three *quarters* confinement, then if we had never been
extant in the greater world, but had
expir'd in an *abortion* ; we are in-
larg'd from the priſon of the womb,
we live, we grow, and give being
to our like : we ſee, we hear, and
outward objects affect our other
ſenſes :

senses : we understand, we will, we imagine, and remember : and yet know no more of the immediate reasons of most of these common functions, then those little *Embryo Anchorites* : We breath, we talk, we move, while we are ignorant of the manner of these vital performances. The *Dogmatist* knows not how he moves his finger ; nor by what art or method he turns his tongue in his vocal expressions. New parts are added to our substance, to supply our continual decayings, and as we *dye* we are *born* daily ; nor can we give a certain account, how the aliment is so prepared for nutrition, or by what *mechanism* it is so regularly distributed ; the turning of it into chyle, by the stomachs heat, is a general, and unsatisfying solution.

We

We love, we hate, we joy, we grieve: paſſions annoy us, and our minds are diſturb'd by thoſe corporal *æſtuations*. Nor yet can we tell how theſe ſhould reach our *unbodyed ſelves*, or how the Soul ſhould be affected by theſe heterogeneous agitations. We lay us down, to ſleep away our diurnal cares; night ſhuts up the Senſes windows, the mind contracts into the Brains *centre*. We *live in death*, and lye as in the *grave*. Now we know nothing, nor can our waking thoughts inform us, who is *Morpheus*, and what that leaden *Key*, that locks us up within our ſenſeleſs Cels: There's a difficulty that pincheth, nor will it eaſily be reſolved. The Soul is awake, and ſolicited by external motions, for

some

some of them reach the perceptive region in the moſt ſilent repoſe, and obſcurity of night. What is't then that prevents our Senſations, or if we do perceive, how is't, that we *know it not?* But we Dream, ſee Viſions, converſe with *Chimæra's*, the one half of our lives is a *Romance*, a fiction. We retain a catch of thoſe pretty ſtories, and our awakened imagination ſmiles in the recollection. Nor yet can our moſt ſevere inquiries finde what did ſo abuſe us, or ſhew the nature, and manner of theſe nocturnal illuſions : When we puzzle our ſelves in the diſquiſition, we do but *dream,* and every *Hypotheſis* is a *phancy.* Our moſt induſtrious conceits are but like their object, and as uncertain as thoſe of midnight.

night. Thus when some dayes,
and nights have gone over us,
the stroak of Fate concludes the
number of our pulses; we take
our leave of the *Sun* and *Moon*,
and bid mortality adieu. The
vital flame is extinct, the Soul
retires into another world, and
the body to dwell with dust. Nor
doth the last Scene yield us any
more satisfaction in our *autogra-*
phy; for we are as ignorant how
the soul leaves the light, as how
it first came into it; we know as
little how the union is dissolved,
that is, the chain of the so differing subsistencies, that compound
us, as how it first commenced.
This then is the creature that so
pretends to *knowledge*, and that
makes such a noise, and bustle for
Opinions.

Opinions. The inſtruction of *Del-phos* may ſhame ſuch confidents into modeſty; and till we have learn't that honeſt *adviſo*, though from *hell*, ΓΝΩΘΙ ΣΕΑΥΤΟΝ; *Confidence* is arrogance, and *Dogmatizing* un-reaſonable preſuming. I doubt not but the opinionative reſolver, thinks all theſe eaſie *Knowables*, and the Theories here accounted *Myſteries,* are to him *Revelations.* But let him ſuſpend that concluſion till he hath weigh'd the conſiderations hereof, which the Diſcourſe it ſelf will preſent him with; and if he can untie thoſe knots, he is able to teach all humanity, and will do well to oblige mankinde by his informations.

I had thought here to have ſhut up my *Preface,* being ſenſible of the

B   *tædium*

tædium of long præliminaries. But
left the Ingenious ftumble at my
threfhold, and take offence at the
feemingly difproportionate excefs,
which I afcribe to *Adam's fenfes*:
I'le fubjoyn a word to prevent the
fcruple. Firft then, for thofe that
go the way of the *Allegorie*, and
affert *pre-exiftence*; I'm fecure e-
nough from their diffatisfaction.
For, that the *ætherial Adam* could
eafily fenfe the moft tender touches
upon his *pafsive vehicle*, and fo
had a clear and full perception of
objects, which we fince plung'd
into the groffer *Hyle* are not at all,
or but a little aware of; can be no
doubt in their *Hypothefis*. Nor can
there as great a difference be fuppofed between the fenfes of *eighty*,
and thofe of *twenty*, between the

Opticks

Opticks of the blind *Bat* and perspi-
cacious *Eagle*, as there was between
those pure un-eclipsed Sensations,
and these of our now-embodyed,
muddied *Sensitive.* Now that the
præ-existent Adam could so advan-
tageously form his vehicle, as to receive better information from the
most distant objects, than we by
the most helpful *Telescopes*; will be
no difficult admission to the friends
of the *Allegory.* So that what may
seem a meer *hyperbolical,* and fanci-
ful display to the *Sons* of the *letter*;
to the *Allegorists* will be but a defective representation of literal realities. And I cannot be obnoxious to
their censure, but for my coming
short in the *description.*

But I am like more dangerously
to be beset by them that go the way

of

of the *plain* : and 'twill be thought
fomewhat hard, to verifie my *Hypothefis* of the *literal Adam.* Indeed,
there is difficulty in the *Mechanical
Defence* ; and *Dioptrical* impugnati-
ons are fomewhat formidable. For
unlefs the conftitution of *Adam's*
Organs was diverfe from ours, and
from thofe of his *fallen* felf, it will
to fome feem impoffible , that he
fhould command diftant objects
by natural, as we do by artificial advantages. Since thofe removed bodies of *Sun* and *Stars* (in which I
inftance) could form but minute
angles in *Adam's Retina,* and fuch as
were vaftly different from thofe they
form in ours affifted by a *Telefcope.*
So that granting *Adam's* eye had no
greater *Diametrical* widenefs of the
pupil, no greater diftance from the
Cornea

Cornea to the *Retiformis*, and no more *filaments* of the *Optick nerves* of which the *tunica Retina* is woven, than we: the unmeasurable odds of *Sensitive* perfections which I assign him; will be conceiv'd *mechanically* impossible. These difficulties may seem irresistibly pressing, and incapable of a satisfactory solution.

But I propound it to the consideration of the Ingenious Objectors, whether these supposed *Organical* defects might not have been supplyed in our unfallen *Protoplast* by the vast perfections of his *Animadversive*, and some other advantageous circumstances: So that though it be granted, that an object at the distance of the *Stars* could not form in the eye of *Adam* any *angles*, as

B 3   wide

wide as thofe it forms by the help
of a *Tube*; yet I think my *Hypothe-*
fis may ftand unfhaken. For fup=
pofe two *Eyes* of an equal and like
figure, in the fame diftance from an
object; fo that it forms equal *angles*
in both : It may come to pafs by
other reafons, that one of thefe *Eyes*
fhall fee this *object* bigger then the
other : yea, if the difference of the
reafons on both fides be fo much
greater, one Eye fhall fee *it* clearly,
and the other not at all : For let one
of thefe *eyes* be placed in an *old* body, or in a body deprived quite, or
in a great meafure of thofe *fpirits*
which are allowed the Inftruments
of fight, or of the due egrefs and re=
grefs of them, in their natural cour-
fes and channels; and let the other
have a body of a clean contrary
quality;

quality; or let the *foul* that actuates one of the said *eyes*, be indued with an higher faculty of *Animadversion* (I mean with a greater degree of the *Animadversive* ability) than the *foul* hath, that actuates the other. In either of thefe cafes, the fore-mention'd difformity of *vifion*, will fall out in the fame uniform cafe of *Dioptrical* advantages. For a little *angle* made in the *Eye*, will make as difcernible an impreffion to a *Soul* of a greater *Animadverfive* power, and affifted by more and meeter inftruments of fight; as a greater *angle* can make to a *foul* of a lefs *power*, and deftitute of thofe other Inftruments, which are as neceffary to fight as thofe *Dioptrical* conveniencies. So that grant that the ob

ject

ject set at the same distance made *angles* in the eye of *Adam*, no wider than those it formes in ours; yet that which we discern not, might have been seen by him, having more and better *spirits*, and being endued with a stronger *Animadversive*, according to mine *Hypothesis*. For there is the same proportion between a great *power*, and a little *help*, or a little *Angle*; which is between a small *power*, and a great *help*, or a great *Angle*.

If all this satisfie not, I begg from the ingenious the favour of this consideration: That some grains must be allow'd to a *rhetorical* display, which will not bear the rigour of a *critical severity*. But whether this mine *Hypothesis*

The Preface.

pothesis stand or fall, my Discourse
is not at all concerned. And I
am not so fond of my conjectures, but that I can lay them
down at the feet of a *convictive*
opposition.

To the Learned Author, of the Eloquent and Ingenious *Vanity* of DOGMATIZING.

POets are but *Libe'lers*, I implore no *Muse*;
  Parnaſſian praiſe is an abuſe.
Call up the *Spirit* of *Philoſophy*:
Your worth's diſgrac't by *Poetry*.
Summon *Des-Cartes*, *Plato*, *Socrates*:
Let this great *Triad* ſpeak your praiſe.
Other Encomiaſts that attempt, ſet·forth
Their own defects, and not your worth.
As if a *Chamber-light* ſhould dare eſſay,
To gloſs the beauty of the *day*.
He that thinks fully to deſcribe it, dreams:
You're only ſeen by your own beams.
And only *Eagle-eyes* can bear that *light*;
Your ſtrength and luſtre blindes weak ſight.
Let *pedants* quarrel with th' light that detects
Their belov'd *vanities* and defects.
And let the *Bat*, aſſoon as day's begun,
Commence a ſuit againſt the *Sun*.
Let reprehended *Dogmatizers* ſtamp;
And the ſcorch't *Moore* curſe Heavens lamp:
While nobler ſouls, that underſtand what's writ,
Are debtors to your *ſtrength* and *wit*.

You

You have remov'd the old *Antipathy*
'Tween *Rhetorick*, and *Philosophy* :
And in your Book have cloath'd *Socratick* sense,
In *Demosthenian* Eloquence.
Yo've smooth'd the *Satyr*, and the *wanton* have
Reform'd and made Rhetorick *grave*.
And since your Pen hath thus oblig'd them
'Tis fit they club t'express your worth. (both,

H. Darsy, Esq;

_____

To

_____

To his Worthy Friend
Mr. *JOSEPH GLANVILL*;
Upon the
Vanity of DOGMATIZING
in *Philosophy*, displayed in his
Ingenious Book.

NO *controversies* do me please,
   Unless they do contend for *Peace* :
Nor scarce a demonstration,
But such as *yours* ; which proves, there's *none.*
Doubtful I liv'd, and doubtful die :
Thus ΑΥΤΟΣ gave ΕΦΗ the lye ;
And with his own more aged *Criticks,*
Expung'd his Youthful *Analyticks.*
To make my Shrift, that certain I
Am only of Uncertainty ;
Is no less glorious, then due,
After the *Stagirite* and *You* :
I am absolved, if the Hand
Of great *Apollo*'s Priest may stand.
You have made *Ignorance* a *Boast* :
Pride hath its ancient channel lost ;
Like *Arethusa*, only found
By those, that follow't under ground,
Title your Book, The *Works* of *MAN* ;
The *Index* of the *Vatican* :

Call

Call it Arts *Encyclopædy* ;
The Universal *Panſophy* ;
The State of all the Queſtions,
Since *Peter Lumbard*, ſolv'd at once ;
Ignorance in a learned dreſs,
Which Volumes teach, but not profeſs ;
The Learning which all Ages knew,
Being Epitomiz'd by you.
You teach us *doubting* ; and no more
Do *Libraries* turn'd o're and o're :
Take up the *Folio*, that comes next,
'Twill prove a *Comment* on your *Text* ;
And the *Quotation* would be good,
If *B OD L E Y* in your *Margin* ſtood.

A. Borfet, M. A.

TO

TO HIS
Ingenious Friend the Author, on his
Vanity of DOGMATIZING.

Let vaunting *Knowledge* now strike sail,
  And unto modest *Ign'rance* vail.
Our firmest *Science* (when all's done)
Is nought but bold *Opinion*.
He that hath conquer'd every Art
Th' *Encyclopædy* all by heart;
Is but some few *conjectures* better
Than he that cannot read a *letter*.
If any certainty there be,
'Tis this, that there's no *certaintie*.
Reason's a draught that do's display,
And cast its aspects ev'ry way.
It do's acknowledge no back parts,
'Tis fac'd like *Janus* : and regard's
Opposite sides; what one frowns on,
T'other face sweetly smiles upon.
Then may the *Sciolist* hereby
Correct his *Metoposcopy*.
Let him, e're censure reason, sound
And view her lineaments all round.
And since that *Science* he has none,
Let him with you his *nescience* owne.

Weakness

Weakneſs acknowledged is beſt :
And imperfection when confeſt.
Meek and unboaſting *Ignorance*,
Is but a ſingle impotence :
But when 'tis clad in high profeſſion,
'Tis then a double imperfection.
A ſilly *Ape* ſtruttingly dreſt,
Would but appear the greater *jeſt*.
But your example teacheth us
To become leſs *ridiculous*.
He that would learn, but what you ſhow,
The narrow bounds of what men *know* :
And would but take a ſerious view,
Of the *foundations* with you :
He'd ſcarce his *confidence* adventure,
On bottomes which are ſo unſure.
In diſquiſitions firſt guſt
It would be Shipwrackt, ſunk, and loſt.

P. H.

READER,

That the *Author* may not be accountable for more faults, then his own ; he defires thee to correct, or at leaft to take notice of thefe *Typographical* miftakes : fome of which are lefs confiderable, but others, if unobferv'd, may difturb the fenfe, and render the meaning lefs obvious : thou art therefore requefted to exercife thine ingenuity, in pardoning the *Printer* ; and thy juftice, in doing right to the *Author.*

ERRATA.

Page.	line.	read.	Page.	line.	read.
20.	5.	unite.	60.	6.	makes.
22.	2.	apprehenders.	67.	16.	and our.
24.	9.	fpirits.	70.	12.	of reafon.
25.	7.	fpontaneous.	99.	25.	mad, that.
27.	7.	principles and.	102.	5.	be what.
28.	27.	motions.	103.	26.	of.
29.	21.	conceive it.	113.	9.	coufenage.
41.	10.	confiderations.	129.	20.	the world.
42.	11.	compofition.	140.	1.	the beft.

Books newly publifhed.

A perfect Hiftory of *The Civil Warrs of* Great Brittain *and* Ireland, by an Impartial pen, in *folio.*

Britannia Baconica, or the Natural Rarities of *England,* Scotland *and* Wales, as they are to be found in every Shire, in *octavo.*

The Vanity of
DOGMATIZING;
OR,
Confidence in Opinions.

CHAP. I.

A display of the Perfections of Innocence, with a conjecture at the manner of Adams knowledge, viz. that it was by the large extent of his Senses : founded upon the supposition of the perfection of his Faculties , and induc'd from two Philosophick principles.

Ur misery is not of yesterday, but as antient as the first Criminal, and the ignorance we are involved in, almost coæval with the humane

C   nature ;

nature; not that we were made so by our God, but our selves; we were his creatures, sin and misery were ours. To make way for what follows, we will go to the root of our antient happiness, and now ruines, that we may discover both what the *Man was*, and what the *Sinner is*.

The Eternal Wisdome having made that Creature whose crown it was to be like his Maker, enrich't him with those ennoblements which were worthy him that gave them, and made no less for the benefit of their receiver, then the glory of their Author. And as the Primogenial light, which at first was difused over the face of the unfashion'd Chaos, was afterwards by Divine appointment gathered into the Sun and Stars, and other lucid bodies, which shine with an underived lustre: so those scatter'd perfections which are divided among the several *cantons* of created beings, were as it were constellated and summ'd up in this Epitome of the greater World, *M A N.* His then blisful injoy-

injoyments anticipated the aspires *to be like G O D S* ; being in a condition not to be added to, as much *as in desire* ; and the unlikeness of it to our now miserable, because Apostate, state, makes it almost as impossible to be conceiv'd, as to be regain'd. A condition which was envied by creatures that nature had plac't a sphære above us, and such as differ'd not much from glory, and blessed immortality, but in perpetuity and duration. For since the most despicable and disregarded pieces of decay'd nature, are so curiously wrought, and adorned with such eminent *signatures* of *Divine wisdome*, as speak *it* their Author, and that after a curse brought upon a disorder'd Universe ; what think we was done unto him whom the King delighted to honour ? and what was the portion of Heavens Favorite, when *Omniscience* it self sat in Councel to furnish him with all those accomplishments which his specifick capacity could contain ? which questionless were as much above the Hyperbolies that fond Poetry bestowes

upon

upon its admired objects, as their flatter'd beauties are really below them. The
moſt refined glories of ſubcœleſtial ex-
cellencieſare but more faint reſemblances of theſe. For all the powers and
faculties of this copy of the Divinity, this
meddal of God, were as perfect as beauty and harmony in Idea. The ſoul was
not clogg'd by the inactivity of its
maſſe, as ours; nor hindered in its
actings, by the diſtemperature of indiſpoſed organs. Paſſions kept their place,
as ſervants of the higher powers, and
durſt not arrogate the Throne, as now:
no countermands came hence, to repeal
the decretals of the Regal faculties; that
Batrachomyomachia of one paſſion againſt
an other, and both againſt reaſon, was yet
unborn. Man was never at odds with himſelf, till he was at odds with the commands of his Maker. There was no jarring
or diſharmony in the faculties, till ſin un-
tun'd them. He could no ſooner ſay to
one power *go*, but it *went*, nor to another *do this*, but it *did it*. Even the
ſenſes, the Souls windows, were without

out any ſpot or opacity ; to liken them
to the pureſt Cryſtal, were to debaſe
them by the compariſon ; for their acu-
men and ſtrength depending on the deli-
cacy and apt diſpoſure of the organs and
ſpirits, by which outward motions are
conveyed to the judgement-ſeat of the
Soul : thoſe of Innocence muſt needs
infinitely more tranſcend ours, then the
ſenſes of ſprightful youth doth them of
frozen decrepit age. *Adam* needed no
Spectacles. The acuteneſs of his natural Opticks (if conjecture may have
credit) ſhew'd him much of the Cœleſtial magnificence and bravery without
a *Galilæo's* tube : And 'tis moſt probable that his naked eyes could reach near
as much of the upper World, as we with
all the advantages of art. It may be
'twas as abſurd even in the judgement
of his ſenſes, that the Sun and Stars
ſhould be ſo very much , leſs then this
Globe, as the contrary ſeems in ours ;
and 'tis not unlikely that he had as clear
a perception of the earths motion, as we
think we have of its quieſcence.

C 3

Thus

Thus the accuracy of his knowledge of natural effects, might probably arise from his sensible perception of their causes. What the experiences of many ages will scarce afford us at this distance from perfection, his quicker senses could teach in a moment. And whereas we patch up a piece of Philosophy from a few industriously gather'd, and yet scarce well observ'd or digested experiments, his knowledge was compleatly built, upon the certain, extemporary notice of his comprehensive, unerring faculties. His sight could inform him whether the Loadstone doth attract by Atomical *Effluviums*; which may gain the more credit by the consideration of what some affirm; that by the help of *Microscopes* they have beheld the subtile streams issuing from the beloved *Mine-rall*. It may be he saw the motion of the bloud and spirits through the transparent skin, as we do the workings of those little industrious *Animals* through a hive of glasse. The Mysterious influence of the Moon, and its causality on the seas motion

motion, was no queſtion in his Philoſophy, no more then a Clocks motion is
in ours, where our ſenſes may inform us
of its cauſe. Sympathies and Antipa-
thies were to him no occult qualities. Cauſes are hid in night and obſcurity from us, which were all *Sun* to him.

Now to ſhew the reaſonableneſs of
this Hypotheſis, I'le ſuppoſe what I
think few will deny ; That God adorn'd
that creature which was a tranſcript of
himſelf, with all the perfections its capacity could bear. And that this great
extent of the ſenſes *Horizon* was a
perfection eaſily competible to ſinleſs
humanity, will appear by the improvement of the two following principles.

Firſt, as far as the operation of nature
reacheth, it works by corporeal inſtruments. If the Cœleſtial lights influence our Earth, and advance the
Production of Minerals in their hidden
beds, it is done by material communications. And if there be any virtue
proceeding from the Pole, to direct the
motion of the enamour'd ſteel (however

unobſerv'd

unobferv'd thofe fecret influences may
be) they work not but by corporal Application.

Secondly, Senfe is made by motion,
caus'd by bodily impreffion on the organ,
and continued to the brain, and centre
of perception. Hence it is manifeft that
all bodies are in themfelves fenfible, in
as much as they can imprefs this motion, which is the immediate caufe of
fenfation: And therefore, as in the
former Principle, the moft diftant efficients working by a corporeal caufality, if it be not perceiv'd, the non-per-
ception muft arife from the dulnefs and
imperfection of the faculty, and not any
defect in the object. So then, is it
probable that the tenuous matter the
inftrument of remoter agents, fhould be
able to move, and change the particles of
the indifpofed *clay or fteel*, and yet not
move the ductile eafie fenfes of perfected man? Indeed we perceive not fuch
fubtile infinuations, becaufe their action
is overcome by the ftrokes of ftronger
impreffors, and we are fo limited in our
                                    per-

perceptions, that we can only attend to the more vigorous impulfe: but this is an imperfection incident to our degraded natures, which infinite wifdom eafily prevented in his innocent Mafter-piece: Upon fuch confiderations, to me it appears to be moft reafonable, that the circumference of our *Protoplaft*'s fenfes, fhould be the fame with that of natures activity: unlefs we will derogate from his perfections, and fo reflect a difparagement on him that made us. And I am the more perfwaded of the concinnity of this notion, when I confider the uncouth harfhnefs either of the way of actuall concreated knowledge, or of infant growing faculties; neither of which methinks feem to be much favour'd by our feverer reafons.

Thus I have given a brief account of what might have been fpun into Volumes; a full defcription of fuch perfections cannot be given but by him that hath them; an attainment which we fhall never reach, till mortality be fwallowed up of life. CHAP.

CHAP. II.

*Our Decay and Ruins by the fall,
defcanted on. Of the now Scant-
nefs of our Knowledge: with a
cenfure of the Schoolmen, and Peripatetick Dogmatifts.*

BUt 'tis a miferable thing to have
been happy: and a felf-contracted
wretchednefs, is a double one. Had
felicity alwayes been a ftranger to humanity, our now mifery had been none;
and had not our felves been the Authors
of our ruines, lefs. We might have
been made unhappy, but fince we are
miferable, we chofe it. He that gave
them, might have taken from us our
extern injoyments, but none could have
robb'd us of innocence but our felves.
That we are below the Angels of God,
is

is no mifery, 'tis the lot of our natures ;
but that we have made our felves like
the beafts that perith, is fo with a witnefs, becaufe the fruit of our fin.
While man knew no fin, he was ignorant of nothing elfe, that it imported
humanity to know : but when he had
finned, the fame trangreffion that opened his eyes to fee his own fhame, fhut
them againft moft things elfe, but it, and
his newly purchafed mifery. With the
nakednefs of his body, he faw that of his
foul ; and the blindnefs, and difaray of
his faculties, which his former innocence
was a ftranger to : and that that fhew'd
them him, made them. Whether our
purer intellectuals, or only our impe-
tuous affections, were the prime authors
of the *anomie*, I difpute not : fin is as
latent in its firft caufe, as vifible in its
effects ; and 'tis the mercy of heaven
that hath made it eafier to know the
cure, then the rife of our diftempers.
This is certain, that our *mafculine powers*
are deeply fharers of the confequential
mifchiefs, and though *Eve* were the firft

in

in the difobedience, yet was *Adam* a joint partaker of the curfe. We are not now like the creatures we were made, and have not only loft our *Makers* image, but *our own*: And do not much more tranfcend the creatures, which God and nature have plac't at our feet, then we come fhort of our antient felves; a proud affecting to be like *Gods*, hath made us unlike *Men*.

For whereas our ennobled underftandings could once take the wings of the morning, to vifit the world above us, and had a glorious difplay of the higheft form of created excellencies, it now lies groveling in this lower region, muffled up in mifts, and darknefs: the curfe of the Serpent is fallen upon *degenerated humanity*, that it fhould go on its belly, and lick the duft. And as in the *Cartefian hypothefis*, the Planets fometimes lofe their light, by the fixing of the impurer *fcum*; fo our impaired intellectuals, which were once as pure *light and flame* in regard of their vigour and activity, are now darkned by thofe groffer

fpots

spots, which our difobedience hath contracted. And our now overfhadow'd
fouls (to whofe beauties ftars were
foils) may be exactly emblem'd , by
thofe *crufted globes,* whofe influential
emiffions are intercepted, by the interpofal of the benighting element, while the
purer effence is imprifon'd within the
narrow compaffe of a centre. For thefe
once glorious lights, which did freely fhed
abroad their harmelefs beams, and wanton'd in a larger circumference, are now
pent up in a few firft principles (the
naked effentials of our faculties) within
the ftraight confines of a Prifon. And
whereas knowledge dwelt in our unde-
praved natures, as light in the Sun, in as
great plenty, as purity ; it is now hidden
in us like fparks in a flint , both in fcarci-
ty, and obfcurity.

For confidering the fhortnefs of our
intellectual fight, the deceptibility and
impofitions of our fenfes, the tumultuary
diforders of our paffions, the prejudices
of our infant educations, and infinite fuch
like (of which an after oecafion will befriend

friend us, with a more full and particular
recital) I say, by reason of these, we may
conclude of the science of the most of
men, truly so called, that it may be truss'd
up in the same room with the *Iliads*, yea
it may be all the certainty of those high
pretenders to it, the voluminous Schoolmen, and Peripatetical Dictators, (bating
what they have of first Principles and the
Word of God) may be circumscrib'd
by as small a circle, as the Creed, when
Brachygraphy had confin'd it within the
compass of a penny.   And methinks the
disputes of those assuming confidents, are
like the controversie of those in *Plato*'s
den, who having never seen but the shadow of an horse trajected against a wall,
eagerly contended, whether its *neighing*
proceeded from the appearing Mane, or
Tail, which they saw moving through
the agitation of the substance, playing in
the winde: so these in the darker cels of
their imagin'd principles, violently differ
about the shadowes and *exuviæ* of
beings, words, and notions, while for the
most part they ignore the substantial
realities;

realities ; and like children make *babies,* for their phancies to play with, while their uſeleſs ſubtilties afford but little intertain to the nobler faculties.

But many of the moſt accompliſh't wits of all ages, whoſe modeſty would not allow them to boaſt of more then they were owners of, have reſolv'd their knowledge into *Socrates* his ſumme total, and after all their pains in queſt of Science, have ſat down in a profeſt *neſcience.* It is the ſhallow unimprov'd intellects that are the confident pretenders to certainty; as if contrary to the *Adage, Science had no friend but Ignorance.* And though when they ſpeak in the general of the weakneſs of our underſtandings, and the ſcantneſs of our knowledge, their diſcourſe may even juſtifie *Scepticiſm* it ſelf; yet in their particular opinions are as aſſertive and dogmatical, as if they were *omniſcient.* To ſuch, as a curbe to confidence, and an evidence of humane infirmities even in the nobleſt parts of Man, I ſhall give the following inſtances of our intellectual blindneſs : not that I intend

to

to poze them with thofe common *Ænigma's* of Magnetifm, Fluxes, Refluxes and the like, thefe are refolv'd into a confeft ignorance, and I fhall not perfue them to their old *Afylum* : and yet it may be there is more knowable in thefe, then in leffe acknowledg'd myfteries : But I'le not move beyond our felves, and the moft ordinary and trivial *Phænomena* in nature, in which we fhall finde enough to fhame confidence, and unplume *Dogmatizing*.

CHAP.

Chap. III.

Inſtances of our Ignorance propounded,
(1) of things within our ſelves.
The nature of the Soul, and its ori-
gine, glanc'd at and paſt by;
(1) It's union with the body is un-
conceivable : So (2) is its moving
the body, conſider'd either in the
way of Sir K. Digby, Des-Cartes,
or Dr. H. More, and the Plato-
niſts. (3) The manner of direction
of the Spirits, as unexplicable.

IN the proſecution of our intendment
wee'll firſt inſtance in ſome things in the
generall, which concern the ſoul in this
ſtate of terreſtriall union; and then ſpeak
more particularly to ſome faculties within us, a ſcientificall account of which

D   mortality

mortality is unacquainted with. Secondly we intend to note fóme myfteries ,
which relate to matter and Body. And
Thirdly to fhew the unintelligible intricacy of fome ordinary appearances.

§ 1. It's a great queftion with fome
what the *foul* is. And unleffe their phancies may have a fight and fenfible palpation of that more clarified fubfiftence,
they will prefer infidelity, it felf to an
unimaginable *Idea*. I'le onely mind fuch,
that the foul is feen, as other things, in
the Mirrour of its effects, and attributes :
But, if like children they'll run behind
the glafs to fee its *naked face*, their expectation will meet with nothing but vacuity & emptinefs. And though a pure Intellectual eye may have a fight of it in reflex
difcoveries ; yet, if we affect a grofser
touch, like *Ixio* we fhal embrace a cloud.

§ 2. And it hath been no lefs a trouble to the world to determine whence
it came, then what it is. Whether it
were made by an immediate creation,
or feminall traduction, hath been a Ball
of contention to the moft learned ages :
And

And yet after all the bandying attempts of refolution it is as much a queſtion as ever, and it may be will be ſo till it be concluded by immortality. Some ingenious ones think the difficulties, which are urged by each ſide againſt the other, to be pregnant proofs of the falſhood of both; and ſubſtitute an hypotheſis, which for probability is ſuppoſed to have the advantage of either. But I ſhall not ſtir in the waters, which have been already mudded by ſo many contentious enquiries. The great *St. Auſtin*, and others of the gray heads of reverend Antiquity have been content to ſit down here in a profeſt neutrality: And I'le not induſtiouſly endeavour to urge men to a confeſſion of what they freely acknowledge; but ſhall note difficulties which are not ſo uſually obſerv'd, but as inſoluble as theſe.

§ 3. It is the ſaying of divine *Plato*, that Man is natures *Horizon*; dividing betwixt the upper *Hemiſphere* of immateriall intellects, and this lower of Corporeity: And that we are a Compound

D 2   of

of beings diſtant in extreams, is as clear as Noon. But how the purer Spirit is united to this clod, is a knot too hard for fallen Humanity to unty. What cement ſhould untie heaven and earth, light and darkneſs, natures of ſo divers a make, of ſuch diſagreeing attributes, which have almoſt nothing, but *Being*, in common ; This is a riddle, which muſt be left to the coming of *Elias*. How ſhould a thought be united to a marble-ſtatue, or a ſun-beam to a lump of clay! The freezing of the words in the air in the northern climes, is as conceivable, as this ſtrange union. That this active ſpark, this σύμφυίον πνεῦμα [as the Stoicks call it] ſhould be confined to a Priſon it can ſo eaſily pervade, is of leſs facill apprehenſion, then that the light ſhould be pent up in a box of Cryſtall, and kept from accompanying its ſource to the lower world : And to hang weights on the wings of the winde ſeems far more intelligible.

In the unions, which we underſtand, the extreams are reconciled by
inter-

interceding participations of natures,
which have fomewhat of either. But
Body and Spirit ftand at fuch a diftance
in their effentiall compofitions, that to
fuppofe an uniter of a middle conftitution, that fhould partake of fome of the
qualities of both, is unwarranted by any
of our faculties, yea moft abfonous to
our reafons; fince there is not any the
leaft affinity betwixt length, breadth and
thicknefs, and apprehenfion, judgement
and difcourfe: The former of which
are the moft immediate refults [if not
effentials] of Matter, the latter of
Spirit.

§ 4. Secondly, We can as little give
an account, how the *Soul moves* the
Body. That, that fhould give motion to
an unwieldy bulk, which it felf hath
neither bulk nor motion; is of as difficil
an apprehenfion, as any myftery in nature. For though conceiving it under
fome phancied appearance, and pinning
on it materiall affections, the doubt doth
not fo fenfibly touch us; fince under
fuch conceptions we have the advan-

tage of our senses to befriend us with
parallels, and grofs apprenhenders may
not think it any more strange, then that
a Bullet should be moved by the rarified
fire, or the clouds carryed before the
invisible winds : yet if we defæcate the
notion from materiality, and abstract
quantity, *locality* and all kind of *cor-*
poreity from it, and reprefent it to our
thoughts either under the notion of the
ingenious Sir *K. Digby* as a pure *Mind*
and *Knowledge*, or as the admir'd *Des-*
Cartes expreffes it, *une chofe qui penfe*, as a
thinking fubftance ; it will be as hard
to apprehend, as that an empty wifh
should remove Mountains : a fuppofition. which if realized, would relieve
Sifyphus. Nor yet doth the ingenious hypothefis of the moft excellent *Canta-*
brigian Philofopher, of the fouls being
an *extended penetrable* fubftance, relieve
us ; fince, how that which penetrates all
bodies without the leaft jog or ob-
ftruction, fhould imprefs a motion on
any, is by his own confeffion alike inconceivable. Neither will its moving the
　　　　　　　　　　　　　　Body

Body by a vehicle of Spirits, avail us;
since they are Bodies too, though of a
purer mould. And to credit the unintelligibility both of this union and motion, we need no more then to consider,
that when we would conceiue any thing
which is not obvious to our senses, we
have recourse to our memories the storehouse of past observations: and turning
over the treasure that is there, seek for
something of like kind, which hath formerly come within the notice of our outward or inward senses. So that we cannot conceive any thing, which comes not
within the verge of our senses ; but either by like experiments which we have
made, or at least by some remoter hints
which we receive from them. And
where such are wanting, I cannot apprehend how the thing can. be conceived.
If any think otherwise , let them carefully examine their thoughts : and, if
they finde a determinate intellection of
any Modes of Being, which were never
in the least hinted to them by their exter-
nall or internall senses ; I'le beleeve that
D 4   such

such can realize *Chimæra's*. But now in the cases before us there are not the least footsteps, either of such an Union, or Motion, in the whole circumference of sensible nature : And we cannot apprehend any thing beyond the evidence of our faculties.

§ 5. Thirdly, How the soul *directs* the *Spirits* for the motion of the Body according to the several animal exigents ; is as perplex in the theory, as either of the former. For the *meatus*, or passages, through which those subtill emissaries are conveyed to the respective members , being so almost infinite , and each of them drawn through so many meanders, cross turnings, and divers roades, wherein other spirits are continually a journeying ; it is wonderfull, that they should exactly perform their regular destinations without losing their way in such a wilderness: neither can the wit of man tell how they are directed. For that they are carried by the manuduction of a Rule , is evident from the constant steddyness and regularity of their motion into the parts,

parts, where their supplies are expected : But, what that regulating efficiency
should be, and how managed ; is not
easily determin'd. That it is performed by meer *Mechanisme*, constant experience confutes ; which assureth us,
that our spontaneous motions are under the Imperium of our will. At least
the first determination of the Spirits into such or such passages, is from the
soul, what ever we hold of the after
conveyances ; of which likewise I think,
that all the philosophy in the world cannot make it out to be purely Mechani-
call. But yet though we gain this, that
the soule is the principle of direction,
the difficulty is as formidable as ever. For
unless we allow it a kinde of inward
sight of the Anatomicall frame of its
owne body of every vein, muscle, and
artery ; of the exact site, and position
of them, with their severall windings,
and secret chanels : it is as unconceivable how it should be the Directrix of
such intricate motions, as that a blind
man should manage a game at Chess.

But

But this is a kinde of knowledge, that we are not in the leaft aware of : yea many times we are fo far from an attention to the inward direction of the fpirits, that our employ'd mindes obferve not any method in the outward performance ; even when 'tis manag'd by variety of interchangeable motions, in which a ftea- dy direction is difficult, and a mifcariage eafy. Thus an Artift will play a Leffon on an inftrument without minding a ftroke; and our tongues will run divifions in a tune not miffing a note, even when our thoughts are totally engaged elfe- where : which effects are to be attributed to fome fecret Art of the Soul, which to us is utterly occult, and without the ken of our Intellects.

CHAP.

Chap. IV.

(4) We can give no account of the manner of Senfation: nor (5) of the nature of the Memory. It is confider'd according to the philofo= phy of Des-Cartes, *Sir* K. Digby, Ariftotle *and* Mr. Hobbs *, and all ineffectuall. Some other unexpli- cables mention'd.*

§ 6. But befides thofe abftrufities, that lie more deep, and are of a more myfterious alloy ; we are at a lofs for a fcientificall account even of our Senfes, the moft knowable of our facul- tyes. Our eyes, that fee other things, fee not themfelves : And thofe principials foundations of knowledge are them- felvs unknown. That the foul is the fole Percipient, which alone hath animad- verfion

verſion and ſenſe properly ſo called ,
and that the Body is only the receiver and conveyer of corporeall impreſſions, is as certain , as Philoſophy can
make it. *Ariſtotle* himſelf teacheth ſo
much in that Maxime of his Νοῦς ὁρᾷ, ᾧ
νοῦς ἀκούει. And *Plato* credits this poſition
with his ſuffrage ; affirming , that 'tis
the ſoul that hath life and ſenſe, but the
body neither. But this is ſo largly pro-
ſecuted by that wonder of men , the
Great *Des-Cartes,* and is a Truth that
ſhines ſo clear in the Eyes of all conſidering men ; that to goe about induſtriouſly to prove it, were to light a candle to
ſeek the Sun : we'll therefore ſuppoſe it,
as that which needs not amuſe us ; but
yet, what are the inſtruments of ſenſible
perceptions and particular conveyers of
outward motions to the ſeat of ſenſe, is
difficult : and how the pure mind can
receive information from that , which
is not in the leaſt like it ſelf, and but
little reſembling what it repreſents ; I
think inexplicable. Whether Senſation
be made by corporall emiſſions and materiall εἴδωλα, or by motions impreſt on the
Æthereall

Æthereall matter , and carryed by the continuity thereof to the Common fenfe ; I'le not revive into a Difpute : The ingenuity of the latter hath already given it almoft an abfolute victory over its Rivall. But fuppofe which we will, there are doubts not to be folv'd by either. For how the foule by mutation made in matter a fubftance of another kind, fhould be excited to action ; and how bodily alterations and motions fhould concern it, which is fubject to neither; is a difficulty which confidence may triumph over fooner, then conquer. For body connot act on any thing but by motion ; motion cannot be received but by quantative dimenfion ; the foul is aftranger to fuch grofs fubftantiality, and hath nothing of quantity, but what it is cloathed with by our deceived phancies ; and therefore how can we conceive under a paffive fubjection to material impreffions ? and yet the importunity of pain, and unavoydablenefs of fenfations ftrongly perfwade, that we are fo. Some fay, that the foul indeed is not paffive under the materiall phantafms ; but doth only intuitively

view

view them by the necessity of her Nature,
and so observes other things in these there
representatives. But how is it, and by what
Art doth the soul read that such an image
or stroke in matter [whether that of
her vehicle, or of the Brain, the case is the
same] signifies such an object ? Did we
learn such an Alphabet in our Embryo-
state ? And how comes it to pass, that we
are not aware of any such congenite apprehensions ? We know what we know;
but do we know any more ? That by diversity of motions we should spell out
figures, distances, magnitudes, colours,
things not resembled by them ; we
must attribute to some secret deduction.
But what this deduction should be, or by
what mediums this Knowledge is advanc'd ; is as dark, as Ignorance it self.
One, that hath not the knowledge of Letters, may see the Figures ; but comprehends not the meaning included in them :
An infant may hear the sounds, and see
the motion of the lips ; but hath no conception conveyed by them, not knowing what they are intended to signify. So
our souls, though they might have perceived

ceived the motions and images themselves by simple sense; yet without some implicit inference it seems inconceivable, how by that means they should apprehend their *Archetypes*. Moreover images and motions are in the Brain in a very inconsiderable latitude of space; and yet they represent the greatest magnitudes. The image of an Hemisphere of the upper Globe cannot be of a wider circumference, then a Wall-nut: And how can such petty impressions notifie such vastly expanded objects, but through some kind of Scientifical method, and Geometry in the Principle? without this it is not conceivable how distances should be perceiv'd, but all objects would appear in a cluster, and lie in as narrow a room as their images take up in our scanter *Craniums*. Nor will the Philosophy of the most ingenious *Des-Cartes* help us out: For that striking upon divers filaments of the brain cannot well be supposed to represent their respective distances, except some such kind of Inference be allotted us in our faculties; the concession of which will only steed

us

us as a Refuge for Ignorance, where we shall meet, what we would seem to shun.

§. 7. The *Memory* is a faculty whose nature is as obscure, and hath as much of Riddle in it as any of the former ; It seems to be an Organical Power, because bodily distempers often marr its *Idea's,* and cause a total oblivion : But what instruments the Soul useth in her review of past impressions, is a question which may drive Enquiry to despair. There are four principal *Hypotheses* by which a Resolution hath been attempted. The first that I'le mention, is that of the incomparable *Des-Cartes,* who gives this account : The *Glandula pinealis,* by him made the seat of Common Sense , doth by its motion impel the Spirits into divers parts of the Brain ; till it find those wherein are some tracks of the object we would remember ; which consists in this, *viz.* That the Pores of the Brain, through the which the Spirits before took their course, are more easily opened to the Spirits which demand re-entrance ; so that finding those pores, they make their way

way through them fooner then through others : whence there arifeth a fpecial motion in the *Glandula* , which fignifies this to be the objeƈt we would *remember*. A fecond is, that of the ingenious Sir *K. Digby* , a fummary of which is, That things are referved in the memory by fome corporeal *exuviæ* and material Images; which having impinged on the Common fenfe, rebound thence into fome vacant cells of the Brain , where they keep their ranks and poftures in the fame order that they entred , till they are again ftirr'd 'up; and then they flide through the *Fancy*, as when they were firft prefented. Thefe are the endeavours of thofe two *Grand Sages* , then whom it may be the Sun never faw a more learned pair. And yet as a fad evidence of the infirmities of laps'd humanity : thefe great *Sophi* fail here of their wonted fuccefs in unridling Nature. And I think Favour it felf can fay no more of either *Hypothefis* , then that they are ingenious attempts. Nor do I fpeak this to derogate from the Grandeur of their Wits us'd to Viƈtory : I fhould rather confer

E   what

what I could to the erecting of such Tro-
phies to them, as might eternize their
Memories. And their coming short here,
I think not to be from defect of their personal abilities, but specifick constitution;
and the doubt they leave us in, proceeds
from hence, that they were no more then
men. I shall consider what is mentioned
from them apart, before I come to the
other two: And what I am here about
to produce, is not to argue either of these
Positions of Falseness; but of Uncon-
ceiveableness. In the general, what hath
been urg'd under the former head, stands
in full force against both these, and them
that follow. But to the first; If *Memo-*
ry be made by the *easie motion* of the *Spi-*
rits through the opened *passages,* according to what hath been noted from *Des-*
Cartes; whence have we a distinct Remembrance of such diversity of Objects,
whose Images without doubt pass through
the same *apertures?* And how should
we recall the distances of Bodies which
lye in a line? Or, is it not likely, that the
impell'd Spirits might light upon other
Pores accommodated to their purpose
                                                        through

through the *Motion* of other Bodies through them ? Yea, in such a *pervious* substance as the *Brain*,they might finde an easie either entrance, or *exit*, almost every where ; and therefore to shake every grain of corn through the same holes of a *Sieve* in repeated winnowings, is as easie to be performed as this to be conckived. Besides, it's difficult to apprehend, but that these *avennues* should in a very short time be stopped up by the pressure of other parts of the matter, through its natural *gravity*, or other alterations made in the *Brain* ; And the opening of other *vicine passages* might quickly obliterate any tracks of these ; as the making of one hole in the yeelding *mud*, defaces the print of another near it ; at least the accession of enlargement, which was derived from such transitions, would be as soon lost, as made. But for the *second*, How is it imaginable, that those active *particles*, which have no *cement* to unite them, nothing to keep them in the order they were set, yea, which are ever and anon justled by the occursion of other bodies, whereof there is an infinite store

E 2   in

in this Repofitory, fhould fo orderly keep
their Cells without any alteration of their
fite or pofture, which at firft was allotted
them? And how is it conceivable, but
that carelefly turning over the Idea's of
our mind to recover fomething we would
remember, we fhould put all the other
Images into a diforderly floating, and
fo raife a little *Chaos* of confufion,
where Nature requires the exacteft order. According to this account, I cannot fee, but that our *Memories* would
be more confufed then our Mid-night
compofitions : For is it likely, that the
divided *Atomes* whieh prefented themfelves together, fhould keep the fame
ranks in fuch a variety of tumultuary agitations, as happen in that liquid *Medium*? An heap of Ants on an Hillock will
more eafily be kept to an uniformity
in motion; and the little bodies which
are inceffantly playing up and down the
Air in their carelefs poftures, are as
capable of Regularity as thefe. Much
more m ght be added, but I intend only a
touch.

But a Third way, that hath been attempted,

tempted, is that of *Ariſtotle*, which ſays, that Objects are conſerved in the *Memory* by certain *intentional* Species, Beings, which have nothing of Matter in their Eſ-ſential Conſtitution, but yet have a necef-ſary ſubjective dependence on it, whence they are called *Material*. To this briefly.

Beſides that theſe Species are made a *Medium* between Body and Spirit, and therefore partake of no more of Being, then what the charity of our Imaginati-ons affords them; and that the ſuppoſi-tion infers a creative *energie* in the object their producent, which Philoſophy allows not to Creature-Efficients: I ſay, beſide theſe, it is quite againſt their na-ture to ſubſiſt, but in the preſence and under the actual influence of their cauſe; as being produc'd by an Emanative Cauſality, the Effects whereof dye in the removal of their Origine. But this ſuper-annuated conceit deſerves no more of our remembrance, then it contributes to the apprehenſion of it. And therefore I paſs on to the laſt.

Which is that of Mr. *Hobbs*, that *Memory* is nothing elſe but the knowledge

of *decaying Senfe*, which is made by the *reaction* of one *body* againft another; or, as he expreffes it in his *Humane Nature*, a *Miſſing of Parts in an Objeƈt*. The foundation of this *Principle* [as of many of its fellows] is totally everſt by the moſt ingenious *Commentator* upon *Immaterial Beings*, Dr. *H. More* in his book *Of Immortality*. I ſhall therefore leave that caufe in the hands of that moſt learned undertaker, and only obferve two things to my prefent purpofe. (1). Neither the *Brain*, nor *Spirits*, nor any other material fubſtance within the *Head* can for any confiderable fpace of time conferve *motion*. The former is of fuch a clammy confiſtence, that it can no more retain it then a *Quagmire* : And the *fpirits* for their liquidity are more uncapable then the fluid *Medium*, which is the conveyer of *Sounds*, to perfevere in the continued repetition of *vocal Airs*. And if there were any other fubſtance within us, as fitly temper'd to preferve *motion*, as the Author of the opinion could defire : Yet (2.) which will equally prefs againſt either of the former, this motion
would

would be quickly deadned even to an utter ceſſation, by *counter-motions*; and we ſhould not remember any thing, but till the next impreſſion. Much leſs can this *Principle* give an account, how ſuch an abundance of *motions* ſhould orderly ſucceed one another, as things do in our *memories*: And to remember a *ſong* or *tune*, it will be required, that our Souls be an *Harmony* more then in a *Metaphor*, continually running over in a ſilent whiſper thoſe *Muſical accents* which our retentive faculty is preſerver of. Which could we ſuppoſe in a ſingle Inſtance; yet a multitude of *Muſical Conſonancies* would be as impoſſible, as to play a thouſand tunes on a *Lute* at once. One motion would croſs and deſtroy another; all would be claſhing and diſcord: And the *Muſicians Soul* would be the moſt *diſharmonious*: For according to the tenour of this opinion, our *memories* will be ſtored with infinite variety of divers, yea contrary motions, which muſt needs interfere, thwart, and obſtruct on another: and there would be nothing within us, but *Ataxy* and diſorder.

E 4   § 8.

§. 8. Much more might be added of the difficulties, which occurr touching the *Understanding*, *Phancy*, *Will*, and *Affections*. But the Controverfies here-about, are fo hotly manag'd by the divided *Schools*, and fo voluminoufly every where handled; that it will be thought better to fay nothing of them, then a little. The fole difficulties about the *Will*, its nature, and fequency to the Underftanding, &c. have almoft quite baffled inquiry, and fhewn us little elfe, but that our *Underftandings* are as *blind* as it is. And the grand queftion depending hereon, Πόθεν τὸ κακόν; I think will not be ended, but by the final abolition of its object. They, that would lofe their *Knowledge* here, let them diligently inquire after it. Search will difcover that *Ignorance*, which is as invincible, as its Caufe. Thefe *Controverfies*, like fome *Rivers*, the further they run, the more they are hid. And I think a lefs account is given of them now, then fome *Centuries* paft; when they were a fubject of debate to the pious *Fathers*,

CHAP.

CHAP. V.

How our Bodies are form'd unexplicable. The Plastick signifies nothing; the Formation of Plants, and Animals unknown, in their Principle. Mechanisme solves it not. A new way propounded, which also fails of satisfaction. (2.) No account is yet given how the parts of Matter are united. Some Considerations on Des-Cartes *his Hypothesis, it fails of Solution. (3.) The Question is unanswerable, whether Matter be compounded of Divisibles, or Indivisibles.*

THerefore we'l pass on to the next, the consideration of our *Bodies*, which though we see, and feel, and con-

continually converse with ; yet its constitution, and inward frame is an *America*, a yet undiscovered *Region*. The
saying of the Kingly Prophet, *I am wonderfully made*, may well be understood
of that *admiration*, which is the *Daughter of Ignorance*. And with reverence
it may be applyed, that in *seeing we see,
and understand not*. Three things I'le
subjoyn concerning this *Sensible matter*,
the other part of our composition.

§. 1. That our *bodies* are made according to the most curious *Artifice*,
and orderly contrivance, cannot be denyed even by them, who are least beholden to *Nature*. The elegance of this
composure, sav'd the great *Æsculapius*,
Galen, from a profest *Atheism*. And I cannot think that the branded *Epicurus*, *Lucretius*, and their fellows were in earnest,
when they resolv'd this composition
into a *fortuitous range* of *Atoms*. To
suppose a *Watch*, or any other the
most curious *Automaton* by the blind
hits of *Chance*, to perform diversity of
orderly *motions*, to indicate the *hour*,
day of the *Moneth*, *Tides*, age of the
                                          Moon,

Moon, and the like, with an unparallel'd exactness, and all without the regulation of Art, this were the more pardonable abfurdity. And that this admirable *Engine* of our Bodies, whofe functions are carryed on by fuch a multitude of *parts*, and *motions*, which neither interfere, nor impede one another in their operations ; but by an *harmonious Sympathy* promote the perfection and good of the whole : That this fhould be an undefign'd effect, is an affertion, that is more then *Melancholies Hyperbole*. I fay therefore, that if we do but confider this *Fabrick* with minds unpoffeft of an affected madnefs ; we will eafily grant, that it was fome skilful *Archeus* who delineated thofe comely *proportions*, and hath expreft fuch exactly *Geometrical elegancies* in its compofitions. But what this hidden *Architect* fhould be, and by what *inftruments* and art this frame is erected ; is as *unknown* to us, as our *Embryo*-thoughts. The *Plaftick* faculty is a fine word : But what it is, how it works, and whofe it is, we cannot learn ; no, not by a return into the *Womb* ; neither will the *Platonick*

nick Principles unriddle the doubt.: For
though the Soul be fuppofed to be the
Bodies *Maker*, and the builder of its own
houfe ; yet by what kind of Knowledge,
Method, or Means, is as unknown : and
that we fhould have a *knowledge* which
we know not of, is an affertion, which
fome fay, hath no commiffion from our
Faculties. The Great *Des-Cartes* will
allow it to be no better, then a downright abfurdity. But yet fhould we
fuppofe it, it would be evidence enough
of what we aim at.

Nor is the compofition of our Bodies
the only wonder : we are as much non-
pluft by the moft contemptible *Worm*,
and *Plant*, we tread on. How is a drop
of Dew organiz'd into an Infect, or a
lump of Clay into animal Perfections ?
How are the Glories of the Field fpun,
and by what Pencil are they limn'd in
their unaffected bravery ? By whofe direction is the nutriment fo regularly
diftributed unto the refpective parts, and
how are they kept to their fpecifick
uniformities ? If we attempt Mechanical
folutions, we fhall never give an account,
why

why the Wood-cock doth not fometimes
borrow colours of the Mag-pye, why
the Lilly doth not exchange with the
Dayfie, or why it is not fometime
painted with a blufh of the Rofe? Can
unguided matter keep it felf to fuch
exact conformities, as not in the leaft fpot
to vary from the *fpecies*? That divers
Limners at a diftance without either
copy, or defigne, fhould draw the fame
Picture to an undiftinguifhable exactnefs,
both in form, colour, and features; this
is more conceivable, then that *matter*,
which is fo diverfified both in quantity, quality, motion, fite, and infinite
other circumftances, fhould frame it felf
fo abfolutely according to the Idea of its
kind. And though the fury of that
Apelles, who threw his Pencil in a
defperate rage upon the Picture he had
effayed to draw, once cafually effected
thofe lively reprefentations, which his
Art could not defcribe; yet 'tis not likely,
that one of a thoufand fuch præcipitancies
fhould be crowned with fo an unexpected
an iffue. For though *blind matter* might
reach fome elegancies in individual effects;

fects ; yet fpecifick conformities can be
no *unadvifed* productions, but in greateft
likelyhood, are regulated by the immediate efficiency of fome *knowing* agent :
which whether it be *feminal Forms* ,
according to the *Platonical* Principles, or
what ever elfe we pleafe to fuppofe ;
the manner of its working is to us *unknown* : or if thefe effects are meerly
Mechanical ; yet to learn the method of
fuch operations may be , and hath indeed been ingenioufly attempted ; but I
think cannot be performed to the fatisfaction of feverer examination.

That all bodies both *Animal, Vegetable,* and *Inanimate,* are form'd out of fuch
particles of matter, which by reafon of
their figures , will not cohære or lie
together, but in fuch an order as is neceffary to fuch a fpecifical formation, and
that therein they naturally of themfelves
concurre, and refide, is a pretty conceit,
and there are *experiments* that credit it.
If after a decoction of *hearbs* in a
Winter-night, we expofe the liquor to
the frigid air ; we may obferve in the
morning under a cruft of Ice, the perfect
appearance

appearance both in *figure*, and *colour*, of the *Plants* that were taken from it. But if we break the *aqueous Cryſtal*, thoſe pretty *images* diſ-appear and are preſently diſſolved.

Now theſe *airy Vegetables* are preſumed to have been made, by the reliques of theſe *plantal emiſſions* whoſe avolation was prevented by the *condenſed incloſure*. And therefore playing up and down for a while within their liquid priſon, they at laſt ſettle together in their natural order, and the *Atomes* of each part finding out their proper place, at length reſt in their methodical Situation, till by breaking the *Ice* they are diſturbed, and thoſe counterfeit *compoſitions* are ſcatter'd into their firſt *Indiviſibles*. This *Hypotheſis* may yet ſeem to receive further confirmation, from the artificial *reſurrection* of *Plants* from their *aſhes*, which *Chymiſts* are ſo well acquainted with: And beſides, that *Salt* diſſolved upon fixation returns to its affected *cubes*, the regular figures of *Minerals*, as the *Hexagonal* of *Cryſtal*, the *Hemi-ſphærical* of the *Fairy-ſtone*, the *ſtellar figure*

of

of the ftone *Afteria,* and fuch like, feem
to look with probability upon this way
of formation. And I muft needs fay 'tis
handfomly conjectur'd. But yet what
thofe figures are, that fhould be thus
mechanically adapted, to fall fo unerringly into regular compofitions, is beyond
our faculties to conceive, or determine.
And how thofe *heterogeneous atomes* (for
fuch their figures are fuppofed) fhould by
themfelves hit fo exactly into their proper
refidence in the midft of fuch tumultuary
motions, crofs thwartings, and *arietations*
of other particles, efpecially when for
one way of hitting right, there are
thoufands of miffing ; there's no *Hypothefis* yet extant can refolve us. And yet
had heaven afforded that miracle of men,
the Illuftrious *Des-Cartes* a longer day
on earth, we might have expected
the utmoft of what ingenuity could perform herein : but his immature Fate hath
unhappily difappointed us ; and prevented
the moft defirable Complement of his
not to be equall'd *Philofophy*.

§. 2. (2.) It's no lefs difficult to give
an account, how the *Parts* of the *Matter*
of

of our Bodies are *united* : For though
superficial Enquirers may easily satisfie
themselves by answering, that it is done
by *muscles, nerves,* and other like *strings*
and *ligaments*, which Nature hath de-
stin'd to that office ; yet, if we seek
for an account how the parts of these do
cohere, we shall find the cause to be as
latent, as the effect of easie discovery.
Nothing with any shew of success hath
yet appeared on the Philosophick Stage,
but the opinion of *Des-Cartes* ; that the
Parts of *Matter* are *united* by Rest.
Neither can I conceive, how any thing
can be substituted in its room, more
congruous to reason ; since *Rest* is most
opposite to *Motion*, the immediate cause
of *disunion*. But yet I cannot see, how
this can satisfie, touching the almost *in-
dissolvible coherence* of some bodies, and
the *fragility* and *solubility* of others :
For if the *Union* of the *Parts* consist
only in *Rest* ; it would seem that a bagg of
dust would be of as firm a consistence
as that of *Marble* or *Adamant :* a Bar
of *Iron* will be as easily broken as a *Tobacco-pipe* ; and *Bajazets* Cage had been

F   but

but a forry *Prifon*. The *Ægyptian Py-ramids* would have been fooner loft, then the Names of them that built them ; and as eafily blown away, as thofe *inverft ones* of *fmoke*. If it be pretended for a difference, that the parts of folid bodies are held together by *hooks*, and *angulous* involutions ; I fay, this comes not home : For the *coherence* of the parts of thefe *hooks* [as hath been noted] will be of as difficult a conception, as the former: And we muft either fuppofe an infinite of them holding together on one another ; or at laft come to *parts*, that are *united* by a meer *juxta-pofition :* Yea, could we fuppofe the former , yet the coherence of thefe, would be like the hanging together of an infinite fuch of *Duft :* which *Hypothefis* would fpoil the *Pro-verb*, and *a rope of fand*, fhould be no more a phrafe for *Labour in vain* : For unlefs there be fomething, upon which all the reft may depend for their *cohefion* ; the hanging of one by another, will fignifie no more then the mutual dependence of *caufes* and *effects* in an *infinite Series*, without a *Firft :* the admiffion of which,

Atheifm

Atheiſm would applaud. But yet to do the *Maſter* of *Mechanicks* right; ſomewhat of more validity in the behalf of this *Hypotheſis* may be aſſign'd : Which is, that the cloſeneſs and compactneſs of the *Parts reſting* together, doth much confer to the ſtrength of the *union* : For every thing continues in the condition, wherein it *is*, except ſomething more powerful *alter it* : And therefore the *parts*, that *reſt* cloſe together, muſt continue in the ſame relation to each other, till ſome other *body* by *motion* disjoyn them. Now then, the more *parts* there are pen't together, the more able they will be for *reſiſtence*; and what hath leſs *compactneſs*, and by conſequence fewer *parts*, according to the *laws* of *motion* will not be able to effect any *alteration* in it. According to what is here preſented, what is moſt *denſe*, and leaſt *porous*, will be moſt *coherent*, and leaſt *diſcerpible*. And if this help not, I cannot apprehend what can give an account of the former inſtances. And yet even this is confuted by experience; ſince the moſt *porous, ſpongy bodies* are

oſt-

oft-times the moſt *tough* in conſiſtence.
'Tis eaſier to break a tube of *Glaſs* or
Cryſtal, then of *Elm* or *Aſh* : And yet
as the *parts* of the former are more, ſo
they are more at *reſt* ; ſince the *liquid
juyce*, which is diffuſed through the *parts*
of the *Wood*, is in a continual agitation,
which in *Des-Cartes* his *Philoſophy* is
the cauſe of *fluidity* ; and a proportion'd
humidity conferr's much to *union* [Sir K.
Digby makes it the *Cement* it ſelf] ; a
dry ſtick will be eaſily broken, when *a
green one* will maintain a ſtrong reſiſtence : and yet in the *moiſt* ſubſtance
there is leſs *reſt*, then in what is, *dryer*
and more *fragill*. Much more might
be added : But I'le content my ſelf
with what's mentioned ; and, notwithſtanding what hath been ſaid, I judge
this account of that moſt *miraculous wit*
to be the moſt *ingenuous* and *rational*,
that *hath* or [it may be] *can* be given. I
ſhall not therefore conclude it falſe ;
though I think the emergent *difficulties*,
which are its attendants, *unanſwerable* :
which is proof enough of the weakneſs
of our *now Reaſons* , which are driven

to such straights and puzzles even in things which are most *obvious*, and have so much the advantage of our *faculties*.

§.3. The composition of bodies, whether it be of *Divisibles* or *Indivisibles*, is a question which must be rank'd with the *Indissolvibles* : For though it hath been attempted by the most illustrious *Wits* of all *Philosophick* Ages; yet they have done little else, but shewn their own *divisions* to be almost as *infinite*, as some suppose those of their Subject. And notwithstanding all their shifts, subtilties, newly invented Words and Modes, sly subterfuges, and studyed evasions ; yet the product of all their endeavours, is but as the Birth of the labouring *Mountains*, *Wind* and *Emptiness*. Do what they can ; *Actual Infinite extension every where, Equality of all bodies*, *Impossibility of Motion*, and a world more of the most palpable absurdities will press the assertors of *infinite divisibility*. Neither can it be avoided, but that all *motions* would be *equal* in *velocity*, the *lines* drawn from side to side in a *Pyramid*, may have more parts then the *Basis*, all bodies would be

swal-

ſwallow'd up in a *point* , and endleſs more inconſiſtences, will be as neceſſarily conſequential to the opinion of *Indiviſibles*. But intending only to inſtance in difficulties , which are not ſo much taken notice of ; I ſhall refer the Reader, that would ſee more of this, to *Oviedo*, *Pontius* , *Ariaga* , *Carelton* , and other *Jeſuites* : whoſe management of this ſubject with equal force on either ſide, is a ſtrong preſumption of what we drive at,

Chap. VI.

Difficulties about the Motion of a Wheel, which admit of no Solution.

BEſides the already mention'd difficulties, even the moſt ordinary trivial *occurrents*, if we contemplate them in the *Theory*, will as much puzzle us, as any of the former. Under this head
I'le

I'le add three rhings touching the Motion of a *wheel,* and conclude this.

§. 1. And firſt, if we abſtractly conſider it, it ſeems impoſſible that a *wheel* ſhould *move :* I mean not the *progreſſive,* but that Motion which is meerly on its own *Centre.* And were it not for the information of Experience , it's moſt likely that *Philoſophy* had long ago concluded it *impoſſible :* For let's ſuppoſe the wheel to be divided according to the *Alphabet.* Now in motion there is a change of place, and in the motion of a *wheel* there is a ſucceſſion of one part to another in the ſame place ; ſo that it ſeems unconceivable that *A.* ſhould move until *B.* hath left its place : For *A.* cannot move, but it muſt acquire ſome place or other. It can acquire none but what was *B*'s , which we ſuppoſe to be moſt immediate to it. The ſame ſpace cannot contain them both. And therefore *B.* muſt leave its place , before *A.* can have it ; Yea, and the nature of ſucceſſion requires it. But now *B.* cannot move, but into the place of *C* ; and *C.* muſt be out, before *B.* can come in : ſo

F 4   that

that the motion of *C*. will be pre-required
likewise to the motion of *A*; & so onward
till it comes to *Z*. Upon the same accounts
Z. will not be able to move, till *A*. moves,
being the part next to it: neither will *A*. be
able to move [as hath been shown] till
Z. hath. And so the motion of every part
will be pre-requir'd to it self. Neither
can one evade, by saying, that all the
parts move at once. For (1.) we
cannot conceive in a *succession* but that
something should be first, and that motion should begin somewhere. (2.) If
the parts may all change places with one
another at the same time without any
respect of *priority*, and *posteriority* to each
others *motion* : why then may not a company of *Bullets* closely crowded together
in a *Box*, as well move together by a
like mutual and simultaneous exchange ?
Doubtless the reason of this ineptitude
to motion in this position is, that they
cannot give way one to another, and
motion can no where begin because of
the *plenitude*. The case is just the same
in the instance before us ; and therefore
we need go no further for an evidence
of

of its [*inconceivableneſs*. But yet to give it one touch more according to the *Peripatetick* niceneſs, which ſays, that one part enters in the ſame *inſtant* that the other goes out: I'le add this in brief: In the *inſtant* that *B.* leaves its place, it's in it, or not: If ſo; then *A.* cannot be in it in the ſame *inſtant* without *quantative penetration*. If not; then it cannot be ſaid to leave it in that *inſtant*, but to have left it before. Theſe difficulties, which pinch ſo in this obvious experiment, ſtand in their full force againſt all Motion on the *Hypotheſis* of *abſolute plenitude*. Nor yet have the Defenders hereof need to take notice of them, becauſe they equally preſs a moſt ſenſible Truth. Neither is it fair, that the oppoſite opinion of *interſpers'd vacuities* ſhould be rejected as abſurd upon the account of ſome *inextricable perplexities* which attend it. Therefore let them both have fair play; and which ſoever doth with moſt caſe and congruity ſolve the *Phænomena*, that ſhall have my vote for the moſt *Philoſophick Hypotheſis.*

§. 2.

§. 2. It's a difficulty no less despe-
rate then the former, that the *parts vicine* to the *centre*, which it may be pass not
over the hundredth part of *space* which
those do of the extreme *circumference*,
should describe their *narrower circle*
but in equal time with those other, that
trace so great a *round*. If they move
but in the same degree of *Velocity* ; here
is then an *equality in time* and *motion*,
and yet a vast *inequality* in the *acquired
space*. A thing which seems flatly impossible : For is it conceivable, that of two
bodies setting forth together, and continuing their motion in the same swift-
ness, the one should so far out-go its
fellow, as to move ten mile an hour,
while the other moves but a furlong ?
If so, 'twill be no wonder, that *the race
is not to the swift*, and the *furthest way
about* may well be the *nearest way home*.
There is but one way that can be attempted to untie this knot ; which is, by saying, that the *remoter* and more out-side
parts move more swiftly then the *central* ones. But this likewise is as unconceivable as what it would avoid :
For

For suppose a right *line* drawn from the *centre* to the *circumference*, and it cannot be apprehended, but that the *line* should be inflected, if some parts of it move faster then others. I say if we do abstractedly from experience contemplate it in the *theory*, it is hard to conceive, but that one part moving, while the other rests, or at least moves slower (which is as rest to a swifter motion) should change its distance from it, and the respect, which it had to it; which one would think should cause an incurvation in the *line*.

§. 3. I'le add only this one, which is an experiment that may for ever silence the most daring confidence. Let there be two *wheels* fixt on the same Axel in *Diameter* ten inches a piece. Between them let there be a *little wheel*, of two inches Diameter, fixed on the same Axel. Let them be moved together on a plane, the great ones on the ground suppose, and the little one on a Table [for because of its parvitude it cannot reach to the same floor with them] And you'l find that the little wheel will move over
the

the fame fpace in equal time with equal
circulations, with the great ones, and defcribe as long a line. Now this feems
bigg of repugnancies, though Senfe it
felf fuffragate to its truth : For fince
every part of the greater wheels make
a proportionable part of the line, as do
the parts of the little one, and the parts
of thofe fo much exceeding in multitude
the parts of this : It will feem neceffary that the line made by the greater
wheels fhould have. as many parts more
then the line made by the lefs, as the
wheels themfelves have in *circumference*,
and fo the line would be as much longer
as the wheels are bigger : fo that one
of thefe abfurdities is unavoidable , either that more parts of the greater wheels
go to the making one part of their lines,
which will inferr a quantitative penetration ; or that the little wheel hath as
many parts as the great ones, though five
times in *Diameter* exceeded by them,
fince the lines they defcribe are of equal
length ; or the lefs wheel's line will
have fewer parts then the others, though
of equal extent with them, fince it can
                                    have

have no more parts then the *less circle,* nor *they* fewer then the *greater.* But thefe are all fuch repugnancies, as that *Melancholy* it felf would fcarfe own them. And therefore we may well enter this among the *unconceivables.* Should I have enlarged on this Subject to the taking in of all things that claim a fhare in't, it may be few things would have been left unfpoken to, but the *Creed.* Philofophy would not have engrofs'd our Pen, but we muft have been forced to anger the *Intelligences* of higher Orbs. But intending only a glance at this rugged Theam, I fhall forbear to infift more on it, though the confideration of the Myfteries of *Motion, Gravity, Light, Colours, Vifion, Sound,* and infinite fuch like [things obvious, yet unknown] might have been plentiful fubject. I come now to trace fome of the *caufes* of our *Ignorance* and Intellectual *weaknefs:* and among fo many it's almoft as great a wonder as any of the former; that we can *fay, we know.*

CHAP.

CHAP. VII.

Mens backwardnefs to acknowledge
their own Ignorance and Error,
though ready to find them in others.
The (1) caufe of the Shortnefs of
our Knowledge, viz. the depth of
Verity difcours't of, as of its ad-
mixtion in mens Opinions with falfe-
hood, and the connexion of truths,
and their mutual dependence : A
fecond Reafon of the fhortnefs of our
Knowledge, viz. becaufe we can per-
ceive nothing but by proportion to
our Senfes.

THe Difeafe of our *Intellectuals* is
too great, not to be its own *Diag-*
noftick : And they that feel it not, are
not lefs fick, but ftupidly *fo.* The weaknefs

nefs of humane underftanding, all will
confefs : yet the confidence of moft in
their own reafonings, practically difowns it : And 'tis eafier to perfwade
them it from others lapfes then their own;
fo that while all complain of our *Ignorance* and *Error*, every one exempts
himfelf. It is acknowledged by all, while
every one denies it. If the foregoing
part of this Difcourfe, have not univerfally concluded our weaknefs : I have
one Item more of my own. If Knowledge can be found in the Particulars
mention'd ; I muft lofe that, which I
thought I had, *That there is none*. But
however, though fome fhould pick
a quarrel with the inftances I alleadged ;
yet the conclufion muft be owned in
others. And therefore befide the general reafon I gave of our intellectual dif-
abilities, The *Fall* ; it will be worth
our labour to defcend to a more particular account : fince it is a good degree of
Knowledge to be acquainted with the
caufes of our *Ignorance*. And what
we have to fay under this head, will be
comprehenfive both of the caufes of
that,

that, and (which are the effects thereof) of our *misapprehensions* and *Errours.*

§. 1. And first, one cause of the little we *know* may be, that Knowledge
lies *deep*, and is therefore difficult; and
so not the acquist of every careless *Inquirer*. *Democritus* his Well hath a
βαθος, and Truth floats not. The useless
froth swims on the surface; but the
Pearl lies cover'd with a mass of Waters. *Verisimilitude* and *Opinion* are an
easie purchase; and these counterfeits
are all the Vulgars treasure: But true
Knowledge is as dear in acquisition, as
rare in possession. Truth, like a *point*
or *line*, requires an acuteness and intention to its discovery; while verisimility,
like the expanded *superficies*, is an obvious sensible on either hand, and affords
a large and easie field for loose enquiry.
And 'tis the more difficult to find out
Verity, because it is in such inconsiderable proportions scattered in a mass of
opinionative uncertainty; like the Silver
in *Hiero's* Crown of Gold : And it is
no easie piece of *Chymistry* to reduce
them

them to their *unmixed selves*. The Elements are no where pure in thefe lower *Regions*; and if there is any free from the admixtion of another, fure 'tis above the *concave* of the *Moon*: Neither can any boaft of a knowledge, which is depurate from the defilement of a contrary, within this *Atmofphear* of flefh; it dwels no where in unblended proportions, on this fide the *Empyreum*. All Opinions have their Truth, and all have what is not fo; and to fay all are *true* and none, is no abfurdity. So that to crown our felfs with fparks, which are almoft loft in fuch a world of *heterogeneous* natures, is as difficult as defirable. Befides, *Truth* is never *alone*; to know one will require the knowledge of many. They hang together in a chain of mutual dependence; you cannot draw one link without many others. Such an Harmony cannot commence from a fingle ftring; diverfity of ftrokes makes it. The beauty of a Face is not known by the Eye, or Nofe; it confifts in a *fymmetry*, and 'tis the comparative faculty which votes it: Thus is Truth *relative*,

G   and

and little confiderable can be attain'd
by *catches*. The Painter cannot tranfcribe
a face upon a Tranfient view ; it requires
the information of a fixt and obfervant
Eye : And before we can reach an exact fight of Truth's uniform perfections,
this *fleeting Tranfitory* our *Life*, is gone.
Thus we fee the face of Truth, but as
we do one anothers, when we walk
the ftreets, in a carelefs *Pafs-by :* And
the moft diligent obfervers, view but
the back-fide o'th' *Hangings* ; the right
one is o'th' other fide the *Grave :* fo
that our Knowledge is but like thofe
broken ends, at beft a moft confufed
adumbration. Nature, that was veil'd
to *Ariftotle*, hath not yet uncover'd, in
almoft two thoufand years. What he
fought on the other fide of *Euripus*, we
muft not look for on this fide *Immortality*. In eafie difquifitions we are often
left to the uncertainty of a guefs : yea
after we have triumph'd in a fuppofed
Εὕρηκα; a new-fprung difficulty marrs
our *Ovations*, and expofeth us to the
Torment of a difappointment : fo that
even the great *Mafter* of *Dogmatifts*
him-

himself concludes the Scene with an *Anxius vixi, Dubius morior*.

§. 2. Another reason of our *ignorance* and the *narrowneſs* of our *apprehenſions* may ariſe hence ; That we cannot perceive the manner of any of Natures operations, but by proportion to our *ſenſes*, and a return to *material phantaſms*. A blind man cannot conceive colours, but either as some *audible*, *guſtable*, *odoriferous*, or *tactile* qualities ; and when he would imagine them, he hath queſtionleſs recourſe to some of *theſe*, in an account of which his other ſenſes befriend him. Thus more perfect apprehenders misconceive *Immaterials* : Our imaginations paint Souls and Angels in as diſſimilar a reſemblance. Thus had there not been any *night*, *ſhadow*, or *opacity* ; we ſhould never have had any determinate conceit of *Darkneſs* ; That would have been as inconceiveable to us , as its contrary is to him that never ſaw it. But now our *ſenſes* being ſcant and limited, and Natures operations ſubtil and various ; they muſt needs tranſcend, and out-run our faculties.

They

They are only Natures groffer wayes of working , which are fenfible ; Her finer threads are out of the reach of our feeble *Percipient* , yea queftionlefs fhe hath many hidden *Energies* , no wayes imitated in her obvious peices : and therefore it is no wonder that we are fo often at a lofs ; an infirmity beyond prevention , except we could ftep by ftep follow the tracks and methods of *Infinite Wifdom,* which cannot be done but by him that owns it.

CHAP.

CHAP. VIII.

*A third reason of our Ignorance and
Error,* viz. *the impostures and deceits of our Senses. The way to
rectifie these mis-informations propounded. Des-Cartes his method
the only way to Science. The difficulty of exact performance.*

§. 3. ANother reason is the *Imposture* and *fallacy of our Senses,*
which impose not only on common
Heads, who scarse at all live to the
higher Principle ; But even more refined
Mercuries, who have the advantages of
an improved reason to disabuse them,
are yet frequently captivated to these
deceiving Prepossessions : appealing to a
Judicature both uncommissioned and unjust ; and when the clearest Truth is to
be tryed by such Judges, its innocence will
not secure it from the condemning award

G 3   of

of that *unintelligent Tribunal :* For since
we live the life of *Brutes ,* before we
grow into *Man ;* and our Underſtandings in this their *Non-age,* being almoſt
meerly Paſſive to ſenſible Impreſſions,
receiving all things in an uncontroverted
and promiſcuous admiſſion : It cannot
be, that our Knowledge ſhould be other,
then an heap of *Miſ-conception* and *Error,*
and conceits as impertinent as the *toys* we
delight *in.* All this while, we have no more
no reaſon, then the εἴδωλον ψυχῆς [as *Plotinus*
cals it] amounts to. And beſides this our
eaſie ſubmiſſion to the ſophiſtications of
ſenſe, and inability to prevent the miſ-
carriages of our *Junior* Reaſons ; that
which ſtrikes the great ſtroke toward
our after-deceptions, is the pertinacious
adherence of many of theſe firſt Impreſſions to our *Graduate* Underſtandings.
That which is early received, if in any
conſiderable ſtrength of *Impreſs ,* as it
were grows into our tender natures,
and is therefore of difficult remove. Thus
a fright in *Minority ,* or an *Antipathy*
then contracted, is not worn out but
with its ſubject. And it may be more
                                        then

then a *Story*, that *Nero* derived much
of his cruelty from the Nurfe that fuck-
led him. Now though our coming
Judgments do in part undeceive us, and
rectifie the grofler Errors which our
unwary Senfitive hath engaged us in ;
yet others are fo flefht in us, that they
maintain their intereft upon the deceptibility of our decayed Natures, and are
cherifh't there , as the legitimate iffues
of our reafonable faculties.

Indeed *Senfe* it felf detects its more
palpable deceits, by a counter-evidence ;
and the more ordinary Impoftures feldom out-live the firft *Experiments*. If
our fight reprefent a Staff as crooked
in the *water* ; the fame faculty rectifies
both it, and us, in the *thinner Element*.
And if a fquare Tower feem round at a
diftance ; the eye, which miftook in the
circumftance of its figure, at that remove,
corrects the miftake in a due approach :
Yea , and befriends thofe who have
learn'd to make the advantage of its
informations, in more remote and difficil difcoveries. And though his *Senfe*
occafion the carelefs *Ruftick* to judge

the

the *Sun* no bigger then a *Cheese-fat* ; yet *sense* too by a frugal improvement of its evidence, grounds the *Astronomers* knowledge, that it's bigger then this *Globe* of *Earth* and *Water*. Which it doth not only by the advantageous assistance of a *Tube*, but by less industrious experiments, shewing in what degrees Distance minorates the Object. But yet in infinite other cases, wherein *sense* can afford none, or but very little help to dis-intangle us ; our first deceptions lose no ground, but rather improve in our riper years : so that we are not weaned from our *child-hood*, till we return to our second *Infancy* ; and even our *Gray* heads out-grow not those Errors, which we have learn't before the *Alphabet*.

Thus our Reasons being inoculated on Sense, will retain a rellish of the stock they grow upon : And if we would endeavour after an unmixed Knowledge ; we must unlive our former lives, and (inverting the practise of *Penelope*) undo in the *day* of our more advanc'd understandings, what we had spun in the *night* of our *Infant-ignorance*. He that
would

would rebuild a decayed *structure*, must first pluck down the former *ruines*. A *fabrick*, though high and beautiful, if founded on *rubbish*, is easily made the triumph of the winds: And the most pompous seeming Knowledge, that's built on the unexamin'd prejudices of *Sense*, stands not, but till the *storm arise*; the next strong encounter discovers its weakness, in a shameful overthrow. And now since a great part of our scientifical *Treasure* is most likely to be *adulterate*, though all bears the image and superscription of *Verity*; the only way to know what is sophisticate, and what is not so, is to bring all to the *Examen* of the Touchstone: For the prepossessions of *sense* having (as is shewen) so mingled themselves with our Genuine Truths, and being as plausible to appearance as they; we cannot gain a true assurance of any, but by suspending our assent from all, till the deserts of each, discover'd by a strict enquiry, claim it. Upon this account I think the *method* of the most excellent *Des-Cartes* not unworthy its Author; and (since

Dog-

Dogmatical Ignorance will call it so) a *Scepticism*, that's the only way to *Science*. But yet this is so difficult in the impartial and exact performance, that it may be well reckon'd among the bare *Possibilities*, which never commence into a *Futurity* : It requiring such a free, sedate, and intent minde, as it may be is no where found but among the *Platonical Idea's*. Do what we can , Prejudices will creep in, and hinder our Intellectual Perfection : And though by this means we may get some comfortable allay to our distempers; yet can it not perfectly cure us of a disease , that sticks as close to us as our natures.

CHAP.

Chap. IX.

*Two Instances of Sensitive deception.
(1) Of the Quiescence of the Earth.
Sense is the great inducement to its
belief; its testimony deserves no credit in this case, though it do move,
Sense would present it as immoveable.
The Sun to Sense is as much devoid
of motion as the Earth. Four Cases
in which motion is insensible, viz.
(1) If it be very swift. (2) If it be
steddy and regular. (3) If very
slow. (4) If the Sentient partake of
it. Applyed to the Earths motion.
The unweildiness of its bulk is no argument of its immobility.*

Now before I leave this, I shall take
the opportunity, which this head
offers, to endeavour the detection of
some

some grand *prejudices* of *sense*, in two instances; the free debate of which I conceive to be of great importance, though hitherto for the most part obstructed, by the peremptory conclusion of *sense*, which yet I shall declare to have no suffrage in the case of either : And the pleasantness and concernment of the *Theories*, if it be one, I hope will attone the *Digreßion*.

§. 2. *First*, it is generally opinion'd, that the *Earth rests* as the Worlds *centre*, while the *Heavens* are the subject of the *Universal Motions* ; And, *as immoveable as the Earth* , is grown into the credit of being *Proverbial*. So that for a man to go about to counter-argue this common belief, is as fruitless as to whistle against the windes. I shall not undertake to maintain the *Paradox*, that stands *diameter* to this almost *Catholick* Opinion. Its assertion would be entertained with the hoot of the Rabble : the very mention of it as possible, is among the most ridiculous ; and they are likely most severely to judge it, who least understand the Cause. But yet the Patronage of

as

as great *Wits*, as it may be e're faw the Sun, such as *Pythagoras*, *Des-Cartes*, *Copernicus*, *Galilæo*, *More*, *Kepler*, &c. hath gain'd it a more favourable cenfure with the learned World; and advanc'd it far above either vain, or contemptible. And if it be a miftake, it's only fo: There's no *Herefie* in fuch an harmlefs aberration; at the worft, with the ingenuous; the probability of it will render it a lapfe of eafie Pardon. Now whether the *Earth* move or reft, I undertake not to determine. My work is to prove, that the common inducement to the belief of it's *quiefcence*, the teftimony of *fenfe*, is weak and frivolous: to the end, that if upon an unprejudiced tryal, it be found more confonant to the *Aftronomical Phænomena*; its *Motion* may be admitted, notwithftanding the feeming contrary evidence of unconcerned *Senfes*. And I think what follows will evince, that this is no fo abfurd an *Hypothefis*, as Vulgar Philofophers account it; but that, though it *move*, its *motion* muft needs be as *infenfible*, as if it were *quiefcent*: and the affertion

of

of it would then be as uncouth and harſh to the ſons of *Senſe*, that is, to the generality of Mankind, as now it is.

That there is a *motion*, which makes the viciſſitudes of day and night, and conſtitutes the ſucceſſive Seaſons of the *Annual Circle*; *Senſe* may aſſure us, or at leaſt the comparative Judgement of an higher faculty, made upon its immediate evidence : But whether the *Sun*, or *Earth*, be the common *Movent*, cannot be determin'd but by a farther appeal. If we will take the literal evidence of our Eyes ; the *Æthereal Coal* moves no more then this *Inferior clod doth* : For where ever in the Firmament we ſee it, it's repreſented to us, as fixt in that part of the enlightened *Hemiſphear*. And though an after-account diſcover, that it hath changed its *Site* and *reſpect* to this our *Globe*; yet whether that were cauſed by its tranſlation from us, or ours from it, Senſe leaves us in an *Ignoramus* : So that if we are reſolved to ſtand to its Verdict, it muſt be by as great a *Miracle* if the *Sun* ever *move*, as it was that it once *reſted*; or
what

what ever elfe was the fubject of that
fupernal change. And if upon a meer
fenfible account we will deny Motion to
the *Earth*; upon the fame inducement
we muft deny it the *Sun*; and the *Heavens* will lofe their *Firft Moveable*. But
to draw up clofer to our main defign,
We may the better conceive that, though
the *Earth move*, yet its *Motion* muft needs
be infenfible; if we confider that in
four cafes *Motion* ftrikes not the
Senfe.

1. The *Velocity* of *Motion* prevents
the *fenfe* of't. Thus a Bullet paffeth by
us, and out-runs the nimbleft *Opticks*;
and the Fly of a Jack in its fwifteft
rounds, gives the Eye no notice of its *circulations*. The reafon is, for that there
is no fenfe without fome ftay of the Object on the faculty: For in Senfe there
are two *confiderables*: The *Motion* made
on the *Brain*; and the *Souls* act confe-
quent thereupon, which we call *Ani-
madverfion*: and in this latter confifts
the formality of *Senfitive Perception*.
Now though poffibly the *Æthereal* Matter might convey the ftroke and motion

made

made on it quite to the Brain, before the
pass of the Object; yet the soul being
taken up with other attendances, per-
ceives not, till engaged to it by iterated
impressions, except the first impulse be
very strong and violent. Thus in the
cleareft night we cannot see some of the
smaller *Stars*, upon the firft caft of the
Eye to their *Celestial Residence* : yet a
more intent view difcovers them ; though
very likely their *Motion* reach't the *Brain*,
affoon as the more noted imprefs of their
Fellows. Thus upon a slight turn of our
fight, we omit many particularities in
nearer objects, which a more fixed look
presents us with. And thus the swifteft
motions, though they knock at the dore;
yet they are gone before the soul can
come, to take an account of their Er-
rand.

2. If *Regularity* and *steddiness* accom-
pany Velocity ; the *motion* then leaves
not the least track in the *sensitive*. Thus
a *French* Top, the common recreation of
School-boys, thrown from a cord which
was wound about it, will stand as it were
fixt on the floor it lighted ; and yet continue

tinue in its repeated *Gyrations*, while the fenfe difcovers not the leaft footfteps of that præcipitate *Rotation*. The reafon is much what the fame with the former : For that meeting no joggs , or counter-motions to interrupt it , the return of the parts is fo quick , that the mind cannot take notice of their fucceffion to each other : For before it can fix to the obfervation of any one, its object is gone : whereas, were there any confiderable thwart in the Motion ; it would be a kind of ftop or arreft, by the benefit of which the Soul might have a glance of the fugitive *Tranfient*. But I pafs thefe ; they concern not our prefent enquiry.

3. If the Motion be very *flow* , we perceive it not. Thus *Vegetables* fpring up from their Mother Earth ; and we can no more difcern their *accretive* Motion, then we can their moft hidden caufe. Thus the fly fhadow fteals away on Times Account-Book the *Dyal* ; and the quickeft Eye can tell no more , but that it's *gone*. If a reafon of this be demanded ; I conceive it may be to fome

H   fatif-

satisfaction return'd, That 'tis because
Motion cannot be perceived without the
perception of its *Terms, viz.* The parts of
space which it immediately left, and those
which it next acquires. Now the space
left and acquir'd in every sensible moment in such slow progressions, is so inconsiderable, that it cannot possibly move
the *sense* ; (which by reason either of
its constitutional dulness, or the importunity of stronger impressions, cannot take
notice of such parvitudes) and therefore
neither can the Motion depending thereon , be any more observable, then
it is.

4. If the *sentient* be carryed *paßibus
æquis* with the body , whose *motion* it
would observe ; [supposing the former
condition, that it be *regular* and *steddy*]
In this case especially the remove is insensible , at least in its proper subject.
Thus, while in a Ship, we perceive it not
to move: but our sense transfers its motion
to the neighbouring shores, as the Poet,
Littus campiq; recedunt. And I question not, but if any were born and bred
under Deck, and had no other information
                                                                but

but what his *fense* affords ; he would without the leaft doubt or *fcruple*, opinion, that the houfe he dwelt in, was as ftable and fixt as ours. To exprefs the reafon according to the Philofophy of *Des-Cartes*, I fuppofe it thus : *Motion* is not perceived, but by the *fucceffive ftrikings* of the object upon divers *filaments* of the *Brain* ; which diverfifie the reprefentation of its *fite* and *diftance*. But now when the motion of the object is common with it, to our felves ; it retains the fame relation to our *fenfe*, as if we both *refted :* For ftriking ftill on the fame *ftrings* of the Brain, it varies not its *fite* or *diftance* from us ; and therefore we cannot poffibly *fenfe* its motion : nor yet upon the fame account our own ; leaft of all, when we are carryed without any *conamen* and endeavour of ours, which in our particular progreffions betrayes them to our notice.

Now then the *Earths motion* (if we fuppofe it to have any) having the joynt concurrence of the two laft, to render it *infenfible* ; I think we fhall need no more proof to conclude the neceffity of its being fo.   H 2   For

For though the *Third* feems not to belong to the prefent cafe, fince the fuppofed motion will be near a thoufand miles
an hour under the *Equinoctial line* ; yet
it will feem to have no *Velocity* to the
fenfe any more then the received *motion*
of the *Sun*, and for the fame reafon. Becaufe the diftant points in the *Celeftial ex-
panfe* [from a various and fucceffive refpect to which the length, and confequently the fwiftnefs of this *motion* muft
be calculated] appear to the Eye in fo
fmall a degree of *elongation* from one
another, as bears no proportion to what
is *real*. For fince the Margin of the *Vifible
Horizon* in the Heavenly *Globe* is Parallel
with that in the Earthly, accounted but
120 miles *diameter* ; Senfe muft needs
meafure the *Azimuths*, or *Vertical Circles*,
by triplication of the fame *diameter* of
120. So that there will be no more proportion betwixt the *fenfible* and *real* celerity of the *Terreftrial Motion*, then
there is between the *vifible* and *rational*
dimenfion of the celeftial *Hemifphear* ;
which is none at all.

But if fenfitive prejudice will yet confidently

fidently maintain the Impossibility of the *Hypothesis*, from the supposed *unwieldiness* of its massy bulk, grounded on our experience of the ineptitude of *great* and *heavy* bodies to *Motion*: I say this is a meer Imposture of our *Senses*, the fallacy of which we may avoid, by considering; that the *Earth* may as easily move, notwithstanding this pretended indisposition of its *magnitude*, as those much vaster *Orbs* of *Sun* and *Stars*. He that made it, could as well give motion to the whole, as to the parts; the constant agitation of which is discover'd in natural productions: and to both as well as Rest to either: Neither will it need the assistance of an *Intelligence* to perpetuate the begun *Rotation*: Since according to the Indispensable *Law* of *Nature* [*That every thing should continue in the state wherein it is, except something more powerful hinder it*] it must persevere in Motion, unless obstructed by a *Miracle*. Neither can *Gravity*, which makes great bodies hard of Remove, be any hinderance to the *Earths motion*: since even the *Peripatetick Maxime, Nihil*

gravitat

gravitat in ſuo loco, will exempt it from this indiſpoſing quality ; which is nothing but the tendency of its parts, which are raviſh't from it, to their deſired *Centre*. And the *French Philoſophy* will inform us, that the *Earth* as well as other bodies is indifferent in it ſelf to *Reſt*, or its contrary. I have done with this inſtance, and my Brevity in the following ſhall make ſome amends for my prolixity in this. He that would be inform'd in this ſubject of the *Earths Mobility*, may find it largely and ingeniouſly diſcuſs'd, in *Galilæo's ſyſtema Coſmicum*.

CHAP.

CHAP. X.

Another instance of the deceptions of our Senses : which is of translating the Idea of our Passions to things without us. Properly and formally heat is not in the fire, but is an expression of our sentiment. Yet in propriety of speech the Senses themselves are never deceived, but only administer an occasion of deceit to the understanding: prov'd by reason, and the Authority of St. Austin.

SEcondly the *best Philosophy* [the deserved Title of the *Cartesian*] derives all sensitive perception from *Motion*, and corporal impress; some account of which we have above given. Not that the Formality of it consists in *material Reaction*, as Master *Hobbs* affirms, totally excluding

H 4   any

any immaterial concurrence : But that
the reprefentations of Objects to the Soul,
the only *animadverfive principle*, are conveyed by motions made upon the immediate Inftruments of Senfe. So that the
diverfity of our Senfations arifeth from
the diverfity of the *motion* or *figure* of
the object ; which in a different manner affect the Brain , whence the Soul
hath its immediate intelligence of the
quality of what is prefented. Thus the
different effects, which *fire* and *water*
have on us, which we call *heat* and *cold*,
refult from the fo differing *configuration* and *agitation* of their *Particles :* and
not from , I know not what *Chimerical
beings*, fuppofed to inhere in the objects, their caufe, and thence to be propagated by many petty *imaginary productions* to the feat of *Senfe*. So that what
we term *heat* and *cold*, and other qualities, are not properly according to *Philofophical* rigour in the Bodies, their Efficients : but are rather *Names* expref-
fing our *paffions* ; and therefore not
ftrictly attributable to any thing without
us, but by *extrinfick denomination*, as
Vifion

Vision to the Wall. This I conceive to be an *Hypothesis*, well worthy a rational belief: and yet is it so abhorrent from the Vulgar, that they would assoon believe *Anaxagoras*, that *snow is black*, as him that should affirm, it is not *white*; and if any should in earnest assert, that the *fire* is not formally *hot*, it would be thought that the heat of his brain had fitted him for *Anticyra*, and that his head were *so* to madness: For it is conceiv'd to be as certain, as our faculties can make it, that the same qualities, which we resent within us, are in the object, their Source, And yet this confidence is grounded on no better foundation, then a delusory prejudice, and the vote of *misapplyed sensations*, which have no warrant to determine either one or other. I may indeed conclude, that I am formally *hot* or *cold*; I feel it. But whether these qualities are *formally*, or only *eminently* in their producent; is beyond the knowledge of the *sensitive*. Even the *Peripatetick Philosophy* will teach us, that *heat* is not in the Body of the *Sun*, but only vertually, and as in

its

its caufe ; though it be the Fountain and
great Diftributour of warmth to the neather Creation: and yet none urge the
evidence of *fenfe* to difprove it : Neither can it with any more Juftice be
alledged againft this *Hypothefis*. For if
it be fo as *Des-Cartes* would have it ;
yet *fenfe* would conftantly prefent it to
us, as *Now*. VVe fhould finde *heat* as
infallible an attendant upon *fire*, and
the increafe thereof by the fame degrees
in our approach to the Fountain *calefaci-
ent*, and the fame excefs within the *Vifible* fubftance, as *Now* ; which yet I
think to be the chief inducements to
the adverfe belief: For *Fire* (I retain
the inftance, which yet may be applyed
to other cafes) being conftant in its fpecifical motions in thofe fmaller derivations of it, which are its inftruments of
action, and therefore in the fame manner
ftriking the fentient, though gradually
varying according to the proportions of
more or lefs quantity or agitation, *&c.*
will not fail to produce the fame effect
in us, which we call *heat*, when ever we
are within the Orb of its activity. And
the

the *heat* muſt needs be augmented by proximity, and moſt of all within the *Flame*, becauſe of the more *violent motion* of the particles there, which therefore begets in us a ſtronger ſenſe. Now if this *motive Energie*, the Inſtrument of this active *Element*, muſt be called *Heat*; let it be *ſo*, I contend not. I know not how otherwiſe to call it: To impoſe names is part of the *Peoples* Charter, and I fight not with *Words*. Only I would not that the *Idea* of our *Paſſions* ſhould be apply'd to any thing without us, when it hath its ſubject no where but in our ſelves. This is the grand deceit, which my deſign is to detect, and if poſſible, to rectifie. Thus we have ſeen two notorious inſtances of *ſenſitive deception*, which juſtifie the charge of *Petron. Arbiter*.

Fallunt nos oculi, vagiq; ſenſus
Oppreſſâ ratione mentiuntur.

And yet to ſpeak properly, and to do our *ſenſes* right, ſimply they are not deceived, but only adminiſter an occaſion

to

to our forward *understandings* to deceive
themselves : and so though they are
some way accessory to our delusion ;
yet the more principal faculties are the
Capital offenders. Thus if the *Senses* represent the *Earth* as *fixt* and *immoveable* ;
they give us the truth of their *Senti-*
ments : To *sense* it is *so,* and it would be
deceit to present it otherwise. For [as
we have shewn] though it do *move* in
it self ; it *rests* to us, who are carry'd
with it. And it must needs be to *sense*
unalterably *quiescent,* in that our Rotation with it, prevents the variety of *suc-*
cessive Impress ; which only renders motion *sensible.* And so if we erroneously
attribute our particular incommunicable
sensations to things, which do no more
resemble them then the *effect* doth its
æquivocal cause ; our *senses* are not in
fault, but our *precipitate judgements.*
We *feel* such, or such a *sentiment* within
us, and herein is no cheat or misprision :
'tis truly so, and our *sense* concludes nothing of its Rise or Origine. But if hence
our Understandings falsly deduct, that
there is the same quality in the *external*
                              Impressor ;

Impreſſor; 'tis, it is *criminal*, our *ſenſe* is *in-nocent*. When the *Ear* tingles, we really hear a *ſound*: If we judge it without us, it's the fallacy of our *Judgments*. The *apparitions* of our frighted *Phancies* are real *ſenſibles*: But if we tranſlate them without the compaſs of our Brains, and apprehend them as external objects; it's the unwary raſhneſs of our *Under-ſtanding* deludes us. And if our diſaf-fected Palates reſent nought but bitterneſs from our choiceſt viands, we truly taſt the unpleaſing quality, though falſly conceive it in that, which is no more then the occaſion of its production. If any find fault with the novelty of the notion; the learned St. *Auſtin* ſtands ready to confute the charge: and they, who revere *Antiquity*, will derive ſatis-faction from ſo venerable a ſuffrage. He tells us, *Si quis remum frangi in aquâ opinatur, &, cùm aufertur, integrari; non malum habet internuncium, ſed ma-lus eſt Judex*. And onward to this pur-poſe, The ſenſe could not otherwiſe per-ceive it in the *water*, neither ought it: For ſince the *Water* is one thing, and the

Air:

Air another ; 'tis requifite and neceffary,
that the *fenfe* fhould be as different as
the *medium :* Wherefore the Eye fees
aright ; if there be a miftake, 'tis the
Judgement's the Deceiver. Elfewhere
he faith,that our Eyes mif-inform us not,
but faithfully tranfmit their refentment
to the mind. And againft the *Scepticks*,
That it's a piece of injuftice to complain
of our *fenfes,* and to exact from them
an account, which is beyond the fphear of
their notice : and refolutely determines,
*Quicquid poffunt videre oculi, verum vi-
dent.* So that what we have faid of the
fenfes deceptions, is rigidly to be charg'd
only on our carelefs Underftandings,
mifleading us through the ill management of fenfible informations. But becaufe fuch are commonly known by the
name of the *Senfes deceipts* (fomewhat
the more juftifiably in that they adminifter the occafion) I have thought good
to retain the ufual way of fpeaking,though
fomewhat varying from the manner of
apprehending.

CHAP.

CHAP. XI.

A fourth reason of our Ignorance and Error, viz. *the fallacy of our Imaginations ; an account of the nature of that faculty ; Inſtances of its deceptions ; Spirits are not in a place ; Intellection, Volition, Decrees, &c. cannot properly be aſcrib'd to God. It is not Reaſon that oppoſeth Faith, but Phancy : the intereſt which Imagination hath in many of our Opinions , in that it impreſſes a perſwaſion without evidence.*

Fourthly, we *erre* and come ſhort of *Science,* becauſe we are ſo frequently miſlead by the evil conduct of our *Imaginations* ; whoſe irregular ſtrength and importunity doth almoſt perpetually abuſe

abuſe us. Now to make a full and clear diſcovery of our *Phancies* deceptions ; 'twill be requiſite to look into the nature of that *myſterious faculty.* In which ſurvey we muſt trace the Soul in the wayes of her *intellectual* actions ; whereby we may come to the diſtinct knowledge of what is meant by *Imagination* , in contradiſtinction to ſome other Powers. But firſt premiſing, that the *Souls nature* (at leaſt as far as concerns our inquiry) conſiſts in *intelligibility:* And ſecondly , that when we ſpeak of *Powers* and *Faculties* of the Soul, we intend not to aſſert with the *Schools,* their *real* diſtinction from it, or each other, but only a *modal* diverſity. Therefore I ſhall diſtribute *Intellectual operations* according to the known *triple* diviſion, though with ſome difference of repreſentation. The firſt is *ſimple apprehenſion,* which denotes no more, then the ſouls naked *Intellection* of an object, without either *compoſition* or *deduction.* The foundation of this act , as to materials, is *ſenſitive perception.* Now our *ſimple* apprehenſion of corporal objects,

if

if present, we call *Sense* ; if absent, we properly name it *Imagination*. Thus when we would conceive a *Triangle* , *Man*, *Horse*, or any other sensible; we figure it in our Phancies, and stir up there its sensible *Idea*. But in our notion of *spirituals*, we, as much as we can, denudate them of all material Phantasmes ; and thus they become the object of our *Intellects*, properly so called. Now all this while the *soul* is, as it were, silent ; and in a more passive way of reception. But the *second act* advanceth propositions from *simple intellections* : and hereby we have the knowledge of the *distinctions* or *identities* of objective representations. Now here, as in the former, where the objects are purely *material*; the Judgment is made by the *Imagination* : if otherwise, we refer it to the *Understanding*. There is yet *a third Act*, which is a connecting of *Propositions* and deducing of *Conclusions* from them : and this the Schools call *Discourse* ; and we shall not miscall it, if we name it, *Reason*. Now this , as it supposeth the two former, so is it grounded on certain

I   *congenite*

congenite propofitions ; which I conceive to be the very *Effentials* of Rationality. Such are, *Quodlibet eft, vel non eft* ; *Impoſſibile eft idem eſſe, & non eſſe* ; *Non entis nulla funt prædicata*, &c. Not that every one hath naturally a *formal* and *explicit* notion of thefe *Principles* : For the Vulgar ufe them, without knowledge of them, under any fuch *exprefs* confideration ; But yet there was never any born to *Reafon* without them. If any ask, how the Soul came by thofe foundation-*Propoſitions* : I return, as Quantity did by *longum, latum, & profundum* ; they being the *Eſſential annexes*, or rather *conſtitutives* of it, as *Reaſonable*. Now then, when the conclufion is deduc'd from the unerring dictates of our faculties ; we fay the Inference is *Rational* : But when from mif-apprehended, or ill-compounded phantafmes ; we afcribe it to the *Imagination*. So we fee, there is a triple operation of the *Phancy* as well as *Intellect* ; and thefe powers are only *circumftantially* different. In this method we intend a diftinct, though fhort account, how the *Imagination* deceives

ceives us. First then, the *Imaginations* which is of *simple* perception, doth never of it self and directly mislead us ; as is at large declared in our former discourse of *Sense*. Yet is it the almost fatal means of our deception, through the unwarrantable *compositions, divisions,* and *applications,* which it occasions the *second Act* to make of the *simple Images.* Hence we may derive the Visions, Voyces, Revelations of the *Enthusiast :* the strong Idea's of which, being conjur'd up into the *Imagination* by the heat of the *melancholized* brain, are judged exterior *Realties ;* when as they are but motions within the *Cranium.* Hence Story is full of the wonders, it works upon *Hypochondriacal Imaginants ;* to whom the grossest absurdities are infallible certainties, and free reason an Impostour. That *Groom,* that conceited himself an *Emperour,* thought all as irrational as disloyal, that did not acknowledge him : And he, that supposed himself made of Glass ; thought them all *mad,* that dis-believed him. But we pity, or laugh at those fatuous *extravagants ;* while yet our

I 2   selves

felves have a confiderable dofe of what
makes them *fo*: and more fober heads
have a fet of mifconceits, which are as
abfurd to an unpaffionated *reafon*, as
thofe to our unabufed *fenfes*. And, as
the greateft counter-evidence to thofe
diftemper'd phancies is none : fo in the
more ordinary deceits, in which our
Imaginations infenfibly engage us, we
give but little credit to the uncorrupted
fuggeftions of the faculty, that fhould
difabufe us. That the *Soul* and *Angels*
are devoid of *quantitative dimenfions*,
hath the fuffrage of the moft ; and that
they have nothing to do with groffer *locality*, is as generally opinion'd : But
who is it, that retains not a great part of
the impofture, by allowing them a *definitive Ubi*, which is ftill but *Imagination ?* He that faid, a *thoufand* might dance
on the *point of a Needle*, fpake but grofly ; and we may as well fuppofe them
to have *wings*, as a proper *Ubi*. We
fay, *Spirits* are where they operate : But
ftrictly to be in a *place*, or *ubi*, is a
material Attribute, and incompatible with
fo depurate a Nature. We ask not,
in

in what place a *thought* is, nor are we
folicitous for the *Ubi* of *Vertue*, or any
other *Immaterial* accident. *Relations*, *Ubications*, *Duration*, the *vulgar* Philofophy
admits into the lift of fomething; and
yet to enquire in what *place* they are,
were a foloecifm. So that, if *to be* and
to be in a place be not reciprocal; I know
not why fpirits may not be exempted,
having as much to plead from the purity
of their nature, as any thing *but one*,
within the circle of being. And yet
Imagination ftands fo ftrongly againft
the notion, that it cannot look for the
favour of a very diffufive entertainment.
But we are more dangeroufly deceiv'd,
when judging the *Infinite Effence* by our
narrow felves; we afcribe *Intellections*,
Volitions, *Decrees*, *Purpofes*, and fuch
like *Immanent actions* to that nature,
which hath nothing in common with us,
as being infinitely above us. Now to
ufe thefe as *Hypothefeis*, as himfelf in his
Word, is pleas'd to *low* himfelf to our
capacities, is allowable: But a ftrict and
rigorous imputation is derogatory to
him, and arrogant in us. To fay, that

God

God doth *eminently* contain all those effects in his glorious *simple Effence*, that the creature can produce or act by such a faculty, power, or affection; is to affirm him to be. what he is, *Infinite*. Thus, to conceive that he can. do all those things in the most perfect manner, which we do upon *underftanding, willing,* and *decreeing*; is an apprehenfion suteable to his *Idea*: But to fix on him the formality of *faculties*, or *affections*; is the Impofture of our *Phancies*, and contradictory to his *Divinity*. 'Tis this deception misleads the contending world; and is the Author of most of that darknefs and confufion, that is upon the face of the *Quinquarticular* debates. Now then, we being thus obnoxious to fallacy in our *apprehenfions* and *judgements*, and so often impofed upon by thefe deceptions; our *Inferences* and *Deductions* muft needs be as unwarrantable, as our *fimple* and *compound* thoughts are deceitful. Thus the *reafon* of the far greateft part of mankind, is but an aggregate of miftaken phantafms; and in things *not fenfible* a conftant delufion. Yea the higheft and
                                    moft

moſt improved parts of Rationality, are
frequently caught in the entanglements of
a tenacious *Imagination* ; and ſubmit to
its obſtinate , but deluſory *Dictamens*.
Thus we are involv'd in inextricable
perplexities about the *Divine Nature*, and
Attributes ; and in our reaſonings about
thoſe ſublimities are puzled with contradictions, which are but the toyings of
our *Phancies*, no abſurdities to our more
defæcate faculties. What work do our
Imaginations make with *Eternity* and
Immenſity ? and how are we gravell'd
by their cutting *Dilemma's ?* I'm confident many have thus *imagin'd* themſelves out of their *Religion* ; and run a
ground on that more deſperate abſurdity, *Atheiſm*. To ſay, *Reaſon* oppoſeth
Faith, is to ſcandalize both : 'Tis *Imagination* is the Rebel ; *Reaſon* contradicts
its impious ſuggeſtions. Nor is our
Reaſon any more accountable for the
Errours of our *Opinions* ; then our *holi-
neſs* for the vitioſity of our *Lives* : And
we may as well ſay, that the *Sun* is the
cauſe f the *ſhadow*, which is the effect
of the intercepting *opacity* , as either.

Reaſon and *Faith* are at perfeƈt *Uniſons :*
The diſharmony is in the *Phancy.* Τὸ λογικόν ἐςι θεῖον, is a ſaying of *Plato*'s ; and
well worthy a Chriſtian ſubſcription,
Reaſon being the Image of the Creators
Wiſdom copyed out in the Creature.
Though indeed, as 'tis now in the ſub-
jeƈt, 'tis but an amaſsment of *imaginary*
conceptions, præjudices, ungrounded opini-
ons, and infinite Impoſtures ; and 'tis
no wonder, if theſe are at odds with
the Principles of our belief : But all this
is but *apiſh Sophiſtry* ; and to give it a
Name ſo *Divine* and *excellent,* is abuſive
and unjuſt.

There is yet another as deplorable a
deceit of our *Imaginations* , as any :
which is, its impreſſing a ſtrong perſwaſion of the Truth of an *Opinion,* where
there is no evidence to ſupport it. And
if it be ſuch, as we never heard queſtion'd
or contradiƈted ; 'tis then held as indu-
bitate, as *firſt principles.* Thus the moſt
of mankind is led by *opinionative* im-
pulſe; and *Imagination* is prædominant.
Hence we have an ungrounded *credu-*
lity cry'd up for *faith* ; and the more
vigorous

vigorous impreſſions of *Phancy*, for the *Spirits* motions. Theſe are the grand deluſions of our Age, and the higheſt evidence of the *Imaginations* deceptions. This is the *ſpirit*, that works in the children of *Phancy*; and we need not ſeek to remoter reſolutions. But the excellent Dr. *H. More* hath follow'd *Enthuſiaſtick effects* to their proper *Origine*, and prevented our endeavours of attempting it. His Diſcourſe of *Enthuſiaſm* compleatly makes good the Title; and 'tis as well a *Victory*, as a *Triumph.*

CHAP.

Chap. XII.

A fifth Reason, the præcipitancy of our Understandings; the reason of it. The most close ingagement of our minds requisite to the finding of truth; the difficulties of the performance of it. Two instances of our præcipitating; as the concluding thing impossible, which to Nature are not so; and the joyning Causes with irrelative Effects.

§.5. AGain another account of the shortness of our *Reasons* and easiness of deception, is, the *forwardness* of our *Understandings assent*, to slightly examin'd *conclusions*, contracting many times a firm and obstinate belief from weak inducements; and that not only in such things, as immediately concern the sense,

fenfe, but in almoft every thing that
falls within the fcope of our enquiry.
For the declarement of this, we are to
obferve, That every being unceffantly
afpires to its own *perfection*, and is reft-
lefs till it obtain it; as is the trembling
Needle, till it find its *beloved North*.
Now the perfection of a Faculty is Union with its Object, to which its refpective
actions are directed, as the fcope and
term of its endeavours. Thus our Underftanding being perfected by Truth,
with all the impatience, which accompanies ftrong defire, breaths after its
enjoyment. But now the *good* and perfection of *being*, which every thing reacheth at, muft be *known*, and that in the
particular inftances thereof; or elfe 'tis
not attain'd: and if it be miftaken, that
being courts deceit and its own delufion.
Now this *Knowledge* of their *Good*, was
at firft as natural to all things, as the
defire on't: otherwife this innate propen-
fion would have been as much a torment and mifery to thofe things that are
capable of it, as a needlefs impertinency to all others. But Nature fhoots
not

not at *Rovers*. Even inanimates, though they know not their perfection them-selves, yet are they not carryed on by a blind unguided *impetus :* But that which directs them, knows it. The next or-ders of being have some sight of it them-selves: And man most perfectly had it, before the *touch* of the *Apple*. So then beside this general propensity to Truth, the *Underſtanding* must know what is so, before it can entertain it with *aſſent*. The former we poſſeſs (it may be) as entire-ly as when Nature gave it us: but of the latter little, but the capacity : And herein have we made our selves of all creatures the moſt miserable. And now such a multitude, such an Infinite of *uncertain opinions*, bare *probabilities*, specious *falſhoods*, spreading themselves before us, and solliciting our belief ; and we being thus greedy of *Truth*, and yet so unable to diſcern it: It cannot be, that we ſhould reach it any otherwiſe, then by the moſt cloſe *meditation* and engage-ment of our minds ; by which we muſt endeavour to eſtrange our aſſent from every thing, which is not clearly, and

distinctly

distinctly evidenc't to our *faculties*. But now, this is so difficult; and as hath been intimated, so almost infeasable; that it may well drive modesty to despair of *Science*. For though possibly Assiduity in the most fixed cogitation be no trouble or pain to *immaterializ'd spirits*; yet is it more, then our *embodyed souls* can bear without lassitude or distemper. For in this terrestrial state there are few things transacted, even in our *Intellectual* part, but through the help and furtherance of *corp.al* Instruments; which by more then ordinary usage lose their edge and fitness for action, and so grow inept for their respective destinations. Upon this account our *senses* are dull'd and spent by any extraordinary intention; and our very *Eyes* will ake, if long fixt upon any difficultly discerned object. Now though *Meditation* be to be reckoned among the most abstracted operations of our minds; yet can it not be performed without a considerable proportion of *Spirits* to assist in the Action, though indeed such as are furnish't out of the bodies purer store. This I

think

think to be hence evidenc't ; in that fixed ferioufnefs herein, heats the brain in
fome to diftraction , caufeth an aking
and dizinefs in founder heads , hinders
the works of Nature in its lower and
animal functions, takes away or leffens
pain in diftemper'd parts, and feldom
leaves any but under a wearyfome dull-
nefs, and inactivity ; which I think to be
arguments of fufficient validity to juftifie
our affent to this, that the *fpirits* are
imploy'd in our moft *intenfe* cogitations,
yea in fuch , whofe objects are moft
elevated above *material.* Now the managing and carrying on of this work by
the *Spirits* inftrumental *co-efficiency* requires, that they be kept together without
diftraction or diffipation ; that fo they
may be ready to receive and execute the
orders and commiffions of the commanding faculty. If either of thefe happen,
all mifcarries : as do the works of
Nature , when they want that *heat,*
which is requifite for their intended
perfection. And therefore, for the prevention of fuch inconveniences in *meditation ,* we choofe recefs and folitude.
But

But now if we confider the *volatile* nature of thofe *officious Affiftants*, and the
feveral caufes which occur continually,
even from the meer *Mechanifm* of our
Bodies to fcatter and diforder them, befides the excurfions of our roving *phancies* (which cannot be kept to a clofe
attendance) ; it will be found very hard
to retain them in any·long fervice, but do
what we can, they'l get loofe from the
Minds *Regimen*. So that it's no eafie matter to bring the body to be what it was
intended for, the *Souls fervant* ; and to
confine the *imagination*, of as facil a performance , as the *Goteham's* defign of
hedging in the *Cuckow*. And though
fome conftitutions are genially difpofited
to this mental ferioufnefs ; yet they can
fcarce fay , *Nos numeri fumus :* yea in
the moft advantag'd tempers, this difpofition is but *comparative* ; when as
the moft of men labour under difadvantages, which nothing can rid them of,
but that which loofens them from this
mafs of flefh. Thus the boyling bloud
of youth, fiercely agitating the fluid Air,
hinders that ferenity and fixed ftayednefs,
which

which is neceſſary to ſo ſevere an intent-
neſs : And the frigidity of decrepite age
is as much its enemy, not only through
penury of *ſpirits*, but by reaſon of its
clogging them with its dulling moiſture.
And even in the temperate *zone* of our
life, there are few bodies at ſuch an
æquipoiz of humours ; but that the prevalency of ſome one indiſpoſeth the *ſpirits* for a work ſo difficult and ſerious :
For *temperamentum ad pondus*, may well
be reckon'd among the *three Philoſophi-
cal unattainables*. Beſides, the buſtle
of buſineſs, the avocations of our ſenſes,
and external pleaſures, and the noyſe
and din of a clamorous world are impediments not to be maſter'd by feeble
endeavours. And to ſpeak the full of
my Sentiments, I think never *Man* could
boaſt it, without the Precincts of *Paradiſe* ; but He, that came to gain us a
better *Eden* then we loſt. So then, to
direct all this to our end, the mind of
man being thus naturally amorous of, and
impatient for *Truth*, and yet averſe to,
and almoſt incapacitated for, that diligent and painful ſearch, which is neceſſary

cessary to its discovery ; it must needs
take up short, of what is really so, and
please it self in the possession of imaginary appearances, which offering themselves to its embraces in the borrowed
attire of that, which the *enamour'd In-*
tellect is in pursuit of, our impatient
minds entertain these counterfeits, without the least suspicion of their couse age.
For as the *Will*, having lost its true and
substantial *Good*, now courts the shadow,
and greedily catches at the vain shews
of *superficial* bliss : so our no less degenerate *understandings* having suffered
as sad a divorce from their dearest object, are as forward to defile themselves
with every meretricious semblance, that
the variety of opinion presents them
with. Thus we see the inconsiderate
vulgar, prostrating their assent to every
shallow appearance : and those , who
are beholden to *Prometheus* for a finer
mould, are not furnisht with so much
truth as otherwise they might be owners
of, did not this *precipitancy* of *concluding*
prevent them : As 'tis said of the industrious *Chymist*, that by catching at

K   it

it too foon, he loft the long expected treafure of the *Philofophical Elixir*. I'le illuftrate this Head by a double inftance,
and clofe it.

1. Hence it is, that we conclude many
things within the lift of *Impoßibilities*,
which yet are eafie *Feafables*. For by an
unadvifed tranfiliency leaping from the
effect to its remoteft caufe, we obferve
not the connexion through the interpofal of more immediate caufalities;
which yet at laft bring the extreams together without a *Miracle*. And here-
upon we haftily conclude that *impoßible*,
which we fee not in the proximate
capacity of its *Efficient*. Hence, that a
fingle *Hair* fhould root up an *Oak* (which
the Mathematicks teach us to be poffible)
will be thought fit to be number'd with
the ftory of the *Brazen-head*, or that
other of the wifhing Hat. The relation
of *Archimedes*'s lifting up the fhips of
Marcellus, among many finds but little
more credit, then that of the *Gyants*
fhouldering *Mountains*: And his other
exploits found no better to common
Ears, then thofe of *Amadis de Gaule*,
and

and the *Knight* of the *Sun*. And yet Mathematicians know, that by multiplying of Mechanical advantages, any power may conquer any refiftance; and the great *Syracufian wit* wanted but *Tools*, and a *place* to ftand on, to remove the *Earth*. So the brag of the *Ottoman*, that he would throw *Malta* into the Sea, might be performed at an eafier rate, then by the fhovels of his *Janizaries*. And from this laft noted head, arifeth that other of joyning *caufes* with *irrelative effects*, which either refer not at all unto them, or in a remoter capacity. Hence the *Indian* conceiv'd fo grofsly of the *Letter*, that difcover'd his Theft; and that other, who thought the Watch an *Animal*. From hence grew the impoftures of *charms*; and *amulets*, and other infignificant ceremonies; which to this day impofe upon common belief, as they did of old upon the *Barbarifm* of the incultivate *Heathen*. Thus effects unufual, whofe caufes run under ground, and are more remote from ordinary difcernment, are noted in the Book of *Vulgar Opinion*; with

K 2 *Digitus*

Digitus Dei, or *Dæmonis* ; though they owe no other dependence to the *first,* then what is common to the whole *Syntax* of beings, nor yet any more to the *second,* then what is given it by the imagination of those unqualifi'd Judges. Thus every unwonted *Meteor* is portentous ; and the appearance of any unobserved *Star,* some divine *Prognostick.* Antiquity thought *Thunder* the immediate voyce of *Jupiter,* and impleaded them of impiety, that referr'd it to natural causalities. Neither can there happen a *storm,* at this remove from *Antique* ignorance, but the multitude will have the *Devil* in't.

CHAP.

CHAP. XIII.

The sixth Reason discours't of, viz. the interest which our Affections have in our Dijudications. The cause why our Affections mislead us; several branches of this mention'd; and the first, viz. Constitutional Inclination largely insisted on.

AGain we owe much of our *Errour* and *Intellectual scarcity* to the Interest in, and power which our *affections* have over, our so easily seducible Understandings. And 'tis a truth well worthy the Pen, from which it dropt; *Periit Judicium, ubi res transiit in Affectum.* That *Jove* himself cannot be *wise* and in *Love*; may be understood in a larger sense, then Antiquity meant it. *Affection* bribes the Judgement to the most notorious inequality; and we

K 3   cannot

cannot expect an equitable award, where the Judge is made a Party : So that, that Underſtanding only is capable of giving a juſt deciſion, which is, as *Ariſtotle* ſaith of the *Law*, Νοῦς ἄνευ ὀρέξεως: But where the *Will*, or *Paſſion* hath the caſting voyce, the caſe of *Truth* is *deſperate*. And yet this is the miſerable diſorder, into which we are laps'd : The lower Powers are gotten uppermoſt ; and we *ſee* like men on our *heads*, as *Plato* obſerv'd of old, that on the *right* hand, which indeed is on the *left*. The *Woman* in us, ſtill proſecutes a deceit, like that begun in the *Garden :* and our *Underſtandings* are wedded to an *Eve*, as fatal as the *Mother* of our *miſeries*. And while all things are judg'd according to their ſuitableneſs, or diſagreement to the *Guſto* of the fond *Feminine* ; we ſhall be as far from the *Tree of Knowledge*, as from that, which is guarded by the *Cherubin*. The deceiver ſoon found this ſoft place of *Adam*'s ; and Innocency it ſelf did not ſecure him from this way of *ſeduction*. The firſt deception enter'd in at this Poſtern, and hath ever ſince kept it open for the entry of of *Legion* : so that we scarse see any thing now but through our *Passions*, the most blind, and sophisticate things about us. Thus the *Monsters* which story relates to have their *Eyes* in their *breasts*, are *pictures* of us in our *invisible selves*. Our *Love* of one Opinion induceth us to embrace it ; and our *Hate* of another, doth more then fit us, for its rejection : And, *that Love is blind*, is extensible beyond the object of *Poetry*. When once the *affections* are engag'd, there's but a short step to the Understanding : and, *Facilè credimus quod volumus*, is a truth, that needs not plead Authority to credit it.

The reason, I conceive, is this : *Love* as it were *uniting* the Object to the *Soul*, gives it a kind of *Identity* with us ; so that the beloved *Idea* is but *our selves* in another *Name :* and when *self* is at the bar, the sentence is not like to be impartial : For every man is naturally a *Narcissus*, and each *passion* in us, no other but *self-love* sweetned by milder Epithets. We can love nothing, but what is agreeable to us ; and our desire of what is

K 4 so,

so, hath its firſt inducement from within us: Yea, we love nothing but what
hath ſome reſemblance within our ſelves ;
and whatever we applaud as good or
excellent, is but *ſelf* in a *tranſcript,* and
è contrà. Thus, to reach the higheſt of
our *Amours,* and to ſpeak all at once :
We love our *friends,* becauſe they are
our *Image* ; and we love our *God* , becauſe we are *his.* So then, the *beloved*
Opinion being thus wedded to the *Intellect* ; the caſe of our *eſpouſed ſelf*
becomes our own : And when we weigh
our ſelves, *Juſtice* doth not uſe to hold
the ballance. Beſides, all things being
double-handed, and having the appearances both of Truth, and Falſhood ;
where our *affections* have engaged us,
we attend only to the former, which we
ſee through a magnifying *Medium :*
while looking on the latter, through the
wrong end of the *Perſpective* , which
ſcants their dimenſions, we neglect and
contemn them. Yea, and as in corrupt
judicial proceedings , the fore-ſtalled
Underſtanding paſſes a peremptory ſentence upon the ſingle hearing of one
Party :

Party ; and so comes under the Poets
censure of him, *Qui statuit aliquid parte
inauditâ alterâ.*

But to give a more particular account
of this Gullery ; Our *affections* engage
us as by our *Love to our selves* , so by
our Love to *others*. Of the former we
have the observable instances of *natural
disposition*, *Custom* and *Education*, *Interest*,
and *our proper Invention :* Of the latter
in that *Homage*, which is payd to *Antiquity*, and *Authority*. I take them up in
order.

1. *Congruity* of Opinions , whether
true or false, to our *natural constitution*,
is one great incentive to their belief,
and reception : and in a sense too the
complexion of the *mind*, as well as *manners*, follows the *Temperament* of the
Body. Thus some men are genially
disposited to some *Opinions*, and naturally as averse to others. Some things
we are inclined to love, and we know
not why : Others we disesteem, and upon no better account then the Poet did
Sabidius, *Hoc tantùm possum dicere, Non
amo te*. Some faces at first sight we admire
and

and dote on : others, in our impartial apprehensions no less deserving our esteem,
we can behold without resentment ; and
it may be with an invincible disregard.
I question not, but intellectual representations are received by us, with as an
unequal a Fate upon a bare *Temperamental* Relish or Disgust : And I believe
the Understanding hath its *Idiosyncrasies,*
as well as other faculties. Some men
are made to *superstition,* others to *fran-
tick Enthusiasm* ; the former by the *cold*
of a timorous *heart ,* the latter by the
heat of a temerarious *brain :* And there
are natures, as fatally averse to either.
And the *opinions ,* which are suited to
their respective *tempers,* will be sure to
find their welcome, and to grow without
manure. Your dull *phlegmatick* Souls
are taken with the dulness of *sensible*
doctrines : and the more *Mercurial* Ge-
niuses calculated to what is more refined,
and *Intellectual.* Thus *opinions* have their
Climes and *National* diversities : And as
some Regions have their proper Vices,
not so generally found in others ; so have
they their mental depravities, which are
                                    drawn

drawn in with the common air of the Countrey. And I take this for one of the moſt conſiderable cauſes of the diverſity of *Laws*, *Cuſtomes*, *Religions*, *natural* and *moral* doctrines, which is to be found in the divided Regions of the inhabited Earth. And therefore I wonder not at the *Idolatry* of the *Jews* of old, or of the ſeveral parts of the world to this day, nor at the *ſenſual expectations* of the *Muſſel-men*, nor at the fopperies of the ſuperſtitious *Romaniſts*, nor the ridiculous devotions of the deluded *Indians :* ſince that the moſt ſenſeleſs conceits and fooleries cannot miſs of Harbor, where *affection*, grown upon the ſtock of a *depraved conſtitution*, hath endeared them. And if we do but more nearly look into our *faculties* , beginning our ſurvey from the loweſt dregs of *ſenſe*, even thoſe which have a nearer commerce with matter, and ſo by ſteps aſcend to our more *ſpiritualiz'd ſelves :* we ſhall throughout diſcover how *conſtitutional partiality* ſways us. Thus to one *Palate* that is *ſweet*, *deſirable*, and *delicious* , which to another is *odious* and *diſtaſtful* ; or more

com-

compendioufly in the Proverb, *One mans meat is anothers poyfon.* Thus what to one is a moft grateful *odour,* to another is *noxious* and *difpleafant* ; 'twere a mifery to fome to lye ftretch't on a bed of Rofes: And in the *fenfe* of *life* ; that's a *welcome touch* to one, which is *difagreeing* to another. And yet to rife a little higher to the *nobler pair* ; the *mufical* Airs, which one entertains with moft *delightful tranfports* , to another are *importune :* and the objects, which one can't fee without an *Extafie,* another is no more mov'd at, than a *Statue.* If we pafs further , the *phancies* of men are fo immediately diverfify'd by the individual *Crafis,* that every man is in this a *Phœnix* ; and owns fomething, wherein none are like him : and thefe are as many , as humane nature hath *fingulars.* Now the *phancies* of the moft, like the *Index* of a Clock, are moved but by the inward *Springs* and wheels of the corporal *Machine* ; which even on the moft fublimate Intellectuals is dangeroufly *influential.* And yet this fits at the Helm of the Worlds belief;

belief; and Vulgar *Reason* is no better then a more *refined Imagination.* So then the *Senses , Phancy ,* and what we call *Reason* it felf, being thus influenc'd by the *Bodies temperament,* and little better then indications of it ; it cannot be otherwife, but that this *love of our felves* fhould ftrongly incline us in our moft abftracted *dijudications.*

CHAP. XIV.

A second thing whereby our Affections ingage us in Error, is the prejudice of Cuftom *and* Education. *A third,* Intereft. *The fourth,* Love *to our own Productions.*

2.   ANother genuine derivation of this *felfifh fondnefs,* by reafon of which we mifcarry of *Science,* is the almoft infuperable *prejudice of Cuftom,* and *Education :* by which our minds are encumber'd,

encumber'd, and the moſt are held in a *Fatal Ignorance*. Now could a man be compoſed to ſuch an advantage of conſtitution, that it ſhould not at all adulterate the images of his mind ; yet this *ſecond nature* would alter the *craſis* of the Uuderſtanding, and render it as obnoxious to aberrances ; as now. And though in the former regard , the *Soul* were a pure ἄγραφον γραμματεῖον ; yet *cuſtom* and *education* will ſo blot and ſcrible on't , as almoſt to incapacitate it for after-impreſſions. Thus we judge all things by our *anticipations* ; and condemn or applaud them, as they agree or differ from our *education-prepoſſeſſions*. One Countrey laughs at the *Laws*, *Cuſtoms*, and *Opinions* of another, as abſurd and ridiculous ; and the other is as charitable to them, in its conceit of theirs. This confirms the moſt ſottiſh *Idolaters* in their accuſtomed adorations, beyond the conviction of any thing, but *Dooms-day*. The impreſſions of a barbarous *education* are ſtronger in them, then *nature* ; when in their cruel *worſhips* they launce themſelves with knifes, and expoſe their

harmleſs

harmleſs *Infants* to the *flames* as a Sacrifice to their *Idols*. And 'tis on this
account, that there's no Religion ſo irrational, but can boaſt its *Martyrs*. This
is it, which befriends the *Talmud* and
Alcoran; and did they not owe their credit more to it, then to any rational inducement, we might expect their *aſhes*:
whereas *Education* hath ſo rooted theſe
miſ-believers in their ungrounded *faith*,
that they may aſſoon be pluck't from
themſelves, as from their obſtinate adherencies; and to convert a *Turk*, or *Iew*,
may be well a *phraſe* for an attempt
impoſſible. We look for it *only* from him,
to whom our *Impoſſibles* are *none*. And
'tis to be feared, that *Chriſtianity* it ſelf by
moſt, that have eſpouſed it, is not held
by any better tenure. The beſt account
that many can give of their *belief*, is,
that they were *bred* in it; which indeed
is no better, then that which we call, the
Womans Reaſon. And thouſands of them,
whom their profeſſion, and our charity
ſtyles *Chriſtians*, are driven to their Religion by *cuſtom* and *education*, as the
Indians are to *Baptiſm*; that is, like a
drove

drove of Cattle to the water. And had our *Stars* determin'd our nativities among the Enemies of the *Cross*, and theirs under a *Christian horoscope*; in all likelyhood *Antichristianism* had not been the object of our aversion, nor *Christianity* of theirs : But we should have exchang'd the Scene of our belief with that of our abode and *breeding*. There is nothing so *monstrous*, to which *education* cannot form our ductile *minority*; it can lick us into shapes beyond the *monstrosities* of those of *Affrica*. And as King *James* would say of *Parliaments*; it can do any thing, but make a *man* a *woman*. For our initial age is like the melted wax to the prepared Seal, capable of any impression from the documents of our Teachers. The *half-moon* or *Cross*, are indifferent to its reception; and we may with equal facility write on this *rasa Tabula*, Turk, or Christian. We came into the world like the unformed *Cub*; 'tis *education* is our *Plastick*: we are baptized into our opinions by our Juvenile nurture, and our growing years confirm those unexamined Principles. For

our

our firſt task is to learn the *Creed* of our Countrey; and our next to maintain it. We ſeldom examine our Receptions, more then children their *Catechiſms*; For *Implicit* faith is a vertue, where *Orthodoxie* is the object. Some will not be at the trouble of a Tryal: others are ſcar'd from attempting it. If we do, 'tis not by a *Sun-beam* or ray of univerſal light; but by a *flame* that's kindled by our *affections*, and fed by the fewel of our *anticipations*. And thus like the *Hermite*, we think the *Sun* ſhines no where, but in our *Cell*; and all the world to be in darkneſs but our ſelves. We judge truth to be circumſcrib'd by the confines of our belief, and the doctrines we were brought up in: and with as ill manners, as thoſe of *China*, repute all the reſt of world, *Monoculous*. So that what ſome *Aſtrologers* ſay of our *Fortunes* and the paſſages of our lives; may by the allowance of a *Metaphor* be ſaid of our *Opinions*: That they are written in our *ſtars*, being to the moſt as fatal as thoſe involuntary occurrences, and as little in their Power as the *placits* of

L   *deſtiny*.

deſtiny. We are bound to our Countreys opinions, as to its laws : and an accuſtomed aſſent is *tantamount* to an infallible concluſion. He that offers to diſſent, ſhall be out-law'd in his reputation : and the fear of guilty *Cain,* ſhall be fulfilled on him, who ever *meets* him *ſhall ſlay him.* Thus *Cuſtom* and *Education* hath ſeal'd the *Canon* ; and he that adds or takes away from the Book of *Orthodox* belief, ſhall be more then in danger of an *Anathema :* And the *Inquiſition* is not confined to the juriſdiction of the *Triple-Crown.* So we prepoſterouſly invert the Precept ; holding faſt what hath the Vote of our antedating apprehenſions, we try all things by theſe our partial *Prolepſes.* He that dares do otherwiſe, is a *Rebel* to *Orthodoxy* ; and expoſeth his credit to *Se-queſtration.* Thus *Cuſtom* conciliates our eſteem to things, no otherwiſe deſerving it : what is in *faſhion*, is handſom and pleaſant ; though never ſo uncouth to an unconcern'd beholder. Their antick deckings with feathers is as comely in the account of thoſe barbarous Nations, which uſe them ; as the Ornaments of Lace,

Lace, and Ribband, are in ours. And the plucking off the *fhooe* is to the *Japanners* as decent a falutation ; as the uncovering of the *head* is to us, and their abhorred *neighbours.* On the other hand we ftart and boggle at what is *unufual :* and like the *Fox* in the fable at his firft view of the *Lyon,* we cannot endure the fight of the *Bug-bear,Novelty.* Hence fome innocent truths have been affix'd with the reproach of *Herefie :* into which, becaufe contrary to the inur'd belief, the violent rejecters would not endure a patient infpection : But as children frighted in the dark, who run away with an out-cry from the *Monfters* of their own imaginations framing ; and will not ftay for the information of a better difcovery : fo they looking on them through their unadvifed fears, and uncharitable fufpicions ; command their Underftandings to a præcipitate flight, figuring their phancies to fhapes *monftrous* and *horrible,* through which they make them the objects of their averfion. Hence there is no truth, but its adverfaries have made it an ugly *Vizard* ; by which it's expofed to the hate and dif-

efteem

efteem of fuperficial examiners : And an opprobrious title with vulgar believers is as good as an *Argument*. 'Tis but writing the name, that cuftomary receptions have difcredited, under the opinions we diflike ; and all other refutation is fuperfluous. Thus fhallow apprehenders are frighted from many fober *Verities*; like the King of *Arabs*, who ran away from the *fmoaking Mince-Py*, apprehending fome dangerous plot in the harmlefs fteam. So then, while we thus miftake the infufions of *education*, for the *principles* of univerfal *nature* ; we muft needs fail of a *fcientifical Theory*. And therefore the two Nations differing about the *antiquity* of their Language, made appeal to an undecifive *experiment* ; when they agreed upon the tryal of a child brought up among the wild Inhabitants of the Defert. The *Language* it fpake, had no reafon to be accounted the moft ancient and natural : And the lucky determination for the *Phrygians* by its pronouncing the word *Beck* , which fignified bread in the dialect of that Countrey, they owed not to *Nature*, but the

the *Goat-herd*; from which the expofed Infant, by accompanying that fort of *animals*, had learnt it.

3. Again, *Intereft* is another thing, by the *magnetifme* of which our *affections* are almoft irrefiftibly attracted. It is the *Pole*, to which we turn, and our *fympa-thizing* Judgements feldom decline from the *direction* of this *Impregnant*. Where *Intereft* hath engaged us; like *Hannibal*, we'l find a way to veritie, or make it. Any thing is a Truth, to one whofe *In-tereft* it is, to have it fo. And therefore Self-defigners are feldom difappointed, for want of the fpecioufnefs of a caufe to warrant them; in the belief of which, they do oft as really impofe upon them-felves, as induftrioufly endeavour it upon others. With what an infinite of *Law-fuits*, *controverfies*, and *litigious cafes* doth the world abound? and yet every man is confident of the truth and goodnefs of his own. And as Mr. *Hobbs* obferves, the reafon that Mathematical demonftra-tions are uncontroverted, is; becaufe *Intereft* hath no place in thofe unquefti-onable *verities*: when as, did the advan-

tage, of any stand against them, *Euclids Elements* would not pass with a *Ne-
mine contradicente.* Sir *H. Blunt* tells us,
that temporal expectations bring in
droves to the *Mahumetan Faith* ; and we
know the same holds thousands in the
Romish. The *Eagles* will be, where the
carcase is; and that shall have the faith
of most, which is best able to pay them
for't. An advantageous cause never wanted *Proselytes.* I confess, I cannot believe
that all the learned *Romanists* profess
against their *conscience* ; but rather, that
their *Interest* brings their *consciences* to
their *Profession* : and self-advantage can
as easily incline some, to believe a
falshood, as profess it. A good *will,*
help'd by a good *wit,* can find truth any
where : and, what the *Chymists* brag of
their *Elixir,* it can transmute any *metal*
into *gold* ; In the hand of a skilful Artificer, in spight of the Adage, *Ex quolibet
ligno Mercurius.* Though yet I think,
that every Religion hath its bare *Nominals* : and that Pope was one with a wit-
ness, whose saying it was, *Quantum nobis
lucri peperit illa fabula de Christo* !

4, Besides

4. Besides, fourthly, *Self-love* engageth us for any thing, that is a *Minerva* of our own. We love the issues of our *Brains*, no less then those of our *bodies* : and fondness of our own *begotten notions*, though *illegitimate*, obligeth us to maintain them. We hugge intellectual deformities, if they bear our Names ; and will hardly be perswaded they are so, when our selves are their Authors. If their *Dam* may be judge, the young *Apes* are the most beautiful things in Nature ; and if we might determine it, our proper conceptions would be all voted *Axioms*. Thus then the *Affections* wear the breeches : and the *Female* rules, while our Understanding governs us, as the story saith *Themistocles* did *Athens.* So that to give the sum of all, most of the contests of the litigious world pretending for *Truth*, are but the bandyings of one mans *affections* against anothers : in which, though their reasons may be foil'd, yet their *Passions* lose no ground, but rather improve by the *Antiperistasis* of an opposition.

L 4   CHAP.

CHAP. XV.

5. *Our Affections are engaged by our Reverence to Antiquity and Authority. This hath been a great hinderer of Theorical improvements; and it hath been an advantage to the Mathematicks, and Mechanicks Arts, that it hath no place in them. Our mistake of Antiquity. The unreasonableness of that kind of Pedantick Adoration. Hence the vanity of affecting impertinent quotations. The Pedantry on't is derided; the little improvement of Science through its successive derivations, and whence that hath hapned.*

ANother thing, that engageth our *affections* to unwarrantable conclusions, and is therefore fatal to *Science*; is our

our doting on *Antiquity*, and the opinions of our *Fathers*. We look with a superstitious reverence upon the accounts of præterlapsed ages: and with a supercilious severity, on the more deserving products of our own. A vanity, which hath possefs'd all times as well as ours; and the *Golden Age* was never *prefent*. For as in *Statick* experiment, an inconsiderable weight by vertue of its diftance from the Centre of the Ballance, will preponderate much greater magnitudes; fo the moft flight and chaffy opinion, if at a great remove from the prefent age, contracts fuch an efteem and veneration, that it out-weighs what is infinitly more ponderous and rational, of a *modern* date. And thus, in another fenfe, we realize what *Archimedes* had only in *Hypothefis*; weighing a fingle *grain* againft the *Globe* of Earth. We reverence gray-headed Doctrines; though feeble, decrepit, and within a ftep of duft : and on this account maintain opinions, which have nothing but our *charity* to uphold them. While the *beauty* of a Truth, as of a *picture*, is not acknowledg'd but at a
diftance;

diſtance ; and that wiſdom is nothing
worth, which is not fetcht from *afar* :
wherein yet we oft deceive our ſelves,
as did that *Mariner*, who miſtaking them
for precious ſtones , brought home his
ſhip fraught with common *Pebbles* from
the remoteſt *Indies*. Thus our Eyes,
like the *prepoſterous Animal's*, are behind
us ; and our Intellectual motions *retrograde*. We adhere to the determinations
of our fathers, as if their *opinions* were
entail'd on us as their *lands* ; or (as ſome
conceive) part of the Parents ſoul were
portion'd out to his off-ſpring, and the
conceptions of our minds were *ex traduce*. The Sages of old live again in us ;
and in opinions there is a *Metempſychoſis*.
We are our re-animated *Anceſtours*, and
antedate their *Reſurrection*.　And thus,
while every age is but another ſhew
of the former ; 'tis no wonder, that Science hath not out-grown the dwarfiſhneſs of its *priſtine ſtature*, and that the
Intellectual world is ſuch a *Microcoſm*. For
while we account of ſome admired
Authours, as the *Seths Pillars*, on which
all knowledge is engraven ; and ſpend
　　　　　　　　　　　　　　that

that time and study in defence of their Placits, which with more advantage to Science might have been employ'd upon the Books of the more ancient, and *univerſal Author:* 'Tis not to be admired, that Knowledge hath receiv'd ſo little improvement from the endeavours of many pretending promoters, through the continued ſeries of ſo many ſucceſ-ſive ages, For while we are ſlaves to the *Dictates* of our *Progenitours*; our diſcoveries, like *water*, will not run higher then the *Fountains*, from which they own their derivation, And while we think it ſo piaculous, to go beyond the *Ancients*; we muſt neceſſarily come ſhort of genuine *Antiquity*, Truth; un-leſs we ſuppoſe them to have reach'd perfection of Knowledge in ſpight of their acknowledgements of ignorance,

Now if we enquire the reaſon, why the *Mathematicks*, and *Mechanick Arts*, have ſo much got the ſtart in growth of other *Sciences:* We ſhall find it probably reſolv'd into this, as one conſiderable cauſe: that their progreſs hath not been retarde dby that reverential aw of former diſcoveries,

difcoveries, which hath been fo great an
hinderance to Theorical improvements.
'Twas never an herefie to out-limn
Apelles ; nor criminal to out-work the
Obelisks.Galilæus without a crime out-faw
all *Antiquity* ; and was not afraid to believe his eyes, in fpight of the *Opticks* of
Ptolomy and *Ariftotle.* 'Tis no difcredit
to that ingenious *Perfpicill,* that Antiquity ne're faw in't : Nor are we fhy of
aſſent to thofe *celeftial* informations, becaufe they were *hid from ages.* We
believe the *verticity* of the *Needle,*without
a Certificate from the *dayes of old* : And
confine not our felves to the fole conduct
of the *Stars* , for fear of being wifer
then our Fathers. Had *Authority* prevail'd here , the Earths *fourth part* had
to us been *none,* and *Hercules* his Pillars
had ftill been the worlds *Non ultra : Se-*
neca's Prophefie had yet been an unfulfill'd
Prediction, and one moiety of our *Globes,*
an empty *Hemifphear.*

In a fenfe, Τὰ ἀρχαῖα κρατείτω, is a wholefom inftruction ; and becoming the Vote
of a *Synod :* But yet, in common acceptation , it's an Enemy to Verity,
which

which can plead the *antiquity* of above *six thousand*; and bears date from before the *Chaos*. For, as the Noble Lord *Verulam* hath noted, we have a mistaken apprehension of *Antiquity*; calling that so, which in truth is the worlds Nonage. *Antiquitas seculi est juventus Mundi.* So that in such appeals, we fetch our knowledge from the *Cradle*; which though it be nearest to *Innocence*, it is so too to the fatal ruines which follow'd it. Upon a true account, the *present age* is the worlds *Grandævity*; and if we must to *Antiquity*, let multitude of days speak. Now for us to supersede further disquisition, upon the infant acquirements of those Juvenile endeavours, is foolishly to neglect the nobler advantages we are owners of, and in a sense to disappoint the expectations of him that gave them. Yet thus we prevent our selves of Science; and our knowledge, though its Age write *thousands*, is still in its *swadlings*. For like School-boys, we give over assoon as we have learn't as far as our Masters can teach us: And had not the undertakings of some glorious He-

roes

roes prevented; *Plato*'s year might have found us, where the days of *Aristotle* left us. For my part, I think it no such arrogance, as our Pedants account it; that almost two thousand years elapsed since, should weigh with the sixty three of the *Stagirite*. If we owe it to him, that we know so much; 'tis long of his Pedantick adorers that we know so little more. I can see no ground, why his Reason should be *textuary* to ours; or that God, or Nature, ever intended him an Universal *Headship*. It was another, in whom were hid all the Treasures of *Wisdom* and *Knowledge :* His reason only is the *Yea* and *Amen*; who is the *Alpha* and *Omega*, the Christian אֱמֶת. 'Twas this vain Idolizing of Authors, which gave birth to that silly vanity of *impertinent citations*; and inducing Authority in things neither requiring, nor deserving it. That saying was much more observable, *That men have beards, and women none*; because quoted from *Beza :* and that other, *Pax res bona est;* because brought in with a, *said St. Austin*. But these ridiculous fooleries, to your more
generous

generous difcerners, fignifie nothing but the Pedantry of the affected Scioliſt. 'Tis an inglorious acquiſt to have our heads or Volumes laden, as were Cardinal *Campeius* his Mules, with old and uſeleſs luggage : And yet the magnificence of many high pretenders to Science, if laid open by a true diſcovery, would amount to no more then the old *Boots* and *Shooes*, of that proud, and expoſed *Embaſſadour*. Methinks 'tis a pitiful piece of Knowledge, that can be learnt from an *Index* ; and a poor Ambition to be rich in the Inventory of anothers Treaſure. To boaſt a *memory* (the moſt that theſe Pedants can aim at) is but an humble oſtentation. And of all the faculties , in which ſome Brutes out-vie us, I leaſt envy them an excellence in that ; deſiring rather to be a *Fountain*, then a *Hogs-head*. 'Tis better to own a Judgment, though but with a *Curta ſupellex* of coherent notions ; then a *memory*, like a Sepulchre , furniſhed with a load of broken and diſcarnate bones. *Authorities* alone with me make no *number*, unleſs Evidence of Reaſon
ſtand

ſtand before them : For all the *Cyphers* of *Arithmetick* , are no better then a ſingle *nothing*. And yet this rank folly of affecting ſuch impertinencies , hath overgrown our Times ; and thoſe that are Candidates for the repute of *Scholars*, take this way to compaſs it. When as multiplicity of reading, the beſt it can ſignifie , doth but ſpeak them to have taken pains for it: And this alone is but the dry, and barren part of learning, and hath little reaſon to denominate. A number of *Receits* at the beſt can but make an *Emperick*.

But again, to what is more perpendicular to our diſcourſe, if we impartially look into the remains of Antique Ages ; we ſhall finde but little to juſtifie ſo groundleſs a Tyranny, as *Antiquity* hath impos'd on the enſlaved world. For if we drive the Current of Science as high, as *Hiſtory* can lead us; we ſhall finde, that through its ſeveral ſucceſſive derivations it hath ſtill lain under ſuch diſadvantages, as have rendred any conſiderable acceſſion unfeaſable. And though

ɩt

it hath oft chang'd its Channel, by its remove from one Nation to another; yet hath it been little more alter'd, then a *River* in its paſſage through differing *Regions, viz.* in *Name* and *Method.* For the ſucceeding times ſtill ſubſcribing to, and copying out thoſe, who went before them, with little more then *verbal* diverſity; *Science* hath ſtill been the ſame *pityful* thing, though in a various *Livery.* Now if we look upon it, either in the hand of the *ſuperſtitious Egyptian, fabulous* and *diſputing Græcian,* or as *garrulous Roman* : what hath it been, but only a pretty toy in an *Hieroglyphick;* a very ſlender ſomething in a *Fable;* or an old nothing in a *diſputation?* And though thoſe former days have not wanted brave *Wits,* that have gallantly attempted, and made Eſſays worthy Immortality; yet by reaſon either of the unqualified capacities of the multitude, (who dote on things ſlight and trivial, neglecting what is more rare and excellent) or the clamorous aſſaults of envious and more popular oppoſers, they have ſubmitted

M   to

to Fate, and are almoſt loſt in Oblivion.
And therefore, as that great man, the
Lord Bacon hath obſerv'd, *Time* as a
River, hath brought down to us what
is more light and ſuperficial; while
things more ſolid and ſubſtantial have
been immerſed. Thus the *Ariſtotelian
Philoſophy* hath prevailed; while the more
excellent *Hypotheſes* of *Democritus* and
Epicurus have long lain buryed under
neglect aud obloquy: and for ought I
know might have ſlept for ever, had
not the ingenuity of this age recall'd
them from their *Urne*. But it is ſomewhat collateral to my ſcope, as well as
diſproportion'd to my abilities, to fall
upon particular Inſtances of the defects
and Errours of the *Philoſophy* of the
Ancients. The foremention'd noble
Advancer of Learning, whoſe name
and parts might give credit to any undertaking; hath handſomly perform'd
it, in his ingenious *Novum Organum*. And
yet, becauſe it may conferr towards the
diſcovery of how little our adherence
to *Antiquity* befriends Truth, and the
encreaſe

encreafe of Knowledge ; as alſo how groundleſs are the *Dogmatiſts* high pretenſions to Science : I ſhall adventure ſome conſiderations on the *Peripatetick Philoſophy* ; which hath had the luck to ſurvive all others, and to build a fame on their *Ruines.*

M 2   C H A P.

CHAP. XVI.

Reflexions on the Peripatetick Philofophy.

The Generality of its Reception, no Argument of its deferts; the firft charge againft that Philofophy ; that it is meerly verbal. A Cenfure of the Peripatetick Jefuites. Materia prima *in that Philofophy fignifies nothing. A Parallel drawn between it and Imaginary Space : this latter pleads more for its reality. Their Form alfo is a meer word, and* potentia Materia *infignificant. An effay to detect Peripatetick Verbofity , by tranflating fome definitions.*

THat *Ariftotles Philofophy* hath been entertain'd by the *moft* ; hath deceiv'd the credulous into a conceit, that
it's

it's *best :* And its intrinfick worth hath
been concluded from the Grandure of its
Retinue. But *Seneca*'s determination,
Argumentum peßimi Turba eft, is more
deferving our credit : and the *feweft,*
that is the *wifeft,* have always ftood
contradictory to that ground of belief;
Vulgar applaufe by feverer Wifdom being held a fcandal. If the numeroufnefs
of a Train muft carry it ; *Vertue* may go
follow *Aftræa,* and *Vice* only will be
worth the courting. The *Philofopher*
defervedly fufpected himfelf of vanity,
when cryed up by the multitude : And
difcreet apprehenders will not think the
better of that *Philofophy,* which hath the
common cry to vouch it. He that writ
counter to the *Aftrologer* in his *Almanack,* did with more truth foretell the
weather : and he that fhall write, *Foul,*
in the place of the Vulgars, *Fair* ; paffes
the jufter cenfure. Thofe in the *Fable,*
who were wet with the fhowre of *folly,*
hooted at the *wife men* that efcap'd it, and
pointed at their actions as *ridiculous* ;
becaufe unlike their own, that were
truly *fo.* If the major Vote may caft it,

Wifdom

Wiſdom and Folly muſt exchange
names; and the way to the one will
be by the other. Nor is it the Rabble
only, which are ſuch perverſe diſcerners;
we are now a ſphear above them: I
mean the πὶ πολὺ, of pretended *Philoſo-*
phers, who judge as odly in their way,
as the *Raſcality* in theirs: and many a
profeſt Retainer to *Philoſophy*, is but an
Ignoramus a in ſuit of *ſecond Notions*.
'Tis ſuch, that moſt revere the Reliques
of the Adored *Sophy*; and, as *Artemeſia*
did thoſe of *Mauſolus*, paſſionately drink
his *aſhes*. Whether the Remains of the
Stagirite deſerve ſuch *Veneration*, we'll
make a brief enquiry.

1. That the *Ariſtotelian Philoſophy* is
an huddle of *words* and *terms inſignifi-*
cant, hath been the cenſure of the wiſeſt:
And that both its Baſis and Superſtructure are *Chimarical*; cannot be unobſerv'd by them, that know it, and are
free to judge it. 'Tis a *Philoſophy*, that
makes moſt accurate Inſpections into the
Creatures of the *Brain*; and gives the
exacteſt *Topography* of the *Extramundane*
ſpaces. Like our late *Politicians*, it makes
discoveries,

difcoveries, and their objects too ; and deals in beings, that are nothing beholden to the *Primitive Fiat*. Thus the fame undivided Effence, from the feveral circumftances of its being and operations, is here multiplied into *Legion*, and emprov'd to a number of fmaller *Entities* ; and thefe again into as many *Modes* and infignificant *formalities*. What a number of words here have nothing anfwering them ? and as many are impofed at random. To wreft names from their known meaning to Senfes moft alien, and to darken *fpeech by words without knowledge* ; are none of the moft inconfiderable faults of this *Philofophy* : To reckon them in their particular inftances, would puzzle *Archimedes*. Now hence the genuine *Idea's* of the Mind are adulterate ; and the Things themfelves loft in a crowd of *Names*, and *Intentional nothings*. Thus thefe *Verbofities* do emafculate the Underftanding ; and render it flight and frivolous, as its objects. Me thinks, the late *Voluminous Jefuites*, thofe *Laplanders* of *Peripateticifm*, do but fubtilly trifle : and their *Philofophick* undertakings

M 4 are

are much like his, who spent his time in darting *Cumming-seeds* through the *Eye* of a *Needle*. One would think they were impregnated, as are the Mares in *Cappadocia*; they are big of words: their tedious Volumes have the *Tympany*, and bring forth the wind. To me, a *curſus Philoſophicus*, is but an Impertinency in *Folio*; and the ſtudying of them a laborious idleneſs. 'Tis here, that things are crumbled into *notional Atomes*; and the ſubſtance evaporated into an *imaginary Æther*. The Intellect, that can feed on this *air*, is a *Chamælion*; and a meer *inflated* skin. From this ſtock grew *School-divinity*, which is but *Peripateticiſm* in a *Theological Livery*. A *Schoolman* is the Ghoſt of the *Stagirite*, in a Body of condenſed Air: and *Thomas* but *Ariſtotle ſainted*. But to make good our charge againſt the *Philoſophy* of the *Schools*, by a more cloſe ſurveying it. That its *Principles* are ſteril, unſatisfying *Verboſities*; cannot eſcape the notice of the moſt ſhallow Inquirer. To begin at the bottom; their *Materia prima* is a meer *chimæra*. If we can fix a determinate
nate

nate conceit of nothing ; that's the *Idea*
on't : And, *Nec quid, nec quale , nec
quantum* , is as as appofite a *definition* of
nothing, as can be. If we would conceive this Imaginary *Matter :* we muſt
deny all things of it, that we can conceive, and what remains is the thing we
look for. And ſhould we allow it all,
which its Aſſertors aſſign it, *viz. Quantity interminate* ; 'tis ſtill but an empty
extended capacity, and therefore at the
beſt , but like that *Space* , which we
imagine was before the beginning of
Time , and will be after the Univerſal
Flames. 'Tis eaſie to draw a *Paralleliſm*
between that *Ancient* , and this more
Modern Nothing ; and in all things to
make good its reſemblance to that *Commentitious Inanity.* The *Peripatetick matter* is a pure unaČtuated Power : and this
conceited *Vacuum* a meer Receptῒbility.
Matter is ſuppos'd *indeterminate :* and
Space is ſo. The pretended *firſt matter* is
capable of all *forms :* And the *imaginary
ſpace* is receptive of any *body.* The *matter*
can be aČtuated at once but by a ſingle
Informant ; and *Space* is repleniſht by
one

one *Corporal Inexiſtence.* *Matter* cannot
naturally ſubſiſt *uninform'd :* And *Nature* avoids *vacuity* in *ſpace.* The *matter*
is *ingenerate,* and beyond corruption :
And the *ſpace* was before, and will be
after either. The *matter* in all things is
but *one* : and the *ſpace* moſt *uniform.*
Thus the Foundation-Principle of *Peripateticiſm* runs but *parallel* to an acknowledg'd *nothing :* and their agreement in
eſſential characters makes rather an *Identity,* then a *Parity* ; but that *Imaginary
ſpace* hath more to ple*a*d for its *reality,*
then the *matter* hath, and herein only
are they *diſſimilar.* For *that* hath no
dependence on the bodies which poſſeſs
it ; but was before them, and will ſurvive them : whereas *this* eſſentially relies on the *form,* and cannot ſubſiſt without it. Which yet, me thinks, is little
better then an *abſurdity :* that the cauſe
ſhould be an *Eleemoſynary* for its ſubſi-
ſtence to its effect, and a nature *poſterior*
to, and dependent on it ſelf. This *dependentia a poſteriori,* though in a diverſe
way of cauſality, my reaſon could never
away with : Yea, one of their own,
Oviedo

Oviedo a *Spanish* Jesuite, hath effectually impugn'd it. So then there's nothing *real*, answering this Imaginary *Proteus*; and *Materia prima* hath as much of being, as *Mons aureus*. But to take a step further, their *Form* is as obnoxious; and as dry a *word*, as the formention'd *Nominal*. I'le not spend time in an industrious confutation: The subject is dry, and I long to be out on't; with a note on its *imaginary Origine*, I'le leave it. It's source is as obscure, as *Nile*'s; and *Potentia materiæ* is a pitiful figment. Did it suppose any thing of the *form* to pre-exist in the *matter*, as the seminal of its being; 'twere tolerable sense to say it were *educed* from it, But by *educing* the affirmers only mean a producing in it, with a subjective dependence on its Recipient: a very fine signification of *Eduction*; which answers not the question whence 'tis derived, but into what it is received. The question is of the *terminus à quo*, and the answer of the *subject*. So that all that can be made of this *power* of the *matter*, is meerly *a receptive capacity*: and we may as well affirm,

that

that the world was *educ'd* out of the
power of the *imaginary space*; and give
that as a sufficient account of its Original.   And in this language, to grow
rich · were to *educe* money out of the
power of the Pocket.   To make a full
discovery of the jejune emptiness of
these *Philosophick Principles*, were a task
as easie for an ordinary undertaker; as
it would be tedious to an Ingenious Reader.   *Gassendus* hath excellently perform'd it , and, I am confident , to the
conviction of those, whom nobler *Principles* have not yet emancipated from that
degenerous flavery.   I shall not attempt
a work that hath been finished by such
an *Apelles*.   Only to give an hint more
of this verbal emptiness ; a short view
of a *definition* or two will be current
evidence : which, though in *Greek* or
Latine they amuse us, yet a *vernacular
translation* unmasks them ; and if we
make them speak *English* , the cheat is
transparent.   Light is ἐνέργεια τῦ διαφάνϛ
saith that *Philosophy*: In *English*, the *Act
of a perspicuous body*. Sure *Aristotle* here
transgress his *Topicks :* and if this definition

finition be clearer, and more known then
the thing defin'd ; *midnight* may vye
for conspicuity with *noon*. Is not *light*
more known then this insignificant *Ener-*
gie ? And what's a *diaphanous* body, but
the *Lights medium*,the *Air ?* so that *light*
is the act of the *Air* : which *definition*
spoils the *Riddle* ; and makes it no wonder, a man should see by *night* as well as
by *day*. Thus is *light* darkned by an *il-*
lustration ; and the *Sun* it self is wrap'd
up in obscuring *clouds* : As if *light* were
best seen by *darkness*, as *light inaccessi-*
ble is known by *Ignorance*. If *Lux* be
Umbra Dei ; this definition is *Umbra*
lucis. The Infant, that was last enlarged
from its *maternal cels* ; knows more what
light is , then this *definition* teacheth.
Again, that motion is ἐντελέχεια τῦ ὄντ۬ ἐν
δυνάμει, *&c.* is as insignificant as the former. By the most favourable interpretation of that unintelligible *Entelechy* ; It
is but an *act* of a being in *power,* as it is in
power : The construing of which to any
real meaning, is beyond the *criticisms* of
a *Mother Tongue* ; except it describes our
modern Acts of Parliaments. Sure that
                              definition

definition is not very *conspicuous*, whose *Genus* pos'd the *Devil*. The *Philosopher*, that prov'd *motion* by walking, did in that action better *define* it : And that puzled *Candidate*, who being ask'd what a *circle* was, describ'd it by the *rotation* of his *hand*; gave an account more satisfying. In some things we must indeed give an allowance for words of Art : But in defining obvious appearances, we are to use what is most plain and easie; that the mind be not misled by *Amphibologies*, or ill conceived notions, into fallacious deductions. To give an account of all the insignificancies of this *Philosophy*, would be almost to transcribe it; a task that I should never engage in, though I ow'd no account for my idle hours. 'Twill need a pardon from the Ingenious for the minutes already spent, though in a *confutation*.

CHAP.

CHAP. XVII.

2. Peripatetick Philosophy is litigious ; it hath no setled constant significati- on of words; the inconveniences here- of. Aristotle intended the cherish- ing Controversies: prov'd by his own double testimony. Some of his imper- tinent arguings derided. Disputes retard, and are injurious to know- ledge. Peripateticks are most exer- cised in the Controversal parts of Philosophy, and know little of the practical and experimental. A touch at School-Divinity.

THat this *Philosophy* is *litigious,* the very spawn of *disputations* and *con- troversies* as undecisive as needless ; is the natural result of the former : Storms are

are the products of vapours. For where words are imposed arbitrariously, having no stated real meaning; or else distorted from their common use, and known significations: the mind must needs be led into confusion and misprision; and so things plain and easie in their naked natures, made full of *intricacy* and disputable *uncertainty*. For we cannot conclude with assurance, but from clearly apprehended *premises*; and these cannot be so conceiv'd, but by a distinct comprehension of the words out of which they are *elemented*. So that, where they are unfixt or ambiguous; our *propositions* must be so, and our *deductions* can be no better. One reason therefore of the uncontroverted certainty of *Mathematical Science* is; because 'tis built upon clear and settled *significations* of *names*, which admit of no *ambiguity* or insignificant *obscurity*. But in the *Aristotelian* Philosophy it's quite otherwise: Words being here carelesly and abusively admitted, and as inconstantly retained; it must needs come to pass, that they will be diversly apprehended by contenders,
and

and so made the subject of *controversies*, that are *endless* both for *use* and *number*. And thus being at their first step out of the way to *Science*, by mistaking in *simple terms*; in the progress of their enquiries they must needs lose both themselves, and the Truth, in a *Verbal Labyrinth*. And now the entangled disputants, as Master *Hobs* ingeniously observeth, like Birds that came down the Chimney; betake them to the false light, seldom suspecting the way they enter'd: But attempting by vain, impertinent, and coincident distinctions, to escape the absurdity that pursues them; do but weary themselves with as little success, as the silly Bird attempts the window. The mis-stated words are the original mistake; and every other essay is a new one. Now these canting contests, the usual entertainment of the *Peripatum*, are not only the accidental *vitiosities* of the *Philosophers*; but the genuine issues of the *Philosophy* it self. And *Aristotle* seems purposely to intend the cherishing of *controversal digladiations*, by his own affectation of an intricate *obscurity*. Himself

N   acknow-

acknowledg'd it, when he faid ; his *Phy-ficks* were *publifh'd*, and not *fo :* And by that double advice in his *Topicks* 'tis as clear as light. In one place, he advifeth his Sectatours in difputations to be *ambiguous :* and in another, to bring forth any thing that occurs, rather then give way to their Adverfary ; Counfel very well becoming an Enquirer after Verity ! Nor did he here advife them to any thing, but what he followeth himfelf, and exactly copies out in his practife. The multitudes of his lame, abrupt, equivocal, felf-contradicting expreffions, will evidence it as to the firft part: which who confiders, may be fatisfied in this ; that if *Ariftotle* found *Nature's face* under covert of a *veil*, he hath not removed the old, but made her a *new one*. And for the latter, his frequent flightnefs in arguing doth abundantly make it good. To inftance, he proves the *world* to be perfect, becaufe it confifts of *bodies* ; and that *bodies* are fo, becaufe they confift of a *triple dimenfion* ; and that a *triple dimenfion* is perfect, becaufe *three* are all ; and that *three* are *all*, becaufe when 'tis

'tis but *one* or *two*, we can't fay *all*, but when 'tis *three*, we may: Is not this an abfolute *demonftration* ? We can fay All at the number *three* : Therefore the *world is perfect*. *Tobit* went forth and his *Dog* follow'd him ; therefore there's a *world* in the *Moon*, were an argument as *Apodictical*. In another place he proves the *world* to be but *one* : For were there another , our Earth would fall unto it. This is a pitiful deduction, from the meer prejudice of Senfe ; and not unlike theirs, who thought, if there were *Antipodes*, they muft needs [as it's faid of *Erafmus*] *in Cœlum defcendere*. As if, were there more *worlds* , each of them would not have its proper *Centre*. Elfewhere fhewing, why the *Heavens* move this way rather then another, he gives this for a reafon : becaufe they move to the more *honourable* ; · and *before* is more *honourable* then *after*. This is like the *Gallant* , who fent his man to buy an *Hat*, that would *turn up behind*. As if, had the Heavens moved the other way ; that term had not been then *before*, which is now the contrary. This Inference is

N 2   founded

founded upon a very weak suppofition, *viz.* That thofe alterable refpects are realities in Nature ; which will never be admitted by a confiderate difcerner. Thus *Aristotle* acted his own inftructions; and his obfequious Sectators have fuper-erogated in obfervance. They have fo difguifed his *Philofophy* by obfcuring *Comments,* that his revived felf would not own it : And were he to act another part with mortals ; he'd be but a pitiful *Peripatetick,* every *Sophifter* would out-talk him.

Now this *difputing* way of Enquiry is fo far from advancing *Science* ; that 'tis no inconfiderable retarder:For in *Scientifical* difcoveries many things muft be confider'd, which the hurrey of a difpute indifpofeth for ; and there is no way to truth, but by the moft clear comprehenfion of *fimple notions* , and as wary an accuracy in *deductions.* If the Fountain be difturb'd , there's no feeing to the bottom ; and here's an exception to the *Proverb,* '*Tis no good fifhing* for Verity *in troubled waters.* One miftake of either *fimple apprehenfion,* or *connexion,* makes an *erroneous conclufion.* So that the precipitancy

cipitancy of *disputation*, and the stir and
noise of Passions, that usually attend it;
must needs be prejudicial to Verity : its
calm insinuations can no more be heard
in such a bustle, then a whisper among
a croud of Saylors in a storm. Nor do
the eager clamors of contending Disputants, yeeld any more relief to eclipsed
Truth ; then did the sounding Brass of
old to the *labouring Moon*. When it's
under question, 'twere as good flip *cross*
and *pile*, as to dispute for't : and to play
a game at *Chess* for an opinion in *Philosophy* [as my self and an ingenious
Friend have sometime sported] is as
likely a way to determine. Thus the *Peripatetick* procedure is inept for *Philosophical* solutions : The *Lot* were as equitable a decision, as their empty *Loquacities*. 'Tis these nugacious *Disputations*,
that have been the great hinderance to
the more improveable parts of Learning :
and the modern Retainers to the *Stagirite* have spent their sweat and pains upon the most litigious parts of his *Philosophy* ; while those , that find less play
for the contending *Genius*, are incultivate.

N 3   Thus

Thus *Logick*, *Physicks*, *Metaphysicks*, are the burden of Volumes, and the dayly entertainment of the *Disputing Schools :* while the more profitable doctrines of the *Heavens*, *Meteors*, *Minerals*, *Animals*; as also the more *practical* ones of *Politicks*, and *Oeconomicks*, are scarce so much as glanc'd at. And the indisputable *Mathematicks*, the only *Science* Heaven hath yet vouchsaf't Humanity; have but few Votaries among the slaves of the *Stagirite*. What, the late promoters of the *Aristotelian Philosophy*, have writ on all these so fertile subjects; can scarce compare with the single disputes about *Materia prima*.

Nor hath Humane Science monopoliz'd the damage, that hath sprung from this Root of Evils: *Theology* hath been as deep a sharer. The Volumes of the *Schoolmen*, are deplorable evidence of *Peripatetick depravations :* And *Luther*'s censure of that *Divinity*, *Quam primum apparuit Theologia Scholastica, evanuit Theologia Crucis*, is neither uncharitable, nor unjust. This hath mudded the Fountain of Certainty with notional and Ethnick ad-

mix-

mixtions; and platted the head of *Evangelical* truth, as the *Jews* did its *Author's*, with a *Crown* of *thorns* : Here, the most obvious Verity is subtiliz'd into niceties, and spun into a thread indiscernible by common *Opticks*, but through the *spectacles* of the adored *Heathen*. This hath robb'd the *Christian* world of its *unity* and *peace* ; and made the Church, the Stage of everlasting contentions : And while *Aristotle* is made the *Centre* of *Truth*, and *Unity*, what hope of reconciling ? And yet most of these Scholastick controversies are ultimately resolv'd into the subtilties of his *Philosophy* : And me thinks an *Athenian* should not be the best guide to the θεὸς ἄγνωσος ; Nor an *Idolater* to that God he neither knew nor owned. When I read the eager contests of these *Notional Theologues* , about things that are not ; I cannot but think of that pair of *wise ones* , that fought for the *middle* : And me thinks many of their Controversies are such , as if *we* and our *Antipodes*, should strive who were *uppermost* ; their title to Truth is equal. He that divided his *Text* into

one

one part ; did but imitate the *Schoolmen*
in their *coincident diſtinctions* : And
the beſt of their *curioſities* are but like
paint on Glaſs , which intercepts and
dyes the light the more deſirable ſplendor. I cannot look upon their elabo-
rate trifles, but with a ſad reflexion on
the degenerate ſtate of our lapſed Intellects ; and as deep a reſentment, of the
miſchiefs of this *School-Philoſophy*.

CHAP,

CHAP. XVIII.

3. *It gives no account of the Phæno-*
mena ; those that are remoter, it at-
tempts not. It speaks nothing perti-
nent in the most ordinary : Its cir-
cular, and general way of Solution.
It resolves all things into occult qua-
lities. The absurdity of the Aristote-
lian Hypothesis of the Heavens. The
Gallaxy is no meteor : the Heavens
are corruptible. Comets are above
the Moon. The Sphear of fire deri-
ded. Aristotle convicted of several
other false assertions.

3. THe *Aristotelian Hypotheses* give
a very dry and *jejune* account
of Nature's *Phænomena*, For as to its
more

more *mysterious* reserves, *Peripatetick*
enquiry hath left them unattempted ; and
the most forward notional Dictators sit
down here in a contented ignorance :
and as if nothing more were knowable
then is already discover'd, they put stop
to all endeavours of their Solution. *Qua-*
lities, that were *Occult* to *Aristotle,* must
be so to us ; and we must not *Philoso-*
phize beyond *Sympathy* and *Antipathy* :
whereas indeed the Rarities of Nature
are in these Recesses , and its most excellent operations *Cryptick* to common
discernment. Modern Ingenuity expects
Wonders from *Magnetick* discoveries :
And while we know but its more sensible
ways of working ; we are but vulgar
Philosophers , and not likely to help the
World to any considerable *Theories.* Till
the *Fountains* of the great *deeps* are
broken up ; *Knowledge* is not likely to
cover the *Earth* as the waters the *Sea.*
Nor is the *Aristotelian Philosophy* guilty
of this sloth and Philosophick penury,
only in remoter abstrusities : but in
solving the most ordinary causalities, it
is as defective and unsatisfying. Even
the

the moſt common productions are here
reſolv'd into *Celeſtial influences*, *Elemental combinations*, *active* and *paſſive*
principles, and ſuch *generalities* ; while
the particular manner of them is as hidden as *ſympathies*. And if we follow
manifeſt qualities beyond the empty ſignification of their Names ; we ſhall find
them as *occult*, as thoſe which are profeſſedly *ſo*. That heavy Bodies deſcend
by *gravity*, is no better an account then
we might expect from a *Ruſtick* : and
again, that *Gravity* is a *quality* whereby
an heavy body deſcends, is an impertinent *Circle*, and teacheth nothing. The
feigned *Central alliciency* is but a word,
and the manner of it ſtill *occult*. That
the *fire* burns by a quality called *heat* ;
is an empty dry return to the Queſtion,
and leaves us ſtill ignorant of the immediate way of *igneous ſolutions*. The accounts that this *Philoſophy* gives by other
Qualities, are of the ſame *Gender* with
theſe : So that to ſay the *Loadſtone* draws
Iron by *magnetick attraction*, and that
the *Sea* moves by *flux* and *reflux* ; were
as ſatisfying as theſe *Hypotheſes*, and the
ſolution

I

solution were as pertinent. In the *Qua-*
lities, this Philosophy calls *manifest*, nothing is *so* but the effects. For the heat,
we feel, is but the *effect* of the *fire* ; and
the pressure, we are sensible of , but the
effect of the descending body. And effects, whose causes are confessedly *occult*,
are as much within the sphear of our
Senses ; and our Eyes will inform us of
the motion of the Steel to its *attrahent*.
Thus *Peripatetick Philosophy* resolves all
things into *Occult qualities* ; and the
Dogmatists are the only *Scepticks*. Even
to them, that pretend so much to *Science*,
the world is circumscrib'd with a *Gyges*
his Ring ; and is *intellectually invisible* :
And , *ὁ καταλαμβάνω*, will best become
the mouth of a *Peripatetick*. For by
their way of disquisition there can no
more be truly comprehended, then what's
known by every common Ignorant : But
ingenious inquiry will not be contented
with such vulgar *frigidities*.

But further, if we look into the *Aristo-*
telian Comments on the largest Volumes
of the Universe : The works of the *fourth*
day are there as confused and disorderly,
                                                        as

as the *Chaos* of the *first :* and more like that, which was before the *light*, then the compleatly finish'd, and gloriously disposed *frame*. What a *Romance* is the story of those impossible *concamerations*, *Interfections*, *Involutions*, and feign'd *Rotations* of *folid Orbs ?* All substituted to salve the credit of a broken ill-contrived *Systeme*. The belief of such disorders *above*, were an advantage to the *oblique Atheism* of *Epicurus :* And such Irregularities in the Celestial motions, would lend an Argument to the *Apotheiofis* of *Fortune*. Had the world been coagmented from that supposed fortuitous Jumble ; this *Hypothefis* had been tolerable. But could the doctrine of *folid Orbs*, be accommodated to *Aftronomical Phænomena ;* yet to afcribe each *Sphear* an *Intelligence* to circumvolve it, were an *unphilofophical* defperate refuge : And to confine the bleffed *Genii* to a Province, which was the *Hell* of *Ixion*, were to rob them of their *Felicities*. That the *Galaxy* is a *Meteor*, was the account of *Aristotle :* But the *Tele-fcope ſcope* hath autoptically confuted it : And he, who is not *Pyrrhonian* to the diſbelief of his Senſes, may ſee ; that it's no exhalation from the Earth , but an heap of ſmaller *Luminaries*. That the *Heavens* are void of *corruption*, is *Ariſtotles* ſuppoſal : But the Tube hath betray'd their impurity ; and *Neoterick Aſtronomy* hath found *ſpots* in the *Sun*. The diſcoveries made in *Venus*, and the *Moon*, diſprove the *Antique Quinteſſence* ; and evidence them of as courſe *materials* , as the *Globe* we belong to. The *Perſpicil* , as well as the *Needle* , hath enlarged the *habitable World* ; and that the *Moon* is an *Earth*, is no improbable conjecture. The *inequality* of its ſurface, *Mountanous protuberance*, the nature of its *Macule*, and infinite other circumſtances [for which the world's beholding to *Galilæo*] are Items not contemptible : *Hevelius* hath *graphically* deſcrib'd it : That *Comets* are of nature Terreſtrial , is allowable : But that they are materiall'd of vapours , and never flamed beyond the *Moon* ; were a conceſſion unpardonable.

able. That in *Caſſiopæa* was in the *Firmament*, and another in our age above the *Sun*. Nor was there ever any as low as the higheſt point of the *circumference*, the Stagyrite allows them. So that we need not be appal'd at *Blazing Stars*, and a *Comet* is no more ground for *Aſtrological preſages* then a *flaming* Chimney. The unparallel'd *Des-Cartes* hath unridled their dark *Phyſiology*, and to wonder ſolv'd their *Motions*. His *Philoſophy* gives them tranſcurſions beyond the *Vortex* we breath in; and leads them through others, which are only known in an *Hypotheſis*. *Ariſtotle* would have fainted before he had flown half ſo far, as that *Eagle-wit*; and have lighted on a *hard name*, or *occult quality*, to reſt him. That there is a *ſphear* of *fire* under the concave of the *Moon*, is a dream: And this, may be, was the reaſon ſome imagin'd *Hell* there, thinking thoſe flames the *Ignis Rotæ*. According to this *Hypotheſis*, the whole *Lunar* world is a *Torrid Zone*; and on a better account, then *Ariſtotle*
                                  thought

thought ours was, may be supposed *in-habitable*, except they are *Salamanders* which dwell in those *fiery Regions*. That the *Reflexion* of the *Solar* Rays, is terminated in the *Clouds*; was the opinion of the *Gracian Sage:* But *Lunar* observations have convicted it of falshood; and that planet receives the *dusky* light, we discern in its *Sextile Aspect*, from the *Earth's* benignity. That the *Rainbow* never describes more then a *semicircle*, is no creditable assertion; since experimental observations have confuted it. *Gassendus* saw one at Sun-setting, whose Supreme *Arch* almost reached our *Zenith*; while the Horns stood in the *Oriental Tropicks.* And that Noble wit reprehends the *School-Idol*, for assigning fifty years at least between every *Lunar Iris.* That *Caucasus* enjoys the Sun-beams three parts of the Nights *Vigils*; that *Danubius* ariseth from the *Pyrenaan* Hills: That the Earth is higher towards the *North:* are opinions truly charged on *Aristotle* by the

Restorer

Restorer of *Epicurus* ; and all easily confutable falsities. To reckon all the *Aristotelian* aberrances, and to give a full account of the lameness of his *Hypotheses*, would swell this *digression* into a Volume. The mention'd shall suffice us.

CHAP. XIX.

4. Aristotle's *Philosophy inept for new discoveries ; it hath been the Author of no one invention : It's founded on vulgarities, and therefore makes nothing known beyond them. The knowledge of Natures out-side confers not to practical improvements. Better hopes from the New Philosophy. A fifth charge against Aristotle's Philosophy, it is in many things impious, and self-contradicting : Instances of both propounded.*

O   *The*

The directing all this to the design of the discourse. A Caution, viz. that nothing is here intended in favour of novelty in Divinity; the reason why we may imbrace what is new in Philosophy, while we reject them in Theologie.

4. THE *Aristotelian Philosophy* is inept for New discoveries; and therefore of no accommodation to the *use* of *life*. That all Arts, and Professions are capable of maturer improvements; cannot be doubted by those, who know the least of any. And that there is an *America* of secrets, and unknown *Peru* of Nature, whose discovery would richly advance them, is more then conjecture. Now while we either sayl by the *Land* of gross aud vulgar Doctrines, or direct our Enquiries, by the *Cynosure* of meer abstract *notions*; we are not likely to reach the Treasures on the other side the *Atlantick :* The directing of the World the way to which, is

the

the noble end of true *Philofohpy*. That the *Ariftotelian Phyfiology* cannot boaft it felf the proper Author of any one Invention ; is prægnant evidence of its infecundous deficiency : And 'twould puzzle the Schools to point at any confiderable difcovery, made by the direct, fole manuduction of *Peripatetick* Principles. Moft of our Rarities have been found out by *cafual emergency* ; and have been the works of Time, and Chance, rather then of *Philofophy*. What *Ariftotle* hath of Experimental Knowledge in his Books of *Animals*, or elfewhere ; is not much tranfcending vulgar obfervation : And yet what he hath of this, was never learnt from his *Hypothefes* ; but forcibly fetch'd in to fuffrage to them. And 'tis the obfervation of the Noble St. *Alban* ; that that *Philofophy* is built on a few Vulgar Experiments : and if upon further enquiry, any were found to refragate, they were to be difcharg'd by a *diftinction*. Now what is founded on, and made up but of *Vulgarities*, cannot make known any thing beyond them. For Nature is

fet

is set a going by the most *subtil* and *hidden* Instruments; which it may be have nothing *obvious* which resembles them. Hence judging by visible appearances, we are discouraged by supposed *Impossibilities* which to *Nature* are none, but within her Sphear of Action. And therefore what shews only the outside, and sensible structure of Nature; is not likely to help us in finding out the *Magnalia*. 'Twere next to impossible for one, who never saw the inward wheels and motions, to make a watch upon the bare view of the *Circle* of *hours*, and *Index :* And 'tis as difficult to trace natural operations to any practical advantage, by the sight of the *Cortex* of sensible Appearances. He were a poor *Physitian*, that had no more *Anatomy*, then were to be gather'd from the *Physnomy*. Yea, the most common *Phænomena* can be neither known, nor improved, without insight into the more *hidden* frame. For *Nature* works by an *Invisible Hand* in all things: And till *Peripateticism* can shew us further, then those gross solutions of *Qualities* and *Elements*; 'twill

never

never make us Benefactors to the World, nor confiderable Difcoverers. But its experienc'd fterility through fo many hundred years, drives Hope to defperation. We expect greater things from *Neoterick* endeavours. The *Cartefian Philofophy* in this regard hath fhewn the World the way to be happy. Me thinks this Age feems refolved to bequeath *pofterity* fomewhat to remember it : And the glorious Undertakers, wherewith Heaven hath bleft our Days, will leave the world better provided then they found it. And whereas in former times fuch generous free-fpirited Worthies were, as the Rare newly obferved *Stars*, a fingle one the wonder of an Age : In ours they are like the lights of the greater fize that twinkle in the *Starry Firmament* : And this laft Century can glory in numerous *conftellations*. Should thofe *Heroe's* go on, as they have happily begun ; they'll fill the world with *wonders*. And I doubt not but pofterity will find many things, that are now but *Rumors*, verified into *practical Realities*. It may be fome Ages hence, a voyage to the

Southern unknown *Tracts*, yea poſſibly the *Moon*, will not be more ſtrange then one to *America.* To them, that come after us, it may be as ordinary to buy a *pair* of *wings* to fly into remoteſt *Regions*; as now a pair of *Boots* to ride a *Journey.* And to conferr at the diſtance of the *Indies* by *Sympathetick* conveyances, may be as uſual to future times, as to us in a *litterary* correſpondence. The *reſtauration* of gray hairs to *Juvenility,* and renewing the exhauſted marrow, may at length be effected without a *miracle :* And the turning of the now comparatively *deſert* world into a *Paradiſe,* may not improbably be expected from late *Agriculture.* Now thoſe, that judge by the narrowneſs of former *Principles,* will ſmile at theſe *Paradoxical expectations :* But queſtionleſs thoſe great Inventions, that have in theſe later Ages altered the face of all things ; in their naked propoſals, and meer ſuppoſitions, were to former times as *ridiculous.* To have talk'd of a *new Earth* to have been diſcovered, had been a *Romance* to *Antiquity :* And to ſayl without ſight of *Stars* or ſhoars

by

by the guidance of a *Mineral*, a *story* more abſurd, then the flight of *Dædalus*. That men ſhould ſpeak after their *tongues* were *aſhes*, or communicate with each other in differing *Hemiſphears*, before the Invention of *Letters*; could not but have been thought a *fiction*. *Antiquity* would not have believed the almoſt incredible force of our *Canons*; and would as coldly have entertain'd the wonders of the Teleſcope. In theſe we all condemn *antique incredulity*; and 'tis likely Poſterity will have as much cauſe to pity *ours*. But yet notwithſtanding this ſtraightneſs of ſhallow obſervers, there are a ſet of enlarged ſouls that are more *judiciouſly credulous*: and thoſe, who are acquainted with the fecundity of *Carteſian Principles*, and the diligent and ingenuous endeavours of ſo many true *Philoſophers*; will deſpair of nothing.

5. But again, the *Ariſtotelian Philoſophy* is in ſome things *impious*, and *inconſiſtent* with *Divinity*; and in many more *inconſiſtent* with it ſelf. That the *Reſurrection* is impoſſible; That *God*

O 4   under

underſtands not all things; That the *world* was from *Eternity*; That there's no *ſubſtantial form*, but moves ſome *Orb*; That the firſt Mover moves by an *Eternal*, *Immutable Neceſſity*; That, if the world and motion were not from Eternity, then *God* was Idle; were all the Aſſertions of *Ariſtotle*, which *Theology* pronounceth impieties. Which yet we need not ſtrange at from one, of whom a *Father* ſaith, *Nec Deum coluit nec curavit*: Eſpecially, if it be as *Philoponus* affirms, that he *philoſophiz'd* by command from the *Oracle*. Of the *Ariſtotelian contradictions*, *Gaſſendus* hath preſented us with a Catalogue: We'll inſtance in a few of them. In one place he ſaith, The *Planets ſcintillation* is not ſeen, becauſe of their *propinquity*; but that of the *riſing* and *ſetting Sun* is, becauſe of its *diſtance*: and yet in another place he makes the *Sun* nearer us, then they are. He ſaith, that the *Elements* are not *Eternal*, and ſeeks to prove it; and yet he makes the *world ſo*, and the *Elements* its parts. In his *Meteors* he ſaith, no Dew is produced in the Wind; and yet

yet afterwards admits it under the *South*,
and none under the *North*. In one place
he defines a vapour *humid* and *cold*; and
in another *humid* and *hot*. He faith, the
faculty of speaking is a *sense*; and yet
before he allow'd but *five*. In one place,
that Nature doth all things *best*; and in
another, that it makes more *evil* then
good. And somewhere he contradicts
himself within a *line*; saying, that an
Immoveable Mover hath no principle of
Motion. 'Twould be tedious to mention
more; and the qualiiy of a *digression* will
not allow it.

Thus we have, as briefly as the subject
would bear, animadverted on the so
much admired *Philosophy* of *Aristotle.* The
nobler Spirits of the Age, are disengaged
from those detected vanities: And the
now Adorers of that *Philosophy* are few,
but such narrow souls, that know no
other; Or if any of them look beyond
the leaves of their *Master*, yet they try
other Principles by a Jury of his, and
scan *Cartes* with *Genus* and *Species*.
From the former sort I may hope,
they'l pardon this attempt; and for
the

the latter, I value not their cènfure.

Thus then we may conclude upon the whole, that the ftamp of *Authority* can make *Leather* as current as *Gold*; and that there's nothing fo contemptible, but *Antiquity* can render it *auguft*, and *excellent*. But, becaufe the Fooleries of fome affected Novelifts have difcredited new difcoveries, and render'd the very mention fufpected of Vanity at leaft; and in points Divine, of *Herefie:* It will be neceffary to add, that I intend not the former difcourfe, in favour of any new-broach'd conceit in *Divinity*; For I own no Opinion there, which cannot plead the prefcription of above *fixteen hundred.* There's nothing I have more fadly refented, then the *phrenetick* whimfies with which our Age abounds, and therefore am not likely to Patron them. In *Theology*, I put as great a difference between our *New Lights,* and *Ancient Truths*; as between the *Sun,* and an unconcocted evanid *Meteor.* Though I confefs, that in *Philofophy* I'm a *Seeker*; yet cannot believe, that a *Sceptick* in *Philofophy* muft be one in *Divinity.*

Divinity. *Gospel-Light* began in it *Zenith;* and, as some say the *Sun,* was created in its *Meridian* strength and lustre. But the beginnings of *Philosophy* were in a *Crepusculous obscurity;* and it's yet scarse past the *Dawn.* *Divine* Truths were most pure in their source; and *Time* could not perfect what *Eternity* began: our *Divinity,* like the Grand-father of *Humanity,* was born in the *fulness* of *time,* and in the strength of its manly vigour: But *Philosophy* and Arts commenced *Embryo's,* and are compleated by Times gradual accomplishments. And therefore, what I cannot find in the leaves of former Inquisitours: I seek in the Modern attempts of nearer Authors. I cannot receive *Aristotle's* Πισότατοι παλαιοί, in so extensive an interpretation, as some would enlarge it to: And that discouraging Maxime, *Nil dictum quod non dictum prius,* hath little room in my *estimation.* Nor can I tye up my belief to the *Letter* of *Solomon:* Except *Copernicus* be in the right, there hath been something *New under* the *Sun;* I'm sure, later times have seen *Novelties* in the Heavens

Heavens *above* it. I do not think, that all Science is *Tautology:* The laſt Ages have ſhewn us, what *Antiquity* never ſaw ; no, not in a *Dream.*

CHAP. XX.

It's queried whether there be any Science in the ſenſe of the Dogma= tiſts : (1) *We cannot know any thing to be the cauſe of another, but from its attending it; and this way is not infallible ; declared by inſtances, eſpecially from the Philoſophy of Des=Cartes. All things are mixt, and 'tis difficult to aſſign each Cauſe its diſtinct Effect.* (2)*There's no demonſtration but where the con- trary is impoſſible. We can ſcarce conclude ſo of any thing : Inſtances of ſuppoſed impoſſibles which are none.*

*none. A story of a Scholar that turn'd
Gipsy ; and of the power of Imagination. Of one mans binding anothers thoughts ; and a conjecture at
the maner of its performance.*

COnfidence of *Science* is one great
reason, we miss it : whereby presuming we have it every where, we seek it
not where it is ; and therefore fall short
of the object of our Enquiry. Now
to give further check to *Dogmatical* pretensions, and to discover the vanity of
assuming *Ignorance* ; we'll make a short
enquiry, whether there be any such thing
as *Science* in the sense of its Assertours.
In their notion then, it is the knowledge
of things in their *true, immediate, necessary*
causes : Upon which I'le advance the following Observations.

1. All Knowledge of Causes is *deductive :* for we know none by simple
intuition ; but through the mediation of
its effects. Now we cannot conclude,
any thing to be the cause of another ;
but

but from its continual accompanying it:
for the *caufality* it felf is *infenfible*. Thus
we gather fire to be the caufe of heat,
and the Sun of day-light : becaufe where
ever fire is, we find there's heat ; and
where ever the Sun is, Light attends it,
and *è contrà*. But now to argue from a
concomitancy to a caufality, is not infallibly conclufive: Yea in this way lies notorious delufion. Is't not poffible, and how
know we the contrary, but, that fomething, which alway attends the groffer
flame, may be the caufe of *heat* ? and
may not it, and its fuppofed caufe, be
only *parallel* effects ? Suppofe the *fire*
had ne're appear'd, but had been ftill
hid in *fmoke* ; and that *heat* did alway
proportionably encreafe and diminifh,
with the greater or lefs quantity of that
fuliginous exhalation : fhould we ever
have doubted, that *fmoke* was the caufe
on't ? Suppofe we had never feen more
Sun, then in a cloudy day, and that the
leffer lights had ne're fhewn us their
lucid fubftance ; Let us fuppofe the *day*
had alway broke with a *wind*, and had
proportionably varyed, as that did : Had
not

not he been a notorious *Sceptick*, that should question the causality? But we need not be beholding to such remote suppositions: The French *Philosophy* furnishes us with a better instance. For, according to the Principles of the illustrious *Des-Cartes*, there would be light, though the Sun and Stars gave none; and a great part of what we now enjoy, is independent on their beams. Now if this seemingly prodigious *Paradox*, can be reconcil'd to the least probability of conjecture, or may it be made but a tolerable supposal; I presume, it may then win those that are of most difficil belief, readily to yeeld; that causes in our account the most palpable, may possibly be but *uninfluential attendants*; since that there is not an instance can be given, wherein we opinion a more certain *efficiency*. So then, according to the tenour of that concinnous *Hypothesis*, light being caused by the *Conamen* of the Matter of the *Vortex*, to recede from the Centre of its Motion: it is easily deducible, that were there none of that fluid *Æther*, which makes the body of the Sun in the Centre

Centre of our world, or should it ceafe from action ; yet the *conatus* of the circling matter would not be considerably lefs, but according to the indifpenfable Laws of Motion , muft prefs the Organs of Senfe as now, though it may be not with fo fmart an impulfe. Thus we fee, how there might be *Light* before the *Luminaries* ; and *Evening* and *Morning* before there was a *Sun*. So then we cannot infallibly affure our felves of the truth of the *caufes*, that moft obvioufly occur ; and therefore the foundation of *fcientifical* procedure , is too weak for fo magnificent a fuperftructure. Befides, That the World's a mafs of *heterogeneous* fubfiftencies, and every part thereof a coalition of diftinguifhable varieties ; we need not go far for evidence : And that all things are mixed, and Caufes blended by mutual involutions ; I prefume, to the Intelligent will be no difficult conceffion. Now to profound to the bottom of thefe *diverfities*, to affign each caufe its diftinct effects , and to limit them by their *juft* and *true* proportions ; are neceffary requifites of *Science*: and

he

he that hath compaft them, may boaft he hath out-done *humanity*. But for us to talk of *Knowledge*, from thofe few indiftinct reprefentations, which are made to our groffer faculties, is a *flatulent vanity*.

2. We hold no *demonstration* in the notion of the Dogmatift, but where the contrary is *impoffible :* For *neceffary* is that, which cannot be otherwife. Now, whether the acquifitions of any on this fide perfection, can make good the pretenfions to fo high ftrain'd an *infallibility*, will be worth a reflexion. And , me thinks, did we but compare the miferable fcantnefs of our capacities, with the vaft profundity of things ; both truth and modefty would teach us a *dialect*, more becoming fhort-fighted mortality. Can nothing be otherwife, which we conceive *impoffible*, to be fo ? Is our knowledge, and things, fo adequately commenfurate, as to juftifie the affirming , that that cannot be, which we comprehend not ? Our demonftrations are levyed upon Principles of our own , not univerfal Nature : And, as my Lord *Bacon* notes, we judge from the *Analogy* of our felves,

P   not

not the *Univerfe.* Now are not many things certain by the *Principles* of one, which are impoffible to the apprehenfions of another? Thus fome things our Juvenile reafons tenacioufly adhere to; which yet our maturer Judgements difallow of : many things to meer fenfible difcerners are *impoffible*, which to the enlarged principles of more advanced *Intellects* are eafie verities: Yea, that's abfurd in one *Philofophy*, which is a worthy Truth in another; and that's a demonftration to *Ariftotle*, which is none to *Des-Cartes.* That every fixt *ftar* is a *Sun*; and that they are as diftant from each other, as we from fome of them; That the *Sun*, which lights us, is in the *Centre* of our World, and our *Earth* a *Planet* that wheels about it; That this *Globe* is a *Star*, only crufted over with the groffer Element, and that its *Centre* is of the fame nature with *the Sun*; That it may recover its *light* again, and fhine amids the other *Luminaries*; That our *Sun* may be fwallow'd up of another, and become a *Planet* : All thefe, if we judge by common Principles or the

Rnles

Rules of Vulgar *Philosophy*, are prodigious *Impoſsibilities*, and their contradictories, as good as *demonſtrable* : But yet to
a reaſon inform'd by *Carteſianiſm* ; theſe
have their probability. Thus, it may be,
the groſseſt abſurdities to the Philoſophies
of *Europe*, may be juſtifiable aſsertions
to that of *China :* And 'tis not unlikely,
but what's impoſsible to all *Humanity*,
may be poſsible in the *Metaphyſicks*, and
Phyſiologie of Angels. Now the beſt
Principles, excepting *Divine* , and *Mathematical*, are but *Hypotheſes* ; within
the Circle of which we may indeed
conclude many things, with ſecurity from
Error : But yet the greateſt certainty,
advanc'd from ſuppoſal , is ſtill but
Hypothetical. So that we may affirm,
things are thus and thus , according to
the *Principles* we have eſpouſed : But
we ſtrangely forget our ſelves, when we
plead a neceſsity of their being ſo in
Nature, and an Impoſsibility of their being otherwiſe.

That one man ſhould be able to bind
the thoughts of another , and determine
them to their particular objects ; will
be

be reckon'd in the firſt rank of *Impoſſi-*
bles : Yet by the power of advanc'd
Imagination it may very probably be effected ; and *ſtory* abounds with Inſtances.
I'le trouble the Reader but with one ;
and the hands from which I had it, make
me ſecure of the truth on't. There was
very lately a Lad in the *Univerſity* of
Oxford, who being of very pregnant and
ready parts, and yet wanting the en-
couragement of preferment ; was by his
poverty forc'd to leave his ſtudies there,
and to caſt himſelf upon the wide world
for a livelyhood. Now, his neceſſities
growing dayly on him, and wanting the
help of friends to relieve him ; he was at
laſt forced to joyn himſelf to a company
of *Vagabond Gypſies* , whom occaſionly
he met with, and to follow their Trade
for a maintenance. Among theſe extravagant people , by the inſinuating
ſubtilty of his carriage, he quickly got
ſo much of their love, and eſteem ; as
that they diſcover'd to him their *Myſtery :*
in the practice of which, by the pregnancy
of his wit and parts he ſoon grew ſo
good a proficient, as to be able to out-do
his

his Inftructours. After he had been a pretty while well exercis'd in the Trade;there chanc'd to ride by a couple of *Scholars* who had formerly bin of his acquaintance. The *Scholars* had quickly fpyed out their old friend, among the *Gypfies* ; and their amazement to fee him among fuch fociety , had well-nigh difcover'd him : but by a fign he prevented their owning him before that Crew : and taking one of them afide privately, defired him with his friend to go to an *Inn* , not far diftant thence, promifing there to come to them. They accordingly went thither , and he follows : after their firft falutations, his friends enquire how he came to lead fo odd a life as that was, and to joyn himfelf with fuch a *cheating beggerly* company. The *Scholar-Gypfy* having given them an account of the neceffity, which drove him to that kind of life ; told them, that the people he went with were not fuch *Impoftours* as they were taken for , but that they had a *traditional* kind of *learning* among them , and could do wonders by the power of *Imagination* , and that himfelf had learnt much of their Art, and

P 3   improved

improved it further then themſelves could. And to evince the truth of what he told them, he ſaid, he'd remove into another room, leaving them to diſcourſe together ; and upon his return tell them the ſum of what they had talked of : which accordingly he perform'd, giving them a full account of what had paſs'd between them in his abſence. The *Scholars* being amaz'd at ſo unexpected a diſcovery, earneſtly deſir'd him to unriddle the *myſtery*. In which he gave them ſatisfaction, by telling them, that what he did was by the power of *Imagination*, his Phancy *binding* theirs ; and that himſelf had dictated to them the diſcourſe, they held together, while he was from them : That there were warrantable wayes of heightening the *Imagination* to that pitch, as to bind anothers ; and that when he had compaſs'd the whole *ſecret*, ſome parts of which he ſaid he was yet ignorant of, he intended to leave their company, and give the world an account of what he had learned.

Now that this ſtrange *power* of the *Imagination* is no *Impoſſibility* ; the
wonderful

wonderful *fignatures* in the *Fœtus* caus'd
by the Imagination of the Mother, is no
contemptible Item. The *fympathies* of
laughing & gaping together, are refolv'd
into this Principle : and I fee not why the
phancy of one man may not determine
the cogitation of another rightly qualified, as eafily as his *bodily motion*. This
influence feems to be no more unreafonable, then that of one *ftring* of a Lute
upon another ; when a *ftroak* on it caufeth a proportionable motion in the *fympathizing* confort, which is diftant from
it and not fenfibly touched. Now if
this notion be ftri&tly verifiable ; 'twill
yeeld us a good account how *Angels*
inje&t thoughts into our minds, and know
our cogitations : and here we may fee
the fource of fome kinds of *fafcination*.
If we are prejudic'd againft the *fpeculation*, becaufe we cannot conceive the
manner of fo ftrange an operation ; we
fhall indeed receive no help from the
common *Philofophy :* But yet the *Hypothefis* of a *Mundane* foul, lately reviv'd
by that incomparable *Platonift* and *Cartefian, Dr. H. More*, will handfomly

relieve us. Or if any would rather have
a *Mechanical* account ; I think it may
probably be made out some such way as
follows. *Imagination* is inward Sense.
To *Sense* is required a motion of certain
Filaments of the Brain ; and consequently in *Imagination* there's the like : they
only differing in this, that the motion of
the one proceeds immediately from external objects ; but that of the other hath
its immediate rise within us. Now then,
when any part of the Brain is strongly
agitated ; that, which is next and most
capable to receive the *motive* Impress,
must in like manner be moved. Now
we cannot conceive any thing more
capable of motion, then the *fluid* matter,
that's interspers'd among all bodies, and
contiguous to them. So then, the agitated
parts of the Brain begetting a *motion* in
the proxime *Æther* ; it is propagated
through the liquid *medium* , as we see
the motion is which is caus'd by a stone
thrown into the water. Now, when the
thus moved *matter* meets with any thing
like that, from which it received its primary *impress* ; it will proportionably
move

move it, as it is in *Muſical ſtrings* tuned
Uniſons. And thus the motion being
convey'd, from the *Brain* of one man to
the *Phancy* of another ; it is there receiv'd from the inſtrument of conveyance,
the *ſubtil* matter ; and the ſame kind of
ſtrings being moved , and much what
after the ſame manner as in the firſt *Imaginant* ; the *Soul* is awaken'd to the ſame
apprehenſions, as were they that caus'd
them. I pretend not to any exactneſs or
infallibility in this account , fore-ſeeing
many ſcruples that muſt be removed to
make it perfect : 'Tis only an hint of the
poſſibility of mechanically ſolving the
Phænomenon ; though very likely it may
require many other circumſtances compleatly to make it out. But 'tis not my
buſineſs here to follow it : I leave it
therefore to receive accompliſhment
from maturer Inventions.

CHAP.

Chap. XXI.

Another instance of a supposed Impossibility which may not be so. Of conference at distance by impregnated Needles. A way of secret conveyance by sympathized hands ; a relation to this purpose. Of the magnetick cure of wounds. This discourse weakens not the certainty of truths Mathematical or Divine. Mathematical Science need not elate us, since by it we know but our own creatures, and are still ignorant of our Makers. (3) We cannot know any thing in Nature, without the knowledge of the first springs of natural motions, and these we are ignorant of. Des-Cartes his Philosophy commended.

BUt yet to advance another instance. That men should confer at very distant removes by an *extemporary* intercourse

courfe is a reputed *'impoffibility* , but
yet there are fome hints in natural operations that give us probability that 'tis
feafible , and may be compaft without
unwarrantable affiftance from *Dæmoniack*
correfpondence. That a couple of *Needles*
equally toucht by the fame *magnet*, being fet in two Dyals exactly proportion'd
to each other, and circumfcribed by the
Letters of the *Alphabet*, may effect this
magnale, hath confiderable authorities to
avouch it. The manner of it is thus reprefented. Let the friends that would
communicate take each a Dyal : and
having appointed a time for their *Sympa-*
thetick conference ; let one move his
impregnate *Needle* to any letter in the
Alphabet, and its affected fellow will
precifely refpect the fame. So that would
I know what my friend would acquaint
me with ; 'tis but obferving the letters
that are pointed at by my *Needle*, and
in their order tranfcribing them from
their *fympathized Index* , as its motion
direct's : and I may be affured that my
friend defcribed the fame with his: and
that the words on my paper, are of his
inditing.

inditing. Now though there will be
some ill contrivance in a circumstance of
this invention, in that the thus *impregnate*
Needles will not move to, but avert from
each other (as ingenious Dr. *Browne* in
his *Pseudodoxia Epidemica* hath observed :) yet this cannot prejudice the main
design of this way of ˏsecret conveyance :
Since 'tis but reading counter to the *mag-*
netick informer ; and noting the letter
which is most distant in the *Abecedarian*
circle from that which the needle turns
to, and the case is not alter'd. Now
though this desirable effect possibly may
not yet answer the expectation of inquisitive *experiment* ; yet 'tis no despicable
item, that by some other such way of
magnetick efficiency, it may hereafter
with success be attempted, when *Magi-*
cal History shall be enlarged by riper
inspections : and 'tis not unlikely, but
that present discoveries might be improved to the performance.

There is besides this another way,
which is said to have advanced the *secret*
beyond *speculation*, and compleated it
in *practice*. That some have conferr'd at
distance

diſtance by *ſympathized* hands, and in a moment have thus tranſmitted their thoughts to each other, there are late ſpecious relations do atteſt it : which ſay, that the hands of two friends being *ſympathized* by a transferring of *fleſh* from one into the other, and the place of the *letters* mutually agreed on ; the leaſt prick in the hand of one, the other will be ſenſible of, and that in the ſame part of his own. And thus the diſtant friend by a new kind of *Chiromancy* may read in his own hand what his correſpondent had ſet down in his. For inſtance, would I in *London* acquaint my intimate in *Paris*, that *I am well* : I would then prick that part where I had appointed the letter [*I·*] and doing ſo in another place to ſignifie that word was done, proceed to [*A,*] thence to [*M*] and ſo on, till I had finiſht what I intended to make known. Now that there have been ſome ſuch practices, I have had a conſiderable relation, which I hold not impertinent to inſert. A Gentleman comes to a *Chirurgeon* to have his arm cut off : The Surgeon perceiving
nothing

nothing that it ailed, was much startled at
the motion; thinking him either in *jest*,
or *besides himself*. But by a more deli-
berate recollection, perceiving that he
was both sober, and in earnest; entreats
him to know the reason of so strange a
desire, since his arm to him seem'd perfectly found: to which the Gentleman
replyes, that his hand was *sympathiz'd*,
and his friend was *dead*, so that if not
prevented by *amputation*, he said, it would
rot away, as did that of his deceased
Correspondent. Nor was this an unrea-
sonable surmise; but, if there be any
such way of manual *Sympathizing*, a
very probable conjecture. For, that
which was so sensibly affected with so
inconsiderable a touch, in all likelyhood
would be more immuted, by those greater
alterations which are in *Cadaverous Solutions*. And no doubt, but that by the
same reason it would have been corrupted, as some times *Warts* are by the decay
of *buryed lard* that was rubb'd upon them.
Now if these wayes of secret conveyance
may be made out to be really practicable;
yea, if it be evincible, that they are as
much

much as poſſibly ſo, it will be a warrantable preſumption of the verity of the
former inſtance : ſince tis as eaſily conceivable, that there ſhould be communications between the *phancies* of men, as
either the *impregnate needles,* or *ſympathized hands.* And there is an inſtance
yet behinde, which is more creditable
than either, and gives probability to
them all.

That there is a *Magnetick* way of
curing *wounds* by anointing the *weapon,*
and that the wound is affected in like
manner as is the *extravenate bloud* by
the *Sympathetick medicine,* is for matter
of fact put out of doubt by the Noble
Sir *K. Digby,* and the proof he gives in
his ingenious diſcourſe on the ſubject, is
unexceptionable. For the reaſon of this
wonder, he attempts it by *Mechaniſm,*
and endeavours to make it out by *atomical aporrheas,* which paſſing from the
cruentate cloth or weapon to the wound,
and being incorporated with the *particles*
of the *ſalve* carry them in their embraces
to the affected part : where the *medicinal atomes* entering together with the
efflu-

effluviums of the bloud, do by their subtle
infinuation better effect the cure, then
can be done by any groffer Application.
The particular way of their conveyance,
and their regular direction is handfomly
explicated by that learned *Knight*, and
recommended to the Ingenious by moft
witty and becoming illuftrations. It is
out of my way here to enquire whether
the *Anima Mundi* be not a better account, then any *Mechanical* Solutions.
The former is more defperate, the later
hath more of ingenuity, then folid fatisfaction. It is enough for me that *de facto*
there is fuch an entercourfe between
the *Magnetick unguent* and the *vulnerated* body, and I need not be folicitous
of the Caufe. Thefe *theories* I prefume will not be importunate to the ingenious : and therefore I have taken the
liberty (which the quality of an Effay
will well enough allow of) to touch
upon them, though feemingly collateral
to my fcope. And yet I think, they
are but feemingly fo, fince they do pertinently illuftrate my defign, *viz.* That
what feems *impoffible* to *us*, may not be
                                        fo

so in *Nature* ; and therefore the *Dogmatist* wants this to compleat his demonstration, that '*tis impossible to be otherwise*.

Now I intend not by any thing here to invalidate the certainty of truths either *Mathematical* or *Divine*. These are superstructed on principles that cannot fail us, except our faculties do constantly abuse us. Our *religious foundations* are fastned at the pillars of the *intellectual* world, and the grand *Articles* of our Belief as demonstrable as *Geometry*. Nor will ever either the subtile attempts of the resolved *Atheist* ; or the passionate Hurricanoes of the *phrentick Enthusiast*, any more be able to prevail against the *reason* our *Faith* is built on, than the blustring *windes* to blow out the *Sun*. And for *Mathematical Sciences*, he that doubts their certainty, hath need of a dose of *Hellebore*. Nor yet can the *Dogmatist* make much of these concessions in favour of his pretended *Science* ; for our discourse comes not within the circle of the former : and for the later, the knowledge we have of the *Mathematicks,*

Q

ticks, hath no reafon to elate us ; fince by them we know but *numbers,* and *figures,* creatures of our own, and are yet ignorant of our *Maker's.*

(3.) We cannot know any thing of *Nature* but by an *Analyfis* of it to its *true initial caufes :* and till we know the firft fprings of natural motions, we are ftill but igrrorants. Thefe are the *Alphabet* of Science, and Nature cannot be *read* without them. Now who dares pretend to have feen the *prime motive caufes,* or to have had a view of *Nature,* while fhe lay in her *fimple Originals ?* we know nothing but *effects,* and thofe but by our Senfes. Nor can we judge of their *Caufes,* but by proportion to palpable caufalities conceiving them like thofe within the fenfible *Horizon.* Now 'tis no doubt with the confiderate, but that the *rudiments* of Nature are very unlike the groffer *appearances.* Thus in things obvious, there's but little refemblance between the *Mucous fperm,* and the compleated *Animal.* The *Egge* is not like the *oviparous* production : nor the corrupted *muck* like the *creature* that creeps
from

from it. There's but little similitude betwixt a *terreous humidity*, and *plantal* germinations; nor do *vegetable* derivations ordinarily resemble their *simple seminalities.* So then, since there's so much dissimilitude between *Cause* and *Effect* in the more palpable *Phænomena*, we can expect no less between them, and their *invisible* efficients. Now had our Senses never presented us with those obvious *seminal* principles of apparent generations, we should never have suspected that a *plant* or *animal* could have proceeded from such unlikely *materials :* much less, can we conceive or determine the uncompounded *initials* of natural productions, in the total silence of our Senses. And though the Grand Secretary of Nature, the miraculous *Des-Cartes* have here infinitely out-done all the Philosophers went before him, in giving a particular and *Analytical* account of the *Universal Fabrick :* yet he intends his Principles but for *Hypotheses*, and never pretends that things are really or necessarily, as he hath supposed them : but that they may be admitted pertinently

to

to folve the *Phænomena,* and are convenient fuppofals for the *ufe of life.* Nor can
any further account be expected from
humanity , but how things poffibly *may
have been made* confonantly to fenfible
nature : but infallibly to determine, how
they truly were effected, is proper to him
only that faw them in the *Chaos* , and
fafhion'd them out of that confufed
mafs. For to fay, the *principles* of Nature muft needs be fuch as our *Philofophy* makes them, is to fet bounds to
Omnipotence , and to confine *infinite*
power and *wifdom* to our fhallow *models.*

CHAP.

Chap. XXII.

(4) Becauſe of the mutual dependence and concatenation of Cauſes, we cannot know any one without knowing all. Particularly declared by inſtances. (5) All our Science comes in at our Senſes; their infallibility inquir'd into. The Authors deſign in this laſt particular.

(4) ACcording to the notion of the *Dogmatiſt*, we *know nothing*, except we *knew all things*, and he that pretends to *Science* affects an *Omniſcience.* For all things being linkt together by an uninterrupted *chain* of *Cauſes*; and every ſingle motion owning a dependence on ſuch a *Syndrome* of præ-required *motors:* we can have no true knowledge of any, except we comprehended all, and

Q 3   could

could diſtinctly pry into the whole *method* of *Cauſal Concatenations*. Thus we cannot *know* the cauſe of any one *motion* in a *watch*, unleſs we were acquainted with all its motive dependences, and had a diſtinctive comprehenſion of the whole *Mechanical* frame. And would we *know* but the moſt contemptible *plant* that grows, almoſt all things that have a being muſt contribute to our *knowledge* : for, that to the perfect *Science* of any thing it's neceſſary to know all its *cauſes* ; is both reaſonable in its ſelf, and the ſenſe of the *Dogmatiſt*. So that, to the knowledge of the pooreſt *ſimple*, we muſt firſt know its *efficient*, the *manner*, and *method* of its *efformation*, and the nature of the *Plaſtick*. To the comprehending of which, we muſt have a full proſpect into the whole *Archidoxis* of Nature's ſecrets, and the immenſe profundities of *occult* Philoſophy : in which we know nothing till we compleatly ken all *Magnetick*, and *Sympathetick* energies, and their moſt hidden cauſes. And (2) if we contemplate a *vegetable* in its *material* principle, and look

look on it as made of *earth*; we must
have the true Theory of the nature of
that Element, or we miserably fail of
our *Scientifical* aspirings, and while we
can only say, 'tis *cold* and *dry*, we are
pitiful *knowers*.

But now, to profound into the *Physicks*
of this heterogeneous masse, to discern
the principles of its constitution, and to
discover the reason of its diversities,
are absolute requisites of the *Science* we
aim at. Nor can we tolerably pretend
to have those without the knowledge of
Minerals, the *causes* and *manner* of their
Concretions, and among the rest, the
Magnet, with its amazing properties.
This directs us to the *pole*, and thence
our disquisition is led to the whole *systeme* of the *Heavens* : to the knowledge
of which, we must know their *motions*,
and the *causes*, and *manner* of their *rotations*, as also the reasons of all the
Planetary Phænomena, and of the *Comets*,
their *nature*, and the *causes* of all their
irregular appearings. To these, the
knowledge of the intricate doctrine of
motion, the *powers, proportions*, and *laws*

thereof, is requifite. And thus we are engaged in the objects of *Geometry* and *Arithmetick*, yea the whole *Mathematicks*, muft be contributary, and to them all *Nature* payes a fubfidy. Befides, *plants* are partly material'd of *water*, with which they are furnifht either from *fubterranean* Fountains, or the *Clouds*. Now to have the true Theory of the former, we muft trace the nature of the *Sea*, its origen ; and hereto its remarkable *motions* of *flux* and *reflux*. This again directs us to the *Moon*, and the reft of the Celeftial *faces*. The moifture that comes from the *Clouds* is drawn up in *vapours* : To the Scientifical difcernment of which, we muft know the *nature* and *manner* of that action, their fufpenfe in the *middle region*, the qualities of that *place*, and the *caufes* and *manner* of their precipitating thence again : and fo the reafon of the *Spharical* figure of the *drops* ; the caufes of *Windes*, *Hail*, *Snow*, *Thunder*, *Lightning*, with all other igneous appearances, with the whole *Phyfiology* of *Meteors* muft be enquired into. And again (3) in our

disquifition

difquifition into the *formal Caufes*, the knowledge of the nature of *colours*, is neceffary to compleat the Science. To be inform'd of this, we muft know what *light* is; and *light* being effected by a motion on the Organs of *fenfe*, 'twill be a neceffary requifite, to underftand the nature of our *fenfitive* faculties, and to them the effence of the *foul*, and other fpiritual fubfiftences. The manner how it is *materially* united, and how it is aware of corporeal *motion*. The feat of *fenfe*, and the place where 'tis *principally* affected: which cannot be known but by the *Anatomy* of our parts, and the knowledge of their Mechanical ftru-cture. And if further (4) we contem-plate the *end* of this minute effect, its principal *final* Caufe, being the glory of its Maker, leads us into *Divinity*; and for its fubordinate, as 'tis defign'd for *alimental* fuftenance to living creatures, and *medicinal* ufes to man, we are con-ducted into *Zoography*, and the whole body of *Phyfick*. Thus then, to the *know-ledge* of the moft contemptible *effect* in nature, 'tis neceffary to know the whole

Syntax

Syntax of Caules, and their particular *circumstances*, and *modes* of action. Nay, we *know nothing*, till we *know our selves*, which are the lummary of all the world without us, and the *Index* of the Creation. Nor can we know our selves without the *Physiology* of corporeal Nature, and the *Metaphysicks* of Souls and Angels. So then, every Science borrows from all the reft; and we cannot attain any fingle one, without the *Encyclopady*.

(5) The *knowledge* we have comes from our *Senses*, and the *Dogmatist* can go no higher for the original of his certainty. Now let the *Sciolist* tell me, why things muft needs be *so*, as his individual *senses* reprefent them? Is he fure, that objects are not otherwife *sensed* by others, then they are by him? and why muft his fenfe be the infallible *Criterion*? It may be, what is *white* to us, is *black* to *Negroes*, and our *Angels* to them are *Fiends*. Diverfity of *conftitution*, or other circumftances varies the *sensation*, and to them of *Java* Pepper is *cold*. And though we agree in a common

mon name, yet it may be , I have the
same reprefentation from *yellow* , that
another hath from *green*. Thus two look
upon an *Alabafter* Statue ; he call's it
white, and I affent to the appellation :
but how can I difcover, that his inward
fenfe on't is the fame that *mine* is ? It
may be, *Alabafter* is reprefented to him,
as *jet* is to me, and yet it is *white* to us
both. We accord in the *name :* but it's
beyond our knowledge, whether we do
fo in the *conception* anfwering it. Yea,
the contrary is not without its probability. For though the *Images, Motions,*
or whatever elfe is the caufe of *fenfe,*
may be alike as from the object ; yet
may the reprefentations be varyed according to the nature and quality of the
Recipient. That's one thing to us looking
through a *tube,* which is another to our
naked *eyes.* The fame things feem otherwife through a *green* glafs, then they do
through a *red.* Thus objects have a different appearance, when the *eye* is violently any way *diftorted,* from that they
have, when our Organs are in their proper *fite* and *figure* , and fome extraordinary

dinary alterations in the Brain duplicate
that which is but a fingle object to our
undiftemper'd *Sentient*. Thus, that's of
one *colour* to us ftanding in *one place*,
which hath a contrary afpect in *another*:
as in thofe verfatile reprefentations in the
neck of a *Dove*, and folds of *Scarlet*. And
as great diverfity might have been exemplified in the other *fenfes*, but for brevity I omit them. Now then, fince
fo many various circumftances concurre
to every *individual* conftitution, and
every mans *fenfes*, differing as much
from others in its *figure*, *colour*, *fite*, and
infinite other *particularities* in the *Organization*, as any one mans can from it
felf, through diverfe *accidental* variations: it cannot well be fuppos'd otherwife, but that the *conceptions* convey'd
by them muft be as *diverfe*. Thus, one
mans *eyes* are more *protuberant*, and
fwelling out; anothers more *funk* and
depreffed. One mans *bright*, and fpark-
ling, and as it were fwimming in a *fubtile*, lucid moifture; anothers more *dull*
and heavy, and deftitute of that *fpirituous*
humidity. The *colour* of mens *eyes* is
various,

various, nor is there lefs diverfity in theii *quantitative proportions*. And if we look further into the more *inward* conftitution, there's more variety in the internal *configurations*, than in the *vifible* out-fide. For let us confider the different qualities of the *Optick* nerves, *humors*, *tunicles*, and fpirits; the divers *figurings* of the brain; the *ftrings*, or *filaments* thereof; their difference in tenuity and aptnefs for motion : and as many other circumftances, as there are individuals in *humane nature*; all thefe are diverfified according to the difference of each *Crafis*, and are as unlike, as our *faces*. From thefe diverfities in all likelyhood will arife as much difference in the manner of the reception of the *Images*, and confequently as various *fenfations*. So then, how objects are reprefented to my *felf*; I cannot be ignorant, being confcious to mine own *cogitations*; but in what manner they are received, and what impreffes they make upon the fo differing *organs* of another, he only *knows*, that *feels* them. There is an obvious an eafie objection, which I have fufficiently
caveated

caveated againſt; and with the conſiderate it will ſignifie no more then the
inadvertency of the Objectors. 'Twill be
thought by ſlight diſcerners a ridiculous
Paradox, that all men ſhould not conceive
of the objects of *ſenſe* alike; ſince their
agreement in the *appellation* ſeems ſo
ſtrong an argument of the identity of the
ſentiment. All, for inſtance, ſay, that
Snow is *white,* and that Jet is *black,* is
doubted by none. But yet 'tis more
then any man can determine, whether
his *conceit* of what he cals *white,* be
the ſame with anothers; or whether,
the notion he hath of one *colour* be not
the ſame another hath of a very *diverſe*
one. So then, to direct all againſt the
knowing Ignorant, what he hath of ſenſible evidence, the very ground-work of
his *demonſtration,* is but the knowledge
of his own *reſentment:* but how the ſame
things appear to others, they only *know,*
that are *conſcious* to them; and how they
are in *themſelves,* only he that *made*
them.

Thus have I in this laſt particular
play'd with the *Dogmatiſt* in a perſonated
Scepticiſm:

Scepticifm: and would not have the defign of the whole *difcourfe* meafur'd by the feeming tendency of this part on't. The *Sciolift* may here fee, that what he counts of all things moft abfurd and irrational, hath yet confiderable fhew of probability to plead its caufe, and it may be more then fome of his prefumed *demonftrations*. 'Tis irreprehenfible in *Phyfitians* to cure their Patient of one difeafe, by cafting him into another, lefs defperate. And I hope, I fhall not deferve the frown of the Ingenuous for my innocent intentions; having in this only imitated the practice of bending a *crooked* ftick as much the other way, to ftraighten it. And if by this verge to the other extream, I can bring the *opinionative Confident* but half the way, *viz.* that difcreet modeft æquipoize of Judgement, that becomes the fons of *Adam*; I have compaft what I aim at.

CHAP.

CHAP. XXIII.

*Considerations against Dogmatizing.
(1) 'Tis the effect of Ignorance.
(2) It inhabits with untamed passi=
ons, and an ungovern'd Spirit.
(3) It is the great Disturber of the
world. (4) It is ill manners, and
immodesty. (5) It holds men captive
in Error. (6) It betrayes a narrowness of spirit.*

I Expect but little success of all this
upon the *Dogmatist*, his opinion'd assurance is paramont to Argument, and
'tis almost as easie to reason him out of
a *Feaver*, as out of this *disease* of the
mind, I hope for better fruit from the
more generous *vertuoso's*, to such I appeal against *Dogmatizing*, in the following
considerations; that's well spent upon
impartial

impartial ingenuity, which is loft upon refolved prejudice.

1. *Opinionative confidence* is the effect of *Ignorance,* and were the *Sciolift* perfwaded fo, I might fpare my further reafons againft it: 'tis affectation of *knowledge,* that makes him confident he hath it, and his confidence is counter evidence to his pretenfions to *knowledge.* He is the greateft *ignorant,* that knows not that he is *fo :* for 'tis a good degree of *Science* , to be fenfible that we *want it.* He that knows moft of himfelf, knows leaft of his knowledge, and the exercifed underftanding is confcious of its difability. Now he that is fo, will not lean too affuredly on that, which hath fo frequently deceived him, nor build the *Caftle* of his intellectual fecurity, *in the Air of Opinions.* But for the fhallow paffive intellects, that were never ingag'd in a through fearch of verity, 'tis fuch are the *confidents* that ingage their irrepealable affents to every flight appearance. Thus meer fenfible conceivers, make every thing they hold a *Sacrament,* and the filly vulgar are *fure* of all things. There was no Theo-

R reme

reme in the *Mathematicks* more certain to *Archimedes*, then the *Earth's* immoveable *quiescence* seems to the multitude : nor then did the impossibility of *Antipodes*, to antique ages. And if great *Philosophers* doubt of many things, which popular dijudicants hold as certain as their *Creeds*, I suppose *Ignorance* it self will not say, it is because they are more *ignorant*. Superficial pedants will swear their controversal uncertainties, while wiser heads stand *in bivio*. Opinions are the *Rattles* of immature intellects, but the advanced Reasons have out-grown them. True knowledge is modest and wary, 'tis ignorance that is so bold, and presuming. Thus those that never travail'd without the *Horizon*, that first terminated their Infant aspects, will not be perswaded that the world hath any Countrey better then their own : while they that have had a view of other Regions, are not so confidently perswaded of the precedency of that, they were bred in, but speak more indifferently of the laws, manners, commodities, and customs of their native soil : So they that

that never peep't beyond the common
belief in which their eafie underftandings
were at firft indoctrinated, are indubi-
tately affur'd of the Truth, and comparative excellency of their receptions,
while the larger Souls, that have travail'd
the divers *Climates* of *Opinions*, are
more cautious in their *refolves*, and more
fparing to determine. And let the moft
confirm'd *Dogmatift* profound far into his
indeared opinions, and I'le warrant him
'twill be an effectual cure of *confidence.*

(2) *Confidence in Opinions* evermore
dwells with untamed *paffions*, and is
maintain'd upon the depraved *obftinacy*
of an ungovern'd *fpirit*. He's but a
novice in the Art of *Autocrafy*, that
cannot caftigate his *paffions* in reference
to thofe *prefumptions*, and will come
as far fhort of *wifdom* as *fcience*: for
the Judgement being the *Hegemonical*
power, and director of action, if it be
led by the *over-bearings* of *paffion*, and
ftor'd with *lubricous opinions* in ftead of
clearly conceived *truths*, and be peremptorily refolved in them, the *practice* will
be as irregular, as the *conceptions* erro-
R 2 neous.

neous. *Opinions* hold the ftirrup, while *vice* mounts into the faddle.

(3) *Dogmatizing* is the great difturber both of our *felves* and the *world* without us : for while we wed an *opinion*, we refolvedly ingage againft every one, that oppofeth it. Thus *every man*, being in fome of his *opinionative* apprehenfions fingular, muft be at variance with *all men*. Now every oppofition of our efpous'd opinions furrows the *fea* within us , and difcompofeth the minds *ferenity*. And what happinefs is there in a *ftorm* of paffions? On this account the *Scepticks* affected an indifferent æquipondious *neutrality* as the only means to their *Ataraxia*, and freedom from *paffionate* difturbances. Nor were they altogether miftaken in the way, to their defign'd felicity, but came *fhort* on't , by going *beyond* it : for if there be a repofe naturally attainable this fide the *Stars*, there is no way we can more hopefully feek it in. We can never be at reft , while our quiet can be taken from us by every thwarting our opinions : nor is that content an happinefs , which every one can
rob

rob us of. There is no *felicity*, but in a *fixed stability*. Nor can genuine *constancy* be built upon *rowling* foundations. 'Tis true staidness of mind, to look with an equal regard on all things, and this unmoved *apathy* in opinionative uncertainties, is a warrantable piece of *Stoicism*. Besides, this *immodest obstinacy* in opinions, hath made the world a *Babel*; and given birth to disorders, like those of the *Chaos*. The primitive fight of *Elements* doth fitly embleme that of *Opinions*, and those *proverbial contrarieties* may be reconcil'd, as soon as peremptory contenders. That hence grow *Schisms*, *Heresies*, and *anomalies* beyond *Arithmetick*, I could with were of more difficult probation. 'Twere happy for a distemper'd *Church*, if evidence were not so near us. 'Tis zeal for *opinions* that hath fill'd our *Hemisphear* with smoke and darkness, and by a dear experience we know the fury of those *flames* it hath kindled. Had not Heaven prevented, they had turn'd our *Paradise* into a *Desert*, and made us the habitation of *Jim*, and *Ohim*. 'Tis lamentable that

Homo

Homo homini Dæmon, should be a *Proverb* among the Professors of the *Cross*, and yet I fear it is as verifiable among them, as of those without the pale of visible *Christianity*. I doubt we have lost *S. John*'s sign of *regeneration*. *By this we know that we are past from death, to life, that we love one another*, is I fear, to few a sign of their spiritual *resurrection*. If our Returning Lord, shall scarse find *faith* on earth, where will he look for *charity*? It is a stranger this side the Region of *love*, and *blessedness*; bitter zeal for opinions hath consum'd it. Mutual agreement and indearments was the badge of Primitive Believers, but we may be known by the contrary *criterion*. The union of a Sect within it self, is a pitiful *charity*: it's no concord of *Christians*, but a conspiracy against *Christ*; and they that love one another, for their *opinionative concurrences*, love for their *own sakes*, not their *Lords*: not because they have his *image*, but because they bear one *anothers*. What a stir is there for *Mint*, *Anise*, and *Cummin controversies*, while the great practical

cal *fundamentals* are unstudyed, unob-
ferved? What eagerness in the profe-
cution of *disciplinarian* uncertainties,
when the *love* of God and our *neighbour*,
those Evangelical *unquestionables*, want
that fervent ardor? 'Tis this hath confum'd
the nutriment of the great and more
necessary Verities, and bred differences
that are past any accommodation, but
that of the *last dayes* decisions. The sight
of that day will resolve us, and make
us asham'd of our pety quarrels. Thus
Opinions have rent the world asunder,
and divided it almost into *indivisibles*.
Had *Heraclitus* liv'd now, he had wept
himself into *marble*, and *Democritus*
would have broke his *spleen*. Who can
speak of such fooleries without a *Satyr*,
to see aged Infants so quarrel at *put-pin*,
and the *doating* world grown child *again*?
How fond are men of a bundle of *opinions*, which are no better then a bagge
of *Cherry-stones*? How do they *scramble*
for their *Nuts*, and *Apples*, and how
zealous for their pety Victories? Methinks those grave contenders about *opinionative trifles*, look like aged *Socrates*

upon his boys *Hobby-horse*, or like something more *ludricous :* since they make things their *feria,* which are scarfe tolerable in their sportful *intervals.*

(4) To be *confident in Opinions* is ill *manners,* and *immodesty* ; and while we are peremptory in our persuasions, we accuse them all of *ignorance* and *Error* that subscribe not our assertions. The *Dogmatist* gives the *lye* to all dissenting apprehenders, and proclaims his judgement fittest, to be the *Intellectual Standard.* This is that spirit of immorality, that saith unto dissenters, *Stand off,* I am more *Orthodox then thou art :* a vanity more capital then Error. He that affirms that things must needs be as he apprehends them, implies that none can be right till they submit to his *opinions,* and take him for their director. This is to invert the *Rule,* and to *account* a mans *self better then all men.*

(5) *Obstinacy in Opinions* holds the Dogmatist in the chains of *Error,* without hope of emancipation. While we are confident of all things, we are fatally deceiv'd in most. He that assures himself
he

he never *erres*, will alwayes *erre* ; and his
prefumptions will render all attempts to
inform him, ineffectual. We ufe not to
feek further for what we think we are
poffeft of ; and when falfhood is without
fufpicion imbrac't in the ftead of truth,
and with confidence retained : Verity
will be rejected as a fuppofed Error, and
irreconcileably be hated , becaufe it oppofeth what is indeed fo.

(6) It betrays a *poverty* and *narrow-
nef* of *fpirit*, in the Dogmatical affertors. There are a fet of Pedants that are
born to flavery. But the generous foul
preferves the liberty of his judgement,
and will not pen it up in an *Opinionative
Dungeon* ; with an equal refpect he examins all things, and judgeth as impartially as *Rhadamanth :* When as the Pedant
can hear nothing but in favour of the
conceits he is amorous of ; and cannot
fee, but out of the grates of his *prifon*. The
determinations of the nobler fpirit , are
but *temporary*, and he holds them, but till
better evidence repeal his former apprehenfions. He won't defile his affent by
proftituting it to every conjecture , or
ftuff

stuff his belief, with the luggage of uncertainties. The modesty of his expression
renders him *infallible* ; and while he only
saith he *Thinks so*, he cannot be deceiv'd,
or ever assert a *falshood*. But the wise
Monsieur *Charron* hath fully discourst of
this *Universal liberty* , and sav'd me the
labour of inlarging. Upon the Review
of my former considerations , I cannot
quarrel with his *Motto :* in a sense *Je ne
scay*, is a justifiable *Scepticism*, and not
mis-becoming a Candidate of *wisdom*.
Socrates in the judgement of the *Oracle*
knew more then *All men*, who in his own
knew the least of *any*.

CHAP.

CHAP. XXIV.

AN APOLOGY
FOR
PHILOSOPHY.

IT is the glory of *Philofophy*, that *Ig-norance* and *Phrenfie* are her Enemies. Now to vindicate this abufed *excellence* from the mif-reports of *ftupid* and *En-thufiaftick Ignorants*, I'le fubjoyn this brief *Apology*: Left thofe unintelligent maligners take an advantage from our difcourfe, to depretiate and detract from what hath been alway the object of their *hate*, becaufe never of their *knowledge*, and *capacities*; Or, which is the greater mifchief, left this fhould difcourage thofe enlarged fouls, who afpire to the knowledge of God, and Nature, which is the moft venial ambition.

bition. If *Philosophy* be *uncertain*, the former will confidently conclude it *vain*; and the later may be in danger of pronouncing the same on their pains, who seek it; if after all their labour they must reap the wind, meer opinion and conjecture.

But there's a part of Philosophy, that owes no answer to the charge. The *Scepticks*, πάντα ἐστὶν ἀβέβαια, must have the qualification of an exception; and at least the *Mathematicks* must be priviledg'd from the endictment. Neither yet are we at so deplorable a loss, in the other parts of what we call *Science*; but that we may meet with what will content ingenuity, at this distance from perfection, though all things will not compleatly satisfie strict and rigid *enquiry*. *Philosophy* indeed cannot immortalize us, or free us from the inseparable attendants on this state, *Ignorance*, and *Error*. But shall we malign it, because it entitles us not to an *Omniscience?* Is it just to condemn the *Physitian*, because *Hephestion* dyed? Compleat knowledge

is

is reserv'd to gratifie our glorified faculties. We are ignorant of some things from our specifical incapacity, as *men* ; of more from our contracted, as *sinners* : and 'tis no fault in the *spectacles*, that the *blind man* sees not. Shall we, like sullen children, because we have not what we would ; contemn what the benignity of Heaven offers us ? Do what we can, we shall be imperfect in all our attainments ; and shall we scornfully neglect what we may reach, because some things to mortality are denyed ? 'Tis madness to refuse the Largesses of divine bounty on *Earth*, because there is not an *Heaven* in them. Shall we not rejoyce at the gladsome approach of day, because it's over-cast with a cloud, and follow'd by the obscurity of night ? All sublunary vouchsafements have their allay of a contrary ; and uncertainty, in another kind, is the annex of all things this side the *Sun*. Even Crowns and Diadems, the most splendid parts of terrene attains ; are akin to that, which *to day is in the field*, and *to morrow is*

cut

cut down, and *wither'd* : He that enjoy'd them, and knew their worth,
excepted them not out of the charge of
Univerſal Vanity. And yet the Politician
thinks they deſerve his pains ; and is
not diſcourag'd at the inconſtancy of
humane affairs, and the lubricity of his
ſubjeƐt.

He that looks perfeƐtion, muſt ſeek
it above the *Empyreum* ; it is reſerv'd
for *Glory.* It's that alone, which needs
not the advantage of a ſoyl: DefeƐts
ſeem as neceſſary to our now-happineſs,
as their Oppoſites. The moſt refulgent
colours are the reſult of light and ſhadows. *Venus* was never the leſs beautiful
for her Mole. And 'tis for the Majeſty
of Nature, like the *Perſian Kings*, ſometimes to cover, and not alway to pro-
ſtrate her beauties to the *naked view* :
yea, they contraƐt a kind of ſplendour
from the ſeemingly obſcuring veil ;
which adds to the enraviſhments of her
tranſported admirers. He alone ſees
all things with an unſhadowed compre-
henſive Viſion, who eminently *is All :*
Only the God of *Nature* perfeƐtly
knows

knows her ; and light without darkneſs is the incommunicable claim of him, that dwells in *Light inacceſſible*. 'Tis no diſparagement to *Philoſophy*, that it cannot *Deiſie* us, or make good the impoſſible promiſe of the *Primitive Deceiver*. It is that, which ſhe owns above her, that muſt perfectly remake us after the Image of our Maker.

And yet thoſe raiſed contemplations of God and Nature, wherewith *Philoſophy* doth acquaint us ; enlarge and ennoble the ſpirit, and infinitely advance it above an ordinary level. The ſoul is alway like the objects of its delight and converſe. *A Prince* is as much above a *Peaſant* in *ſpirit*, as *condition :* And man as far tranſcends the Beaſts in largeneſs of deſire, as dignity of Nature and employment. While we only converſe with *Earth*, we are *like* it ; that is, unlike our ſelves : But when engag'd in more refin'd and intellectual entertainments ; we are ſomewhat more, then this narrow circumference of fleſh ſpeaks us. And, me thinks, thoſe generous Vertuoſo's, who dwell in an
higher

higher Region then other Mortals; should make a middle species between the *Platonical* Θεοὶ, and *common Humanity*. Even our Age in variety of glorious examples, can confute the conceit, that souls are equal: And the sole Instances of those illustrious Heroes, *Cartes, Gaßendus, Galilæo, Tycho, Harvey, More, Digby*; will strike dead the opinion of the worlds decay, and conclude it, in its *Prime*. And upon the review of these great Sages, me-thinks, I could easily opinion; that *men* may differ from *men*, as much as *Angels* from *unbodyed Souls*: And, it may be, more can be pleaded for such a Metaphysical innovation, then can for a specifical diversity among our *Predicamental Opposites*. Such as these, being in a great part freed from the entanglements of a drossie Vehicle, are imploy'd like the Spirits above; in taking a survey of Natures Riches, and beginning those *Anthems* to their Maker, which Eternity must consummate. This is one part of the life of Souls.

While

While we indulge to the *Sensitive* or *Plantal* Life, our delights are common to us with the creatures *below us :* and 'tis likely, they exceed us as much as in them, as in the senses their subjects ; and that's a poor happiness for man to aim at, in which Beasts are his Superiours. But those *Mercurial* souls, which were only lent the Earth to shew the world their folly in admiring it ; possess delights, which as it were antedate Immortality, and [though at an humble distance] resemble the *joys above.* The Sun and Stars, are not the worlds *Eyes,* but these : The *Celestial Argus* cannot glory in such an universal view. These out-travel theirs, and their *Monarchs* beams : skipping into *Vortexes* beyond their Light and Influence ; and with an easie twinkle of an Intellectual Eye look into the Centre, which is obscur'd from the upper Luminaries. This is somewhat like the Image of *Omnipresence :* And what the *Hermetical Philosophy* saith of *God,* is in a sense verifiable of the thus *ennobled soul,* That *its Centre is every where, but it's circumference no where.*

S   This

This is the ἀληθινὸς ἄνϑρωπΘ; and what
Plotinus calls fo, the *divine life*, is fomewhat more. Thofe that live but to the
lower *concupifcible*, and relifh no delights but *fenfual* ; it's by the favour of
a *Metaphor*, that we call them *Men*. As
Ariftotle faith of Brutes , they have but
the Μιμήμαⱡα ἀνϑρωπίνης ζωῆς, only fome
fhews and *Apifh imitations* of *Humane* ;
and have little more to juftifie their Title to Rationality , then thofe *Mimick
Animals*, the fuppofed *Pofterity* of *Cham :*
who, had they retain'd the priviledge
of Speech , which fome of the Fathers
fay they they own'd before the *Fall* ; it
may be they would plead their caufe
with them, and have laid ftrong claim
to a Parity. Such, as thefe, are *Philofo-
phies* Maligners,. who computing the
ufefulnefs of all things , by what they
bring to their *Barns* , and *Treafures* ;
ftick not to pronounce the moft generous contemplations, needlefs unprofitable fubtilties : and they might with as
good reafon fay, that the *light* of their
Eyes was a fuperfluous provifion of Nature, becaufe it fills not their *Bellies*.
                                    Thus

Thus the greatest part of miserable Humanity is lost in Earth : and, if Man be an *inversed Plant* ; these are *inversed Men*, who forgetting that *Sursum*, which Nature writ in their Foreheads, take their Roots in this sordid Element. But the *Philosophical soul* is an *inverted Fyramid* ; Earth hath but a point of this *Æthereal Cone*. *Aquila non captat muscas*, The Royal Eagle flyes not but at noble Game ; and a young *Alexander* will not play but with Monarchs. He that hath been cradled in Majesty, and used to Crowns and Scepters ; will not leave the Throne to play with Beggars at *Put-pin*, or be fond of *Tops* and *Cherry-stones :* neither will a Soul, that dwells with Stars, dabble in this impurer Mud ; or stoop to be a Play-fellow and Copartner in delights with the Creatures, that have nought but *Animal*. And though it be necessitated by its relation to flesh to a Terrestrial converse ; yet 'tis, like the *Sun*, without contaminating its Beams. For, though the body by a kind of *Magnetism* be drawn down to this *sediment* of universal dreggs ; yet the thus impregnate spi-

rit

rit contracts a *Verticity* to objects above the *Pole :* And, like as in a falling Torch, though the groſſer Materials haſten to their Element ; yet the flame aſpires, and, could it maſter the dulneſs of its load would carry it beyond the central activity of the *Terraqueous Magnet.* Such ſouls juſtifie *Ariſtotles,* Νᾶς ϑύεꞃϑεν ϗ ϑᾶῷ μόνον; and in allayed ſenſe that title, which the Stoicks give it, of ἀπόσπασμα Θεᾶ. If we ſay, they are not in their bodies, but their bodies in them ; we have the Authority of the divine *Plato* to vouch us : And by the favour of an eaſie ſimile we may affirm them to be to the body, as the light of a Candle to the groſs, and fæculent ſnuff ; which, as it is not pent up in it, ſo neither doth it partake of its ſtench and and impurity. Thus, as the Roman Oratour elegantly deſcants, *Erigimur, & latiores fieri videmur ; humana deſpicimus, contemplanteſq; ſupera & cœleſtia, hæc noſtra, ut exigua & minima, contemnimus.*

And yet there's an higher degree, to which *Philoſophy* ſublimes us. For, as it teacheth a generous contempt of what the grovelling deſires of *creeping* Mortals
Idolize

Idolize and dote on ; so it raiseth us to love and admire an Object, that is as much above terrestrial, as *Infinity* can make it. If *Plutarch* may have credit, the observation of Natures Harmony in the *celestial motions* was one of the first inducements to the belief of *a God :* And a greater then he affirms, that the visible things of the Creation declare him, that made them. What knowledge we have of them, we have in a sense of their Authour. His face cannot be beheld by Creature-Opticks, without the allay of a reflexion ; and Nature is one of those mirrours, that represents him to us. And now the more we know of him, the more we love him, the more we are like him, the more we admire him. 'Tis here, that *knowledge wonders*; and there's an *Admiration*, that's not the *Daughter* of *Ignorance*. This indeed stupidly gazeth at the unwonted *effect :* But the Philosophick passion truly admires and adores the supreme *Efficient.* The *wonders* of the Almighty are not seen, but by those that go *down into the deep.* The *Heavens* declare their *Makers Glory* ; and *Philosophy theirs*,

S 3 which

which by a grateful rebound returns to
its *Original source*. The twinkling span-
gles, the Ornaments of the upper world;
lose their beauty and magnificence;
while they are but the objects of our narrow'd senses: By them the *half* is not
told us; and Vulgar spectators see them,
but as a confused huddle of pety *Illuminants*. But *Philosophy* doth right to those
immense sphears; and advantagiously
reprefents their Glories, both in the vaft-
ness of their *proportions*, and regularity
of their *motions*. If we would see the
wonders of the *Globe* we dwell in; *Philosophy* muft reare us above it. The works
of God speak forth his mighty praife: A
fpeech not underftood, but by thofe that
know them. The moft Artful melody receives but little tribute of Honour from
the *gazing beafts*; it requires skill to relifh *it*. The moft delicate mufical accents of the *Indians*, to us are but *inarticulate hummings*; as queftionlefs are
ours to their otherwise *tuned Organs*. Ignorance of the Notes and Proportions,
renders all *Harmony* unaffecting. A gay
Puppet pleafeth children more, then the
exacteft

exactest piece of *unaffected Art:* it requires some degrees of *Perfection*, to admire what is truly *perfect*; as it's said to be an advance in Oratory to relish *Cicero.* Indeed the unobservant Multitude, may have some general confus'd apprehensions of a kind of *beauty*, that guilds the outside frame of the Universe : But they are Natures courser *wares*, that lye on the *stall*, expos'd to the transient view of every *common Eye*; her choicer *Riches* are lock't up only for the sight of *them*, that will buy at the expence of *sweat* and *Oyl.* Yea, and the visible Creation is far otherwise apprehended by the *Philosophical Inquirer*, then the *unintelligent Vulgar.* Thus the *Physitian* looks with another Eye on the *Medicinal hearb*, then the *grazing Oxe*, which swoops it in with the common *grass* : and the Swine may see the *Pearl*, which yet he values but with the *ordinary muck*; it's otherwise pris'd by the skilful *Jeweller.*

And from this last Article, I think, I may conclude the charge, which hotbrain'd folly lays in against *Philosophy*; that it leads to *Irreligion*, frivolous and

vain

vain. I dare fay, next after the *divine Word*, it's one of the beft friends to *Piety*. Neither is it any more juftly accountable for the impious irregularities of fome, that have payd an homage to its fhrine ; then *Religion* it felf for the finful extravagances both *opinionative* and *practical* of high pretenders to it. It is a vulgar conceit, that *Philofophy* holds a confederacy with *Atheifm* it felf ; but moft *injurious :* for nothing can better antidote us againft it ; and they may as well fay, that *Phyfitians* are the only *murtherers*. A *Philofophick Atheift,* is as good fenfe as a *Divine one :* and I dare fay the Proverb, *Ubi tres Medici, duo Athei*, is a fcandal. I think the Original of this conceit might be ; That the Students of Nature, confcious to her more *cryptick* ways of working, refolve many ftrange effects into the nearer efficiency of *fecond caufes* ; which common Ignorance and Superftition attribute to the Immediate caufality of the *firft :* thinking it to derogate from the Divine Power, that any thing which is above their apprehenfions, fhould not be reckon'd above *Natures* activity ; though

it be but his Inftrument, and works nothing but as impower'd from him. Hence
they violently declaim againft all, that will
not acknowledge a *Miracle* in every extraordinary effect, as fetting Nature in
the Throne of *God*; and fo it's an eafie ftep
to fay, they deny him. When as indeed,
Nature is but the chain of fecond caufes;
and to fuppofe fecond caufes without a
firft, is beneath the *Logick* of *Gotham*.
Neither can they [who, to make their reproach of Philofophy more *authentick*, alledge the Authority of an *Apoftle* to conclude it *vain*] upon any whit more reafonable terms make good their charge;
fince this allegation ftands in force but
againft its *abufe*, *corrupt fophiftry*, or *traditionary impofitions*, which lurk'd under
the mask of fo ferious a name : At the
worft, the Text will never warrant an
univerfal conclufion any more; then that
other, where the Apoftle fpeaks of *filly
women*, (who yet are the moft rigid urgers of this) can juftly blot the *fex* with
an unexceptionable note of *infamy*.

Now, what I have faid here in this
fhort *Apology* for *Philofophy*, is not fo
ftrictly

ſtrictly verifiable of any that I know, as the *Carteſian.* The entertainment of which among truly ingenuous unpoſſeſt *Spirits,* renders an after-commendation ſuperfluous and impertinent. It would require a *wit* like its Authors, to do it right in an *Encomium.* The ſtrict Rationality of the *Hypotheſis* in the main, and the *critical* coherence of its parts, I doubt not but will bear it down to Poſterity with a *Glory,* that ſhall know no *term,* but the *Univerſal ruines.* Neither can the *Pedantry,* or prejudice of the preſent Age, any more obſtruct its motion in that *ſupreme ſphear,* wherein its deſert hath plac'd it ; then can the howling Wolves pluck *Cynthia* from her *Orb* ; who regardleſs of their noiſe, ſecurely glides through the undiſturbed *Æther.* Cenſure here will diſparage it ſelf, not *it.* He that accuſeth the *Sun* of *darkneſs,* ſhames his own *blind eyes* ; not its *light.* The barking of *Cynicks* at that *Hero's* Chariot-wheels, will not ſully the glory of his *Triumphs.* But I ſhall ſuperſede this *endleſs* attempt : *Sun-beams* beſt commend themſelves.

F I N I S.

The Contents.

CHAP. I.

CHAP.

The Contents.

CHAP. V.

CHAP. VI.

CHAP. VII.

CHAP. VIII.

CHAP.

The Contents.

The Contents.

CHAP

The Contents.

CHAP. XVIII.

CHAP. XIX.

CHAP. XX.

The Contents.

FINIS.

Collegium Mertonense
in Universitate Oxon

Scepsis Scientifica.

Scepsis Scientifica:

OR,

Confest *Ignorance*, the way to *Science*;

In an *Essay* of

The Vanity of DOGMATIZING,

AND

CONFIDENT Opinion.

WITH

A REPLY to the EXCEPTIONS

Of the Learned

THOMAS ALBIUS.

By JOSEPH GLANVILL, M.A.

LONDON:

Printed by *E. Cotes*, for HENRY EVERSDEN at the *Gray-Hound* in St. Paul's *Church-yard*. M. DC. LXV.

NVLLIVS IN VERBA

TO THE
ROYAL SOCIETY.

Illustrious Gentlemen,

THE name of your Honorable Society is so August and Glorious, and this trifle to which I have prefixt it, of so mean, and so unsuitable a quality; that

'tis

'tis fit I ſhould give an account of an action ſo ſeemingly obnoxious. And I can expect no other from thoſe, that judge by firſt ſights and raſh meaſures, then to be thought fond or inſolent; or, as one that hath unmeet thoughts of himſelf, or YOU. But if a naked profeſſion may have credit in a caſe wherein no other evidence can be given of an intention, I adventured not on this Addreſs upon the uſual Motives of Dedications. It was not upon deſign to credit theſe Papers (which yet derive much accidental Honour from the occaſion.) Nor to complement a Society ſo much above Flattery, and the regardleſs air of common Applauſes. I intended not your Illuſtrious Name the diſhonour of being Fence againſt detraction for a performance, which poſſibly deſerves it. Nor was it to publiſh how much I honour You; which were to fancy my ſelf conſiderable. Much leſs was I ſo fond, to think I could contribute any thing

to

to a Conſtellation of Worthies *from whom
the Learned World expects to be informed. But, conſidering how much it is the intereſt of Mankinde in order to the* advance
of Knowledge, *to be ſenſible they have not
yet attain'd it ; or at leaſt, but in* poor *and*
diminutive meaſures ; *and regarding Your*
Society *as the ſtrongeſt* Argument *to perſwade a* modeſt *and* reſerved diffidence *in
opinions, I took the boldneſs to borrow that
deſervedly celebrated* name, *for an* evidence
*to my Subject ; that ſo what was wanting
in my* Proof, *might be made up in the* Example. *For If we were yet arriv'd to* certain *and* infallible *Accounts in Nature,
from whom might we more reaſonably expect
them then from a Number of* Men, *whom,
their impartial* Search, *wary* Procedure,
deep Sagacity, *twiſted* Endeavours, *ample*
Fortunes, *and all other advantages, have
renderd infinitely more likely to have ſuccee-
ded in thoſe Enquiries; then the* ſloath, haſte,
and

and babble *of talking* Diſputants; *or the greateſt induſtry of* ſingle *and leſs qualified Attempters?* If therefore thoſe (*whom,* I am *in no danger of being disbelieved by any that* underſtand the world *and them, if* I call the moſt learned and ingenious Society in Europe.) *if they,* I ſay, confeſs the narrowneſs of humane attainments, *and dare not* confide *in the moſt plauſible of their* Sentiments; *if* ſuch great *and* inſtructed Spirits *think we have not as yet* Phænomena *enough to make as much as* Hypotheſeis; *much leſs, to fix* certain Laws *and preſcribe* Methods *to* Nature *in her Actings:* what inſolence is it *then in the* leſſer ſize of Mortals, *who* poſſibly know *nothing but what they* glean'd *from* ſome little Syſteme, *or the* Diſputes *of Men that love to* ſwagger *for* Opinions, *to* boaſt Infallibility of Knowledge, *and* ſwear *they* ſee *the* Sun *at* Midnight!

Nor

Nor was this the only inducement to the dishonour I have done you in the direction of these worthless Papers; But I must confess I design'd hereby to serve my self in another interest. For having been so hardy as to undertake a charge against the Philosophy of the Schools, and to attempt upon a name which among some is yet very Sacred, I was lyable to have been overborne by a Torrent of Authorities, and to have had the voyce of my single reason against it, drown'd in the noise of Multitudes of Applauders: That I might not therefore be vapour'd down by insignificant Testimonies, or venture bare reasons against what the doating world counts more valuable, I presumed to use the great Name of your Society to annihilate all such arguments. And I cannot think that any, that is but indifferently impudent, will have the confidence to urge, either the greatness of the Authour, or the number of its Admirers in behalf of

(a)   that

that Philoſophy, *after the* ROYAL SOCIETY *is mention'd.* For though *your Honourable and ingenious* Aſſembly *hath not ſo little to do*, *as to* Diſpute with Men *that count it a great attainment to be able to talk much*, *and little to the purpoſe:* And though *you have not thought it worth your labour to enter a profeſs'd diſſent a- gainſt a* Philoſophy *which the greateſt part of the* Virtuoſi, *and* enquiring ſpirits of Europe *have deſerted*, *as a meer* maze of words, *and* uſeleſs contrivance: Yet the credit which the Mathematicks have with you, *your* experimental way of Enqui- ry, *and* Mechanical Attempts *for ſolving the* Phænomena; *beſides that ſome of you* (*to whoſe excellent works the learned world is deeply indebted*) *publickly own the* Carteſian, *and* Atomical Hypotheſeis; Theſe, I ſay, *are arguments of your no great favour to the* Ariſtotelian. For indeed *that* diſputing phyſiology *is of no accommoda- tion*

tion to your designs; *which are not. to teach* Men *to* cant *endlesly about* Materia, *and* Forma; *to hunt* Chimæra's *by rules of* Art, *or to dress up* Ignorance *in words of* bulk *and* sound, *which shall stop the mouth* of enquiry, *and make* learned fools *seem* Oracles *among the* populace: *But the improving the minds of Men in* solid *and* useful notices of *things, helping them to such* Theories *as may be serviceable to* common life, *and the searching out the true* laws of Matter *and* Motion, *in order to the securing of the* Foundations of Religion *against* all attempts of Mechanical Atheism.

In order to the Furtherance (*according to my poor measure*) *of which great and worthy purposes, these* Papers *were first intended. For perceiving that several* ingenious persons *whose assistance might be conducive to the Advance* of real *and* useful Knowledge, *lay under the prejudices of* Education *and* Customary Belief; *I thought that* the

the enlarging them to a ſtate of more generous Freedom by ſtriking at the root of Pedantry and opinionative Aſſurance would
be no hinderance to the Worlds improvement. For Such it was then that the enſuing
Eſſay was deſigned; which therefore wears
a dreſs, that poſſibly is not ſo ſuitable to the
graver Geniuſſes, who have outgrown all
gayeties of ſtyle and youthful reliſhes;
But yet perhaps is not improper for the perſons, for whom it was prepared. And there
is nothing in words and ſtyles but ſuitableneſs, that makes them acceptable and effe-
ctive. If therefore this Diſcourſe, ſuch as
it is, may tend to the removal of any accidental diſadvantages from capable Ingenu-
ities, and the preparing them for inquiry,
I know you have ſo noble an ardour for the
benefit of Mankind, as to pardon a weak
and defective performance to a laudable
and well-directed intention. And though,
if you were acted by the ſpirit of common
Mortals,

Mortals, *you need not care for the propagation of that* gallantry *and* intellectual grandeur *which you are so eminently owners of*, *since 'tis a greater* credit, *and possibly* pleasure, *to be* wise *when* few *are* so ; *yet you being no* Factors *for* Glory *or* Treasure, *but* disinteressed Attempters *for the* universal good, *cannot but favourably regard any thing, that in the least degree may do the considering* World *a* kindness ; *and to enoble it with the spirit that inspires the* ROYAL SOCIETY, *were to advantage it in one of the best* Capacities *in which it is improveable. These* Papers *then* (as I have intimated) *having been directed to an* End *subordinate to this, viz. the disposing the less* stupid Minds *for that honour and improvement* ; *I thought it very proper to call up their eyes to you, and to fix them on their* Example : *That so natural* Ambition *might take part with* reason *and their* interest *to encourage* imitation. *In*

(a 3) *order*

order to which, I think it needless to endeavour to celebrate you in a profest Encomium; since customary Strains and affected Juvenilities have made it difficult to commend, and speak credibly in Dedications; And your deserts, impossible in this. So that he that undertakes it, must either be wanting to your merits, or speak things that will find but little credit among those that do not know You. Or, possibly such, as will be interpreted only as what of course is said on such occasions, rather because 'tis usual, then because 'tis just. But the splendour of a Society, illustrious both by blood and vertue, excuseth my Pen from a subject, in which it must either appear vain, or be defective. I had much rather take notice therefore, how providentially you are met together in Dayes, wherein people of weak Heads on the one hand, and vile affections on the other, have made an unnatural divorce between
being

being Wise *and* Good. These *conceiving* Reason *and* Philosophy *sufficient* vouchees *of* Licentious practices *and their secret* scorn *of* Religion; *and* Those *reckoning it a great instance of* Piety *and devout* Zeal, vehemently *to declaim against* Reason *and* Philosophy. *And what result can be expected from such supposals, That tis a piece of* Wit *and* Gallantry *to be an* Atheist, *and of* Atheism *to be a* Philosopher, *but* Irreligion *on the one side, and* Superstition *on the other, which will end in open irreclaimeable* Atheism *on* both? *Now it seems to me a signality in* Providence *in erecting your most* Honourable Society *in such a juncture of* dangerous Humours, *the very mention of which is evidence, that* Atheism *is* impudent *in pretending to* Philosophy; *And* Superstition *sottishly* ignorant *in phancying, that the* knowledge *of* Nature *tends* to Irreligion. *But to leave this latter to it's conceits, and the*

the little impertinencies of humour. and folly it is fond of: The former is more dangerous, though not more reaſonable. For where 'tis once preſumed, that the whole Fabrick of Religion is built upon Ignorance of the Nature of things; And the belief of a God, ariſeth from unacquaintance with the Laws of Matter and Motion; what can be the iſſue of ſuch preſumptions, but that thoſe that are ſo perſwaded, ſhould deſire to be wiſe in a way that will gratiſie their Appetites: And ſo give up themſelves to the ſwinge of their unbounded propenſions? Yea, and thoſe, the impiety of whoſe lives makes them regret a Deity, and ſecretly wiſh there were none, will greedily liſſen to a Doctrine that ſtrikes at the exiſtence of a Being, the ſenſe of whom is a reſtraint and check upon the licence of their Actions. And thus all wickedneſs and debauches will flow in upon the world like a mighty deluge,

deluge, and beat down all the Banks of Laws, Vertue, and Sobriety before them.

Now though few have yet arrived to that pitch of Impiety, or rather Folly, openly to own such sentiments; yet, I doubt, this concealment derives rather from the fear of Man, then from the love or fear of any Being above him. And what the confident exploding of all immaterial Substances, the unbounded prerogatives are bestowed upon Matter, and the consequent assertions, signifie, you need not be informed. I could wish there were less reason to suspect them branches of a dangerous Cabbala. For the ingenious World being grown quite weary of Qualities and Formes, and declaring in favour of the Mechanical Hypothesis, (to which a person that is not very fond of Religion is a great pretender) divers of the brisker Geniusses, who desire rather to be accounted Witts, then endeavour to be so, have been willing to accept

Me-

Mechaniſm *upon* Hobbian *conditions, and many others were in danger of following them into the* precipice. *So that 'tis not conceivable how a more ſuitable* remedy *could have been provided againſt the* deadly influence *of that* Contagion, *then your Honourable* Society, *by which the meaneſt intellects may perceive, that* Mechanick Philoſophy *yields no ſecurity to* irreligion, *and that thoſe that would be* gentilely *learned and ingenious, need not purchaſe it, at the* dear *raie of being* Atheiſts. *Nor can the* proleptical notions *of Religion be ſo well defended by the* profeſt Servants *of the* Altar, *who uſually ſuppoſe them, and are leſs furniſhed with* advantages *for ſuch* ſpeculations; *ſo that their* Attempts *in this kind will be interpreted by ſuch as are not willing to be convinced, as the* products *of* intereſt, *or* ignorance *in* Mechanicks; *which ſuſpicions can never be deriv'd upon a* Society *of perſons of* Quality *and* Honour,

nour, *who are embodied for no other in-*
tereſt *but that of the* Publique, *and*
whoſe abilities in this kind are too bright
to *admit the leaſt* ſnadow *of the other*
Cenſure. *And 'tis to be hoped, that the*
eminence *of your* condition, *and the* gallantry *of your* Principles, *which are* worthy *thoſe that own them, will invite* Gentlemen *to the* uſeful *and* enobling *ſtudy* of
Nature, *and make* Philoſophy faſhionable;
whereas while that which the World *call'd*
ſo, *conſiſted of nought but* dry Spinoſities,
lean Notions, *and* endleſs Alterations *a-*
bout things of nothing, *all unbecoming* Men
of generous Spirit *and* Education; *of* uſe
no where but where folkes are bound to
talk *by a* Law, *and profeſt by few but per-*
ſons of ordinary *condition*; *while*, I *ſay*,
Philoſophy *was of* ſuch *a* nature, *and* cloathed *with ſuch* circumſtances, *how could*
it be otherwiſe then 'conteptible *in the*
eſteem of the more enfranchiſed *and* ſpright-

ly

ly *tempers*? *So that your* Illuſtrious Society *hath* redeemed *the* credit of Philoſophy; *and I hope to ſee it accounted
a piece of none of the* meaneſt breeding *to
be acquainted with the* Laws of Nature *and
the* Univerſe. *And doubtleſs there is nothing wherein men* of birth *and* fortune
would better conſult their treble intereſt
of PLEASURE, ESTATE, *and* HO-
NOUR, *then by ſuch* generous reſearches. *In which* (1.) *they'l find all the
innocent* ſatisfactions *which uſe to follow*
victory, variety, *and* ſurpriſe, *the uſual
ſources of our beſt taſted* pleaſures. *And
perhaps* humane nature *meets few more*
ſweetly reliſhing *and* cleanly joyes, *then
thoſe, that derive from the* happy iſſues *of*
ſucceſsful Tryals: *Yea, whether they ſucceed to the anſwering the particular* aim *of
the* Naturaliſt *or not; 'tis however a* pleaſant
ſpectacle *to behold the* ſhifts, windings *and*
unexpected Caprichios *of diſtreſſed* Nature,
when

when purſued by a cloſe *and* well managed Experiment. *And the* delights *which re-ſult from theſe* nobler entertainments *are ſuch,* as our cool *and* reflecting thoughts *need not be* aſhamed of. *And which are dogged by no ſuch ſad ſequels as are the pro-ducts of thoſe* titillations *that reach no higher then* Phancy *and the* Senſes. *And* that *alone deſerves to be call'd ſo,* which is plea-ſure *without* guilt or pain. *Nor* (2.) *have the* frugaller Sons *of* fortune *any reaſon to object the* Coſtlineſs *of the* delights *we ſpeak of, ſince, in all likelyhood, they fre-quently* pay dearer *for leſs* advantagious pleaſures. *And it may be there are few bet-ter wayes of* adding *to what they are affraid to* waſte, *then* inquiries *into* Nature. *For by* a skilful application *of thoſe* notices, *may be gain'd in ſuch* reſearches, *beſides the* accelerating *and* bettering of Fruits, emptying Mines, drayning Fens *and* Marſhes, *which may hereby be* effected,

at

at much more eaſie and leſs expenſive rates,
then by the common methods of ſuch performances : I ſay, beſides theſe, Lands
may be advanced to ſcarce credible degrees
of improvement, and innumerable other
advantages may be obtain'd by an induſtry
directed by Philoſophy and Mechanicks,
which can never be expected from drudg-
ing Ignorance. But though thoſe inquiſi-
tive purſuits of things ſhould make out no
pretence to Pleaſure or Advantage; yet
upon the laſt Account (3.) of Honour, they
are infinitely recommendable to all that
have any ſenſe of ſuch an intereſt. For 'tis
a greater credit, if we judge by equal meaſures, to underſtand the Art whereby the
Almighty Wiſdom governs the Motions of the great Automaton, and to know
the wayes of captivating Nature, and making her ſubſerve our purpoſes and deſign-
ments ; then to have learnt all the intrigues
of Policy, and the Cabals of States and
King-

Kingdoms; *yea, then to* triumph *in the* head *of* victorious Troops *over* conquer'd Empires. *Those* succeſſes *being more* glorious *which bring* benefit *to the World;* then *such* ruinous ones *as are dyed in* humane blood, *and* cloathed *in the* livery *of* Cruelty *and* Slaughter.

*N*or *are theſe all the* advantages *upon the Account of which we owe* acknowledgments *to* Providence *for your* erection; *ſince from your* promiſing *and* generous endeavours, *we may hopefully expect a conſiderable* inlargement *of the* Hiſtory *of* Nature, *without which our* Hypotheſeis *are but* Dreams *and* Romances, *and our* Science *meer* conjecture *and* opinion. *For while we frame* Scheames *of things without conſulting the* Phænomena, *we do but* build *in the* Air, *and* deſcribe *an* Imaginary World *of our* own making, *that is but little a kin to the* real one *that* God made. *And 'tis poſſible that all the* Hypotheſeis

theſeis *that yet have been contrived, were built upon too narrow an* inſpection of things, *and the* phaſies *of the* Univerſe. *For the advancing* day of experimental knowledge *diſcloſeth ſuch* appearances, *as will not lye* even, *in any* model *extant. And perhaps the newly diſcovered* Ring *about* Saturn, *to mention no more, will ſcarce be accounted for by any* ſyſteme *of things the World hath yet been acquainted with. So that little can be looked for towards the* advancement of natural Theory, *but from thoſe, that are likely to mend our* proſpect of events *and* ſenſible appearances; *the defect of which will ſuffer us to proceed no further towards* Science, *then to* imperfect gueſſes, *and* timerous ſuppoſals. *And from whom can this* great *and* noble Acquiſt *be expected, if not from a* Society *of perſons that can command both* Wit *and* Fortune *to ſerve them, and profeſſedly ingage* both *in* experimental *purſuits of* Nature? *The deſired*

desired success *of which kind of ingagements cannot so reasonably be looked for from any in the known* Universe, *as from your most* Honourable Society, *where* fondness of preconceiv d opinions, sordid Interests, or affectation of strange Relations, *are not like to render your* reports suspect *or* partial, *nor* want of Sagacity, Fortune, or Care, *defective:* some of which possibly have been *ingredients in most former experiments. So that the relations of your* Tryals *may be received as undoubted* Records of certain events, *and as securely be depended on, as the* Propositions of Euclide. *Which* advantage *cannot be hoped from* private undertakers, or Societies *less qualified and conspicuous then* Yours. *And how great a benefit such a* Natural History *as may be confided in, will prove to the whole* stock of learned Mankinde, *those that understand the interest of the* inquiring World *may conjecture. Doubtless, the success of those your* great *and* Catholick Endeavours *will*

(c)

pro

promote the Empire *of* Man *over* Nature, *and bring plentiful acceſſion of* Glory *to your* Nation; *making* BRITAIN *more juſtly famous then the once celebrated* GREECE; *and* LONDON *the wiſer* ATHENS. For You really *are what former Ages could contrive but in* wiſh *and* Romances; *and* Solomons Houſe *in the* NEW ATLANTIS, *was a* Prophetick Scheam *of the* ROYAL SOCIETY. *And though ſuch* Auguſt *deſigns as inſpire your enquiries, uſe to be derided by* drolling phantaſticks, *that have only wit enough to make others and themſelves* ridiculous: Yet there's *no reproach in the ſcoffs of* Ignorance; *and thoſe that are wiſe enough to underſtand* your worth, *and the* merit *of* your endeavours, *will contemn the* ſilly taunts *of* fleering Buffoonry; *and the* jerks *of that* Wit, *that is but a* kind *of* confident, *and* well-acted folly. And *'tis none of the leaſt conſiderable expectations that may be reaſonably had of* your

your Society, *that 'twill discredit that* toyish-ness *of* wanton fancy ; *and pluck the misap-plyed name of the* W I T S, *from those con-ceited* Humourists *that have assum'd it; to be-stow it upon the more* manly spirit *and* geni-us , *that playes not tricks with* words, *nor frolicks with the* Caprices *of* froathy ima-gination : *But imployes a* severe reason *in enquiries into the momentous concernments of the* Universe.

On consideration of all which Accounts, I *think it just you should have acknowledgments from all the* Sons *and* Favourers *of* Wisdom : *and I cannot believe it a crime for me to own my part of those obligations (though in a slen-der offering) for which all the thoughtful and awakened World is your* debtour ; *no more then 'twas a fault to pay the* tribute penny *to* Cæsar, *or is a piece of* guilt *to be* dutiful. *And though perhaps I have not so well consul-ted the repute of my* intellectuals, *in bringing their weaknesses and* imperfections *into such*

(c 2)   discerning

diſcerning preſences; *yet I am well content,
if thereby I have given any proof of an* honeſt
will, *and well-meaning* Morals; *And I think,
I can without repugnance Sacrifice the former, to an occaſion of gaining my ſelf this* lat-
ler *and* better *Teſtimony; of which diſpoſition,
I ſay, I am now giving an inſtance in preſenting
ſo* Illuſtrious *an* Aſſembly *with a* Diſcourſe,
that hath nothing to recommend it, but the devotion *wherewith tis offer'd them. And really when I compare this* little *and* mean performance, *with the* vaſtneſs *of my* ſubject; *I
am* diſcourag'd *by the* diſproportion: *And
me thinks I have brought but a* Cockle-ſhell
of water from the Ocean: *Whatever I look
upon within the* amplitude *of* heaven *and*
earth, *is evidence of* humane ignorance; *For
all things are a* great darkneſs *to us, and we
are* ſo *unto our ſelves: The* plaineſt *things
are as* obſcure, *as the moſt* confeſſedly myſterious; *and the* Plants *we tread on, are as much*
above *us, as the* Stars *and* Heavens. *The
things*

things that touch *us are as* diſtant *from us, as*
the Pole; *and we are as much* ſtrangers *to*
our ſelves, *as to the inhabitants* of America.
On review of *which, me thinks* I *could begin*
a new to deſcribe the poverty *of our* intellectual acquiſitions, *and the* vanity *of* bold
opinion; *Which the* Dogmatiſts *themſelves*
demonſtrate in all the controverſies they are
engaged in; each *party being* confident *that*
the others confidence *is* vain; *from which a*
third *may more reaſonably conclude the* ſame
of the confidence *of* both. *And me thinks*
there ſhould need no more to reduce diſputing
men to modeſt *acknowledgments, and more be-*
coming temper, then the conſideration; *That*
there is not any thing about which the reaſon
of Man *is capable of being imployed, but hath*
been the ſubject *of* Diſpute, *and* diverſity *of*
apprehenſion. *So that, as the excellent* Lord
Mountaigne *hath obſerved,* [Mankind is
agreed in nothing; no, not in this, that the
heavens are over us;] every man *almoſt*
diffe-

differing *from* another; *Yea*, *and* every man *from* himſelf: *And yet* every man *is* aſſur'd *of his own* Scheams *of* conjecture, *though he cannot hold this* aſſurance, *but by this* proud abſurdity, *That he alone is in the right*, *and all the reſt of the World miſtaken*. *I ſay then*, *there being ſo much to be produced both from the* natural *and* moral *World to the* ſhame *of* boaſting Ignorance; *the enſuing Treatiſe*, *which with a* timerous *and* un-aſſur'd countenance *adventures into your* preſence, *can pride it ſelf in no higher title*, *then that of an E S S A Y*, *or imperfect offer at a Subject*, *to which it could not do right but by diſcourſing all things*. On *which con-ſideration*, I *had once reſolv'd to ſuffer this Trifle to paſs both out of* Print *and* Memo-ry; *But another thought ſuggeſting*, *that the* inſtances *I had given of* humane Igno-rance *were not only* clear *ones*, *but* ſuch *as are not ſo ordinarily* ſuſpected; *from which to our* ſhortneſs *in moſt things elſe*, 'tis *an* eaſie

eafie inference, *and* a potiori, I *was perfwaded, and fomewhat by* experience, *that it*
might *not be altogether* unufeful *in the capacities 'twas intended for* : *And on thefe Accounts I fuffer'd this* Publication; *to which*
(without *vanity I fpeak it*) *I found fo faint an
inclination, that I could have been well content to fuffer it to have flipt into the flate of*
eternal filence *and* oblivion. *For* I *muft
confefs that* way of writing *to be lefs agreeable to my* prefent relifh *and* Genius; *which
is more gratified with* manly fenfe, *flowing
in a* natural *and* unaffected Eloquence, *then
in the* mufick *and curiofity of* fine Metaphors
and dancing periods. *To which meafure of
my prefent humour, I had indeavour'd to reduce the flyle of thefe* Papers; *but that* I
*was loth to give my felf that trouble in an
Affair, to which I was grown too* cold *to be
much concern'd in. And this* inactivity *of temper perfwaded me, I might reafonably expect a
pardon from the* ingenious, *for* faults *commit-
ted*

ted in an immaturity of Age *and* Judgment *that would excuſe them*; *and perhaps* I *may have ſtill need to plead it to attone for the imperfections of this* Adreſs: *By which, though* I *have expoſed* deformities *to the* cleareſt Sunſhine, *that ſome others* prudence *would have directed into the* ſhades *and* more private receſſes; *Yet* I *am ſecure to loſe nothing by the adventure that is comparably valued by me as is the* Honour *of declaring my ſelf,*

Illuſtrious Gentlemen,

The moſt humble Admirer

of *Your* Auguſt Society,

Joſ. Glanvill.

Imprimatur,

Tho. Grigg. R. P. D. Humfr.
Ep. Lond. à Sac. Dom.

Octob. 18.
1664.

(d)   ADVER.

ADVERTISEMENT.

IN the Author's absence, these Mistakes crept into the Press; the Grosser of which are mark't with an Asterisk, that they may not escape the Readers notice.

ERRATA.

In the Discourse.

For	Read	Page	Line.
* Ignorance	Innocence.	1	2
* the in first	first in the	5	13
the	this	16	3
purpose, the motion	purpose, by the motion	26	10
own	one	48	3
and	are	52	6
shott	short	82	penul.
tempers, then	tempers, they	147	4
have	hath	155	17
* Refute,	refuse	174	25
* And	All	175	1
He	she	176	1
at at	at an	177	14
bren cradled	been cradled.	178	26

In the APPENDIX.

In the Apology.

deserved	deserted	2	6

In the Letter to Albius.

confest	confess	2	15
* causes want	causes of want	4	17

In the Answer.

* Inquiry	Empire	8	13
Yet	Yea	12	13
* Tassus	Fastus	12	30
Ad	And	17	21
To	For	22	29
Mechanicks	Mechanick	26	20
* Manifest	Immanifest	30	17
unapproved	unprov'd	30	19
difficulty	a difficulty	34	11
difficult	as difficult	34	13
Prain	Brain	34	14
* myriate	minute	38	18
Arbitrariness	Arbitrariness.	57	20

Scepsis Scientifica:

OR,

The Vanity of *DOGMATIZING*.

CHAP. I.

A general Description of the state of Primitive ~~Ignorance~~ *innocence ; by way of* Introduction.

Hat ever is the *Ignorance* and *Infelicity* of the present *state*, we cannot, without affronting the *Divine Goodness*, deny, but that at first we were made *wise* and *happy* ; For nothing of *specifick imperfection* or deformity could come from the hands that were directed by an *Almighty Wisdome* ; so that, whatever disorders have since befallen them, all things were at first disposed by an

B

Omniscient

Omniscient Intellect that cannot contrive *ineptly*; and our selves exactly formed according to the *Idea's* of that *Mind*, which frames things confonantly to the Rules of their respective Natures. But a particular knowledge of the bleft advantages, and happy circumstances of our primitive condition, is loft with *Innocence*; and there are fcarce any hints of conjecture from the *prefent*. How ever, this perhaps we may fafely venture on by way of *general* Defcription;

That the *Æternal Wifdome* from which we derive our beings, inrich't us with all thofe enoblements that were fuitable to the meafures of an unftraightned *Goodnefs*, and the *capacity* of fuch a *kind* of Creature. And as the *primogenial* Light which at firft was diffufed over the face of the unfafhion'd *Chaos*, was afterwards contracted into the Fountain *Luminaryes*; fo thofe fcattered perfections which were divided among the feveral ranks of inferiour Natures, were fumm'd up, and conftellated in *ours*. Thus the then happy temper of our condition and affairs anticipated the Afpires to be *Like Gods*; and poffibly was fcarce to be added to as much as in defire. But the unlikenefs of It to our now *miferable*, becaufe *Apoftate*, State, makes it almoft as impoffible to be *conceiv'd*, as to be *regained*. 'Twas a condition envied by Creatures that nature had placed a Sphear above us; and fuch as differ'd not much from *Glory* and bleffed *Immortality* but in *perpetuity* and *duration*.

For

For since the moſt deſpicable and diſregarded pieces of decayed nature are ſo curiouſly wrought, and adorned with ſuch eminent ſignatures of Divine *Wiſdome* as ſpeak *It* their Authour, and that after a Curſe brought upon a diſorder'd Univerſe: with how rich an *Embroydery* then think we were the nobler compoſures dignified in the days of ſpotleſs Innocence? And of how ſublime a quality were the *perfeƈtions* of the Creature that was to wear the *Image* of the Prime *perfeƈtion?* Doubtleſs, they were as much above the *Hyperbolies* that Fond Poetry beſtowes upon it's admired objeƈts, as their flatter'd imperfeƈt beauties are really below them. And the moſt refined Glories of *Subcœleſtial* excellencies are but more faint reſemblances of *theſe.* For all the powers and faculties of this *Copy* of the *Divinity,* this *Meddal* of *God,* were as perfeƈt, as *beauty* and *harmony* in *Idœa.* The *ſoul* being not cloy'd by an unaƈtive maſs, as *now;* nor hindered in it's aƈtings, by the *diſtemperature* of indiſpoſed Organs. *Paſſions* kept their place, and tranſgreſt not the boundaries of their proper Natures; Nor were the diſorders began which are occaſion'd by the licence of unruly *Appetites.* Now though perhaps ſome will not allow ſuch vaſt advantages to the *terreſtrial Adam,* which they think not conſiſtent with the *Hiſtory,* and circumſtances of his *Defeƈtion:* Yet thoſe that ſuppoſe the *Allegory* and *Præ=exiſtence,* will eaſily admit all this, and more of the *Æthereal* Condition. But I'le not determine any thing in matters of ſo high and difficult a Nature; which ever is the truth, this general Accompt I have given is not concerned; I asserting only what both will acknowledge, That the first condition of our natures was a state of blessedness and perfection.

CHAP. II.

Our Decay and Ruines by the Fall; *particularly those of our Intellectual Powers.*

BUt, 'tis a *miserable* thing to have been *happy*. And a self contracted wretchedness, is a double one. Had *Felicity* alwayes been a stranger to our natures, our *now misery* had been *none*; And had not our selves been the Authours of our Ruines, *less*. We might have been *made unhappy*, but since we are *miserable* we *chose* it. He that gave them, might have taken from us our other enjoyments, but nothing could have rob'd us of *innocence* but our *selves*. That we are below the Angels of God is no *misery*, 'tis the *lot* of our *Natures*: But that we have made our selves like the *beasts that perish*, is severely *so*, because the Fruit of a voluntary defection. While Man was *innocent* he was likely *ignorant* of nothing, that imported him to know. But when he had *transgrest*, the Fault that opened his eyes upon his *shame*, shut them up from most things else, but his newly purchased *misery.*

sery. He saw the *Nakedness* of his *soul* with that of his *body*, and the blindness and disarray of his Faculties, which his former innocence was a stranger to. And what disclosed this *Poverty* and these *Disorders*, caused them, whether the *understanding* and *affections* were the most criminal Authours of that unhappy defailance, need not be disputed. And how evils should commence in so blessed a Constitution of affairs, and advantageous temper of them both, will perhaps difficultly be determined: Merciful Heaven having made it easier to know the *cure*, then the *rise* of our distempers. This is certain, that our *Masculine powers* are deeply sharers of the *consequential* mischiefs; and though *Eve* were the first *in the disobedience*, yet was *Adam* a joynt partaker of the *Curse*: So that we are not now like the Creatures we were made, but have lost both our Makers *image*, and our own. And possibly the Beasts are not more inferiour to us, then we are to our antient selves: A proud affecting to be like *Gods*, having made us unlike *Men*. For (to pass the other instances of our degradation, which indeed were a plentiful Subject, but not so press to my design) our *intellectual* and Highest *Faculties* are deplorable evidence of our Ruins. And upon these I shall fix my Observations.

For whereas our ennobled understandings could once take the wings of the morning, to visit the World above us, and had a glorious display of the highest form of created excellencies, they now lye groveling in this lower

region,

region, muffled up in miſts, and darkneſs : the curſe of
the Serpent is fallen upon *degenerat·d* Man , *To go on
his belly and lick the duſt.* And as in the *Carteſian hypotheſis,*
the Planets ſometimes loſe their light, by the fixing of
the impurer *ſcum* ; ſo our impaired intellectuals, which
were once as pure *light and flame* in regard of their vigour
and activity , are now darkned by thoſe groſſer *ſpots,*
which diſobedience hath contracted.   And our now
overſhadow'd ſouls (to whoſe beauties Stars were foils)
may be exactly emblem'd, by thoſe *cruſted globes,* whoſe
influential emiſſions are intercepted, by the interpoſal of
the benighting element, while the purer eſſence is im-
priſon'd by the groſs and impervious Matter. For theſe
once glorious lights, which did freely ſhed abroad their
harmleſs beams, and wanton'd in a larger circumference,
are now pent up in a few *firſt principles* (the *naked eſſentials* of our *faculties*) within the ſtraight confines of a
Priſon. And whereas knowledge dwelt in our undepra-
ved natures, as light in the *Sun,* in as great plenty, as purity ; it is now hidden in us like ſparks in a flint, both in
ſcarcity and obſcurity.

For, conſidering the *ſhortneſs* of our *intellectual ſight,*
the *deceptibility* and impoſitions of our *ſenſes,* the tumultuary *diſorders* of our *paſſions,* the *prejudices* of our *infant
educations,* and infinite ſuch like (of which an after occaſion will befriend us, with a more full and particular
recital) I ſay, by reaſon of theſe, we may conclude of the
ſcience of the moſt of men, truly ſo called, that it may
be

be trufs'd up in the fame room with the *Iliads*, yea it may be all the certainty of thofe high pretenders to it, the voluminous Schoolmen, and Peripatetical Dictators, (bating what they have of the firft Principles and the Word of God) may be circumfcrib'd by as fmall a circle, as the Creed, when *Brachygraphy* had confin'd it within the compafs of a penny. And methinks the difputes of thofe affuming *confidents*, that think fo highly of their Attainments, are like the controverfie of thofe in *Plato*'s den, who having never feen but the fhadow of an horfe trajected againft a wall, eagerly contended, whether its *neighing* proceeded from the appearing Mane, or Tail, ruffled with the winds. And the *Dogmatift's* are no lefs at odds in the darker cells of their *imaginary* Principles, about the *fhaddows* and *exuviæ* of beings; when for the moft part they are ftrangers to the fubftantial *Realities.* And like children are very buifie about the Babyes of their *Phancies,* while their ufelefs fubtilties afford little entertainment to the nobler Faculties.

But many of the moft accomplifh't wits of all ages, whofe modefty would not allow them to boaft of more then they were owners of, have refolv'd their knowledge into *Socrates* his fumme total, and after all their pains in queft of *Science,* have fat down in a profeffed *nefcience.* It is the fhallow unimprov'd intellects that are confident pretenders to certainty; as if contrary to the *Adage,* Science had no friend but Ignorance. And though their general acknowledgments of the weaknefs

of

of *humane understanding*, and the *narrowness* of what
we know, look like *cold* and *sceptical* discouragements;
yet the particular expressions of their *sentiments* and *opi-*
nions, are as *Oracular*, as if they were *Omniscient*. To
such, as a curb to confidence, and as an evidence of
humane infirmities even in the noblest parts of Man,
I shall give the following instances of our intellectual
blindness: not that I intend to poze them with those
common *Ænigma's* of *Magnetism*, *Fluxes*, *Refluxes*,
and the like; these are resolv'd into a *confest* ignorance, and I shall not persue them to their old *Asylum*:
and yet it may be there is more knowable in these,
then in less acknowledg'd mysteries: But I'le not
move beyond our selves, and the most ordinary and
trivial *Phænomena* in nature, in which we shall finde
enough to shame *Confidence*, and unplume *Dogmati-*
zing.

CHAP. III.

A general Account of our Ignorance of our own Natures.

TO begin then with the *Theory* of our own *Natures* ; we ſhall find in them too great evidence of *intellectual* deficience, and deplorable confeſſions of *humane ignorance*. For we came into the world, and we *know* not *how* ; we live in't in a *ſelf-neſcience*, and go hence again and are as ignorant of our *receſs*. We *grow*, we *live*, we *move* at firſt in a *Microcoſm*, and can give no more *Scientifical* account, of the ſtate of our three *quarters* confinement, then if we had never been extant in the greater world, but had expir'd in an *abortion*; we are enlarg'd from the priſon of the womb, our *ſences* are affected, we *imagine* and *remember* ; and yet know no more of the *immediate* reaſons of theſe common functions, then thoſe little *Embryo Anchorites* : We *breath*, we *talk*, we *move*, while we are ignorant of the manner of theſe vital performances. The *Dogmatiſt* knows not how he ſtirrs his finger; nor by what art or method he directs his tongue in articulating *ſounds* into *voyces*. *New* parts are added to our ſubſtance, to ſupply our continual *decayings*, and as we *dye* we are *born* dayly; nor can we give a cer-

C   tain

tain account, how the *aliment* is fo prepared for *nutri-tion*, or by what *mechanifm* it is fo regularly diftributed; we are tranfported by *Paſſions*; and our *mindes* ruffled by the diforders of the *body* : Nor yet can we tell how thefe fhould reach our *immaterial felves*, or how the *Soul* fhould be affected by fueh kind of *agitations*. We lay us down, to *fleep* away our cares; night fhuts up the Senfes windows, the mind contracts into the Brains *centre* ; We *live* in *death*, and *lye* as in the *grave*. Now we know no-thing, nor can our waking thoughts inform us, who is *Morpheus*, and what that leaden *Key* that locks us up within our fenfelefs Cels : There's a difficulty that pin-cheth, nor will it eafily be refolved. The Soul is awake, and folicited by external motions, for fome of them reach the perceptive region in the moft filent repofe, and obfcu-rity of night. What is't then that prevents our *Senfations*; or if we do perceive, how is't that we *know it not* ? But we *Dream*, fee *Vifions*, converfe with *Chimæra's* ; the one half of our lives is a *Romance*, a fiction. We retain a catch of thofe pretty ftories, and our awakened imagination fmiles in the recollection. Nor yet can our moft fevere inquiries finde what did fo abufe us, or fhew the nature and manner of thefe nocturnal *illufions* : When we puzzle our felves in the difquifition, we do but *dream*, and every *Hypothefis* is a *phancy*. Our moft induftrious conceits are but like their object, and as uncertain as thofe of mid-night. Thus when fome dayes and nights have gone over us, the ftroak of Fate concludes the number of

our

our pulſes; we take our leave of the *Sun* and *Moon*, and lay our Heads in *Aſhes*. The vital flame goes out, the *Soul* retires into another world, and the *body* to dwell in *darkneſs*. Nor doth the laſt Scene yield us any more ſatisfaction in our *autography*; for we are as ignorant how the Soul leaves the light, as how it firſt came into it; we know as little how the *union* is *diſſolved*, that is the chain of the ſo differing *ſubſiſtencies* that compound us, as how it firſt *commenced*. This then is the proud creature that ſo highly pretends to *knowledge*, and that makes ſuch a noiſe and buſtle for *Opinions*. The inſtruction of *Delphos* may ſhame ſuch *confidents* into *modeſty*; and till we have learn't that honeſt *adviſo*, though from *hell*, ΓΝΩΘΙ ΣΕΑΥΤΟΝ, *Confidence* is arrogance, and *Dogmatizing* unreaſonable preſuming. I doubt not but the opinionative reſolver, thinks all theſe eaſie *Problems*, and the Theories here accounted *Myſteries*, are to him *Revelations*. But let him ſuſpend that concluſion till he hath weigh'd the conſiderations hereof, which the proceſs of our Diſcourſe will preſent him with; and if he can unty thoſe knots, he is able to teach all humanity, and will do well to oblige mankinde by his informations.

Chap. IV.

Some great Instances of our Ignorance dis-
cours't of, (1) of things within our selves.
The Nature of the Soul and it's Origine,
glanc't at and past by: (1) It's union with
the body is unconceivable: So (2) is its
moving the body, consider'd either in the
way of Sir K. Digby, Des-Cartes, *or*
Dr. H. More, *and the* Platonists. (3) *The*
manner of direction of the Spirits, as un-
explicable.

BUt that I may more closely pursue the design I am
engag'd on, I shall discourse some great *Instances* of
our *Ignorance* in a way of more press and strict
survey. And those I shall insist on are such as (1) concern the *S O U L*, both in its *common* Nature, and *parti-*
cular Faculties. Or (2) such as are drawn from the consideration of *our own*, other *organical B O D I E S*, and
M A T T E R in the general. And (3) some *trite* and
common A P P E A R A N C E S. Of which I discourse in
order.

If

If certainty were anywhere to be expected, one would think it fhould be in the Notices of our *Souls,* which are indeed our *felves,* and whofe *fentiments* we are intimately acquainted with. In things without us , ignorance is no wonder; fince we cannot profound into the *hidden things* of Nature, nor fee the firft fprings and wheeles that fet the reft a going. We view but fmall pieces of the *Univerfal* Frame, and want *Phænomena* to make intire and fecure *Hypothefes.* But if *that* whereby we *know* other things, know not it felf; if our Souls are ftrangers to things within them, which they have far greater advantages of being acquainted with, than matters of external nature; I think then this firft inftance will be a Fair one, for the extorting a Confeffion of that *Ignorance* I would have acknowledg'd.

(1) I take notice then that the learned world hath been at an infinite uncertainty about the fpeculation of the *Souls Nature.* In which every man almoft held a diftinct opinion. *Plato* call'd it, only in the general, *A felf-moving fubftance. Ariftotle* an *Entilechie,* or, An Hee knew not what. *Hefiod* and *Anaximander* compounded It of *Earth* and *Water. Heraclides* made It *Light. Zeno* the *Quinteffence* of the *four Elements. Xenocrates* and the *Ægyptians* a *Moving Number.* The *Chaldæans* a *Vertue* without *Form. Parmenides* compofed It of *Earth* and *Fire. Empedocles* of *Blood. Galen* held It an *hot Complexion. Hippocrates* a *Spirit* diffufed through the *body. Varro* fuppofed It an heated and difperfed *Aire. Thales* a Nature

C 3 without

without reft. And *Crates* and *Decæarchus, Nothing.* **Thus**
have the greateft Sages differ'd in the firft Theory of humane Nature; which yet perhaps is not fo defperate an
Inquiry, as fome others that are apprehended lefs difficult. And poffibly moft have been deceived in this *Speculation*, by feeking to grafp the *Soul* in their *Imaginations*; to which grofs faculty, that purer effence is unpalpable: and we might as well expect to *tafte* the *Sun-
beams.* Such therefore are to be minded, that the *Soul* is
feen, like other things, in the *mirrour* of it's *effects* and
attributes: But if like Children, they'l run behind the
glafs to catch it, their expectations will meet with nothing but *vacuity* and *emptinefs.* And though a pure *intellectual* eye may have a fight of it in *reflex* difcoveries;
yet if we affect a groffer touch, like *Ixion* we fhall embrace
a Cloud.

(2) It hath been no lefs a trouble to determine the
Soul's *Original*, than *Nature.* Some thought It was from
the beginning of the World, and one of the firft things
created. Others, that 'tis an extract from the univerfal
foul of all things. Some believe It came from the *Moon*,
others from the *Stars*, or vaft fpaces of the *Æther* above
the *Planets*; fome that 'tis made by *God*, fome by *Angels*,
and fome by the *Generant.* Whether it be immediately
created, or *traduced*, hath been the great ball of contention to the Later Ages. And yet, after all the bandying
attempts of refolution; 'Tis as much a Queftion as **ever**;
and it may be will be fo till it be concluded by *Immortality.*

tality. The Patrons of Traduction accufe their Adverfaries of affronting the *Attributes* of *God;* and the Affer-
tours of *Creation* impeach *Them* of violence to the *Nature* of *Things.* Either of the opinions ftrongly oppofeth
the other ; but very feebly defends *it felf.* Which occafions fome to think, that both are *right,* and both *miftaken* : *Right* in what they fay againft each other ; but
Miftaken in what they plead for their refpective felves.
But I fhall not ftirr in the waters which have been already mudded by fo many contentious Inquiries. The
great St. *Auftin,* and others of the grey heads of Reverend
Antiquity, have been content to fit down here in a pro-
feft Neutrality: And I'le not induftrioufly endeavour
to urge men to a confeffion of what they freely acknowledge ; but fhall note difficulties which are not fo ufually
obferv'd, though as unaccountable as *thefe.*

§. I. IT is the faying of divine *Plato*, that Man is
natures *Horifon;* dividing betwixt the upper
Hemifphere of *immaterial intellects,* and this lower of *Corporeity* : And that we are a Compound of beings diftant
in extreams, is as clear as Noon. But how the purer
Spirit is united to this *clod,* is a knot too hard for our
degraded intellects to unty. What *cement* fhould unite
heaven and *earth,* light and darknefs, natures of fo divers
a make, of fuch difagreeing attributes, which have almoft nothing, but *Being,* in common : This is a riddle,
which muft be left to the coming of *Elias.* How fhould

a

a thought be united to a marble-ſtatue, or a ſun-beam to a
lump of clay ? The freezing of the words in the air in the
Northern climes, is as conceivable, as the ſtrange union.
That this *active ſpark,* this *συμφυῖον πνεῦμα* (as the Stoicks
call it) ſhould be confined to a Priſon it can ſo eaſily
pervade, is of leſs facil apprehenſion, then that the light
ſhould be pent up in a box of Cryſtal, and kept from accompanying its ſource to the lower world: And to
hang weights on the wings of the winde ſeems far more
intelligible.

In the *unions,* which we underſtand, the extreams are
reconciled by interceding participations of natures,
which have ſomewhat of either. But *Body* and *Spirit*
ſtand at ſuch a diſtance in their eſſential compoſitions,
that to ſuppoſe an uniter of a middle conſtitution, that
ſhould partake of ſome of the qualities of both, is unwarranted by any of our faculties, yea moſt abſonous to
our reaſons; ſince there is not any the leaſt affinity betwixt *length*, *breadth* and *thickneſs*; and *apprehenſion*,
judgement and *diſcourſe*: The former of which are the
moſt immediate reſults (if not eſſentials) of *Matter*, the
latter of *Spirit*.

§. 2. SEcondly, We can as little give an account, how
the *Soul moves* the *Body.* That, that ſhould
give motion to an unwieldy *bulk*, which it ſelf hath
neither *bulk* nor *motion*; is of as difficil an apprehenſion,
as any myſtery in nature. For though conceiving it under
some

some phancied appearance, and pinning on it material affections, the doubt doth not so sensibly touch us ; since under such conceptions we have the advantage of our senses to befriend us with parallels ; and gross apprehenders may not think it any more strange, then that a Bullet should be moved by the rarified fire , or the clouds carryed before the invisible winds : yet if we defæcate the notion from *materiality*, and abstract *quantity*, *place*, and all kind of *corporeity* from it, and represent it to our thoughts either under the notion of the ingenious Sir *K. Digby* ; as, A pure *Mind* and *Knowledge* ; or, as the admir'd *Des-Cartes* expresses it, *Une chose qui pense*, as, *A thinking substance* ; it will be as hard to apprehend, as that an empty wish should remove Mountains : a supposition which if realized, would relieve *Sisyphus*. Nor yet doth the ingenious hypothesis of the most excellent *Cantabrigian* Philosopher, of the *Soul's* being an *extended penetrable* substance, relieve us ; since, how that which penetrates all bodies without the least jog or obstruction, should impress a motion on any, is by his own confession alike inconceivable. Neither will its moving the Body by a *vehicle* of Spirits, avail us ; since they are Bodies too, though of a purer mould.

And to credit the unintelligibility both of this *union* and *motion* , we need no more then to consider that when we would conceive any thing which is not obvious to our senses, we have recourse to our memories the storehouse of past observations : and turning over the treasure

D   that

that is there, feek for fomething of like kind, which hath
formerly come within the notice of our outward or inward fenfes. So that we cannot conceive any thing,
that comes not within the verge of fome of thefe ; but
either by like *experiments* which we have made, or at leaft
by fome remoter hints which we receive from them.
And where fuch are wanting, I cannot apprehend how
the thing can be conceived. If any think otherwife, let
them carefully perufe their perceptions : and, if they
finde a determinate intellection of the Modes of Being,
which were never in the leaft hinted to them by their *external* or *internal* fenfes ; I'le believe that fuch can realize
Chimæra's. But now in the cafes before us there are not
the leaft footfteps, either of fuch an *Union*, or *Motion*, in
the whole circumference of fenfible nature : And we cannot apprehend any thing beyond the evidence of our
faculties.

§. 3. THirdly, How the *Soul directs* the *Spirits* for
the motion of the Body according to the
feveral animal exigents ; is as perplex in the Theory, as
either of the former. For the *meatus*, or paffages, through
which thofe fubtill emiffaries are conveyed to the refpective members, being fo almoft infinite, and each of
them drawn through fo many Meanders, crofs turnings,
and divers roads, wherein other fpirits are continually a
journeying ; it is wonderful, that they fhould exactly
perform their regular deftinations without lofing their
way

way in fuch a wildernefs : neither can the wit of man tell how they are directed. For that they are carryed by the manuduction of a Rule, is evident from the conftant fteadynefs and regularity of their motion into the parts, where their fupplies are expected : But, what that regulating efficiency fhould be, and how managed ; is not eafily determin'd. That it is performed by meer *Mecha-nifme*, conftant experience confutes ; which affureth us, that our *fpontaneous* motions are under the *Imperium* of our *will*. At leaft the firft determination of the Spirits into fuch or fuch paffages, is from the *Soul*, what ever we hold of the after conveyances ; of which likewife I think, that all the Philofophy in the world cannot make it out to be purely *Mechanical*. But yet though we gain this, that the Soul is the principle of direction, the difficulty is as formidable as ever. For unlefs we allow it a kinde of inward fight of the *Anatomical* frame of its own body of every *vein*, *mufcle*, and *artery* ; of the exact fite, and pofition of them, with their feveral windings, and fecret chanels : it is as unconceivable how it fhould be the *Directrix* of fuch intricate motions, as that a blind man fhould manage a game at Chefs, or Marfhal an Army. But this is a kinde of *knowledge*, that we are not in the leaft aware of : yea many times we are fo far from an attention to the inward *direction* of the *Spirits*, that our employ'd mindes obferve not any method in the outward performance ; even when 'tis manag'd by variety of interchangeable motions , in which a fteady

D 2   direction

direction is difficult, and a miſcariage eaſie. Thus an Artiſt will play a Leſſon on an Inſtrument without minding a ſtroke; and our tongues will run diviſions in a tune not miſſing a note, even when our thoughts are totally engaged elſewhere: which effects are to be attributed to ſome ſecret *Art* of the Soul, which to us is utterly occult, and without the ken of our Intellects.

Chap. V.

(4) *We can give no account of the manner of* Senſation.

§. 4.   BUt beſides the *difficulties* that lye more deep, and are of a more myſterious alloy; we are at a loſs for a *ſcientifical* account even of our *Senſes*, the moſt knowable of our faculties. Our *eyes*, that ſee other things, ſee not themſelves: And the foundations of knowledge are themſelves unknown. That the *Soul* is the ſole Percipient, which alone hath *animadverſion* and *ſenſe* properly ſo called, and that the *Body* is only the receiver and conveyer of corporeal impreſſions, is as certain, as Philoſophy can make it. *Ariſtotle* himſelf teacheth ſo much in that Maxime of his Νοῦς ὁρᾷ, κ̀ νοῦς ἀκούει. And *Plato* credits this poſition with his ſuffrage; affirming, that 'tis the *Soul* that hath *life* and *ſenſe*, but the
body

body neither. But this is fo largely profecuted by the the Great *Des-Cartes,* and is a Truth that fhines fo clear in the Eyes of all confidering men; that to go about induftrioufly to prove it, were to light a candle to feek the the Sun : we'll therefore fuppofe it, as that which needs not arreft our motion ; but yet, what are the inftruments of fenfible perceptions and particular conveyers of outward motions to the *feat* of *fenfe,* is difficult : and how the pure mind can receive information from that, which is not in the leaft like it felf, and but little refembling what it reprefents; I think inexplicable. Whether *Senfation* be made by *corporal emiſsions* and *material* ΕΙΔΩΛΑ, or by notions impreft on the *Æthereal* matter, and carryed by the continuity thereof to the Common fenfe; I'le not revive into a Difpute : The ingenuity of the latter hath already given it almoft an abfolute victory over its Rival. But fuppofe which we will, there are doubts not to be folv'd by either. For how the foul by mutation made in *matter* a fubftance of another kind, fhould be excited to action ; and how bodily alterations and motions fhould concern *that* which is fubject to neither ; is a difficulty, which confidence may fooner triumph on, then conquer. For *body* cannot act on any thing but by *motion*; motion cannot be received but by *quantity* and *matter*; the *Soul* is a ftranger to fuch grofs *fubftantiality* , and ownes nothing of thefe, but that it is cloathed with by our deceived phancies; and therefore how can we conceive it fubject to *material impreſsions* ? and yet the

impor-

importunity of pain, and unavoydableneſs of *ſenſations* ſtrongly perſwade, that we are *ſo*.

Beſides, how is it, and by what *Art* doth it read that ſuch an *image* or ſtroke in *matter* (whether that of her vehicle, or of the Brain, the caſe is the ſame) ſignifies ſuch an *object*? Did we learn an Alphabet in our *Embryo-*ſtate? And how comes it to paſs, that we are not aware of any ſuch congenite apprehenſi= ons? *We know what we know*; but do we *know* any more? That by diverſity of *motions* we ſhould ſpell out *figures, diſtances, magnitudes, colours*, things not reſembled by them; we muſt attribute to ſome *ſecret deduction*. But what this *deduction* ſhould be, or by what *mediums* this Knowledge is advanc'd; is as dark, as Ignorance. One, that hath not the knowledge of Letters, may ſee the *Figures*; but comprehends not the meaning included in them: An infant may hear the ſounds, and ſee the motion of the lips; but hath no conception conveyed by them, no knowing what they are intended to ſignifie. So our *Souls*, though they might have perceived the *motions* and *images* themſelves by *ſimple ſenſe*; yet without ſome *implicit inference* it ſeems inconceivable, how by that means they ſhould apprehend their *Ar= chetypes.*

Moreover, *Images* and *Motions* are in the Brain in a very inconſiderable latitude of ſpace; and yet they repreſent the greateſt *magnitudes*. The image of an
Hemiſphere

Hemifphere of the upper Globe cannot be of a wider circumference, then a Wall-nut: And how can such petty impreffions notifie fuch vaftly expanded objects, but through fome kind of *Scientifical* method, and *Geometry* in the Principle? without this it is not conceivable how *diftances* fhould be perceiv'd, but all objects would appear in a clufter, and lye in as narrow a room as their images take up in our fcanter *Craniums.* Nor will the Philofophy of the moft ingenious *Des-Cartes* help us out: For, *The ftriking of divers filaments of the brain,* cannot well be fuppofed to reprefent *Diftances*, except fome fuch kind of *Inference* be allotted us in our faculties: the conceffion of which will only fteed us as a Refuge for *Ignorance*; where we fhall meet, what we would feem to fhun.

CHAP.

Chap. VI.

The nature of the Memory *unaccountable.*
'Tis conſider'd particularly according to
the Ariſtotelian, Carteſian, Digbæan *and*
Hobbian *Hypotheſis.*

§. 5. THe *Memory* alſo is a faculty whoſe nature
is as obſcure, and hath as much of Riddle
in it as any of the former : It ſeems to
be an *Organical* Power , becauſe bodily diſtempers
often marr its *Idea's,* and cauſe a total oblivion : But
what inſtruments the Soul uſeth in her review of paſt
impreſſions, is a queſtion which may drive Enquiry
to deſpair. There are four principal *Hypotheſes* by which
a Reſolution hath been attempted.

The *Peripatetick,* the *Carteſian,* the *Digbæan,* and the
Hobbian. We'l examine theſe Accounts of the *Magnale.*
And I begin with that which will needs have it
ſelf believ'd the moſt venerable for *Antiquity* and
Worth.

(1) Then according to *Ariſtotle* and his *Peripatum,*
Objects are conſerved in the *Memory* by certain *intenti=*
onal Species, Beings, which have nothing of Matter in
their

their Effential Conftitution, but yet have a neceffary fubjective dependence on it, whence they are called *Material*. To this briefly.

Befides that thefe Species are made a *Medium* between *Body* and *Spirit*, and therefore partake of no more of Being, then what the charity of our Imaginations affords them; and that the fuppofition infers a creative *energie* in the object their producent, which Philofophy allows not to Creature-Efficients : I fay, befide thefe, it is quite a-gainft their nature to fubfift, but in the prefence and under the actual influence of their caufe; as being produc'd by an *Emanative Caufality*, the Effects whereof dye in the removal of their Origine. But this fuperannuated conceit deferves no more of our remembrance, then it contributes to the apprehenfion of it. And therefore I pafs on to the *Cartefian* which fpeaks thus :

The *Glandula Pinealis*, in this Philofophy made the feat of Common Senfe, doth by its motion impel the Spirits into divers parts of the Brain; till it find thofe wherein are fome tracks of the object we would remember; which confifts in this, *viz*. That the Pores of the Brain, through the which the Spirits before took their courfe, are more eafily opened to the Spirits which demand re-entrance; fo that finding thofe pores, they make their way through them fooner then through others : whence there arifeth a fpecial motion in the *Glandula*, which fignifies this to be the object we would *remember*.

E   But

But I fear there is no ſecurity neither in this *Hypotheſis* ; For if *Memory* be made by the *eaſie motion* of the *Spirits* through the opened *paſſages*, according to what hath been noted from *Des-Chartes* ; whence have we a diſtinct Remembrance of ſuch diverſity of Objects, whoſe Images without doubt paſs through the ſame *apertures*? And how ſhould we recal the diſtances of Bodies which lye in a line ? Or, is it not likely, that the impell'd Spirits might light upon other Pores accommodated to their purpoſe, the *Motion* of other Bodies through them ? Yea, in ſuch a *pervious* ſubſtance as the *Brain*, they might finde an eaſie either entrance, or *exit*, almoſt everywhere ; and therefore to ſhake every grain of corn through the ſame holes of a Sieve in repeated winnowings, is as eaſie to be performed, as this to be perceived. Beſides, it's difficult to apprehend, but that theſe *avennues* ſhould in a ſhort time be ſtopped up by the preſſure of other parts of the matter, through its natural *gravity*, or other alterations made in the *Brain* :   And the opening of other *vicine paſſages* might quickly obliterate any tracks of theſe ; as the making of one hole in the yielding *mud*, defaces the print of another near it ; at leaſt the acceſſion of enlargement, which was derived from ſuch tranſitions, would be as ſoon loſt, as made.

We are ſtill to ſeek then for an *Oedipus* for the Riddle ; wherefore we turn our eyes to the *Digbæan* Account, of which this is the ſumme ; That things are reſerved in the *Memory* by ſome corporeal *exuviæ* and material Images ; which

which having impinged on the Common fenfe, rebound thence into fome vacant cells of the Brain, where they keep their ranks and poftures in the fame order that they entred, till they are again ftirr'd up; and then they flide through the *Fancy*, as when they were firft prefented.

But, how is it imaginable, that thofe active *particles*, which have no *cement* to unite them, nothing to keep them in the order they were fet, yea, which are ever and anon juftled by the occurfion of other bodies, whereof there is an infinite ftore in this Repofitory, fhould fo orderly keep their *Cells* without any alteration of their fite or pofture, which at firft was allotted them? And how is it conceivable, but that carelefly turning over the *Idea's* of our mind to recover fomething we would re-member, we fhould put all the other Images into a difor-derly floating, and fo raife a little *Chaos* of confufion, where Nature requires the exacteft order. According to this account, I cannot fee, but that our *Memories* would be more confufed then our Mid-night compofitions: For is it likely, that the divided *Atomes* which prefented themfelves together, fhould keep the fame ranks in fuch a variety of tumultuary agitations, as happen in that liquid *Medium*? An heap of Ants on an Hillock will more eafily be kept to an uniformity in motion; and the little bodies which are inceffantly playing up and down the Air in their carelefs poftures, are as capable of Regularity as thefe.

The

The laſt **Account** of the *Faculty* we are inquiring of is the *Hobbian*, according to which *Hypotheſis*; *Memory* is nothing elſe but the knowledge of *decaying Senſe*, made by the *reaction* of one *body* againſt another; or, as the Author expreſſes it in his *Humane Nature*, *A miſſing of Parts in an Object*. The foundation of which *Principle* (as of many of its fellows) is totally everſt by the moſt ingenious *Commentator* upon *Immaterial Beings*, Dr. *H. More* in his book *Of Immortality*. I ſhall therefore leave that cauſe in the hands of that moſt learned undertaker, and only obſerve two things to my preſent purpoſe. (1) Neither the *Brain*, nor *Spirits*, nor any other material ſubſtance within the *Head* can for any conſiderable ſpace of time conſerve *motion*. The former is of ſuch a clammy conſiſtence, that it can no more retain it then a *Quagmire*: And the *ſpirits* for their liquidity are more uncapable then the fluid *Medium*, which is the conveyer of *Sounds*, to perſevere in the continued repetition of *vocal Ayres*. And if there were any other ſubſtance within us, as fitly temper'd to preſerve *motion*, as the **Author** of the opinion could deſire: Yet (2) which will equally preſs againſt either of the former, this motion would be quickly deadned by *counter-motions*; and we ſhould not *remember* any thing, but till the next impreſſion. Much leſs can this *Principle* give an account, how ſuch an abundance of *motions* ſhould orderly ſucceed one another, as things

things do in our *memories*: And to remember a *song* or *tune*, it will be required, that our Souls be an *Harmony* more then in a *Metaphor*, continually running over in a filent whisper those *Musical accents* which our retentive faculty is preserver of. Which could we suppose in a fingle Inftance; yet a multitude of *Musical Confonancies* would be as impoffible, as to play a thousand tunes on a *Lute* at once. One motion would cross and deftroy another; all would be clashing and discord: And the *Musicians Soul* would be the most *disharmonious*: For, according to the tenour of this opinion, our *memories* will be stored with infinite variety of divers, yea contrary motions, which must needs interfere, thwart, and obftruct one another: and there would be nothing within us, but *Ataxy* and disorder.

§. 6. **M**Uch more might be added of the difficulties, which occur concerning the *Underftanding, Phancy, Will,* and *Affections.* But the Controversies hereabout, are so hotly manag'd by the divided *Schools*, and so voluminously everywhere handled; that it will be thought better to say nothing of them, then a little. The sole difficulties about the *Will*, its *nature*, and *sequency* to the *Underftanding*, &c have almoft quite baffled inquiry, and shewn us little else, but that our *Underftandings* are as *blind* as *it* is. And the grand queſtion depending hereon, Πόϑεν τὸ κακόν; I think will not be ended, but by the final abolition of its object. They, that would loſe their *Knowledge* here, let them diligently inquire after it. Search will diſcover that *Ignorance*, which is as invincible, as its Cauſe. Theſe *Controverſies*, like ſome *Rivers*, the further they run, the more they are hid. And it may be a poorer account is given to them now, then ſome *Centuries* paſt, when they were a ſubject of debate to the pious *Fathers*.

Chap.

CHAP. VII.

How our Bodies *are* form'd *unexplicable.*
The Plastick *signifies nothing;* the Formation *of* Plants, *and* Animals *unknown,*
in their Principle. Mechanisme *solves*
it not. A new way propounded, which
also fails of satisfaction. (2.) *No ac-*
count is yet given how the parts of Matter *are* united. *Some Consideration on*
Des-Cartes *his Hypothesis, it fails of So-*
lution. (3.) *The Question is unanswerable,*
whether Matter *be compounded of* Divisibles, *or* Indivisibles.

BUt from these I pass to the *Second* General, the
consideration of *Bodies*, our own and others.
For *our* own, though we *see*, and *feel*, and continually converse with them; yet their constitution,
and inward frame is an *America*, a yet undiscovered *Re-*
gion. And the saying of the Kingly Prophet, *I am won-*
derfully made, may well be understood of that *admira-*
tion, which is the *Daughter of Ignorance*. Three things
The

I'le fubjoyn concerning this *Senfible matter*, the other part of our compofition.

§. 1. THat our *Bodie's* are made according to the moft curious *Artifice*, and orderly contrivance, cannot be denyed even by them, who are leaft beholden to *Nature*. The elegance of this compofure, fav'd *Galen* from *Atheifm*. And I cannot think that the branded *Epicurus, Lucretius*, and their fellows were in earneft, when they refolv'd this compofition into a *fortuitous range* of *Atoms*. To fuppofe a *Watch*, or any other the moft curious *Automaton* by the blind hits of *Chance*, to perform diverfity of orderly *motions*, to fhew the *hour*, *day* of the *Month*, *Tides*, *age* of the *Moon*, and the like, with an unparallel'd exactnefs, and all without the regulation of *Art*; this were the more pardonable abfurdity. And that this admirable *Engine* of our Bodies, whofe functions are carryed on by fuch a multitude of *parts*, and *motions*, which neither interfere, nor impede one another in their operations; but by an *harmonious Sympathy* promote the perfection and good of the whole: That this fhould be an undefign'd effect, is an affertion, that is more then *Melancholies Hyperbole*. I fay therefore, that if we do but confider this *Fabrick* with free and unpoffeft mindes; we fhall eafily grant, that it was fome skilful *Archeus* who delineated thofe comely *proportions*, and hath expreft fuch exactly *Geometrical elegancies* in its compofitions. But what
this

this hidden *Architect* should be, and by what *instruments* and art this frame is erected; is as *unknown* to us, as the thoughts of our cradles. The *Plastick* faculty is a fine word, and will do well in the mouth of a puzled *Emperick* : But what it is, how it works, and whose it is, we cannot learn; no, not by a return into the *Womb*; neither will the *Platonick* Principles unriddle the doubt : For though the Soul be supposed to be the Bodies *Maker*, and the builder of its own house; yet by what kind of *Knowledge*, *Method*, or *Means*, is as unknown : and that we should have a *knowledge* which we know not of, is an assertion which hath no commission from our Faculties. The Great *Des-Cartes* will allow it to be no better, then a downright absurdity. But yet should we suppose it, it would be evidence enough of what we aim at.

§. 2. NOr is the composition of our *own Bodies* the only wonder : we are as much nonplust by the most contemptible *Worm*, and *Plant*, we tread on. How is a drop of Dew organiz'd into an Insect? or, a lump of Clay into a more perfect *Animal* ? How are the Glories of the Field spun, and by what Pencil are they limn'd in their unaffected bravery ? By whose direction is the nutriment so regularly distributed unto the respective parts, and how are they kept to their specifick uniformities ? If we attempt *Mechanical* solutions, we shall never give an account, why the *Wood-cock* doth not sometimes borrow colours of the *Mag-pye*; why the *Lilly*

F doth

doth not exchange with the *Daysie*; or why it is not ſometime painted with a bluſh of the *Roſe*? Can *un-guided matter* keep it ſelf to ſuch exact conformities, as not in the leaſt ſpot to vary from the *ſpecies*? That divers Limners at a diſtance without either copy, or deſigne, ſhould draw the ſame *Picture* to an undiſtinguiſhable ex-actneſs, both in *form, colour,* and *features*; is more con-ceivable, then that *matter*, which is ſo diverſified both in *quantity, quality, motion, ſite,* and infinite other circum-ſtances, ſhould frame it ſelf ſo unerringly according to the *Idea* of its kind. And though the fury of that *Apel-les,* who threw his Pencil in rage upon the Picture he had eſſayed to draw, once caſually effected thoſe lively re-preſentations, which his Art could not deſcribe; yet 'tis not likely, that one of a thouſand ſuch *præcipitancies* ſhould be crowned with ſo an unexpected an iſſue. For though *blind matter* might reach ſome *elegancies* in indi-vidual effects; yet *ſpecifick conformities* can be no *unad-viſed* productions, but in greateſt likelyhood, are regula-ted by the immediate efficiency of ſome *knowing* agent: which whether it be *ſeminal Formes*, according to the *Platonical* Principles, or whatever elſe we pleaſe to ſup-poſe; the manner of its working is to us *unknown*: or if theſe effects are meerly *Mechanical*; yet to learn the method of ſuch operations may, and hath indeed been, ingeniouſly attempted; but I think cannot be performed to the ſatisfaction of ſeverer examination.

That all bodies both *Animal, Vegetable,* and *Inanimate,* are

are form'd out of fuch particles of matter, which by reafon of their figures, will not cohære or lye together, but
in fuch an order as is neceffary to fuch a fpecifical formation, and that therein they naturally of themfelves concurre, and refide, is a pretty conceit, and there are *experiments* that credit it. If after a decoction of *hearbs* in
a Winter-night, we expofe the liquor to the frigid air ;
we may obferve in the morning under a cruft of Ice, the
perfect appearance both in *figure*, and *colour*, of the *Plants*
that were taken from it. But if we break the *aqueous
Cryftal*, thofe pretty *images* dif-appear and are prefently
diffolved.

Now thefe *airy Vegetables* are prefumed to have been
made, by the reliques of thefe *plantal emiſsions* whofe
avolation was prevented by the *condenfed inclofure*. And
therefore playing up and down for a while within their
liquid prifon, they at laft fettle together in their natural
order, and the *Atomes* of each part finding out their proper place, at length reft in their methodical Situation ;
till by breaking the *Ice* they are difturbed, and thofe
counterfeit *compofitions* are fcatter'd into their firft *Indivifibles*. This *Hypothefis* may yet feem to receive further
confirmation, from the artificial *refurrection* of *Plants*
from their *afhes*, which *Chymifts* are fo well acquainted
with : And befides, that *Salt* difolved upon fixation, returns to its affected *cubes*, the regular figures of *Minerals*,
as the *Hexagonal* of *Cryftal*, the *Hemi-fphærical* of
the *Fairy-ftone*, the *ftellar figure* of the ftone *Afteria*,

and

and ſuch like, ſeem to look with probability upon this way of formation. And I muſt needs ſay 'tis handſomly conjectur'd. But yet what thoſe figures are, that ſhould be thus mechanically adapted, to fall ſo unerringly into regular compoſitions, is beyond our faculties to conceive or determine. And now thoſe *heterogenous atomes* (for ſuch their figures are ſuppoſed) ſhould by themſelves hit ſo exactly into their proper reſidence in the midſt of ſuch tumultuary motions, croſs thwartings, and *arietations* of other particles, eſpecially when for one way of hitting right, there are thouſands of miſſing; there's no *Hypo-theſis* yet extant can reſolve us. And yet had heaven af-forded that miracle of men, the Illuſtrious *Des-Cartes* a longer day on earth, we might have expected the utmoſt of what ingenuity could perform herein : but his imma-ture Fate hath unhappily diſappointed us; and preven-ted the moſt deſirable Complement of his not to be equall'd *Thiloſophy.*

§. 3. (2) IT's no leſs difficult to give an account, how the *Parts* of *Matter* and *Bodies* are *united* : For though ſuperficial Enquirers may eaſily ſatisfie themſelves by anſwering, that it is done by *muſcles*, *nerves*, and other like *ſtrings*, and *ligaments*, which Na-ture hath deſtin'd to that office; yet, if we ſeek for an account how the parts of theſe do cohere, we ſhall find our ſelves loſt in the enquiry. Nothing with any ſhew of ſucceſs hath yet appeared on the *Philoſophick Stage*, but the

the opinion of *Des-Cartes* ; that the Parts of *Matter* are *united* by Reſt. Neither can I conceive, how any thing can be ſubſtituted in its room, more congruous to rea-ſon ; ſince *Reſt* is moſt oppoſite to *Motion*, the immediate cauſe of *diſunion*. But yet I cannot ſee, how this can ac-count for the almoſt *indiſſolvible coherence* of ſome bodies, and the *fragility* and *ſolubility* of others : For if the *Union* of the *Parts* conſiſt only in *Reſt* ; it would ſeem, that a bagg of *duſt* would be of as firm a conſiſtence as that of *Marble* or *Adamant* : a Bar of *Iron* will be as eaſily broken as a *Tobacco-pipe* ; and *Bajazets* Cage had been but a ſorry *Priſon*. The *Ægyptian Pyramids* would have been ſooner loſt, then the Names of them that built them ; and as eaſily blown away, as thoſe *inverſt ones* of *ſmoke*. Nor can it be pretended for a difference, that the parts of ſolid bodies are held together by *hooks*, and *angulous* involu-tions ; ſince the *coherence* of the parts of theſe will be of as difficult a conception, as the former : And we muſt either ſuppoſe an infinite of them holding together on one another ; or at laſt come to *parts*, that are *united* by a meer *juxta-poſition* : Yea, could we ſuppoſe the former, yet the coherence of theſe, would be like the hanging to-gether of an infinite ſuch of *Duſt* : which *Hypotheſis* would ſpoil the *Proverb*, and *a rope of ſand*, ſhould be no more a phraſe for *Labour in vain* : For unleſs there be ſomething , upon which all the reſt may depend for their *coheſion* ; the hanging of one by another, will ſig-nifie no more then the mutual dependence of *cauſes* and

effects

effects in an *infinite Series*, without a *First*: the admiffion of which, *Atheifm* would applaud. But yet to do the *Mafter* of *Mechanicks* right; fomewhat of more validity in the behalf of this *Hypothefis* may be affign'd: Which is, that the clofenefs and compactnefs of the *Parts refting* together, doth much confer to the ftrength of the *union*: For *every thing continues in the condition, wherein it is, except fomething more powerful alter it*: And therefore the *parts*, that *reft* clofe together, muft continue in the fame relation to each other, till fome other *body* by *motion* disjoyn them. Now then, the more *parts* there are pen't together, the more able they will be for *refiftence*; and what hath lefs *compactnefs*, and by confequence fewer *parts*, according to the *laws* of *motion* will not be able to effect any *alteration* in it. According to what is here prefented, what is moft *denfe*, and leaft *porous*, will be moft *coherent*, and leaft *difcerpible.* And if this help not, I cannot apprehend what can give an account of the former inftances. And yet even this is confuted by experience; fince the moft *porous fpongie bodies* are oft-times the moft *tough* in confiftence. 'Tis eafier to break a tube of *Glaſs* or *Cryftal*, then of *Elm* or *Afh*: And yet as the *parts* of the former are more, fo they are more at *reft*; fince the *liquid juyce*, which is diffufed through the *parts* of the *Wood*, is in a continual agitation, which in *Des-Cartes* his *Philofophy* is the caufe of *fluidity*; and a proportion'd *humidity* confer's

much

much to *union* (Sir *K. Digby* makes it the *Cement it self*); *A dry stick* will be easily broken, when *a green one* will maintain a strong resistence : and yet in the *moist* substance there is less *rest*, then in what is *dryer* and more *fragill.* Much more might be added: But I'le content my self with what's mentioned; and, notwithstanding what hath been said, I judge this account of that *miraculous wit* to be the most *ingenious* and *rational*, that *hath* or (it may be) *can* be given. I shall not therefore conclude it false; though I think the emergent *difficulties*, which are its attendants, *unanswerable* : proof enough of the weakness of our *now Reasons*, which are driven to such straights and puzzles even in things which are most *obvious*, and have so much the advantage of our faculties.

&. 4. (3.) THe *composition* of *Bodies*, whether it be of *Divisibles* or *Indivisibles*, is a question which must be rank'd with the *Indissolvibles* : For though it hath been attempted by the most illustrious *Wits* of all *Philosophick* Ages ; yet they have done little else, but shewn their own *divisions* to be almost as *infinite*, as some suppose those of their Subject. And notwithstanding all their shifts, subtilties, newly invented Words and Modes, sly subterfuges, and studyed evasions; yet the product of all their endeavours,

vours, is but as the Birth of the labouring *Mountains*, *Wind*, and *Emptineſs*. Do what they can; *Actual Infinite extenſion every where*, *Equality of all bodies*, *Impoſsibility of Motion*, and a world more of the moſt palpable abſurdities will preſs the aſſertors of *infinite diviſibility*. Neither can it be avoided, but that all *motions* would be *equal* in *velocity*; the *lines* drawn from ſide to ſide in a *Pyramid*, may have more parts then the *Baſis*, all bodies would be ſwallow'd up in a *point* and endleſs more inconſiſtences, will be as neceſſarily conſequential to the opinion of *Indiviſibles*. But intending only to inſtance in difficulties, which are not ſo much taken notice of; I ſhall refer the Reader, that would ſee more of this, to *Oviedo, Pontius, Ariaga, Carelton*, and other *Jeſuites*: whoſe management of this ſubject with equal force on either ſide, is a ſtrong preſumption of what we drive at.

CHAP.

Chap. VIII.

Difficulties about the Motion of a Wheel, *which admit of no Solution.*

BEſides the already mention'd difficulties, even the moſt ordinary trivial *occurrents*, if we contemplate them in the *Theory*, will as much puzzle us, as any of the former. Under this head I'le add three things concerning the Motion of a *Wheel*, and conclude this branch of my ſubject.

§. 1. FIrſt then in the abſtract conſideration, it ſeems impoſſible that a *wheel* ſhould *move* : I mean not the *progreſſive*, but that Motion which is meerly on its own *Centre*. And were it not for the information of Experience , it's moſt likely that *Philoſophy* had long ago concluded it *impoſſible* : For let's ſuppoſe the wheel to be divided according to the *Alphabet*. In motion then there is a change of place, and in the motion of a *wheele* there is a ſucceſſion of one part to another in the ſame place ; ſo that it ſeems unconceivable that *A.* ſhould move until *B.* hath left his place : For *A.* cannot move, but it muſt acquire ſome place or other. It can acquire none but what was *B's*, which we

G ſuppoſe

suppose to be most immediate to it. The same space cannot contain them both. And therefore *B*. must leave its place, before *A* can have it; Yea, and the nature of succession requires it. But now *B*. cannot move, but into the place of *C*; and *C*. must be out, before *B*. can come in: so that the motion of *C*. will be pre-required likewise to the motion of *A*; and so onward till it comes to *Z*. Upon the same accounts *Z*. will not be able to move, till *A* moves, being the part next to it: neither will *A*. be able to move (as hath been shewn) till *Z*. hath. And so the motion of every part will be pre-requir'd to it self. Neither can one evade, by saying, that all the parts move at once. For (1.) we cannot conceive in a *succession* but that something should be first, and that motion should begin somewhere. (2.) If the parts may all change places with one another at the same time without any respect of *priority* and *posteriority* to each others *motion*: why then may not a company of *Bullets* closely crowded together in a *Box*, as well move together by a like mutual and simultaneous exchange? Doubtless the reason of this ineptitude to motion in this position is, that they cannot give way one to another, and motion can no where begin because of the *plenitude*. The case is just the same in the instance before us; and therefore we need go no further for an evidence of its *inconceivableness*. But yet to give it one touch more according to the *Peripatetick* niceness, which sayes, that one part enters in the same *instant* that the other goes out: I'le add

this

this in brief: In the inftant that *B.* leaves its place, it's in it, or not: If fo; then *A.* cannot be in it in the fame *in-ftant* without a *penetration.* If not; then it cannot be faid to leave it in that *inftant*, but to have left it before. Thefe difficulties, which pinch fo in this obvious experi-ment, ftand in their full force againft all Motion on the *Hypothefis* of *abfolute plenitude.* Nor yet have the Defen-ders hereof need to take notice of them, becaufe they equally prefs a moft fenfible Truth. Neither is it fair, that the oppofite opinion of *interfpers'd vacuities* fhould be rejected as abfurd upon the account of fome *inextricable perplexities* which attend it. Therefore let them both have fair play; and whichfoever doth with moft eafe and congruity folve the *Phænomena,* that fhall have my vote for the moft *Philofophick Hypothefis.*

§. 2. IT's a difficulty no lefs defperate then the for-mer, that the *parts vicine* to the *centre*, which it may be pafs not over the hundredth part of *fpace* which thofe do of the extreme *circumference*, fhould defcribe their *narrower circle* but in equal time with thofe other, that trace fo great a *round.* If they move but in the fame degree of *Velocity*; here is then an *equality in time* and *motion*, and yet a vaft *inequality* in the *acquired fpace.* A thing which feems flatly impoffible: For is it con-ceivable, that of two bodies fetting forth together, and continuing their motion in the fame fwiftnefs, the one fhould fo far out-go its fellow, as to move ten mile an

hour,

hour, while the other moves but a furlong ? If ſo, 'twill be no wonder, that *the race is not to the ſwift*, and the *fur-theſt way about* may well be the *neareſt way home*. There is but one way that can be attempted to untie this knot ; which is, by ſaying, that the *remoter* and more out-ſide parts move more ſwiftly than the *central* ones. But this likewiſe is as unconceiveable as what it would avoid : For ſuppoſe a right *line* drawn from the *centre* to the *circumference*, and it cannot be apprehended, but that the *line* ſhould be inflected, if ſome parts of it move faſter than others. I ſay if we do abſtractedly from experience contemplate it in the *theory*, it is hard to conceive, but that one part moving, while the other reſts, or at leaſt moves ſlower (which is as reſt to a ſwifter motion) ſhould change its diſtance from it, and the reſpect, which it had to it; which one would think ſhould cauſe an incurvation in the *line*.

§. 3. LEt there be two *Wheels* fixt on the ſame Axel in *Diameter* ten inches a piece. Between them let there be a *little wheel*, of two inches Diameter, fixed on the ſame Axel. Let them be moved together on a plane, the great ones on the ground ſuppoſe, and the little one on a Table (for becauſe of its par-vitude it cannot reach to the ſame floor with them) And you'l find that the little wheel will move over the ſame ſpace in equal time with equal *circulations*, with the great ones, and deſcribe as long a line. Now
this

this seems bigg of repugnancies, though Sense it self suffragate to its truth : For since every part of the greater wheels make a proportionable part of the line, as do the parts of the little one, and the parts of those so much exceeding in multitude the parts of this : It will seem necessary that the line made by the greater wheels should have as many parts more then the line made by the less, as the wheels themselves have in *circumference*, and so the line would be as much longer as the wheels are bigger : so that one of these absurdities seems unavoidable, either that more parts of the greater wheels go to the making one part of their lines, which will infer a *penetration* of *dimensions*; or that the little wheel hath as many parts as the great ones, though five times in *Diameter* exceeded by them, since the lines they describe are of equal length; or the less wheel's line will have fewer parts then the others, though of equal extent with them, since it can have no more parts then the *less circle*, nor *they* fewer then the *greater*. What offers have been made towards the resolving this difficulty, by the ingenious *Tacquett* and others, and with what success; will be considered in the Appendix; to which, that I may pursue other matters, I remit the Inquisitive Reader.

Should I have enlarged on this Subject to the taking in of all things that claim a share in't, it may be few things would have been left unspoken to, but the *Creed.* Philosophy would not have engross'd our Pen, but we must have been forced to anger the *Intelligences* of higher Orbs. But intending only a glance at this rugged Theam, I shall forbear to insist more on it, though the consideration of the Mysteries of *Motion, Gravity, Light, Colours, Vision, Sound,* and infinite such like (things *obvious,* yet *unknown*) might have been plentiful subject. I come now to trace some of the *causes* of our *Ignorance* and Intellectual *weakness:* and among so many it's almost as great a wonder as any of the former; that we can *say, we know.*

CHAP.

Chap. IX.

Mens backwardnefs to acknowledge their own Ignorance and Error, though ready to find them in others. The (1) *caufe of the Shortnefs of our Knowledge,* viz. *the* depth of Verity *difcours't of, as of its admixtion in Mens Opinions with falfehood, and the connexion of truths, and their mutual dependence: A fecond Reafon of the fhortnefs of our Knowledge,* viz. *becaufe we can perceive nothing but by proportion to our Senfes.*

THe Difeafe of our *Intellectuals* is too great, not to be its own evidence: And they that feel it not, are not lefs *fick*, but ftupidly *fo* The weaknefs of humane underftanding, all will confefs: yet the confidence of moft in their own reafonings, practically difowns it: And 'tis eafier to perfwade them it from others lapfes then their own; fo that while all complain of our *Ignorance* and *Error*, every one exempts himfelf. It is acknowledged by *all*, while

every

every one denies it. If the foregoing part of this Diſcourſe, have not univerſally concluded our weakneſs:
I have own Item more of mine. If knowledge can be
found in the Particulars mentioned; I muſt loſe that,
which I thought I had, *That there is none.* But however,
though ſome ſhould pick a quarrel with the inſtances
I alleadged; yet the concluſion muſt be owned in others.
And therefore beſide the general reaſon I gave of our
intellectual diſabilities, The *Fall* ; it will be worth our
labour to deſcend to a more particular account : ſince
it is a good degree of *Knowledge* to be acquainted with
the *cauſes* of our *Ignorance.* And what we have to ſay
under this head, will equally concern our *miſapprehen-
ſions* and *Errors.* And the particulars I intend are *Cauſes*
and *Evidences* of both.

§. I. (1) THen we owe much of our *Ignorance* to
the *depth* of *Knowledge;* which is not
the acquiſt of *ſuperficials* and *ſupine* enquirers. *Democritus* his Well hath a Βάθος, and Truth floats not.
The uſeleſs froth ſwims on the ſurface; but the Pearl
lies cover'd with a maſs of Waters. *Veriſimilitude* and
Opinion are an eaſie purchaſe : But true *Knowledge* is
dear and *difficult.* Like a *point* or *line,* it requires an
acuteneſs and intention to its diſcovery; while *veriſimi-
lity,* like the expanded *ſuperficies,* is an obvious ſenſible,
and affords a large and eaſie field for looſe enquiry.
And 'tis the more difficult to find out Truth, becauſe it
is

is in ſuch inconſiderable proportions ſcattered in a maſs
of *opinionative uncertainties* ; like the Silver in *Hiero*'s
Crown of Gold : And it is no eaſie piece of *Chymiſtry* to
reduce theſe *Minutes* to their *unmixed ſelves*. The Elements are no where pure in theſe lower *Regions* ; and
if there is any free from the admixtion of another, ſure
'tis above the *concave* of the *Moon* : Neither can any
boaſt a *knowledge* depurate from the defilement of a
contrary, within this *Atmoſphear* of fleſh ; it dwels no
where in unblended proportions , on this ſide the
Empyreum. All Opinions have their *Truth*, and all
have what is not *ſo* ; and to ſay *all* are *true* and *none*,
is no abſurdity. So that to crown our ſelfs with ſparks,
which are almoſt loſt in ſuch a world of *heterogeneous*
natures, is as difficult as deſirable. Beſides, *Truth* is
never *ſingle* ; to know one will require the knowledge of many. They hang together in a chain of
mutual dependence ; you cannot draw one linke without attracting others. Such an Harmony cannot commence from a ſingle ſtring ; diverſity of ſtrokes makes
it. The beauty of a Face is not known by the *Eye*,
or *Noſe* ; it conſiſts in a *ſymmetry*, and 'tis the comparative faculty which votes it : Thus is Truth *relative*, and little conſiderable can be attained by *catches*.
The Painter cannot tranſcribe a face upon a Tranſi-
ent view ; it requires the information of a fixt and
obſervant Eye : And before we can reach an exact
ſight of Truth's uniform perfections , this *fleeting*

H   *Tran-*

Tranfitory our *Life*, is gone. So that we fee the face
of Truth, but as we do one anothers, when we walk
the ftreets, in a carelefs *Pafs-by*: And the moft diligent obfervers, view but the back-fide o'th' *Hang-*
ings; the right one is on the other fide the *Grave*:
And our Knowledge is but like thofe *broken ends*; at
beft a moft confufed *adumbration*. Nature, that was
veil'd to *Ariftotle*, hath not yet uncover'd, in almoft
two thoufand years. What he fought on the other
fide of *Euripus*, we muft not look for on this fide
Immortality. In *eafie* difquifitions we are often left to
the uncertainty of a guefs: yea after we have triumph'd in a fuppofed Εὕρηκα; a new-fprung difficulty
marrs our *Ovations*, and expofeth us to the Torment
of a difappointment: fo that even the great *Mafter* of
Dogmatifts himfelf concludes the Scene with an *Anxius*
vixi, Dubius morior.

§. 2. A Nother reafon of our *Ignorance* and the
narrownefs of our *apprehenfions* is; That we
cannot perceive the manner of any of Natures operations, but by proportion to our *fenfes*, and return to
material phantafms. A blind man conceives not *colours*,
but under the notion of fome other *fenfible*; and more
perfect apprehenders as grofly mifconceive *Immaterials*:
Our imaginations painting *Souls* and *Angels* in as
little agreeing a refemblace. And had there not been
any *night, fhadow*, or *opacity*; we fhould never have
had

had any determinate conceit of *Darkneſs*; *That* would have been as inconceiveáble to us, as its contrary is to him that never ſaw it.

But now our *ſenſes* being ſcant and limited, and Natures operations ſubtil and various; they muſt needs tranſcend, and out-run our faculties. They are only Natures groſſer wayes of working, which are *ſenſible*; Her finer threads are out of the reach of our dull *Percipient*. Yea queſtionleſs ſhe hath many hidden *Energies*, no wayes imitated in her obvious pieces: and therefore it is no wonder that we are ſo often at a loſs; an infirmity beyond prevention, except we could ſtep by ſtep follow the tracks and Methods of *Infinite Wiſdom*, which cannot be done but by him that owns it.

CHAP. X.

A third reaſon of our Ignorance *and* Error, viz. *the impoſtures and deceits of our* Senſes. *The way to rectiſie theſe miſ-informations propounded.* Des-Chartes *his method the only way to Science. The difficulty of exact performance.*

§. 3.   ANother reaſon is the *Impoſture* and *fallacy of our Senſes*, which impoſe not only on common Heads, who ſcarce at all live to the *higher Principle*; But even more refined *Mercuries*, who have the advantages of an improved reaſon to diſ-abuſe them, and yet frequently captivated to theſe de-ceiving Prepoſſeſſions: appealing to a Judicature both uncommiſſioned and unjuſt; and when the cleareſt Truth is to be tryed by ſuch Judges, its innocence will not ſecure it from the condemning award of that *unintel-ligent Tribunal*: For ſince we live the life of *Brutes*, be-fore we grow into *Man*; and our underſtandings in this their *Non-age*, being almoſt meerly Paſſive to ſenſi-

ble

ble Impreſſions, receiving all things in an uncontroverted and promiſcuous admiſſion : It cannot be, that our
Knowledge ſhould be other, then an heap of *Miſ-
conception* and *Error*, and conceits as impertinent as
the *toys* we delight *in*. All this while we have no
more reaſon, then the ΕΙΔΩΛΟΝ ΨΥΧΗΣ (as *Plotinus* calls it) amounts to. And beſides this our eaſie
ſubmiſſion to ſophiſtications of *ſenſe*, and inability
to prevent the miſcariages of our *Junior* Reaſons;
and that which ſtrikes the great ſtroke toward our
after-deceptions, is the pertinacious adherence of many of theſe firſt impreſſions, to our advanc't Underſtandings. That which is early received, if in any
conſiderable ſtrength of *Impreſs*, as it were grows into our tender natures, and is therefore of difficult
remove. Thus a fright in *Minority*, or an *Antipathy* then contracted, is not worn out but with its
ſubject. And it may be more then a *Story*, that
Nero derived much of his cruelty from the Nurſe that
ſuckled him. Now though our coming Judgements
do in part undeceive us, and rectifie the groſſer Errors which our unwary Senſitive hath engaged us
in; yet others are ſo fleſht in us, that they maintain
their intereſt upon the deceptibility of our decayed Natures, and are cheriſh't there, as the legitimate iſſues of
our reaſonable faculties.

H 3 Indeed

Indeed *Senſe* it ſelf detects its more palpable deceits, by a counter-evidence; and the more ordinary Impoſtures ſeldom out-live the firſt *Experiments.*
If our *ſight* repreſent a Staff as crooked in the *wa-*
ter; the ſame faculty rectifies both it, and us, in
the *thinner Element.* And if a ſquare Tower ſeem
round at a diſtance; the eye, which miſtook in the
circumſtance of its figure, at that remove, corrects
the miſtake in a due approach: Yea, and befriends
thoſe who have learn'd to make the advantage of its
informations, in more remote and difficil diſcoveries. And though his *Senſe* occaſion the careleſs
Ruſtick to judge the *Sun* no bigger then a *Cheeſe-fat*;
yet *ſenſe* too by a frugal improvement of its evidence, grounds the *Aſtronomers* knowledge, that it's
bigger then this *Globe* of *Earth* and *Water.* Which
it doth not only by the advantageous aſſiſtance of a
Tube, but by leſs induſtrious experiments, ſhew-
ing in what degrees Diſtance minorates the Object. But yet in infinite other caſes, wherein *ſenſe*
can afford none, or but very little help to diſ-in-
tangle us; our firſt deceptions loſe no ground, but
rather improve in our riper years: ſo that we are
not weaned from our *child-hood*, till we return to
our ſecond *Infancy*; and even our *Gray* heads out-
grow not thoſe Errors, which we have learn't before
the *Alphabet.*

Thus

Thus our *Reasons* being inoculated on *Sense*, will retain a relish of the stock they grew on : And if we would endeavour after an unmixed Knowledge; we must *unlive* our former *lives*, and (inverting the practice of *Penelope*) undo in the *day* of our more advanc'd understandings , what we had spun in the *night* of our *Infant-ignorance*. He that would rebuild a decayed *structure*, must first pluck down the former *ruines*. A *fabrick*, though high and beautiful , if founded on *rubbish* , is easily made the triumph of the winds : And the most pompous seeming Knowledge, that's built on the unexamin'd prejudices of *Sense*, stands not, but till the *storm ariseth*; the next strong encounter discovers its weakness , in a shameful over-throw. Since then , a great part of our scientifical *Treasure* is most likely to be *adulterate* , though all bears the image and superscription of *Truth*; the only way to know what is sophisticate, and what is not so, is to bring all to the *Examen* of the Touchstone : For the prepossessions of *sense* having (as is shewen) so mingled themselves with our Genuine Truths , and being as plausible to appearance as they; we cannot gain a true assurance of any , but by suspend-ing our assent from all , till the deserts of each, discover'd by a strict enquiry , claim it. Upon this account I think the *method* of the most excellent *Des-Cartes* not unworthy its Author; and (since

Dog=

Dogmatical Ignorance will call it ſo) a *Scepticiſm*, that's the only way to *Science.* But yet this is ſo difficult in the impartial and exact performance, that it may be well reckon'd among the bare *Poſſibilities*, which never commence into a *Futurity* : It requiring ſuch a *free, ſedate,* and *intent* minde, as it may be is no where found but among the *Platonical Idæa's.* Do what we can, Prejudices will creep in, and hinder our Intellectual Perfection : And though by this means we may get ſome comfortable allay to our diſtempers ; yet can it not perfectly cure us of a diſeaſe, that ſticks as cloſe to us as our Natures.

C H A P.

CHAP. XI.

Two Inſtances of Senſitive *deception.* (1) *Of the* Quieſcence *of the* Earth. *Senſe is the great inducement to its belief ; its teſtimony deſerves no credit in this caſe, though it do move, Senſe would preſent it as immoveable. The Sun to Senſe is as much devoid of moti- on as the* Earth. *The Caſes wherein* mo- tion *is* inſenſible, *Applyed to the Earths motion. The unweildineſs of its bulk is no argument of its imraobility.*

TO Illuſtrate the Particular I am diſcourſing of, I'le indeavour to deteƈt the unlucky influence of *Sen- ſitive* prejudice by a double Inſtance ; the free debate of which I conceive to be of importance, though hitherto for the moſt part obſtruƈted, by the peremptory concluſion of a faculty which I ſhall make appear to have no ſuffrage in the caſe of either : And the pleaſant- neſs and concernment of the *Theories,* if it be one, I hope will attone the *Digreſſion.*

I

§. 2. FIrſt, it is generally opinion'd , that the *Earth reſts* as the Worlds *centre,* while the *Heavens* are the ſubject of the *Univerſal Motions* ; And, *as immoveable as the Earth,* is grown into the credit of being *Proverbial.* So that for a man to go about to counter-argue this belief, is as fruitleſs as to whiſtle againſt the windes. I ſhall not undertake to maintain the *Paradox,* that confronts this almoſt *Catholick* Opinion. Its aſſertion would be entertained with the hoot of the Rabble : the very mention of it as poſſible, is among the moſt ridiculous ; and they are likely moſt ſeverely to judge it, who leaſt underſtand what it is they cenſure. But yet the Patronage of as great *Wits,* as it may be e're ſaw the Sun, ſuch as *Pythagoras, Des-Cartes, Copernicus, Galileo, More, Kepler,* and generally the *vertuoſi* of the awakened world, hath gain'd it a more favourable cenſure with learned mankind ; and advanc'd it far above either vain, or contemptible. And if it be a miſtake, it's only ſo : There's no *Hereſie* in ſuch an harmleſs aberration ; at the worſt, with the ingenuous, the probability of it will render it a lapſe of eaſie Pardon.

Now whether the *Earth* move or reſt, I undertake not to determine. My work is to prove, that the common inducement to the belief of its *quieſcence,* the teſtimony of *ſenſe,* is weak and frivolous : to the end, that if upon an unprejudiced tryal, it be found more conſonant to the *Aſtronomical Phænomena* ; its *Motion* may

may be admitted, notwithſtanding the ſeeming contrary evidence of unconcerned *Senſes*. And I think what
follows will evince, that this is no ſo abſurd an *Hypotheſis*, as Vulgar Philoſophers acount it; but that,
though it *move*, its *motion* muſt needs be as *inſenſible*,
as if it were *quieſcent*: and the aſſertion of it would then
be as uncouth and harſh to the ſons of *Senſe*, that is, to
the generality of Mankind, as now it is.

That there is a *motion*, which makes the viciſſitudes
of day and night, and conſtitutes the ſucceſſive Seaſons
of the year; *Senſe* may aſſure us; or at leaſt the comparative Judgment of an higher faculty, made upon its
immediate evidence: But whether the *Sun*, or *Earth*,
be the common *Movent*, cannot be determin'd but by
a further appeal. If we will take the literal evidence
of our Eyes; the *Æthereal Coal* moves no more then
this *Inferior clod doth*: For where ever in the *Firmament*
we ſee it, it's repreſented to us, as fixt in that part of
the enlightened *Hemiſphear*. And though an after-
account diſcover, that it hath changed it's *Site* and
reſpect to this our *Globe*; yet whether that were cauſed
by its tranſlation from us, or ours from it, Senſe leaves
us in an *Ignoramus*: So that if we are reſolved to ſtand
to its Verdict, it muſt be by as great a *Miracle* if the
Sun ever *move*, as it was that it once *reſted*, or what
ever elſe was the ſubject of that ſupernal change. And
if upon a meer ſenſible account we will deny Motion
to the *Earth*; upon the ſame inducement we muſt deny

it the *Sun*; and the *Heavens* will lofe their *Firft Moveable.* But to draw up clofer to our main defign, We may the better conceive that, though the *Earth move*, yet its *Motion* muft needs be infenfible; if we confider that in thefe cafes relating to our purpofe, *Motion* ftrikes not the *Senfe.*

(1.) Then if the *Motion* be very flow, we perceive it not. We have no fenfe of the *accretive* motion of *Plants* or *Animals*; And the fly *fhaddow* fteals away upon the *Dyal*; And the quickeft Eye, can difcover no more but that *'tis gone.* Which *infenfibility* of flow motions I think may thus be accounted for; *Motion* cannot be perceived without the perception of its *Terms, viz.* The parts of fpace which it immediately left, and thofe which it next acquires. Now the fpace left and acquir'd in every fenfible moment in fuch flow progreffions, is fo inconfiderable, that it cannot poffibly move the *fenfe*; (which by reafon either of its conftitutional dulnefs, or the importunity of ftronger impreffions, cannot take notice of fuch parvitudes) and therefore neither can the Motion depending thereon, be any more obfervable, then we find it.

2. If the *fentient* be carryed *pafsibus æquis* with the body, whofe *motion* it would obferve; (fuppofing that it be *regular* and *fteddy*) In this cafe the remove is infenfible, at leaft in its proper fubject. We perceive not a Ship to move, while we are in it; but our fenfe transfers its motion to the neighbouring fhores, as the Poet, *Littus campiq; recedunt.* And I queftion not, but if any were

born

born and bred under Deck, and had no other information but what his *sense* affords; he would without the
least doubt or scruple, opinion, that the house he dwelt
in, was as stable and fixt as ours To express the reason
according to the Philosophy of *Des-Cartes* , I suppose
it thus : *Motion* is not perceived , but by the *successive
strikings* of the object upon divers *filaments* of the *Brain*;
which diversifie the representation of its *site* and *distance.*
But now when the motion of the object is common
with it, to our selves; it retains the same relation to our
sense , as if we both *rested* : For striking still on the
same *strings* of the Brain, it varies not its *site* or *distance*
from us; and therefore we cannot possibly perceive its
motion : nor yet upon the same account our own; least
of all, when we are carryed without any *conamen* and
endeavour of ours, which in our particular progressions
betrayes them to our notice.

Now then, The *Earths motion* (if we suppose it to
have any) hath the concurrence of both , to render it
insensible; And therefore we need no more proof to
conclude the necessity of its being so.

For though the First seems not to belong to the present case, since the supposed motion will be near a thousand miles an hour under the *Equinoctional line*; yet it
will seem to have no *Velocity* to the *sense* any more
then the received *motion* of the *Sun* , and for the same
reason. Because the distant points in the *Celestial ex-*
panse

panſe (from a various and ſucceſſive reſpect to which the length, and conſequently the ſwiftneſs of this *motion* muſt be calculated) appear to the Eye in ſo ſmall a degree of *elongation* from one another, as bears no proportion to what is *real*. For ſince the Margin of the *Viſible Horizon* in the Heavenly *Globe* is Parallel with that in the Earthly, accounted but 120 miles *diameter*; Senſe muſt needs meaſure the *Azimuths*, or *Vertical Circles*, by triplication of the ſame *diameter* of 120. So that there will be no more proportion betwixt the *ſenſible* and *real* celerity of the *Terreſtrial Motion*, then there is between the *viſible* and *rational dimenſion* of the celeſtial *Hemiſphear*, which is none at all.

But if ſenſitive prejudice will yet confidently maintain the Impoſſibility of the *Hypotheſis*, from the ſuppoſed *unwieldineſs* of its maſſie bulk, grounded on our experience of the ineptitude of *great* and *heavy* bodies to *Motion*: I ſay this is a meer Impoſture of our *Senſes*, the fallacy of which we may avoid, by conſidering; that the *Earth* may as eaſily move, notwithſtanding this pretended indiſpoſition of its *magnitude*, as thoſe much vaſter *Orbs* of *Sun* and *Stars*. He that made it, could as well give motion to the whole, 'as to the parts; the conſtant 'agitation of which is diſcover'd in natural productions : and to *both*, as well as *Reſt* to either : Neither will it need the aſſiſtance of an *Intelligence* to perpetuate the begun

Rotation :

Rotation : Since according to the Indifpenfible *Law* of *Nature* (*That every thing fhould continue in the* |*ftate wherein it is, except fomething more powerful hinder it*) it muft perfevere in Motion, unlefs obftructed by a *Miracle.* Neither can *Gravity*, which makes great bodies hard of Remove, be any hinderance to the *Earths* motion : fince even the *Peripatetick Maxime*, *Nihil gravitat in fuo loco*, will exempt it from the indifpofition of that *Quality*; which is nothing but the tendency of its parts, which are ravifh't from it, to their defired *Centre.* And the *French Philofophy* will inform us, that the *Earth* as well as other bodies is indifferent in it felf to *Reft*, or its contrary.

Снар.

CHAP. XII.

Another instance of the deceptions *of our* Senses: *which is of translating the* Idea *of our* Passions *to things without us.* Properly and formally heat is not in the fire, but is an expression of our sentiment. Yet in proprity of speech the Senses themselves are never deceived, but only administer an occasion of deceit to the understanding: prov'd by reason, and the Authority of St. Austin.

SEcondly the *Best Philosophy* (the deserved Title of the *Cartesian*) derives all *sensitive perception* from *Motion*, and corporal impress; some account of which we have above given. Not that the Formality of it consists in *material Reaction*, as Master *Hobbs* affirms, totally excluding any immaterial concurrence: But that the representations of Objects to the Soul, the only *animadversive principle*, are conveyed by motions made upon the immediate Instruments of Sense. So that the diversity of our Sensations ariseth from the diversity

diversity of the *motion* or *figure* of the object; which in a different manner affect the Brain, whence the Soul hath its immediate intelligence of the quality of what is presented. Thus the different effects, which *fire* and *water*, have on us, which we call *heat* and *cold*, result from the so differing *configuration* and *agitation* of their *Particles*; and not from, I know not what *Chimerical beings*, supposed to inhere in the objects, their cause, and thence to be propagated by many petty *imaginary productions* to the seat of *Sense*. So that what we term *heat* and *cold*, and other qualities, are not properly according to *Philosophical* rigour in the Bodies, their Efficients: but are rather *Names* expressing our *passions*; and therefore not strictly attributable to any thing without us, but by *extrinsick denominations*, as *Vision* to the Wall.

This I conceive to be an *Hypothesis*, well worthy a rational belief: and yet is it so abhorrent from the Vulgar, that they would as soon believe *Anaxagoras*, that *snow is black*, as him that should affirm, it is not *white*; and if any should in earnest assert, that the *fire* is not formally *hot*, it would be thought that the heat of his brain had fitted him for *Anticyra*, and that his head were *so* to madness: For it is conceived to be as certain, as our faculties can make it, that the same qualities, which we resent within us, are in the object, their Source. And yet this confidence is grounded on no better foundation, then a delusory prejudice, and the vote of *misapplyed sensations*, which have no warrant to determine either one or other.

K   I may

I may indeed conclude, that I am formally *hot* or *cold*; I feel it. But whether thefe qualities are *formally*, or only *eminently* in their producent; is beyond the knowledge of the *fenfitive.* Even the *Peripatetick Philofophy* will teach us, that *heat* is not in the Body of the *Sun*, but only *virtually*, and as in its caufe; though it be the Fountain and great Diftributour of warmth to the neather Creation : and yet none urge the evidence of *fenfe* to difprove it : Neither can it with any more Juftice be alledged againft this *Hypothefis.* For if it be fo as *Des-Cartes* would have it ; yet *fenfe* would conftantly prefent it to us, as *Now.* We fhould feel heat as *conftantly* from *Fire* ; it would increafe in the fame degrees, in our approach, and we fhould finde the fame excefs within the flame : which yet I think to be the chief inducements to the adverfe belief : For *Fire* (I retain the inftance, which yet may be applyed to other cafes) being conftant in its fpecifical motions in thofe fmaller derivations of it, which are its inftruments of action, and therefore in the fame manner ftriking the fentient, though gradually varying according to the proportions of more or lefs quantity or agitation, *&c.* will not fail to produce the fame effect in us, which we call *heat*, when ever we are within the Orb of its activity. So that the *heat* muft needs be augmented by proximity, and moft of all within the *Flame*, becaufe of the more *violent motion* of the particles there, which therefore begets in us a ftronger fentiment. Now if this *motive Energie*, the inftrument of this active

Element,

Element, muſt be called *Heat* ; let it be ſo, I contend not.
I know not how otherwiſe to call it : To impoſe names
is part of the *Peoples* Charter, and I fight not with *Words*.
Only I would not that the *Idea* of our *Paſſions* ſhould be
apply'd to any thing without us, when it hath its ſubject
no where but in our ſelves. This is the grand deceit,
which my deſign is to detect, and if poſſible, to rectifie.

We have ſeen then two notorious inſtances of *ſenſitive
deception*, which juſtifie the charge of *Petron. Arbiter.*

> *Fallunt nos oculi, vagiq; ſenſus
> Oppreſſâ ratione mentiuntur.*

And yet to ſpeak properly, and to do our *ſenſes* right,
ſimply they are not deceived, but only adminiſter an
occaſion to our forward *underſtandings* to deceive themſelves : and ſo though they are ſome way acceſſory to our
deluſion ; yet the more principal faculties are the *Capital
offenders.* If the *Senſes* repreſent the *Earth* as *fixt* and
immoveable; they give us the truth of their *Sentiments.*
To *ſenſe* it is *ſo*, and it would be deceit to preſent it otherwiſe. For (as we have ſhewn) though it do *move* in
it ſelf; it *reſts* to us, who are carry'd with it. And it
muſt needs be to *ſenſe* unalterably *quieſcent*, in that our
own Rotation prevents the variety of *ſucceſſive Impreſſ* ;
which only renders motion *ſenſible.* And ſo if we erro-
neouſly attribute our particular incommunicable ſenſations to things, which do no more reſemble them then

the *effect* doth its *æquivocal cauſe*; our *ſenſes* 'are not in fault, but our *precipitate judgments*. We *feel* ſuch, or ſuch a *ſentiment* within us, and herein is no cheat or miſpriſion : 'tis truly ſo, and our *ſenſe* concludes nothing of its Riſe or Origine. But if hence our Underſtandings falſly deduct, that there is the ſame quality in the *external impreſſor*; 'tis, it is *criminal*, our *ſenſe* is *innocent*. When the *Ear* tingles, we really hear a *ſound* : If we judge it without us, it's the fallacy of our *Judgments*. The *apparitions* of our frighted *Phancies* are real *ſenſibles* : But if we tranſlate them without the compaſs of our Brains , and apprehend them as external objects; it's the unwary raſhneſs of our *Underſtanding* deludes us. And if our diſaffected Palates reſent nought but bitterneſs from our choiceſt viands, we truly taſt the unpleaſing quality, though falſly conceive it in that, which is no more then the occaſion of its production. If any find fault with the novelty of the notion; the learned St. *Auſtin* ſtands ready to confute the charge : and they who revere *Antiquity*, will derive ſatisfaction from ſo venerable a ſuffrage. He tells us, *Si quis remum frangi in aquâ opinatur, &, cùm aufertur , integrari; non malum habet internuncium , ſed malus eſt Judex.* And onward to this purpoſe , The ſenſe could not otherwiſe perceive it in the *water ,* neither ought it : For ſince the *Water* is one thing, and the *Air* another ; 'tis requiſite and neceſſary , that the *ſenſe* ſhould be as different as the *medium* : Wherefore the Eye ſees aright ; if there be a miſtake, 'tis the Judgement's

the

the Deceiver. Elfewhere he faith, that our Eyes mif-inform us not, but faithfully tranfmit their refentment to the mind. And againft the *Scepticks*, That it's a piece of injuftice to complain of our *fenfes*, and to exact from them an account, which is beyond the fphear of their notice : and refolutely determines, *Quicquid poſſunt videre oculi, verum vident.* So that what we have faid of the *fenfes deceptions*, is rigidly to be charg'd only on our carelefs Underftandings, mifleading us through the ill management of fenfible informations. But becaufe fuch are commonly known by the name of the *Senfes deceipts* (fomewhat the more juftifiably in that they adminifter the occafion) I have thought good to retain the ufual way of fpeaking, though fomewhat varying from the manner of apprehending.

Chap.

CHAP. XIII.

A fourth Reafon *of our* Ignorance *and* Error, viz. *the fallacy of our* Imaginati- ons; *an account of the nature of that faculty;* Inftances of its deceptions; *Spirits are not in a place;* Intellection, Volition, Decrees, *&c. cannot properly be afcrib'd to* God. *It is not* Reafon *that oppofeth* Faith, *but* Phancy: *the intereft which Imagination hath in many of our Opinions, in that it impreffes a perfwafion without evidence.*

Ourthly, we *erre* and come fhort of *Science,* becaufe we are fo frequently miflead by the evil conduct of our *Imaginations;* whofe irregular ftrength and importunity doth almoft perpetually abufe us. Now to make a full and clear difcovery of our *Phancies* decep- tions; 'twill be requifite to look into the nature of that *myfterious faculty.* In which furvey we muft trace the Soul in the wayes of her *intellectual* actions; whereby we may come to the diftinct knowledge of what is

meant

meant by *Imagination*, in contradiftinction to fome other
Powers. But firft premifing, that the *Souls nature* (at
leaft as far as concerns our inquiry) confifts in *intelli-*
gibility: And fecondly, that when we fpeak of *Powers*
and *Faculties* of the Soul, we intend not to affert with
the *Schools*, their *real* diftinction from it, or each other,
but only a *modal* diverfity. Therefore I fhall diftribute
Intellectual operations according to the known *triple* divi-
fion, though with fome difference of reprefentation.

The firft is *fimple apprehenfion*, which denotes no more,
then the fouls naked *Intellection* of an object, without
either *compofition* or *deduction*. The foundation of this
act, as to materials, is *fenfitive preception*. Now our *fimple*
apprehenfion of corporal objects, if *prefent*, we call
Senfe; if abfent, we properly name it *Imagination*. When
we would conceive a *material* object, our *phancies* prefent
us with it's *Idæa*. But in our Notion of *fpirituals*, we,
as much as we can, ftrip them of all *material Phantafmes*;
and thus they become the object of our *Intellects*, properly fo called. All this while the *foul* is, as it were, *filent*;
and in a more paffive way of reception.

But the *fecond act* advanceth propofitions from *fimple*
intellections: and hereby we have the knowledge of the
diftinctions or *identities* of objects. Now here, as in the
former, where they are purely *material*, the Judgment is
made by the *Imagination*: if otherwife, we refer it to the
Underftanding.

The

The *third Act*, is that which connects *Propoſitions* and deduceth *Concluſions* from them : and *this* the Schools call *Diſcourſe* ; and we ſhall not miſcal it, if we name it, *Reaſon*. *This* as it ſuppoſeth the two former, ſo is it grounded on certain *congenite propoſitions* ; which I conceive to be the very *Eſſentials* of Rationality. Such are, *Quodlibet eſt, vel non eſt* ; *Impoſſibile eſt idem eſſe, & non eſſe* ; *Non entis nulla ſunt prædicata*, and ſuch like. Not that every one hath naturally a *formal* and *explicit* notion of theſe *Principles* : For the Vulgar uſe them, without knowledge of them, under any ſuch *expreſs* conſideration ; But yet there was never any born to *Reaſon* without them. Now when the concluſion is deduc'd from the unerring dictates of our faculties ; we ſay the Inference is *Rational* : But when from miſ-apprehended, or illcompounded phantaſmes ; we aſcribe it to the *Imagination*. So we ſee, there is a triple operation of the *Phancy* as well as *Intellect* ; and theſe powers are only *circumſtantially* different. In this method we intend a diſtinct, though ſhort account, how the *Imagination* deceives us.

Firſt then, the *Imagination*, which is of *ſimple* perception, doth never of it ſelf and directly miſlead us ; as is at large declared in our former diſcourſe of *Senſe*. Yet is it the almoſt fatal means of our deception, through the unwarrantable *compoſitions*, *diviſions*, and *applications*, which it occaſions the *ſecond Act* to make of the *ſimple Images*. Hence we may derive the *Viſions*, *Voyces*, *Revelations* of
the

the *Enthufiaft* : the ftrong Idea's of which, being conjur'd up into the *Imagination* by the heat of the *melancholized* brain, are judged exterior *Realities* ; when as they
are but motions within the *Cranium*. Hence Story is full
of the wonders, it works upon *Hypochondriacal Imaginants* ; to whom the groffeft abfurdities are infallible certainties, and free reafon an Impoftour. That *Groom*, that
conceited himfelf an *Emperour*, thought all as irrational
as difloyal, that did not acknowledge him : And he, that
fuppofed himfelf made of Glafs, thought them all *mad*, that
dif-believed him. But we pity, or laugh at thofe fatuous
Extravagants ; while yet our felves have a confiderable
dofe of what makes them *fo* : and more fober heads have
a fet of mifconceits, which are as abfurd to an unpaffionated *reafon*, as thofe to our unabufed *fenfes*. And as the
greateft counter-evidence to thofe diftemper'd phancies
is none : fo in the more ordinary deceits, in which our
Imaginations infenfibly engage us, we give but little
credit to the uncorrupted fuggeftions of the faculty, that
fhould difabufe us.

That the *Soul* and *Angels* are devoid of *quantity* and
dimenfion, hath the fuffrage of the moft ; and that they
have nothing to do with groffer *locality*, is as generally
opinion'd : but who is it, that retains not a great part
of the impofture, by allowing them a *definitive Ubi*,
which is ftill but *Imagination* ? He that faid, a *thoufand*
might dance on the *point of a Needle*, fpake but grofsly ;
and we may as well fuppofe them to have *wings*, as a

L   proper

proper *Ubi.* We say, *Spirits* are where they operate:
But strictly to be in a *place*, or *ubi*, it may be is a
material Attribute, and incompatible with so pure a
Nature. We ask not, in what place a *thought* is, nor
are we solicitous for the *Ubi* of *Vertue*, or any other
Immaterial accidents. *Relations, Ubications, Duration,* the
vulgar Philosophy admits to be *Something*; and yet to
enquire in what *place* they are, were gross and in-
congruous. So that, if *to be,* and *to be in a place* be not
reciprocal; I know not why *Spirits* may not be exempted, having as much to plead from the *purity* of
their essence, as any thing in nature. And yet *Imagination* stands so strongly against the notion, that it
cannot look for the favour of a very diffusive entertainment.

But we are more dangerously deceiv'd, when judging
the *Infinite Essence* by our narrow selves; we ascribe *Intellections, Volitions, Decrees, Purposes,* and such like *Immanent
actions* to that nature, which hath nothing in common
with us, as being infinitely above us. Now to use these as
Hypotheseis, as himself in his Word, is pleas'd to low himself to our capacities, is allowable: But a strict and rigorous imputation is derogatory to him, and arrogant in
us. To say, that *God* doth *eminently* contain all those
effects in his glorious *simple Essence,* that the creature
can produce or act by such a *faculty, power,* or *affection*; is to affirm him to be what he is, *Infinite.*
Thus, to conceive that he can do all those things in
the

the moſt perfeſt manner , which we do upon *under-*
ſtanding, *willing*, and *decreeing*; is an apprehenſion
ſuteable to his *Idea*: But to fix on him the formality
of *faculties*, or *affeſtions*; is the Impoſture of our
Phancies, and contradiſtory to his *Divinity*. 'Tis this
deception miſleads the contending world; and is the
Author of moſt of that darkneſs and confuſion, that is
upon the face of the Controverſies of *Dort*. We being
then thus obnoxious to fallacy in our *apprehenſions*
and *judgments*, and ſo often impoſed upon by theſe
deceptions; our *Inferences* and *Deduſtions* muſt needs
be as unwarrantable, as our *ſimple* and *compound*
thoughts are deceitful. So that the *reaſon* of the far
greateſt part of mankind, is but an aggregate of miſtaken phantaſms; and in things *not ſenſible*, a conſtant deluſion. Yea the higheſt and moſt improved
Spirits, are frequently caught in the entanglements of
a tenacious *Imagination*; and ſubmit to its obſtinate,
but deluſory ſuggeſtions. Thus we are involv'd in
inextricable perplexities about the *Divine Nature*, and
Attributes; and in our reaſonings about thoſe ſublimities are puzled with contradictions, which are but
the toyings of our *Phancies*, no abſurdities to our
more *defæcate* faculties. What work do our *Imaginati-*
ons make with *Eternity* and *Immenſity*? and how are
we gravell'd by their cutting *Dilemma's*? I'm confident many have thus *imagin'd* themſelves out of their

L 2   *Religion*;

Religion: and run a ground on that more defperate abfurdity, *Atheifm*. To fay, *Reafon* oppofeth *Faith*, is to fcandalize both: 'Tis *Imagination* is the Rebel; *Reafon* contradicts its impious fuggeftions. Nor is our *Reafon* any more accountable for the Errours of our *Opinions*; then our *holinefs* for the *immoralities* of our *Lives*: And we may as well fay, that the *Sun* is the caufe of the *fhadow*, which is the effect of the inter-cepting *opacity*, as either. *Reafon* and *Faith* are at perfect *Unifons*: The difharmony is in the *Phancy*. Tὸ λογικόν ἐςι ϑεῖον, is a faying of *Plato's*; and well wor-thy a Chriftian fubfcription, *Reafon* being the Image of the Creators Wifdom copied out in the Creature. Though indeed, as 'tis now in the fubject, 'tis but an amafsment of *imaginary conceptions*, *præjudices*, *ungroun-ded opinions*, and infinite Impoftures; and 'tis no wonder, if thefe are at odds with the Principles of our belief: But all this is but *apifh Sophiftry*, and to give it a Name fo *Divine* and *excellent*, is abufive and unjuft.

There is yet another as deplorable a deceit of our *Imaginations*, as any: which is, its impreffing a ftrong perfwafion of the Truth of an *Opinion*, where there is no evidence to fupport it. And if it be fuch, as we never heard queftion'd or contradicted, 'tis then unfufpected. The moft of mankind is led by *opinio-native* impulfe, and *Imagination* is prædominant. An un-

ungrounded *credulity* is cry'd up for *faith* ; and the more vigorous impreſſions of *Phancy*, for the *Spirits* motions. Theſe are the grand deluſions of our Age , and the higheſt evidence of the *Imaginations* deceptions. This is the *ſpirit* , that works in the children of *Phancy* ; and we need not ſeek to remoter reſolutions. But the excellent Dr. *H. More* hath follow'd *Enthuſiaſtick effeᶜts* to their proper *Origine* , and prevented our endeavours of attempting it. His Diſcourſe of *Enthuſiaſm* compleatly makes good the Title ; and 'tis as well a *Victory* , as a *Triumph.*

L 3   CHAP.

Chap. XIV.

A fifth Reaſon, the præcipitancy of our Underſtandings; *the reaſon of it. The moſt cloſe engagement of our minds requiſite to the finding of truth; the difficulties of the performance of it. Two inſtances of our præcipitating; as the concluding things* impoſſible, *which to Nature are not ſo; and the joyning Cauſes with irrelative Effects.*

§. 5. AGain, another account of the *ſhortneſs* of of our *Reaſons* and eaſineſs of deception, is, the *forwardneſs* of our *Underſtandings aſſent*, to ſlightly examin'd *concluſions*, contracting many times a firm and obſtinate belief from weak inducements; and that not only in ſuch things, as immediately concern the *ſenſe*, but in almoſt every thing that falls within the ſcope of our enquiry. For the declarement of this, we are to obſerve, That every being unceſſantly aſpires to its own *perfection*, and is reſtleſs till it obtain it; as is the trembling *Needle*, till it find its
beloved

beloved North. Now the perfection of a Faculty is Union with its Object, to which its reſpective actions are
directed, as the ſcope and term of its endeavours. Thus
our Underſtanding being prefected by *Truth,* with all
the impatience, which accompanies ſtrong deſire,
breaths after its enjoyment. But now the *good* and perfection of *being,* which every thing reacheth at, muſt be
known, and that in the particular inſtances thereof; or
elſe 'tis not attain'd : and if it be miſtaken, that *being*
courts deceit and its own deluſion. This *Knowledge* of
their *Good,* was at firſt as natural to all things, as the
deſire on't : otherwiſe this innate propenſion would
have been as much a torment and miſery to thoſe things
that are capable of it, as a needleſs impertinency to all
others. But Nature ſhoots not at *Rovers.* Even *inanimates,*though they know not their perfection themſelves,
yet are they not carryed on by a blind unguided *impetus* :
But that which directs them, knows it. The next or-
ders of being have ſome ſight of it themſelves : And
man moſt perfectly had it, before his unhappy defection. So then beſide this generel propenſity to Truth ,
the *Underſtanding* muſt know what is *ſo,* before it can
aſſent. The former we poſſeſs (it may be) as entirely as
when Nature gave it us : but of the latter , little but
the capacity : So that herein have we made our ſelves
of all creatures the moſt miſerable. And now, ſuch an
Infinite of *uncertain opinions,* bare *probabilities* , ſpecious
falſhoods, ſpreading themſelves before us, and ſolliciting
our

our belief, and we being thus greedy of *Truth*, and yet so unable to discern it: it cannot be, that we should reach it any otherwise, then by the most close *meditation* and engagement of our minds; by which we must endeavour to estrange our assent from every thing, which is not *clearly* and *distinctly* evidenc't to our *faculties*. But this is so difficult; and as hath been intimated, so almost infeasable; that it may well drive modesty to despair of *Science*. For though possibly Assiduity in the most fixed cogitation be no trouble or pain to *immaterializ'd spirits*; yet is it more, then our *embodyed souls* can bear without lassitude or distemper. For in this terrestrial state there are few things transacted, even in our *Intellectual* part, but through the help and furtherance of *corporal* Instruments; which by more then ordinary usage lose their edge and fitness for action, and so grow inept for their respective destinations. Upon this account our *senses* are dull'd and spent by any extraordinary intention; and our very *Eyes* will ake, if long fixt upon any difficultly discerned object. Now though *Meditation* be to be reckoned among the most abstracted operations of our minds; yet can it not be performed without a considerable proportion of *Spirits* to assist the Action, though indeed such as are furnish't out of the bodies purer store. Which I think to be clear from hence, in that fixed seriousness herein, heats the brain in some to distraction, causeth an aking and diziness in sounder heads, hinders the works of Nature in its lower and

animal

animal functions, takes away or leſſens pain in diſtemper'd parts, and ſeldom leaves any but under a wearyſome dulneſs, and inactivity : Arguments of ſufficient validity to juſtifie our aſſent to this, that the *ſpirits* are imploy'd in our moſt *intenſe* cogitations, yea in ſuch, whoſe objects are leaſt *material*. Now the managing and carrying on of this work by the *Spirits* inſtrumental *co-efficiency* requires, that they be kept together without diſtraction or diſſipation ; that ſo they may be ready to receive and execute the orders and commiſſions of the commanding faculty. If either of theſe happen, all miſcarries : as do the works of Nature, when they want that *heat*, which is requiſite for their intended *perfection*. And therefore, for the prevention of ſuch inconveniences in *meditation*, we chooſe receſs and ſolitude.

But now if we conſider the *volatile* nature of thoſe *officious Aſſiſtants*, and the ſeveral cauſes which occur continually, even from the meer *Mechaniſm* of our Bodies to ſcatter and diſorder them, beſides the excurſions of our roving *phancies* (which cannot be kept to a cloſe attendance) ; it will be found very hard to retain them in any long ſervice, but do what we can, they'l get looſe from the Minds *Regimen*. So that it's no eaſie matter to bring the body to be what it was intended for, the *Souls ſervant*; and to confine the *imagination*, of as facil a performance, as the *Goteham's* deſign of hedging in the *Cuckow*. And though ſome conſtitutions are genially diſpoſited to this mental ſeriouſneſs;

M   yet

yet they can fcarce fay, *Nos numeri fumus:* yea in the moft advantag'd tempers, this difpofition is but *comparative*; when as the moft of men labour under difadvantages, which nothing can rid them of, but that which loofens them from this mafs of flefh. Thus the boyling blood of youth, fiercely agitating the fluid Air, hinders that ferenity and fixed ftayednefs, which is neceffary to fo fevere an intentnefs: And the frigidity of decrepit age is as much its enemy, not only through penury of *fpirits,* but by reafon of its dulling moifture. And even in the temperate *zone* of our life, there are few bodies at fuch an *æquipoiz* of humours; but that the prevalency of fome one indifpofeth the *Spirits* for a work fo difficult and ferious: For *temper amentum ad pondus,* may well be reckon'd among the *Philofophical unattainables.* Befides, the buftle of bufinefs, the avocations of our fenfes, and external pleafures, and the noyfe and din of a clamorous world, are impediments not to be mafter'd by feeble endeavours. And to fpeak the full of my Sentiments, I think never man could boaft it, without the Precincts of *Paradife*; but *He,* that came to gain us a better *Eden* then we loft.

So then, to direct all this to our end, the mind of man being thus naturally amorous of, and impatient for *Truth,* and yet averfe to, and almoft incapacitated for that diligent and painful fearch, which is neceffary to its difcovery; it muft needs take up fhott, of what is really *fo,* and pleafe it felf in the poffeffion of imaginary appearances,

pearances, which offering themfelves to its embraces in the borrowed attire of that, which the *enamour'd Intellect* is in purfuit of, our impatient minds entertain thefe counterfeits, without the leaft fufpicion of their coufe-nage. For as the *Will*, having loft its true and fubftantial *Good*, now courts the fhadow, and greedily catches at the vain fhews of *fuperficial* blifs : fo our no lefs degenerate *underftandings* having fuffered as fad a divorce from their deareft object, are as forward to defile themfelves with every meretricious femblance, that the variety of opini-on prefents them with. Thus we fee the inconfiderate vulgar, proftrating their affent to every fhallow appea-rance : and thofe, who are beholden to *Prometheus* for a finer mould, are not furnifht with fo much truth as otherwife they might be owners of, did not this *pre-cipitancy* of *concluding* prevent them : As 'tis faid of the induftrious *Chymift*, that by catching at it too foon, he loft the long expected treafure of the *Philofophical Elixir*. Now this precipitancy of our underftandings is an oc-cafion of a double error, very injurious to the encreafe of Knowledge. To inftance,

(1.) Hence we conclude many things *Impoßibilities*, which yet are eafie *Feafables*. For by an unadvifed tran-filiency leaping from the effect to its remoteft caufe, we obferve not the connexion through the interpofal of more immediate caufalities; which yet at laft bring the extreams together without a *Miracle*. And here-

M 2

upon we haſtily conclude *that impoſſible*, which we ſee not in the proximate capacity of its *Efficient.* That a ſingle *Hair* ſhould root up an *Oak* (which the Mathematicks teach us to be poſſible) by common heads will be thought an abſurd and extravagant expectation. And the relation of *Archimedes's* lifting up the ſhips of *Marcellus*, among many finds but little more credit, then that of the *Gyants* ſhouldering *Mountains* : And yet Mathematicians know, that by multiplying of Mechanical advantages, any power may conquer any reſiſtance, and the great *Syracuſian wit* wanteth but *Tools*, and a *place* to ſtand on, to remove the *Earth.* So that the brag of the *Ottoman*, [*That he would throw* Malta *into the Sea*] might be performed at an eaſier rate, then by the ſhovels of his *Janizaries.*

And (2.) from this laſt noted head, ariſeth that other of *joyning cauſes with irrelative effects*, which either refer not at all unto them, or in a remoter capacity. Hence the *Indian* conceiv'd ſo groſly of the *Letter*, that diſcover'd his *Theft*; and that other, who thought the Watch an *Animal.* From hence grew the impoſtures of *Charmes*, and *Amulets*, and other inſignificant ceremonies ; which to this day impoſe upon common belief, as they did of old upon the *Barbariſm* of the incultivate *Heathen.* Thus effects unuſual, whoſe cauſes run under ground, and are

more

more remote from ordinary discernment, are noted in the Book of *Vulgar Opinion*, with *Digitus Dei*, or *Dæmonis*; though they owe no other dependence to the *first*, then what is common to the whole *Syntax* of beings, nor yet any more to the *second*, then what is given it by the imagination of those unqualifi'd Judges. Thus every unwonted *Meteor* is portentous; and the appearance of any unobserved *Star*, some divine *Prognostick*. Antiquity thought *Thunder* the immediate voyce of *Jupiter*, and impleaded them of impiety, that referr'd it to natural causalities. Neither can there happen a *storm*, at this remove from *Antique* ignorance, but the multitude will have the *Devil* in't.

M 3　　　Chap.

CHAP. XV.

*The ſixth Reaſon diſcours't of, viz. the in-
tereſt which our* Affections *have in our*
*Dijudications. The cauſe why our Af-
fections miſlead us: ſeveral branches of
this mention'd; and the firſt, viz.* Conſtitutional Inclination *largely inſiſted on.*

A Gain (6.) we owe much of our *Erronr* and *Intellectual ſcarcity* to the Intereſt in, and power
which our *affections* have over our ſo eaſie ſedu-
cible Underſtandings. And 'tis a truth well worthy the
Pen, from which it dropt; *Periit Judicium, ubi res
tranſiit in Affectum.* That *Jove* himſelf cannot be *wiſe*
and in *Love*, may be underſtood in a larger ſenſe,
then Antiquity meant it. *Affection* bribes the Judgement
to the moſt notorious inequality; and we cannot expect an equitable award, where the Judge is made a
Party: So that, that underſtanding only is capable of
giving a juſt deciſion, which is, as *Ariſtotle* ſaith of the
Law, Νους ἄνευ ὀρέξεως: But where the *Will*, or *Paſſion*
hath the caſting voyce, the caſe of *Truth* is *deſperate.*
And yet this is the miſerable diſorder, into which we
are

are laps'd: The lower Powers are gotten uppermost; and we *see* like men on our *heads*, as *Plato*. observ'd of old, that on the *right* hand, which indeed is on the *left*. The *Woman* in us, still prosecutes a deceit, like that begun in the *Garden*: and our *Understandings* are wedded to an *Eve*, as fatal as the *Mother* of our *miseries*. And while all things are judg'd according to their suitableness, or disagreement to the *Gusto* of the fond *Feminine*; we shall be as far from the *Tree of Knowledge*, as from that which is guarded by the *Cherubin*. The deceiver soon found this soft place of *Adam*'s; and Innocency it self did not secure him from this way of *seduction*. The first deception enter'd in at this Postern, and hath ever since kept it open for the entry of *Legion*: so that we scarce see any thing now but through our *Passions*, the most blind, and sophisticate things about us. The *Monsters* which story relates to have their *Eyes* in their *breasts*, are *pictures* of us in our *invisible selves*. Our *Love* of one Opinion induceth us to embrace it; and our *Hate* of another, doth more then fit us, for its rejection: And, *that Love is blind*, is extensible beyond the object of *Poetry*. When once the *affections* are engag'd, there's but a short step to the Understanding: and, *Facilè-credimus quod volumus*, is a truth, that needs not plead Authority to credit it.

The reason, I conceive, is this: *Love* as it were *uniting* the Object to the *Soul*, gives it a kind of *Identity* with us; so that the beloved *Idea* is but *our selves* in another

Name:

Name: and when *ſelf* is at the bar, the ſentence is not like to be impartial: For every man is naturally a *Narciſſus*, and each *paſſion* in us, no other but *ſelf-love* ſweetned by milder Epithets. We can love nothing, but what we find agreeable to our ſelves; and our deſire of what is *ſo*, hath its firſt inducement from within us: Yea, we love nothing but what reſembleth us; and whatever we applaud as good or excellent, is but *ſelf* in a *tranſcript*, and *è contrà*. Thus to reach the higheſt of our *Amours*, and to ſpeak all at once: We love our *friends*, becauſe they are our *Image*; and we love our *God*, becauſe we are *His*. So then, the *beloved* Opinion being thus wedded to the *Intellect*; the caſe of our *eſpouſed ſelf* becomes our own: And when we weigh our ſelves, *Juſtice* doth not uſe to hold the ballance.

Beſides, all things being double-handed, and having the appearances both of *Truth*, and *Falſhood*; where our *affections* have engaged us, we attend only to the former, which we ſee through a magnifying *Medium*: while looking on the latter, through the wrong end of the *Perſpective*, which ſcants their dimenſions, we neglect and contemn them. Yea, and as in corrupt judicial proceedings, the fore-ſtalled Underſtanding paſſes a peremptory ſentence upon the ſingle hearing of one Party; and ſo though it may chance to be right in the *concluſion*; is yet unjuſt and miſtaken in the method of *Inference*.

But

But to give a more particular account of this Impoſture; our Affections engage us either,

    (1.) By our Love to our Selfs : or,

    (2.) By our Love to Others.

The former, in the Inſtances of,

    (1.) *Natural diſpoſition.*

    (2.) *Cuſtome* and *Education.*

    (3.) *Intereſt.* And

    (4.) Love of our own *Productions.*

The latter, in the homage which is paid to *Antiquity,*
    and *Authority.*

Theſe are cauſes of our Miſtakes, and Arguments
that we can ſcarce do otherwiſe. And therefore I ſpeak
to them in their order.

    1. *Congruity* of Opinions, whether true or falſe, to
our *natural conſtitution,* is one great incentive to their
reception : For in a ſenſe the *complexion* of the *mind,*
as well as *manners,* follows the *Temperament* of the
Body. On this account ſome men are genially diſpoſed
to ſome *Opinions,* and naturally as averſe to others.
And we *love* and *hate* without a known cauſe of
either. Some Faces both of Perſons and Things, we
admire and dote on : others, in our impartial apprehenſions no leſs deſerving our eſteem, we can behold
without reſentment; yea it may be with an invincible diſregard. And I queſtion not, but *intellectual* re-
        N   preſen-

prefentations are received by us, with as unequal a
Fate upon a bare *Temperamental* Relifh or Difguft:
The *Understanding* alfo hath its *Idiofyncrafies*, as well
as other faculties. So that the great ftirrs of the difputing World, are but the conflicts of the humours.
Superftition, *Atheifm*, and *Enthufiafm*, are tempers; not
meer infufions of *Education*, and *Opinion*. Indeed the
dull and unactive fpirits that concern not themfelves
in *Theory*, follow the fwinge of the common belief in which they were firft inftructed: But the more
vigorous and *ftirring* will fall into *that* of their particular *Crafis*. And when the humour is awakened,
all the bonds of Cuftome and Education cannot hold
them. The opinions which are fuited to their refpective tempers will make way to their affent, in
fpight of accidental preingagements. Thus *opinions*
have their *Climes* and *National* diverfities: And as
fome Regions have their proper Vices, not fo generally found in others; fo have they their mental depravities, which are drawn in with the air of their
Countrey. And perhaps this is a confiderable caufe
of the diverfity of *Lawes*, *Cuftomes*, *Religions*, *natural* and *moral* Doctrines, which is to be found in
the divided Regions of the inhabited Earth. Wherefore I wonder not at the *Idolatry* of the *Jewes* of old,
or of the feveral parts of the world to this day, at
the *fenfual expectation* of the *Muffel-men*, the *circumftan-*
tial

tial follies of the *Papists*, or the antick devotions of the barbarous *Indians*; since that the most senselesse conceits and fooleries cannot miss of Harbor, where *affection* grown upon the stock of a *depraved constitution*, hath endeared them.

And if we do but more nearly look into our *faculties*, beginning our survey from the lowest dregs of *sense*, even those which have a nearer commerce with *matter*, and so by steps ascend to our more *spiritualiz'd selves*: we shall throughly discover how *constitutional partiality* swayes us. To begin then at the *Sences*; that to one *Palate* is *sweet*, and *delicious*, which to another, is *odious* and *distastful*; or more compendiously in the Proverb, *One mans meat, is anothers poyson*. What to one is a most grateful *odour*, to another is *noxious* and *displeasant*; and 'twere a misery to some to lye stretch't on a bed of Roses: That's a *welcome touch* to one, which is *disagreeing* to another; The same *Aires* which some entertain with most delightful transports, to others are importune; and the objects which *this* man can't *see* without an *Extasie*, *that* is no more mov'd at than a *Statue*. If we pass further, the *phancies* of men are so immediately diversify'd by the individual *Crasis*, that every man is in this a *Phœnix*; and owns something wherein none are like him: and these are as many, as humane nature hath *singulars*. Now the *phancies* of the most,

like

like the *Index* of a Clock, are moved but by the inward *Springs* and *Wheels* of the corporal *Machine*; which even on the moſt ſublimed Intellectuals is dangerouſly *influential*. And yet this ſits at the **Helm** of the Worlds belief; and Vulgar *Reaſon* is no better then a more *refined Imagination.* So then the *Senſes*, *Phancy*, and what we call *Reaſon* it ſelf, being thus influenc'd by the *Bodies temperament*, and little better then indications of it; it cannot be otherwiſe, but that this *Love of our ſelves* ſhould ſtrongly incline us in our moſt *Abſtracted Dijudications.*

CHAP.

CHAP. XVI.

A second thing whereby our Affections ingage us in Error; is the prejudice of Custom *and* Education. *A third,* Interest. *The fourth,* Love *to our own* Productions.

2. **A** Nother branch of this *selfish fondness*, by reason of which we miscarry of *Science*, is the almost insuperable *prejudice* of *Custom*, and *Education*: by which our minds are encumber'd, and the most are held in a *Fatal Ignorance* Yea could a man be composed to such an advantage of constitution, that it should not at all adulterate the images of his mind; yet this *second nature* would alter the *crasis* of the Understanding, and render it as obnoxious to aberrances, as now. And though in the former regard, the *Soul* were a pure ἄγραφον γραμμάτιον; yet *custom* and *education* would scrible into an incapacity of new *impressions*. Thus we judge all things by our *anticipations*; and condemn or applaud them, as they agree or differ from our *first receptions*. One Countrey laughs at the *Laws, Customs,* and *Opinions* of another,

as

as abſurd and ridiculous; and the other is as charitable to them, in its conceit of theirs. This confirms the moſt ſottiſh *Idolaters* in their accuſtomed adorations, beyond the conviction of any thing, but *Dooms-day.* The impreſſions of a barbarous *education* are ſtronger in them, then *nature*; when in their cruel *worſhips* they launce themſelves with knifes, and expoſe their harmleſs *Infants* to the *flames* as a Sacrifice to their *Idols.* And 'tis on this account, that there's no Religion ſo irrational, but can boaſt its *Martyrs.* This is it, which befriends the *Talmud* and *Alcoran*; and did they not owe their credit more to cuſtomary and præingag'd Aſſent, then to any rational inducement, we might expect their *aſhes*: whereas *Education* hath ſo rooted theſe miſ-believers in their ungrounded *faith*, that they may aſſoon be pluck't from themſelves, as from their obſtinate adherencies; and to convert a *Turk*, or *Jew*, may be well a *phraſe* for an attempt *impoſſible.* We look for it *only* from him, to whom our *Impoſſibles* are *none.* And 'tis to be feared, that *Chriſtianity* it ſelf by moſt, that have eſpouſed it, is not held by any better tenure. The beſt account that many can give of their *belief*, is, that they were *bred* in it; and the moſt are driven to their Religion by *cuſtom* and *education*, as the *Indians* are to *Baptiſm*; that is, like a drove of Cattle to the water. So that had *Providence* determin'd our nativities among the Enemies of the *Croſs*, and theirs under a *Chriſtian horoſcope*; in all likely-hood we ſhould have exchang'd the Scene of our belief

lief with that of our abode and *breeding*. There is nothing ſo abſurd, to which *education* cannot form our
ductile *minority* ; it can lick us into ſhapes beyond the
monſtroſities of *Africa*. And as King *James* would ſay of
Parliaments, *It can do any thing but make a Man a Woman*. For our initial age is like the melted wax to the
prepared Seal, capable of any impreſſion from the documents of our Teachers. The *half-moon* or *Croſs*, are indifferent to its reception ; and we may with equal facility write on this *Raſa Tabula*, Turk, or Chriſtian. To
determine this indifferency, our firſt task is to learn the
Creed of our Countrey ; and our next to maintain it. We
ſeldom examine our Receptions, more then children
do their *Catechiſms* ; but by a *careleſs greedineſs* ſwallow
all at a venture. For *Impiicit* faith is a vertue, where *Orthodoxie* is the object. Some will not be at the trouble
of a Tryal : others are ſcar'd from attempting it. If
we do, 'tis not by a *Sun-beam* or ray of univerſal light ;
but by a *flame* that's kindled by our *affections*, and fed
by the fewel of our *anticipations*. And thus like the
Hermite, we think the *Sun* ſhines no where, but in our
Cell ; and all the world to be darkneſs but our ſelves.
We judge truth to be circumſcrib'd by the confines of
our belief, and the doctrines we were brought up in : and
with as ill manners, as thoſe of *China*, repute all the
reſt of the world, *Monoculous*. So that what ſome *Aſtrologers* ſay of our *Fortunes* and the paſſages of our lives ;
may by the allowance of a *Metaphor* be ſaid of our
Opinions :

Opinions : That they are written in our *stars,* being to the moſt as fatal as thoſe involuntary occurrences, and as little in their Power as the *placits* of *deſtiny.* We are bound to our Countreys *Opinions,* as to its *Laws* : and an accuſtomed aſſent is *tantamount* to an infallible con- cluſion. He that offers to diſſent, ſhall be an *Out-law* in reputation : and the fears of guilty *Cain,* ſhall be fulfil- led on him, who ever *meets* him *ſhall ſlay him.* Thus *Cuſtome* and *Education* have ſealed the *Canon* ; and he that adds or takes away from the Book of *Orthodox* be- lief, ſhall be more then in danger of an *Anathema* : And the *Inquiſition* is not confined to the juriſdiction of the *Triple-Crown.* The rankeſt follies are *Sacred,* if *cuſtoma- ry* ; and the *Faſhion* is *handſome,* and *agreeable* , though never ſo *uncouth* to an unconcern'd beholder. Their *antick* deckings with *feathers* is as comly in the account of thoſe barbarous Nations , which uſe them ; as the Ornaments of *Lace,* and *Ribband,* are in ours. And the plucking off the ſhooe is to the *Japonians* as decent a ſa- lutation, as the uncovering of the *head* is to us, and their abhorred *neighbours.* And as we are fond of every thing with which *cuſtom* hath acquainted us ; ſo on the other hand we ſtart and boggle at every *unuſual* appearance, and cannot endure the ſight of the *bug-bear,* *Novelty.* On this account very innocent truth's are often affix't with the reproach of *Hereſie* ; and made terrible things in the imaginations of their miſinform'd and frighted enemies ; who like children ſcared in the dark, fly the

Monſters

Monsters of their *Phancies*, and dare not stay to take a true account of the object of their fears. So that there is scarce any truth, but it's adversaries have made it an ugly *Vizard*; by which it's exposed to the hate and disesteem of superficial examiners: For an opprobrious title with vulgar believers is as good as an *Argument*. And 'tis but writing the name, that customary receptions have discredited, under the opinions we dislike; and all other refutation is superfluous. Thus shallow apprehenders are frighted from many sober *Verities*; like the King of *Arabs*, who ran away from the *smoaking Mince-Py*, apprehending some dangerous plot in the harmless steam.

So then, while we thus mistake the infusions of *education*, for the *principles* of universal *nature*; we must needs fail of a *scientifical Theory*. And therefore the two Nations differing about the *antiquity* of their Language, made appeal to an undecisive *experiment*; when they agreed upon the tryal of a child brought up among the wild Inhabitants of the Desert. The *Language* it spake, had no reason to be accounted the most ancient and natural: And the lucky determination for the *Phygians* by its pronouncing the word *Beck*, which signified Bread in the dialect of that Countrey, they owed not to *Nature*, but the *Goat-herd*; from which the exposed Infant, by accompanying that sort of *animals*, had learnt it.

Again

Again (3.) *Intereſt* is another thing, by the *magnetiſme* of which our *affections* are almoſt irreſiſtibly attracted. It is the *Pole*, to which we turn, and our *ſympathizing* Judgements ſeldom decline from the *direction* of this *Impregnant.* Where *Intereſt* hath engaged men; they'l find a way to Truth, or make one. Any thing is *good* and *true*, to one whoſe *Intereſt* it is, to have it ſo. And therefore Self-deſigners are ſeldome diſappointed, for want of the ſpeciouſneſs of a cauſe to warrant them; in the belief of which, they do oft as really impoſe upon themſelves, as they induſtriouſly endeavour it upon others. With what an infinite of *Law-ſuits, controverſies*, and *litigious caſes* doth the world abound? and yet every man is confident of the truth and goodneſs of his own. And it may be as Maſter *Hobbs* obſerves, one reaſon that Mathematical demonſtrations are uncontroverted, is, becauſe *Intereſt* hath no place in thoſe unqueſtionable *verities*: when as, did the advantage, of any ſtand againſt them, perhaps *Euclids Elements* would not paſs with ſo univerſal a ſuffrage. Sir *H. Blunt* tells us, that temporal expectations bring in droves to the *Mahumetan Faith*; and we know the ſame holds thouſands in the *Romiſh*. The *Eagles* will be, where the *carcaſe* is; and that ſhall have the faith of moſt, which is beſt able

to

to pay them for't. An advantagious caufe never wanted *Profelytes.* I confefs, I cannot believe all the learned *Romanifts* profefs againft their *confcience*; but rather, that their *Intereft* brings their *confciences* to their *Profeſſion*: and felf-advantage can as eafily incline fome, to believe a falfhood, as profefs it. A good *will*, help'd by a good *wit*, can find Truth any where: and, what the *Chymifts* brag of their *Elixir*, it can tranflate any *metal* into *gold*, in the hand of a skilful Artificer, in fpight of the Adage, *Ex quo= libet ligno Mercurius.* Though yet I think, that every Religion hath its bare *Nominals*: and that Pope was one with a witnefs, whofe faying it was, *Quantum nobis lucri peperit illa fabula de Chrifto!*

4. Befides, fourthly, *Self=love* engageth us for any thing, that is a *Minerva* of our own. And thereby detains us in the fnares of *ignorance* and *folly.* We love the iſſues of our *Brains*, no lefs then thofe of our *bodies*: and fondnefs of our own *begotten notions*, though *illegitimate*, obligeth us to maintain them. We hugge intellectual deformities, if they bear our Names; and will hardly be perfwaded they are fo, when our felves are their Authors. If their *Dam* may be judge, the young *Apes* are the moft beautiful things in Nature; and if we might determine it, our proper conceptions would be all voted *Axioms.* Thus then

O 2   the

the *Female* rules, and our *Affections* wear the breeches : while our *Understandings* govern, as the story saith *Themistocles* did *Athens.* So that to give the sum of all, most of the contests of the litigious world pretending for *Truth*, are but the bandyings of one mans *affections* against anothers : in which, though their reasons may be foil'd, yet their *Passions* lose no ground, but rather improve by the *Antiperistasis* of an opposition.

CHAP.

CHAP. XVII.

5. *Our* Affections *are engaged by our Reverence to* Antiquity *and* Authority. *This hath been a great hinderer of Theorical improvements; and it hath been an advantage to the* Mathematicks, *and* Mechanicks *Arts, that it hath no place in them. Our mistake of* Antiquity. *The unreasonableness of that kind of Pedantick Adoration. Hence the vanity of affecting impertinent quotations. The Pedantry on't is derided; the little improvement of* Science *through its successive derivations, and whence that hath hapned.*

ANother thing, that engageth our *affections* to unwarrantable conclusions, and is therefore fatal to *Science;* is our doting on *Antiquity,* and the opinion of our *Fathers.* We look with a superstitious reverence upon the accounts of præterlapsed ages : and with a supercilious severity, on the more deserving

products

products of our own. A vanity, which hath poſſeſs'd all times as well as ours; and the *golden Age* was never *preſent*. For as in *Statick* experiment, an inconſiderable weight by virtue of its diſtance from the Centre of the Ballance, will preponderate much greater magnitudes; ſo the moſt ſlight and chaffy opinion, if at a greater remove from the preſent age, contracts ſuch an eſteem and veneration, that it out-weighs what is infinitely more ponderous and rational, of a *modern* date. And thus, in another ſenſe, we realize what *Archimedes* had only in *Hypotheſis*; weighing a ſingle *grain* againſt the *Globe* of Earth. We reverence gray-headed Doctrines; though feeble, decrepit, and within a ſtep of duſt: and on this account maintain opinions, which have nothing but our *charity* to uphold them. While the *beauty* of a Truth, as of a *picture*, is not acknowledg'd but at a *diſtance*; and that wiſdom is nothing worth, which is not fetcht from *afar*: wherein yet we oft deceive our ſelves, as did that *Mariner*, who miſtaking them for precious ſtones, brought home his ſhip fraught with common *Pebbles* from the remoteſt *Indies*. Thus our Eyes, like the *preposterous Animals*, are behind us; and our Intellectual motions *retrograde*. We adhere to the determinations of our fathers, as if their *opinions* were entail'd on us as their *lands*; or (as ſome conceive) part of the Parents ſoul were portion'd out to his off-ſpring, and the conceptions of our minds were *ex traduce*. The Sages of old live again in us; and in opinions there is a *Metempſychoſis*.

tempſychoſis. We are our re-animated *Anceſtours,* and antedate their *Reſurrection.*

And thus, while every age is but another ſhew of the
former ; 'tis no wonder, that Science hath not out-grown
the dwarfiſhneſs of its *priſtine ſtature,* and that the *Intelle-*
ctual world is ſuch a *Microcoſm.* For while we account of
ſome admired Authors, as the *Seths Pillars,* on which all
knowledge is engraven ; and ſpend that time and ſtudy
in defence of their Placits, which with more advantage
to Science might have been employ'd upon the Books
of the more ancient, and *univerſal Author* : 'Tis not to
be admired, that Knowledge hath receiv'd ſo little improvement from the endeavours of many pretending
promoters, through the continued ſeries of ſo many ſucceſſive ages. For while we are ſlaves to the *Dictates* of
our *Progenitours* ; our diſcoveries, like *water,* will not
run higher then the *Fountains,* from which they own
their derivation. And while we think it ſo piaculous, to
go beyond the *Ancients* ; we muſt neceſſarily come ſhort
of genuine *Antiquity, Truth* ; unleſs we ſuppoſe them to
have reach'd perfection of Knowledge in ſpight of their
own acknowledgements of *Ignorance.*

Now if we enquire the reaſon, why the *Math. maticks,*
and *Mechanick Arts,* have ſo much got the ſtart in
growth of other *Sciences* : we ſhall find it probably
reſolv'd into this, as one conſiderable cauſe : that their
progreſs hath not been retarded by that reverential aw
of former diſcoveries, which hath been ſo great an
hinderance

hinderance to Theorical improvements. 'Twas never an
herefie to out=limn *Apelles* ; nor criminal to out-work
the *Obelisks*. *Galilæus* without a crime out-faw all *Anti=
quity*, and was not afraid to believe his eyes, in fpight
of the *Opticks* of *Ptolomy* and *Ariftotle*. 'Tis no difcredit
to the *Telefcope* that Antiquity ne're faw in't : Nor are
we fhy of affent to thofe *celeftial* informations, becaufe
they were *hid from ages*. We believe the *verticity* of the
Needle, without a Certificate from the *dayes of old* : And
confine not our felves to the fole conduct of the *Stars*,
for fear of being wifer then our Fathers. Had *Authority* prevail'd here, the Earths *fourth part* had to us
been none, and *Hercules* his Pillars had ftill been the
worlds *Non ultra* : *Seneca's* Prophefie had been an un•
fulfill'd Prediction, and one moiety of our *Globes*, an
empty *Hemifphere*.

In a fenfe, Τὰ ἀϱχαῖα ϰϱατείτω, is a wholefom inftruction ; and becoming the Vote of a *Synod* : But yet, in
common acceptation, it's an Enemy to Verity, which
can plead the *antiquity* of above *fix thoufand* ; and bears
date from before the *Chaos*. For, as the Noble Lord
Verulam hath noted, we have a miftaken apprehenfion
of *Antiquity* ; calling that fo, which in truth is the worlds
Nonage. *Antiquitas feculi eft juventus Mundi*. So that
in fuch appeals, we fetch our knowledge from the
Cradle ; which though it be nearest to *Innocence*,
it is fo too to the fatal ruines which follow'd it.
Upon a true account, the *prefent age* is the worlds *Grandævity* ;

dævity ; and if we muſt to *Antiquity, Let multitude of dayes speak.* Now for us to ſuperſede further diſquiſition, upon the immature acquirements of thoſe Juvenile endeavours, is fooliſhly to neglect the nobler advantages we are owners of, and in a ſenſe to diſappoint the expectations of him that gave them. Yet thus hath the world prevented it ſelf of *Science.* And *aged* Knowledge, is ſtill an *Infant.* We *ſuperſtitiouſly* ſit down in the Acquiſitions of our Fathers ; and are diſcouraged from attempting further then they have gone before us. So that, but for the undertakings of ſome glorious perſons, who now and then ſhine upon the world, *Plato's* year might have found us, where the dayes of *Ariſtotle* left us. For my part, I think it no ſuch arrogance, as ſome are pleaſed to account it, that almoſt two thouſand years elapſed ſince, ſhould *weigh* with the *ſixty three* of the *Stagirite.* If we owe it to him, that we know ſo much ; 'tis perhaps long of his fond adorers that we know ſo little more. I can ſee no ground, why his Reaſon ſhould be *textuary* to ours ; or that God, or Nature, ever intended him an Univerſal *Headſhip.* 'Twas this vain Idolizing of Authors, which gave birth to that ſilly vanity of *impertinent citations* ; and inducing *Authority* in things neither requiring, nor deſerving it. That ſaying was much more obſervable, *That men have beards, and women none* ; becauſe quoted from *Beza* : and that other, *Pax res bona eſt* ; becauſe brought in with a, *ſaid* St. *Auguſtine.* But theſe ridiculous fooleries, ſignifie no-

P   thing

thing to the more generous difcerners, but the *Pedantry* of the affected *Sciolift*. 'Tis an inglorious acquift to have our heads or Volumes laden, as were Cardinal *Campeius* his Mules, with old and ufelefs luggage : And yet the magnificence of many high pretenders to Science, if laid open by a true difcovery, would amount to no more then the old *Boots* and *Shooes*, of that proud, and expofed *Embaffadour*. Methinks 'tis a pitiful piece of Knowledge, that can be learnt from an *Index*; and a poor Ambition to be rich in the Inventory of anothers Treafure. To boaft a *memory* (the moft that thefe Pedants can aim at) is but an humble oftentation. And of all the faculties, in which fome Brutes out-vie us, I leaft envy them an excellence in that; defiring rather to be a *Fountain*, then an *Hogs-head*. 'Tis better to own a Judgment, though but with a *Curta fupellex* of coherent notions ; then a *memory*, like a Sepulchre, furnifhed with a load of broken and difcarnate bones. *Authorities* alone with me make no *number*, unlefs Evidence of Reafon ftand before them : For all the *Cyphers* of *Arithmatick*, are no better then a fingle *nothing*. And yet this rank folly of affecting fuch impertinencies, hath overgrown our Times; and thofe that are Candidates for the repute of *Scholars*, take this way to compafs it. When as multiplicity of reading, the beft it can fignifie, doth but fpeak them to have taken pains for it : And this alone is but the dry and barren part of Knowledge, and hath little reafon to denominate. A number of *Receipts* at the beft can but make an *Emperick*.

But

But again, to what is more perpendicular to our difcourfe, if we impartially look into the remains of *Antique* Ages; we fhall finde but little to juftifie fo groundlefs a Tyranny, as *Antiquity* hath impos'd on the enflaved world. For if we take an account of the ftate of *Science*, beginning as high as Hiftory can carry us; we fhall find it ftill to have lain under fuch unhappy difadvantages as have hindred it's advance in any confiderable degrees of improvement. And though it hath oft chang'd its Channel, by its remove from one Nation to another; yet hath it been little more alter'd, then a *River* in its paffage through differing *Regions*, *viz.* in *Name* and *Method.* For the fucceeding times ftill fubfcribing to, and copying out thofe, who went before them, with little more then *verbal* diverfity; *Science* hath ftill been the fame *pitiful* thing, though in a various *Livery.* The *Grœcian* learning was but a tranfcript of the *Chaldœan* and *Ægyptian*; and the *Roman* of the *Grœcian.* And though thofe former dayes have not wanted brave *Wits*, that have gallantly attempted, and made Effays worthy Immortality; yet by reafon either of the unqualified capacities of the multitude, (who dote on things flight and trivial, neglecting what is more rare and excellent) or the clamorous affaults of envious and more popular oppofers, they have fubmitted to Fate, and are almoft loft in *Oblivion.* And therefore, as that great man, the *Lord Bacon* hath obferv'd, *Time* as a *River*, hath brought down to us what is more light and fuperficial; while things more folid and fubftantial have been im-

merfed

merfed. Thus the *Ariftotelian Philofophy* hath prevailed; while the more excellent and more *Antient Atomical Hypothefis* hath long lain buryed in neglect and darknefs; aud for ought I know, might have flept for ever, had not the ingenuity of the prefent age, recal'd it from its *urne* and *filence*. But it is fomewhat collateral to my fcope, as well as difporportion'd to my abilities, to fall upon particular Inftances of the defects and Errours of the *Philofophy* of the *Antients*. The foremention'd noble *Advancer of Learning*, whofe name and parts might give credit to any undertaking; hath handfomly perform'd it, in his ingenious *Novum Organum*. And yet, becaufe it may conferr towards the difcovery of how little our adherence to *Antiquity* befriends *Truth*, and the encreafe of Knowledge; as alfo how groundlefs are the *Dogmetifts* high pretenfions to *Science* : I fhall adventure fome confiderations on the *Peripatetick Philofophy*; which hath had the luck to furvive all others, and to build a fame on their *Ruines*.

CHAP. XVIII.

REFLEXIONS on the PERIPATETICK PHILOSOPHY.

The Generality of its Reception, no Argument of its deserts; the first charge against that Philosophy; that it is meerly verbal. Materia prima in that Philosophy signifies nothing. A Parallel drawn between it and Imaginary Space: this latter pleads more for its reallity. Their Form also is a meer word, and potentia Materiæ insignificant. Privation no principle. An essay to detect Peripatetick Verbosity, by translating some definitions.

HOw *Aristotles Philosophy* came so universally to obtain in these later Ages, to the silencing the *Zoroastrian, Pythagorean, Platonical,* and *Epicurean* Learning, is not my business here to inquire. Worth is not to be judg'd by Success, and Retinue; only we may

P 3   take

take notice, that the *Generality* of it's *reception* is with many the *perfwading* Argument of it's *fuperlative* defert. And common Judges meafure *excellency* by *Name* and *Numbers*. But *Seneca's* determination, *Argumentum peſsimi Turba eſt*, is more deſerving our credit : and the *feweſt*, that is the *wiſeſt*, have alwayes ſtood contradictory to that ground of belief; Vulgar applauſe by ſeverer Wiſdom being held a ſcandal. If the numerouſneſs of a Train muſt carry it; *Virtue* may go follow *Aſtræa*, and *Vice* only will be worth the courting. The *Philoſopher* deſervedly ſuſpected himſelf of vanity, when cryed up by the multitude : And diſcreet apprehenders will not think the better of that *Philoſophy*, which hath the common cry to vouch it. He that writ counter to the *Aſtrologer* in his *Almanack*, did with more truth foretell the *weather* : and he that ſhall write *Foul*, in the place of the Vulgars *Fair*; paſſes the juſter cenſure. Thoſe in the *Fable*, who were wet with the ſhowre of *folly*, hooted at the *wiſe men* that eſcap'd it, and pointed at their actions as *ridiculous*; becauſe unlike their own, that were truly *ſo*. If the major Vote may caſt it, *Wiſdom* and *Folly* muſt exchange names; and the way to the one will be by the other. Nor is it the Rabble only, which are ſuch perverſe diſcerners; we are now a ſphear above them : I mean the το πολυ of pretended *Philoſophers*, who judge as odly in their way, as the *Raſcality* in theirs; and many a profeſt Retainer to *Philoſophy*, is but an *Ignoramus* in a ſuit of *ſecond Notions*. 'Tis ſuch, that moſt revere the

Reliques

Reliques of the Adored *Sophy*; and, as *Artemesia* did those of *Mausolus*, paſſionately drink his *aſhes*. Whether the Remains of the *Stagarite* deſerve ſuch *Veneration*, we'll make a brief enquiry.

In the conduct of which deſign, 6 Things I offer againſt that *Philoſophy*, *viz.* (1.) That 'tis meerly *Verbal*, and (2.) *Litigious*. That (3.) It gives no account of the *Phænomina*. Nor (4.) doth it make any *diſcoveries* for the *uſe* of common *Life*. That (5.) 'tis inconſiſtent with *Divinity*, and (6.) with it *ſelf*. Which charges how juſt they are, I think will appear in the ſequell.

To the *Firſt* then. That the *Ariſtotelian Philoſophy* is an huddle of *words* and *terms inſignificant*, hath been the cenſure of the wiſeſt : And that both its *Baſis* and *Superſtructure* are *Chimærical*; cannot be unobſerv'd by them, that know it, and are free to judge it. To detect the verbal Emptineſs of this *Philoſophy*, I'le begin at the Foundation of the *Hypotheſis*. For I intend but *few*, and thoſe ſhall be *ſignal Inſtances*.

(1.) Therefore the *Materia prima* of this *Philoſophy*, ſhall be that of my *Reflections*. In the conſideration of which I ſhall need no more then the notion wherein *Ariſtotle* himſelf hath dreſt it; for evidence of what I aim at; for, *Nec quid, nec quale, nec quantum,* is as oppoſite a difinition of *Nothing*, as can be. So that if we would conceive this *Imaginary Matter* : we muſt deny all things of it, that we can conceive, and what remains is the thing we look for. And allowing all which its

Aſſertors

Affertors affign it, *viz. Quantity interminate* ; 'tis ftill but
an empty extended capacity , and therefore at the beft ,
but like that *Space* , which we imagine was before the
beginning of *Time*, and will be after *It*. 'Tis eafie to
draw a *Parallelifm* between that *Ancient*, and this more
Modern Nothing ; and in all things to make good its refemblance to that *Commentitious Inanity*. The *Peripatetick matter* is a pure unactuated Power : and this conceited *Vacuum* a meer Receptibility. *Matter* is fuppos'd
indeterminate : and *Space* is *fo*. The pretended *firft matter* is capable of all *forms* : And the *imaginary fpace* is
receptive of any *body*. *Matter* cannot naturally fubfift
uninform'd : And *Nature* avoids *vacuity* in *fpace*. The
matter is *ingenerate* , and beyond corruption : And the
fpace was before, and will be after either. The *matter* in
all things is but *one* : and the *fpace* moft *uniform*. Thus
the Foundation-Principle of *Peripateticifm* is exactly parallel to an acknowledg'd *nothing* : and their agreement
in effential characters makes rather an *Identity*, then a
Parity ; but that *Imaginary fpace* hath more to plead for
its *reality*, then the *matter* hath, and in this confifts the
greateft diffimilitude. For *that* hath no dependence on
the bodies which poffefs it ; but was before them, and
will furvive them : whereas *this* effentially relies on the
form and cannot fubfift without it. Which yet, me
thinks, is little better then an *abfurdity* : that the caufe
fhould be an *Eleemofynary* for its fubfiftence to its effect,
and a nature *pofterior* to, and dependent on it felf. This

depen-

dependentia a pofteriori, though in a diverfe way of caufality, my reafon could never away with : yea, a Sectator of
this *Philofophy,* *Oviedo* a *Spanifh* Jefuite, hath effectually
impugn'd it. So then there's nothing *real,* anfwering
this Imaginary *Proteus* ; and *Materia prima* hath as much
of being, as *Mons aureus.*

(2.) The *Peripatetick Forms* are as obnoxious, and
on the fame account lyable to our Reflections as the former Principle. I'le not fpend time in an induftious confutation of what the Votaries of that *Philofophy* themfelves can fcarce tell what to make of : And the fubject
being dry and lefs futable to thofe more *Mercurial* tempers for whom I intend thefe Papers : I'le only pafs a
Reflection on it, and proceed to what may be lefs importunate.

The *Form* then, according to this *Hypothefis,* is a new
fubftance produced in all generations to actuate the *Mat-*
ter and *Paffive* Principle ; out of whofe *Power* 'tis faid
to be educed. And were it fuppofed to contain any thing
of the *Form* præexifting in it, as the feed of the *Being* to
be produced ; 'twere then fenfe to fay, It was *Educed*
from it ; but by *Educing,* the affirmers only mean a
producing in it, with a fubjective dependence on its Recipient : a *worthy* fignification of *Eduction* ; which an-
fwers not the queftion whence 'tis derived, but into what
it is received. The queftion is of the *terminus à quo,* and
the anfwer of the *fubject.* So that all that can be made
of this *power* of the *matter,* is meerly *a receptive capacity* :

Q   and

and we may as well affirm, that the world was *educ'd* out of the *power* of the *imaginary space* ; and give that as a sufficient account of its Original. And in this language, to grow rich were to *educe* money out of the *power* of the Pocket. Wherefore, notwithstanding this *Imaginary Eduction* out of the *power* of the *Matter* ; we are still to seek whether these *Forms* be produced out of *something*, or *nothing* ; either of which supposed, bids defiance to the *Hypothesis*. For according to the first, all possible Forms will be actually latent in the Matter ; which is contrary to the stream of the *Peripatetick* Doctors. And the latter as opposite to their Master's *Ex Nihilo Nihil*, and he acknowledged no *Creation*.

(3.) The third *Principle* of *Bodies* according to the *Aristotelian Philosophy* is *Privation* ; concerning which, I'le add nothing but the words of the excellent Lord *Montaigne*, *Qu'est-il plus vain que de faire l' inanité mesme, cause la production des choses ? La privation c'est une negative : de quel humeur en a-il peu faire la cause & origine des choses qui sont ?*

But yet further, to give an hint more of the *Verbosities* of this *Philosophy*, a short view of a definition or two will be sufficient evidence ; which, though in *Greek* or *Latin* they amuse us ; yet a Translation unmaskes them. And if we make them speak *English*, the cheat is transparent.

Light is ΕΝΕΡΓΙΑ ΤΟΥ ΔΙΑΦΑΝΟΥ saith that *Philosophy* : In English, the *Act of a perspicuous Body.* Sure
Aristotle

Ariftotle here tranfgres't his own *Topicks,* and if this *De-finition* be clearer and more known then the thing *defi-ned, Midnight* may vie for *confpicuity* with *Noon.* Is not Light more known then this infignificant *Energy*? And what's a *diaphanous* body, but the Lights *medium* the *Air*? fo that *Light* is the *Act of the Air.* And if *Lux* be *Umbra Dei,* this definition is *Umbra Lucis.* Thus is Light darkened by an Illuftration, and the *fymbol* of *evidence,* cloathed in the Livery of *Midnight*: As if *light* were beft feen by *darknefs,* as *Light inacceffible* is beft *known* by *Iguorance.*

Again (2.) That *Motion* is ΕΝΤΕΛΕΧΕΙΑ ΤΟΥ ΟΝΤΟΣ ΕΝ ΔΥΝΑΜΕΙ, *&c.* is a definition of *Ariftotle's,* and as culpable as the former. For, by the moft favourable interpretation of that unintelligible *Entelechy*: It is but, *An act of a being in power, as it is in power*; the con-ftruing of which into palpable fenfe or meaning would poze a Critick. Sure that *Definition* is not very *con-fpicuous,*whofe *Genus* puzzled the *Devil.* The *Philofopher* that prov'd *motion* by walking, did in that action bet-ter *define* it: And that puzled *Candidate,* who being ask'd what a *circle* was, defcrib'd it by the *rotation* of his *hand*; gave an account more fatisfying. In fome things we muft indeed give an allowance for words of Art: But in defining obvious appearances, we are to ufe what is moft plain and eafie; that the mind be not mifled by *Amphibologies,* or ill conceived notions, into fallacious deductions: which whether it be not the method of

Peripa-

Peripatetick Philosophy let the indifferent determine. **To** give an account of all the insignificancies, and verbal nothings of this *Philosophy*, would be almost to transcribe it. 'Tis a *Philosophy*, that makes most accurate Inspections into the *Creatures* of the *Brain*; and gives the exactest *Topography* of the *Extramundane spaces.* Like our late *Polititians*, it makes discoveries, and their objects too; and deals in beings, that owe nothing to the *Primitive Fiat.* The same undivided Essence, from the several circumstances of its being and operations, is here multiplyed into *Legion*, and emprov'd to a number of smaller *Entities*; and these again into as many *Modes* and insignificant *formalities.* What a number of words here have nothing answering them? and as many are imposed at random. To wrest names from their known meaning to Senses most alien, and to darken *speech by words without knowledge*; are none of the most inconsiderable faults of this *Philosophy* : To reckon them in their particular instances, would puzzle *Archimedes.* Now hence the genuine *Idea's* of the Mind are adulterate: and the Things themselves lost in a crowd of *Names*, and *Intentional nothings.* Besides, these *Verbosities* emasculate the understanding; and render it slight and frivolous, as its objects.

Methinks, the late *Voluminous Jesuits*, those *Laplanders* of *Peripateticism*, do but subtilly trifle, and their *Philosophick* understandings are much like his, who spent his time in darting *Cumming-seed* through the *Eye* of a *Needle.*

One

One would think they were impregnated, as are the Mares in *Cappadocia*; they are big of words: their tedious Volumes have the *Tympany*, and bring forth nought but wind, and vapour. To me, a *curſus Philoſophicus*, is but an Impertinency in *Folio*; and the ſtudying them a *laborious idleneſs*. 'Tis here, that things are crumbled into *notional Atomes*; and the ſubſtance evaporared into an *imaginary Æther*. The intellect that can feed on this air, is a *Chamæleon*; and a meer *inflated* skin. From this ſtock grew *School-Divinity*, which is but *Peripateticiſm* in a *Theological Livery*. A *School-man* is the Ghoſt of the *Stagirite*, in a Body of condenſed Air: and *Thomas* but *Ariſtotle Sainted*.

CHAP.

CHAP. XIX.

2. Peripatetick Philofophy *is* Litigious; *it hath no fetled conftant fignification of words; the inconveniences hereof.* Arifto-tle *intended the cherifhing Controverfies: prov'd by his own double teftimony. Some of his impertinent arguings inftanc't in. Difputes retard, and are injurious to knowledge.* Peripateticks *are moft exer-cifed in the* Controverfal *parts of* Philo-*fophy, and know little of the* practical *and* experimental. *A touch at School-Di-vinity.*

BUt (2.) this *Philofophy* is *litigious,* the very fpawn of *difputations* and *controverfies* as undecifive as needlefs. This is the natural refult of the former: *Storms* are the products of *vapours.* For where *words* are impofed *arbitrarioufly,* having no ftated real mea-ning; or elfe diftorted from their common ufe, and known fignifications: the mind muft needs be led into
confufion

confufion and mifprifion ; and fo things plain and eafie in their naked natures, made full of *intricacy* and difputable *uncertainty.* For we cannot conclude with affurance, but from clearly apprehended *premifes* ; and thefe cannot be fo conceiv'd, but by a *diftinct* comprehenfion of the *words* out of which they are *elemented.* So that, where thefe are unfixt or ambiguous ; our *propofitions* muft be fo, and our *deductions* can be no better. One reafon therefore of the uncontroverted certainty of *Mathematical Science* is ; becaufe 'tis built upon clear and fettled *fignifications* of *names,* which admit of no *ambiguity* or infignificant *obfcurity.* But in the *Ariftotelian* Philofophy it's quite otherwife : Words being here carelefly and abufively admitted, and as inconftantly retained ; it muft needs come to pafs, that they will be diverfly apprehended by contenders, and fo made the fubject of *Controverfies,* that are *endlefs* both for *ufe* and *number.* And thus being at their firft ftep out of the way to *Science,* by miftaking in *fimple terms* ; in the progrefs of their enquiries they muft needs lofe both themfelves, and the Truth, in a *Verbal Labyrinth.* And now the entangled Difputants, as Mafter *Hobs* ingenioufly obferveth, like Birds that came down the Chimney ; betake them to the falfe light, feldom fufpecting the way they entr'd : But attempting by vain, impertinent, and coincident diftinctions, to efcape the abfurdity that purfues them ; do but weary themfelves with as little fuccefs, as the filly Bird attemps the window.

The

The mif-ftated words are the original miftake; and every other effay is a new one.

Now thefe canting contefts, the ufual entertainment of the *Peripatum,* are not only the accidental *vitiofities* of the *Philofophers;* but the genuine iffues of the *Philofophy* it felf. And *Ariftotle* feems purpofely to intend the cheri= fhing of *controverfal digladiations* , by his own affectation of an intricate *obfcurity.* Himfelf acknowledg'd, when he faid; his *Phyficks* were *publifh'd,* and not *fo* : And by that double advice in his *Topicks* 'tis as clear as light. In one place, he advifeth his Sectatours in difputations to be *ambiguous* : and in another, to bring forth any thing that occurs, rather then give way to their Adverfary : Counfel very well becoming an Enquirer into Truth and Nature. Nor did he here advife them to any thing, but what he followeth himfelf, and exactly copies out in his practice : The multitudes of the *lame, abrupt, equivo-cal, felf=contradicting* expreffions, will evidence it as to the firft part : which who confiders, may be fatisfied in this; that if *Ariftotle* found *Natures face* under covert of a *veil,* he hath not removed the old, but made her a *new* one. And for the latter, his frequent flightnefs in arguing doth abundantly make it good. To inftance :

He proves the *world* to be perfect, becaufe it confifts of *bodies;* and that *bodies* are fo, becaufe they confift of a *triple dimenfion* ; and that a *triple dimenfion* is perfect, becaufe *three* are *all* ; and that *three* are *all,* becaufe when 'tis but *one* or *two,* we can't fay *all,* but when 'tis *three,* we may : Is not
                                                              this

this an abfolute *demonftration?* We can fay All at the number *three* : Therefore the *world is perfect*. *Tobit* went forth and his *Dog* follow'd him; therefore there's a *world* in the *Moon*, were an argument as *Apodictical*. In another place (2.) he proves the *world* to be but *one* : For were there another, our Earth would fall unto it. Which is but a pitiful deduction, from the meer prejudice of *Senfe* ; and not unlike theirs, who thought, if there were *Antipodes*, they muft needs (as it's faid of *Erafmus*) in *Cælum defcendere*. As if, were there more *worlds*, each of them would not have its proper *Centre*. Elfe-where (?.) fhewing, why the *Heavens* move this way rather then another, he gives this for a reafon : becaufe they move to the more *honourable* ; and *before* is more *honourable* then *after*. This is like the *Gallant*, who fent his man to buy an *Hat*, that would *turn up behind*. As if, had the Heavens moved the other way ; that term had not been then *before*, which is now the contrary. This Inference is founded upon a very weak fuppofition, *viz.* That thofe alterable refpects are realities in Nature; which will never be admitted by a confiderate difcerner. Thus *Ariftotle* acted his own inftructions; and his obfequious Sectators have fuper-erogated in obfervance. They have fo difguifed his *Philofophy* by obfcuring *Comments*, that his revived felf would not own it : And were he to act another part with mortals, he'd be but a pitiful *Peripatetick* ; every *Sophifter* would out-talk him.

Now this *difputing* way of Enquiry is fo far from advancing

R

vancing *Science*; that 'tis no inconfiderable retarder : For in *Scientifical* difcoveries many things muft be confider'd, which the hurrey of a difpute indifpofeth for; and there is no way to *Truth*, but by the moft clear comprehenfion of *fimple notions*, and as wary an accuracy in *deduttions*. If the Fountain be difturb'd, there's no feeing to the bottom; and here's an exception to the Proverb, *'Tis no good fifhing for* Verity *in troubled waters*. One miftake of either *fimple apprehenfion*, or *connexion*, makes an *erroneous conclufion*. So that the precipitancy of *difputation*, and the ftir and noife of Paffions, that ufually attend it, muft needs be prejudicial to Verity : its calm infinuations can no more be heard in fuch a buftle, then a whifper among a croud of Say-lors in a ftorm. Nor do the eager clamors of contending Difputants, yield any more relief to eclipfed Truth; then did the founding Brafs of old to the *labouring Moon*. When it's under queftion, 'twere as good flip *crofs* and *pile*, as to difpute for't : and to play a game at *Chefs* for an opinion in *Philofophy* (as my felf and an ingenious Friend have fometime fported) is as likely a way to determine. Thus the *Peripatetick* procedure is inept for *Philofophical* foluti-ons : The *Lot* were as equitable a decifion, as their empty *Loquacities*.

'Tis thefe ungracious *Difputations* that have been the great hinderance to the more improvable parts of Lear-ning : and the modern Retainers to the *Stagirite* have fpent their fweat and pains upon the moft litigious parts of his *Philofophy*; while thofe, that find lefs play for the

contending

contending *Genius,* are incultivate. Thus *Logick,* *Physicks,* and *Metaphysicks,* are the burden of Volumes, and the dayly entertainment of the *Disputing Schools* : while the more profitable doctrines of the *Heavens, Meteors, Minerals, Animals* ; as also the more *practical* ones of *Politicks,* and *Oeconomicks,* are scarce so much as glanc'd at. And the indisputable *Mathematicks,* the only *Science* Heaven hath yet vouchsaf't Humanity, have but few Votaries among the slaves of the *Stagirite.* What, the late promoters of the *Aristotelian Philosophy,* have writ on all these so fertile subjects, can scarce compare with the single disputes about *Materia prima.*

Nor hath **Humane** Science monopoliz'd the damage, that hath sprung from this Root of Evils : *Theology* hath been as deep a sharer. The Volumes of the *Schoolmen* , are deplorable evidence of *Peripatetick depravations* : And *Luther's* censure of that *Divinity , Quam primum apparuit Theologia Scholastica, evanuit Theologia Crucis,* is neither uncharitable, nor unjust. This hath mudded the Fountain of Certainty with notional and Ethnick admixtions, and platted the head of *Evangelical* truth, as the *Jews* did its *Author's,* with a *Crown* of *Thorns* : Here, the most obvious Verity is subtiliz'd into niceties, and spun into a thread indiscernible by common *Opticks,* but through the *spectacles* of the adored *Heathen.* This hath robb'd the *Christian* world of its *unity* and *peace,* and made the Church, the Stage of everlasting contentions : And while *Aristotle* is made the *Center* of *Truth* , and *Unity,*

what

what hope of reconciling ? And yet moſt of theſe Scho-
laſtick controverſies are ultimately reſolv'd into the ſubtilties of his *Philoſophy* : whereas me thinks an *Athenian*
ſhould not be the beſt guide to the ΘΕΟΣ ΑΓΝΩΣΤΟΣ;
Nor an *Idolater* to that God he neither knew nor owned.
When I read the eager conteſts of thoſe *Notional Theo=
logues*, about things that are not; I cannot but think of
that pair of *wiſe ones*, that fought for the *middle* : And me
thinks many of their Controverſies are ſuch, as if *we* and
our *Antipodes*, ſhould ſtrive who were *uppermoſt*; their
title to Truth is equal. He that divided his *Text* into *one*
part; did but imitate the *Schoolmen* in their *coincident di=*
ſtinctions : And the beſt of their *curioſities* are but like
paint on Glaſs, which intercepts and dyes the light the
more deſirable ſplendor. I cannot look upon their ela-
borate trifles, but with a ſad reflexion on the degenerate
ſtate of our lapſed Intellects; and as deep a reſentment,
of the miſchiefs of this *School-Philoſophy*.

Chap. XX.

3. *It gives no account of the* Phænomena; *thoſe that are remoter, it attempts not. It ſpeaks nothing pertinent in the moſt ordinary:* Its *circular, and general way of* Solution. *It reſolves all things into* occult qualities. *The abſurdity of the* Ariſtotelian *Hypotheſis of the Heavens. The* Galaxy *is no* Meteor: *the* Heavens *are* corruptible. Comets *are above the* Moon. *The* Sphear *of* fire *derided.* Ariſtotle *convicted of ſeveral other falſe aſſertions.*

3.   THe *Ariſtotelian Hypotheſes* give a very dry and jejune account of Nature's *Phænomena.*

For (1.) as to its more *myſterious* reſerves, *Peripatetick* enquiry hath left them unattempted; and the moſt forward notional Dictators ſit down here in a contented ignorance: and as if nothing more were knowable then is already diſcover'd, they put ſtop to all endeavours of their Solution. *Qualities,* that were *Oc-cult* to *Ariſtotle* , muſt be *ſo* to us ; and we muſt not *Philoſophize* beyond *Sympathy* and *Antipathy* : whereas indeed the *Rarities* of Nature are in theſe *Receſſes,* and its moſt excellent operations *Cryptick* to common diſcern-ment. Modern Ingenuity expects Wonders from *Mag-netick* diſcoveries : And while we know but its more. ſenſible wayes of working ; we are but vulgar *Philoſo-phers,* and not likely to help the *World* to any conſiderable *Theories.* Till the *Fountains* of the great *deeps* are broken up ; *Knowledge* is not likely to cover the *Earth* as the waters the *Sea.*

Nor (2.) is the *Ariſtotelian Philoſophy* guilty of this ſloth and Philoſophick penury, only in remoter abſtruſities : but in ſolving the moſt *ordinary cauſalities* , it is as de-fective and unſatisfying. Even the moſt common pro-ductions are here reſolv'd into *Celeſtial influences, Elemental combinations, active* and *paſsive* principles, and ſuch *generali-ties ;* while the particular manner of them is as hidden as *ſympathies.* And if we follow *manifeſt qualities* beyond the empty ſignification of their Names ; we ſhall find them as *occult,* as thoſe which are profeſſedly *ſo.* That heavy Bodies deſcend by *gravity,* is no better an account then we might expect from a *Ruſtick* : and again, that *Gravity* is a *quality* whereby an heavy body deſcends, is an imper-tinet *Circle,* and teacheth nothing. The feigned *Central alliciency* is but a word, and the manner of it ſtill *occult.* That the *fire* burns by a quality called *heat ;* is an empty
dry

dry return to the Queftion, and leaves us ftill ignorant of the immediate way of *Igneous folutions*. The accounts that this *Philofophy* gives by other *Qualities*, are of the fame *Gender* with thefe: So that to fay the *Loadftone* draws *Iron* by *magnetick attraction*, and that the *Sea* moves by *flux* and *reflux*; were as fatisfying as thefe *Hypothefes*, and the folution were as pertinent. In the *Qualities*, this Philofophy calls *manifeft*, nothing is *fo* but the effects. For the *heat*, we feel, is but the *effect* of the *fire*; and the *preffure*, we are fenfible of, but the *effect* of the *defcending* body. And effects, whofe caufes are confeffedly *occult*, are as much within the fphear of our Senfes; and our Eyes will inform us of the motion of the Steel to its *attrahent*. Thus *Peripatetick Philofophy* refolves all things into *Occult qualities*; and the *Dogmatifts* are the only *Scepticks*. Even to them, that pretend fo much to *Science*, the world is circumfcrib'd with a *Gyges his ring*; and is *intellectually invifible*: And, ΟΥ ΚΑΤΑΛΑΜΒΑΝΩ, is a fit Motto for the *Peripatum*. For by their way of difquifition there can no more be truly comprehended, then what's known by every common Ignorant. And ingenious inquiry will not be contented with fuch vulgar *frigidities*.

But further, (3.) if we look into the *Ariftotelian* Comments on the largeft Volums of the Univerfe: The works of the *fourth day* are there as confufed and diforderly, as the *Chaos* of the *firft*: and more like that, which was before the *light*, then the compleatly finifh'd, and glorioufly difpofed *frame*. What a *Romance* is the ftory of thofe

thofe impoffible *concamerations*, *InterfeEtions*, *Involutions*, and feign'd *Rotations* of *folid Orbs* ? All fubftituted to falve the credit of a broken ill-contrived *Syfteme*. The belief of fuch diforders *above*, were an advantage to the *oblique Atheifm* of *Epicurus*: And fuch Irregularities in the Celeftial motions, would lend an Argument to the *Apotheiofis* of *Fortune*. Had the world been coagmented from that fuppofed fortuitous Jumble ; this *Hypothefis* had been tolerable. But to intitle fuch *abrupt*, *confufed* motions to *Almighty wifdom*, is to degrade it below the fize of humane forecaft and contrivance. And could the doctrine of *folid Orbs*, be accommodated to *Aftronomical* *Phænomena*; yet to afcribe each *Sphear* an *Intelligence* to circumvolve it, were an *unphilofophical* defperate refuge : And to confine the bleffed *Genii* to a Province, which was the *Hell* of *Ixion*, were to rob them of their *Felicities*. That the *Galaxy* is a *Meteor*, was the account of *Ariftotle* : But the *Telefcope* hath autoptically confuted it : And he, who is not *Pyrrhonian* to the dif-belief of his Senfes, may fee, that it's no exhalation from the Earth, but an heap of fmaller *Luminaries*. That the *Heavens* are void of *corruption*, is *Ariftotles* fuppofal : But the Tube hath betray'd their impurity ; and *Neoterick Aftronomy* hath found *fpots* in the *Sun*. The difcoveries made in *Venus*, and the *Moon*, difprove the *Antique Quinteffence* ; and evidence them of as courfe *materials*, as the *Globe* we belong to. The *Perfpicil*, as well as the *Needle*, hath enlarged the *habitable* *World*; and that the *Moon* is an *Earth*, is no improbable

con-

conjecture. The *inequality* of its furface, *Mountanous protuberance*, the nature of its *Maculæ*, and infinite other circumftances (for which the world's beholding to *Galilæo*)
are Items not contemptible : *Hevelius* hath *graphically*
defcribed it : That *Comets* are of nature Terreftrial, is
allowable : But that they are material'd of vapours, and
never flamed beyond the *Moon ;* were a conceffion unpardonable. That in *Cuffiopæa* was in the *Firmanent,* and
another in our age above the *Sun.* Nor was there ever any
as low as the higheft point of the *circumference,* the Stagyrite allows them. So that we need not be appall'd at
Blazing Stars, and a *Comet* is no more ground for *Aftro-
logical prefages* then a *flaming* Chimney. The unparallel'd
Des-Cartes hath unridled their dark *Phyfiology,* and to
wonder folv'd their *Motions.* His *Philofophy* gives them
tranfcurfions beyond the *Vortex* we breath in ; and leads
them through others, which are only known in an *Hypothefis. Ariftotle* would have fainted before he had flown
half fo far, as that *Eagle-wit ;* and have lighted on a *hard
name,* or *occult quality,* to reft him. That there is a *fphear* of
of *fire* under the concave of the *Moon,* is a dream : And
this, may be, was the reafon fome imagin'd *Hell* there,
thinking thofe flames the *Ignis Rotæ.* According to this
Hypothefis, the whole *Lunar* world is a *Torrid Zone ;* and
on a better account, then *Ariftotle* thought ours was, may
be fuppofed *inhabitable,* except they are *Salamanders* which
dwell in thofe *fiery Regions.* That the *Reflexion* of the *Solar*
Rays, is terminated in the *Clouds ;* was the opinion of

the *Græcian Sage* : But *Lunar* obfervations have convicted
it of falfhood ; and that Planet receives the *dusky* light,
we difcern in its *Sextile Afpect*, from the *Earth's* benignity.
That the *Rainbow* never defcribes more then a *femicircle*,
is no credible affertion ; fince experimental obfervations
have confuted it. *Gaffendus* faw one at Sun-fetting, whofe
Supreme *Arch* almoft reached our *Zenith*, while the Horns
ftood in the *Oriental Tropicks.* And that Noble wit reprehends the *School-Idol*, for affigning fifty years at leaft between every *Lunar Iris.* That *Caucafus* enjoys the Sun-
beams three parts of the Nights *Vigils* ; that *Danubius* arifeth from the *Pyrenæan* Hills : That the Earth is higher
towards the *North* : are opinions truly charged on *Ariftotle* by the *Reftorer* of *Epicurus* ; and all eafily confutable
falfities. To reckon all the *Ariftotelian* aberrances, and to
give a full account of the lamenefs of his *Hypothefes* ,
would fwell this *digreffion* into a Volume. The mention'd fhall fuffice us.

CHAP.

CHAP. XXI.

4. *Ariftotle's Philofophy inept for new dif-coveries; it hath been the Author of no one invention: It's founded on vulgarities, and therefore makes nothing known beyond them. The knowledge of Natures out-fide confers not to practical improvements. Better hopes from the New Philofophy. The directing all this to the defign of the Difcourfe. A Caution, viz. that nothing is here intended in favour of novelty in Di-vinity; the reafon why we may embrace what is new in Philofophy, while we re-ject them in Theologie.*

4. 　THe *Ariftotelian Philofophy* is inept for New dif-coveries; and therefore of no accommodation to the *ufe* of *üfe.* That all Arts, and Profeffi-ons are capable of mature improvements; cannot be doubted by thofe, who know the leaft of any. And that there is an *America* of fecrets, and unknown *Peru* of

Nature, whose discovery would richly advance them, is more then conjecture. Now while we either sayl by the *Land* of gross and vulgar Doctrines, or direct our Enquiries by the *Cynosure* of meer abstract *notions* ; we are not likely to reach the Treasures on the other side the *Atlantick*: The directing of the World the way to which, is the noble end of true *Philosophy.* That the *Aristotelian Physiology* cannot boast it self the proper Author of any one Invention, is prægnant evidence of its infecundous deficiency : And 'twould puzzle the Schools to point at any considerable discovery, made by the direct, sole manuduction of *Peripatetick* Principles. Most of our Rarities have been found out by *casual emergency* ; and have been the works of Time, and Chance, rather then of *Philosophy.* What *Aristotle* hath of Experimental Knowledge in his Books of *Animals*, or else-where ; is not much transcending vulgar observation : And yet what he hath of this, was never learnt from his *Hypotheses* ; but forcibly fetch'd in to suffrage to them. And 'tis the observation of the Noble St. *Alban* ; that that *Philosophy* is built on a few Vulgar experiments : and if upon further enquiry, any were found to refragate, they were to be discharg'd by a *distinction.* Now what is founded on, and made up but of *Vulgarieties*, cannot make known any thing beyond them. For Nature is set a going by the most *subtil* and *hidden* Instruments ; which it may be have nothing *obvious* which resembles them. Hence judging by visible appearances, we are discouraged by suppoſed *Impoſſibilities* which.

which to *Nature* are none, but within her Sphear of
Action. And therefore what shews only the outside, and
sensible structure of Nature; is not likely to help us in
finding out the *Magnalia.* 'Twere next to impossible for
one, who never saw the inward wheels and motions, to
make a watch upon the bare view of the *Circle* of *hours*,
and *Index* : And 'tis as difficult to trace natural operations
to any practical advantage, by the sight of the *Cortex* of
sensible Appearances. He were a poor *Physitian*, that had
no more *Anatomy*, then were to be gather'd from the
Physnomy. Yea, the most common *Phænomena* can be
neither known, nor improved, without insight into the
more *hidden* frame. For *Nature* works by an *Invisible
Hand* in all things : And till *Peripateticism* can shew us
further, then those gross solutions of *Qualities* and *Elements*; 'twill never make us Benefactors to the World,
nor considerable Discoverers. But its experienc'd steri-
lity through so many hundred years, drives hope to de-
speration.

We expect greater things from *Neoterick* endeavours.
The *Cartesian Philosophy* in this regard hath shewn the
World the way to be happy. And me thinks this Age
seems resolved to bequeath *posterity* somewhat to remember it : The glorious Undertakers, wherewith
Heaven hath blest our dayes, will leave the world better
provided then they found it. And whereas in former
times such generous free-spirited Worthies were as the
Rare newly observed *Stars*, a single one the wonder of

an Age: In ours they are like the lights of the greater
ſize that twinkle in the *Starry Firmament*: And this laſt
Century can glory in numerous *conſtellations.* Should
thoſe *Heroes* go on‘ as they have happily begun, they’ll
fill the world with *wonders.* And I doubt not but poſterity will find many things, that are now but *Rumors*, verified into *practical Realities.* It may be ſome Ages hence,
a voyage to the *Southern* unknown *Tracts*, yea poſſibly
the *Moon*, will not be more ſtrange then one to *America.*
To them, that come after us, it may be as ordinary to buy
a *pair* of *wings* to fly into remoteſt *Regions*; as now a
pair of *Boots* to ride a *Journey.* And to conferr at the
diſtance of the *Indies* by *Sympathetick* conveyances, may
be as uſual to future times, as to us in a *litterary* correſpondence. The *reſtauration* of gray hairs to *Juvenility*, and
renewing the exhauſted marrow, may at length be effected without a *miracle*: And the turning of the now
comparative *deſert* world into a *Paradiſe*, may not improbably be expected from late *Agriculture.*

Now thoſe, that judge by the narrowneſs of former
Principles and *Succeſſes*, will ſmile at theſe *Paradoxical
expectations*: But queſtionleſs thoſe great Inventions,
that have in theſe later Ages altered the face of all things;
in their naked propoſals, and meer ſuppoſitions, were
to former times as *ridiculous.* To have talk’d of a *new
Earth* to have been diſcovered, had been a *Romance* to
Antiquity: And to ſayl without ſight of *Stars* or *ſhoars*
by the guidance of a *Mineral*, a *ſtory* more abſurd then
the

the flight of *Dædalus*. That men should speak after their *tongues* were *ashes*, or communicate with each other in differing *Hemisphears*, before the Invention of *Letters*; could not but have been thought a *fiction*. *Antiquity* would not have believed the almost incredible force of our *Canons*; and would as coldly have entertain'd the wonders of the Telescope. In these we all condemn *antique incredulity*; and 'tis likely Posterity will have as much cause to pitty *ours*. But yet notwithstanding this straightness of shallow observers, there are a set of enlarged souls that are more *judiciously credulous*: and those, who are acquainted with the fecundity of *Cartesian Principles*, and the diligent and ingenuous endeavours of so many true *Philosophers*; will despair of nothing.

CHAP.

CHAP. XXII.

(5.) *The* Aristotelian Philosophy *incon-*
sistent with Divinity; *and* (6.) *with it*
self. The Conclusion of the Reflexions.

BUt again (5.) the *Aristotelian Philosophy* is in some
things *impious,* and *inconsistent* with *Divinity.* That
the *Resurrection* is impossible : That *God* understands not all things : That the *world* was from *Eterni-*
ty : That there's no *substantial form,* but moves some
Orb : That the first Mover moves by an *Eternal, Immu-*
table Necessity : That, if the world and motion were
not from Eternity, then *God* was Idle : were all the
Assertions of *Aristotle,* and such as *Theology* pronounceth
impieties. Which yet we need not strange at from one,
of whom a *Father* saith, *Nec Deum coluit nec curavit* :
Especially, if it be as *Philoponus* affirms, that he *philoso-*
phiz'd by command from the *Oracle.* But besides those
I have mention'd, I might present to view a larger Catalogue of *Aristotle's* Impious opinions; of which take
a few :

He makes one *God* the *First Mover,* but 56 others, mo-
vers of the *Orbs.* He calls *God* an *Animal* : and affirms,
that

that He *knows* not *particulars*. He denies that *God* made any thing, or can do any thing but *move* the *Heavens*. He affirms, that 'tis not *God* but *Nature*, *Chance*, and *Fortune* that rule the *World*. That he is tyed to the *first Orb*; and *preserves* not the World, but only *moves* the *Heavens*; and yet elfewhere, that the World and Heavens have infinite power to move themfelves. He affirms, the *Soul* cannot be *separated* from the *Body*, becaufe 'tis it's *Form*. That *Prayers* are to no purpofe, becaufe God underftands not particulars. That God hears no *Prayers*, nor loves any man. That the *Soul perifheth* with the *body*: And that there is neither *ftate*, nor *place* of Happinefs after this life is ended. All which *Dogmata*, how contrary they are to the Fundamental Principles of *Reafon* and *Religion*, is eafily determin'd: and perhaps, never did any worfe drop from the Pens of the moft vile contemners of the Deity. So that the Great and moft Learned *Origen*, was not unjuft in præferring *Epicurus* before the adored *Stagyrite*. And poffibly there have been few men in the world have deferv'd lefs of *Religion*, and thofe that profefs it. How it is come about then, that the Affertour of fuch *impieties*, fhould be fuch an Oracle among *Divines* and *Chriftians*; is I confefs to me, matter of fome aftonifhment. And how *Epicurus* became fo infamous, when *Ariftotle* who fpake as *ill*, and did *worfe*, hath been fo *facred*, may well be wondred at.

T   Again

AGain (6.) The *Peripatetick Philoſophy* is repugnant to it *Self*; as alſo it was contrary to the more *antient Wiſdom*. And therefore the learned *Patritius* ſaith of *Ariſtotle*, *Ob eam rem multos è patribus habuit oppugnatores, celebratorem neminem*. And within the ſame period of ſenſe affirms, *Ipſe ſibi ipſi non conſtat; immo ſæpiſſimè, immo ſemper ſecum pugnat*. Of the *Ariſtotelian contradictions*, *Gaſſendus* hath preſented us with a Catalogue : We'll inſtance in a few of them. In one place he ſaith, The *Planets ſcintillation* is not ſeen, becauſe of their *propinquity*; but that of the *riſing* and *ſetting Sun* is, becauſe of its *diſtance*: and yet in another place he makes the *Sun* nearer us, then they are. He ſaith, that the *Elements* are not *Eternal*, and ſeeks to prove it; and yet he makes the *world ſo*, and the *Elements* its parts. In his *Meteors* he ſaith, no **Dew** is produced in the Wind; and yet afterwards admits it under the *South*, and none under the *North*. In one place he defines a vapour *humid* and *cold*; and in another *humid* and *hot*. He ſaith, the *faculty* of ſpeaking is a *ſenſe*; and yet before he allow'd but *five*. In one place, that Nature doth all things *beſt*; and in another, that it makes more *evil* then *good*. And ſomewhere he contradicts himſelf within a *line*; ſaying, that an *Immoveable Mover* hath no principle of *Motion*. 'Twould be tedious to mention more; and the quality of a *digreſſion* will not allow it.

Thus we have, as briefly as the ſubject would bear, animadverted on the ſo much admired *Philoſophy* of *Ariſtotle*.

ſtotle. The nobler Spirits of the Age, are diſengaged from thoſe detected vanities : And the now Adorers of that *Philoſophy* are few, but ſuch as know no other : Or if any of them look beyond the leaves of their *Maſter*, yet they try other Principles by a Jury of his, and ſcan *Des-Cartes* by *Genus* and *Species*. From the former ſort I may hope, they'l pardon this attempt; ſince nothing but the Authors weakneſs hindred his obliging them. And for the latter, I value not their cenſure.

WE may conclude upon the whole then, that the ſtamp of *Authority* can make *Leather* as current as *Gold*; and that there's nothing ſo *contemptible*, but *Antiquity* can render it *auguſt*, and *excellent*. But, becauſe the Fooleries of ſome affected Novelists have diſcredited new diſcoveries, and render'd the very mention ſuſpected of *Vanity* at leaſt; and in points Divine, of *Hereſie* : It will be neceſſary to add, that I intend not the former diſcourſe, in favour of any new-broach'd conceit in *Divinity* : For I own no Opinion there, which cannot plead the preſcription of above *ſixteen hundred*. There's nothing I have more ſadly reſented, then the craſie whimſies with which our Age abounds, and therefore am not likely to Patron them. In *Theology*, I put as great a difference between our *New Lights*, and *antient Truths*, as between the *Sun*, and an unconcocted evanid *Meteor*. Though I confeſs, that in *Philoſophy* I'm a *Seeker*; yet cannot believe, that a *Sceptick* in *Philoſophy* muſt be one in *Divinity*. *Goſpel-light*

began

began in its *Zenith* ; and, as ſome ſay the *Sun*, was created in its *Meridian* ſtrength and luſtre. But the beginnings of *Philoſophy* were in a *Crepuſculous obſcurity* ; and It's yet ſcarce paſt the *Dawn*. *Divine* Truths were moſt pure in their ſource ; and *Time* could not perfect what *Eternity* began : our *Divinity*, like the Grand-father of *Humanity*, was born in the *fulneſs* of *time*, and in the ſtrength of its manly vigour : But *Philoſophy* and Arts commenced *Embryo's*, and are by Times gradual accompliſhments. And therefore, what I cannot find in the leaves of former Inquiſitours : I ſeek in the Modern attempts of nearer Authors. I cannot receive *Ariſtotle*'s ΠΙΣΤΟΤΑΤΟΙ ΠΑΛΑΙΟΙ, in ſo extenſive an interpretation, as ſome would enlarge it to : And that diſcouraging Maxime, *Nil dictum quod non dictum prius*, hath little *room* in my *eſtimation*. Nor can I tye up my belief to the *Letter* of *Solomon* : Except *Copernicus* be in the right, there hath been ſomething *New under* the *Sun* ; I'm ſure, later times have ſeen *Novelties* in the Heavens *above* it. I do not think, that all Science is *Tautology* : The laſt Ages have ſhewn us, what *Antiquity* never ſaw ; no, not in a *Dream*.

CHAP.

CHAP. XXIII.

It's queried whether there be any Science in the fenfe of the Dogmatifts: (1.) We cannot know any thing to be the caufe of another, but from its attending it; and this way is not infallible; declared by in-ftances, efpecially from the Philofophy of Des-Cartes. All things are mixt; and 'tis difficult to affign each Caufe its diftinct Effects. (2.) There's no demonftration but where the contrary is impoffible. And we can fcarce conclude fo of any thing.

COnfidence of *Science* is one great reafon, we mifs it: For on this account prefuming we have it every where, we feek it not where it is; and therefore fall fhort of the object of our Enquiry. Now to give further check to *Dogmatical* pretenfions, and to difcover the vanity of affuming *Ignorance*; we'll make a fhort enquiry, whether there be any fuch thing as *Science* in

the

the sense of its Assertours. In their notion then, *It is the knowledge of things in their true, immediate, necessary causes :* Upon which I'le advance the following Observations.

1. All Knowledge of Causes is *deductive* : for we know none by simple intuition ; but through the mediation of their effects. So that we cannot conclude, any thing to be the cause of another; but from its continual accompanying it : for the *causality* it self is *insensible*. But now to argue from a concomitancy to a causality, is not infallibly conclusive : Yea in this way lies notorious delusion. For suppose, for instance, we had never seen more *Sun*, then in a cloudy day; and that the lesser lights had ne're appeared : Let us suppose the *day* had alway broke with a *wind*, and had proportionably varyed, as *that* did : Had not he been a notorious *Sceptick*, that should question the causality ? But we need not be beholding to so remote a supposition : The French *Philosophy* furnishes us with a better instance. For, according to the Principles of the illustrious *Des-Cartes*, there would be *light*, though the Sun and Stars gave *none*; and a great part of what we now enjoy, is independent on their beams. Now if this seemingly prodigious *Paradox*, can be reconcil'd to the least probability of conjecture, or may it be made but a tolerable supposal ; I presume, it may then win those that are of most difficult belief, readily to yield, that causes in our account the most palpable, may possibly be but *uninfluential attendants* ; since that there is not an instance

can

can be given, wherein we opinion a more certain *efficiency*. So then, according to the tenour of that concinnous *Hypothefis*, light being caufed by the *Conamen* of the Matter of the *Vortex*, to recede from the Centre of its Motion : it is an eafie inference, that were there none of that fluid *Æther*, which makes the body of the Sun in the Centre of our world, or fhould it ceafe from action ; yet the *conatus* of the circling matter would not be confiderably lefs, but according to the indifpenfable Laws of Motion, muft prefs the Organs of Senfe as now ; though it may be, not with fo fmart an impulfe. Thus we fee, how there might be *Light* before the *Luminaries* ; and *Evening* and *Morning* before there was a *Sun.* So then we cannot infallibly affure our felves of the truth of the *caufes*, that moft obvioufly occur ; and therefore the foundation of *fcientifical* procedure, is too weak for fo magnificent a fuperftructure.

Befides, That the World's a mafs of *heterogeneous* fubfiftencies, and every part thereof a coalition of diftinguifhable varieties ; we need not go far for evidence : And that all things are *mixed*, and Caufes blended by mutual involutions ; I prefume, to the Intelligent will be no difficult conceffion. Now to profound to the bottom of thefe *diverfities*, to affign each caufe its diftinct effects, and to limit them by their *juft* and *true* porportions ; are neceffary requifites of *Science* : and he that hath compaft them, may boaft he hath out-done *humanity.* But for us to talk of *Knowledge*, from thofe few indiftinct reprefentations, which

which are made to our grosser faculties, is a *flatulent vanity.*

2. We hold no *demonstration* in the notion of the *Dogmatist*, but where the contrary is *impossible*: For *necessary is that, which cannot be otherwise*. Now, whether the acquisitions of any on this side perfection, can make good the pretensions to so high *strain'd* an *infallibility*, will be worth a reflexion. And methinks, did we but compare the miserable *scantness* of our *capacities*, with the vast *profoundity* of *things*; both truth and modesty would teach us a more wary and becoming language. Can nothing be otherwise, which we conceive *impossible* to be so ? Is our knowledge, so adequately commensurate with the nature of things, as to justifie such an affirmation, that that cannot be, which we comprehend not ? Our demonstrations are levyed upon Principles of our *own*, not *universal* Nature: And, as my Lord *Bacon* notes, we judge from the *Analogy* of our *selves*, not the *Universe*. Now are not many things *certain* by one man's *Principles*, which are *impossible* to the apprehensions of another ? Some things our Juvenile reasons tenaciously adhere to; which yet our maturer Judgements disallow of: And that to meer sensible discerners is *impossible*, which to the enlarged principles of more advanced *Intellects* is an easie variety : Yea, that's absurd in one *Philosophy*, which is a worthy Truth in another ; and that is a demonstration to *Aristotle*, which is none to *Des-Cartes*. That every fixt *star* is a *Sun*; and that they are as distant from each other, as we from some

of

of them : That the *Sun*, which lights us, is in the *Centre* of our World, and our *Earth* a *Planet* that wheels about it : That this *Globe* is a *Star*, only crusted over with the grosser Element, and that its *Centre* is of the same nature with the *Sun* : That it may recover its light again, and shine amids the other *Luminaries* : That our *Sun* may be swallow'd up of another, and become a *Planet* : All these, if we judge by common Principles, or the Rules of Vulgar *Philosophy*, are prodigious *Impossibilities*, and their contradictories, as good as *demonstrable* : But yet to a reason inform'd by *Cartesianism*, these have their probability. Thus, it may be, the grossest absurdities to the Philosophies of *Europe*, may be justifiable assertions to that of *China* : And tis not unlikely, but what's impossible to all *Humanity*, may be possible in the *Metaphysicks*, and *Physiologie* of Angels. For the best Principles, excepting *Divine*, and *Mathematical*, are but *Hypotheses*; within the Circle of which, we may indeed conclude many things, with security from Error : But yet the greatest certainty, advanc'd from supposal, is still but *Hypothetical*. So that we may affirm, that things are thus and thus, according to the *Principles* we have espoused : But we strangely forget our selves, when we plead a necessity of their being so in *Nature*, and an Impossibility of their being otherwise.

U   CHAP.

CHAP. XXIV.

Three Inſtances of reputed Impoſſibilities, *which likely are not ſo, as* (1.) *of the power of* Imagination. (2.) Secret Conveyance. (3.) Sympathetick Cures.

NOw to ſhew how raſhly we uſe to conclude things *impoſſible* ; I'le inſtance in ſome reputed *Impoſſibilities,* which are only ſtrange and difficult performances. And the Inſtances are Three : (1.) The power of one man's imagination upon anothers. (2.) *Momentous* conveyance at almoſt any diſtance. (3.) *Sympathetick Cures.*

(1.) That the *Phancy* of one Man ſhould *bind* the Thoughts of another, and determine them to their particular objects, will be thought *impoſſible* : which yet, if we look deeply into the matter, wants not it's probability. The judicious Naturaliſt my Lord *Bacon,* ſpeaks not unfavourably of this way of *ſecret influence* : And that the ſpirit of one man hath ſometimes a power over that of another, I think is well atteſted by experience. For ſome preſences daunt and diſcourage us , when others raiſe us to a brisk aſſurance. And I believe there
are

are few but find that fome Companies benumn and cramp them, fo that in them they can neither fpeak nor do any thing that is handfom: whereas among more congruous and fuitable tempers then find themfelves very lucky and fortunate both in Speech and Action. Which things feem to me pretty confiderable evidence of immaterial intercourfes between our Spirits. And that this kind of fecret influence may be advanc't to fo ftrange an operation in the Imagination of one upon another, as to fix and determine it. Methinks the wonderful *fignatures* of the *Fœtus* caufed by the Imagination of the Mother, is no contemptible Item. The *fympathies* of laughing and gaping together, are refolv'd into this Principle : and I fee not why the *phancy* of one man may not determine the cogitation of another rightly qualified, as eafily as his *bodily motion.* Nor doth this influence feem more unreafonable, then that of one *ftring* of a Lute upon another , when a *ftroak* on it caufeth a proportionable motion in the *fympathizing* confort, which is diftant from it and not fenfibly touched. And if there be truth in this notion; 'twill yield us a good account how *Angels* inject thoughts into our minds, and know our cogitations : and here we may fee the fource of fome kinds of *fafcination.*

Now, though in our inquiry after the Reafon of this operation, we can receive no affiftance from the common *Philofophy*; yet the *Platonical Hypothefis* of a *Mundane Soul* will handfomely relieve us. Or if any would

rather have a *Mechanical* account ; I think it may probably be made out fome fuch way as follows. *Imagination* is inward Senfe ; To *Senfe* is required a motion of
certain *Filaments* of the Brain ; and confequently in *Imagination* there's the like : they only differing in this, that
the motion of the one proceeds immediately from external objects ; but that of the other hath its immediate
rife within our felves. Now then, when any part of
the Brain is ftrongly agitated ; that, which is next and
moft capable to receive the *motive* Imprefs, muft in like
manner be moved. And we cannot conceive any thing
more capable of motion, then the *fluid* matter, that's interfpers'd among all bodies, and contiguous to them.
So then, the agitated pars of the Brain begetting a *motion* in the proxime *Æther* ; it is propagated through the
liquid *medium* ; as we fee the motion is which is caus'd
by a ftone thrown into the water. And when the thus
moved *matter* meets with any thing like that, from which
it received its primary *imprefs* ; it will in like manner
move it ; as it is in *Mufical ftrings* tuned *Unifons*. And
thus the motion being convey'd, from the *Brain* of one
man to the *Phancy* of another ; it is there receiv'd from
the inftrument of conveyance, the *fubtil* matter ; and
the fame kind of *ftrings* being moved, and much what
after the fame manner as in the firft *Imaginant* ; the
Soul is awaken'd to the fame apprehenfions, as were
they that caus'd them. I pretend not to any exactnefs
or infallibility in this account, fore-feeing many fcruples
                                                    that

that muſt be removed to make it perfect : 'Tis only an hint of the *poſsibility* of mechanically ſolving the *Phæno-menon*; though very likely it may require many other circumſtances compleatly to make it out. But 'tis not my buſineſs here to follow it : I leave it therefore to re-ceive accompliſhmet from maturer Inventions.

But (2.) to advance another inſtance. That Men ſhould confer at very diſtant removes by an *extemporary* intercourſe, is another reputed *impoſsibility* ; but yet there are ſome hints in Natural operations, that give us pro- bability that it is feaſible, and may be compaſt without unwarrantable correſpondence with the people of the Air. That a couple of *Needles* equally touched by the ſame *magnet*, being ſet in two Dyals exactly proporti-on'd to each other, and circumſcribed by the Letters of the *Alphabet*, may effect this *Magnale*, hath conſiderable authorities to avouch it. The manner of it is thus re-preſented. Let the friends that would communicate, take each a Dyal : and having appointed a time for their *Sympathetick* conference , let one move his im- pregnate *Needle* to any letter in the *Alphabet*, and its affected fellow will preciſely reſpect the ſame. So that would I know what my friend would acquaint me with ; 'tis but obſerving the letters that are pointed at by my *Needle*, and in their order tranſcribing them from their *ſympathizing Index*, as its motion direct's : and I may be aſſured that my friend deſcribed the ſame with

his :

his : and that the words on my paper, are of his inditing. Now though there will be some ill contrivance in a circumstance of this invention, in that the thus *impregnate Needles* will not move to, but avert from each other (as ingenious Dr. *Browne* in his *Pseudodoxia Epidemica* hath observed:) yet this cannot prejudice the main design of this way of secret conveyance : Since 'tis but reading counter to the *magnetick* informer ; and noting the letter which is most distant in the *Abecedarian circle* from that which the Needle turns to, and the case is not alter'd. Now though this pretty contrivance possibly may not yet answer the expectation of inquisitive *experiment* ; yet 'tis no despicable item, that by some other such way of *magnetick efficiency*, it may hereafter with success be attempted, when *Magical* History shall be enlarged by riper inspections : and 'tis not unlikely, but that present discoveries might be improved to the performance.

Besides this there is another way of secret conveyance that's whisper'd about the World, the *truth* of which I vouch not, but the *possibility* : it is conference at distance by sympathized handes.. For say the relatours of this strange secret : The hands of two friends being allyed by the transferring of *Flesh* from one into another, and the place of the Letters mutually agreed on ; the least prick in the hand of one, the other will be sensible of, and that in the same part of his own. And thus the distant friend, by a new kind of

Chiro-

Chiromancy, may read in his own hand what his correspondent had set down in his. For instance, would I in *London* acquaint my intimate in *Paris*, that *I am well*: I would then prick that part where I had appointed the letter [*I* :] and doing so in another place to signfie that word was done, proceed to [*A*,] thence to [*M*] and so on, till I had finisht what I intended to make known.

Now if these seemingly prodigious Phancies of secret conveyances prove to be but *possible*, they will be warrantable presumption of the verity of the former instance : since tis as easily conceivable, that there should be communications between the *phancies* of men, as either the *impregnate needles*, or *sympathized hands*. And there is an instance still behind, which is more credible than either, and gives probability to them all.

(3.) Then there is a *Magnetick* way of curing *wounds* by anointing the *weapon*, and that the wound is affected in like manner as is the *extravenate blood* by the *Sympathetick medicine*, as to matter of fact is with circumstances of good evidence asserted by the Noble Sir *K. Digby* in his ingenious discourse on the subject. The reason of this *magnale* he attempts by *Mechanism*, and endeavours to make it out by *atomical aporrheas*, which passing from the *cruentate* cloth or weapon to the wound, and being incorporated with the *particles* of the *salve* carry them in their embraces to the affected part : where the
medicinal

medicinal atomes entering together with the *effluviums* of the blood, do by their ſubtle inſinuation better effect the cure, then can be done by any groſſer Application. The particular way of their conveyance, and their regular direction is handſomely explicated by that learned *Knight*, and recommended to the Ingenious by moſt witty and becoming illuſtrations. It is out of my way here to enquire whether the *Anima Mundi* be not a better account, then any *Mechanical* Solutions. The former is more deſperate; the latter perhaps hath more of ingenuity, then good ground of ſatisfaction. It is enough for me that *de facto* there is ſuch an entercourſe between the *Magnetick unguent* and the *vulnerated* body, and I need not be ſolicitous of the Cauſe. Theſe *Theories* I preſume will not be importunate to the ingenious: and therefore I have taken the liberty (which the quality of a Eſſay will well enough allow of) to touch upon them, though ſeemingly collateral to my ſcope. And yet I think, they are but ſeemingly ſo, ſince they do pertinently illuſtrate my deſign, *viz.* That what ſeems *impoſſible* to *us*, may not be ſo in *Nature*; and therefore the *Dogmatiſt* wants this to compleat his demonſtration, that *'tis impoſſible to be otherwiſe.*

Now I intend not any thing here to invalidate the certainty of truths either *Mathematical* or *Divine*. Theſe are ſuperſtructed on principles that cannot fail us, except our faculties do conſtantly abuſe us. Our *religious foundations* are faſtened at the pillars of the *intellectual* world,

and

and the grand *Articles* of our Belief as demonstrable as *Geometry.* Nor will ever either the subtile attempts of the resolved *Atheist* , or the passionate Hurricanoes of the wild *Enthusiast,* any more be able to prevail against the *reason* our *Faith* is built on, than the blustring *winds* to blow out the *Sun.* And for *Mathematical Sciences* , he that doubts their certainty, hath need of a dose of *Hellebore.* Nor yet can the *Dogmatist* make much of these concessions in favour of his pretended *Science* ; for our discourse comes not within the circle of the former : and for the later, the knowledge we have of the *Mathematicks,* hath no reason to elate us ; since by them we know but *numbers,* and *figures,* creatures of our own, and are yet ignorant of our *Maker's.*

X   C H A P.

CHAP. XXV.

(3.) We cannot know any thing in Nature without knowing the first springs of Natural Motions; and these we are ignorant of. (4.) Causes are so connected that we cannot know any without knowing all, declared by Instances.

BUt (3.) we cannot know any thing of *Nature* but by an *Analysis* of it to its *true initial causes*: and till we know the first springs of natural motions, we are still but Ignorants. These are the *Alphabet* of Science, and Nature cannot be *read* without them. Now who dares pretend to have seen the *prime motive causes*, or to have had a view of *Nature*, while she lay in her *simple Originals?* we know nothing but *effects*, and those but by our *Senses*. Nor can we judge of their *Causes*, but by proportion to palpable causalities, conceiving them like those within the sensible *Horizon*. Now t'is no doubt with the considerate, but that the *rudiments* of Nature are very unlike the grosser *appearances*. Thus in things obvious, there's but little resemblance between

tween

tween the *Mucous sperm*, and the compleated *Animal*. The
Egge is not like the *oviparous* production : nor the corrupted *muck* like the *creature* that creeps from it. There's
but little similitude betwixt a *terreous humidity*, and *plantal* germinations; nor do *vegetable* derivations ordinarily resemble their *simple seminalities*. So then, since there's
so much dissimilitude between *Cause* and *Effect* in the
more palpable *Phænomena* , we can expect no less between them, and their *invisible* efficients. Now had our
Senses never presented us with those obvious *seminal*
principles of apparent generations, we should never have
suspected that a *plant* or *animal* could have proceeded
from such unlikely *materials* : much less, can we conceive or determine the uncompounded *initials* of natural productions, in the total silence of our *Senses*. And
though the Grand Secretary of Nature, the miraculous
Des=Cartes have here infinitely out-done all the Philosophers went before him, in giving a particular and *Analytical* account of the *Universal Fabrick* : yet he intends
his Principles but for *Hypotheses,* and never pretends
that things are really or necessarily, as he hath supposed
them : but that they may be admitted pertinently to
solve the *Phænomena,* and are convenient supposals for
the *use of life.* Nor can any further account be expected
from humanity, but how things possibly *may have been
made* consonantly to sensible nature : but infallibly to
determine how *they truly were effected,* is proper to him
only that saw them in the *Chaos,* and fashion'd them out

of that confused *mass*. For to say, the *principles* of Nature must needs be such as our *Philosophy* makes them, is to set bounds to *Omnipotence*, and to confine *infinite power* and *wisdom* to our shallow *models*.

(4.) According to the notion of the *Dogmatist*, we *know nothing*, except we *knew all things*; and he that pretends to *Science* affects an *Omniscience*. For all things being linkt together by an uninterrupted *chain* of *Causes*; and every single motion owning a dependence on such a *Syndrome* of præ-required *motors*: we can have no true knowledge of any, except we comprehend all, and could distinctly pry into the whole *method* of *Causal Concatenations*. Thus we cannot *know* the cause of any one *motion* in a *watch*, unless we were acquainted with all its motive dependences, and had a distinctive comprehension of the whole *Mechanical* frame. And would we *know* but the most contemptible *plant* that grows, almost all things that have a being, must contribute to our *knowledge*: for, that to the perfect *Science* of any thing it's necessary to know all its *causes*; is both reasonable in its self, and the sense of the *Dogmatist*. So that, to the knowledge of the poorest *simple*, we must first know its *efficient*, the *manner*, and *method* of its *efformation*, and the nature of the *Plastick*. To the comprehending of which, we must have a full prospect into the whole *Archidoxis* of Nature's secrets, and the immense profundities of *occult* Philosophy: in which we know nothing till we compleatly ken all *Magnetick*, and *Sympathetick*

ener-

energies, and their moſt hidden cauſes. And (2.) if we contemplate a *vegetable* in its *material* principle, and look on it as made of *Earth*; we muſt have the true Theory of the nature of that Element, or we miſerably fail of our *Scientifical* aſpirings, and while we can only ſay, 'tis *cold* and *dry*, we are pitiful *knowers.* But now, to profound into the *Phyſicks* of this heterogeneous maſs, to diſcern the principles of its conſtitution, and to diſcover the reaſon of its diverſities, are abſolute requiſites of the *Science* we aim at. Nor can we tolerably pretend to have thoſe without the knowledge of *Minerals,* the *cauſes* and *manner* of their Concretions, and among the reſt, the *Magnet*, with its amazing properties. This directs us to the *pole,* and thence our diſquiſition is led to the whole *ſyſteme* of the *Heavens* : to the knowledge of which, we muſt know their *motions,* and the *cauſes,* and *manner* of their *rotations,* as alſo the reaſons of all the *Planetary Phænomena,* and of the *Comets,* their *nature,* and the *cauſes* of all their *irregular appearings.* To theſe, the knowledge of the intricate doctrine of *motion,* the *powers,* *proportions,* and *laws* thereof, is requiſite. And thus we are engaged in the objects of *Geometry* and *Arithmetick;* yea the whole *Mathematicks,* muſt be contributary, and to them all *Nature* payes a ſubſidy. Beſides, *plants* are partly material'd of *water,* with which they are furniſht either from *ſubterranean* Fountains, or the *Clouds.* Now to have the true Theory of the former, we muſt trace the nature of the *Sea,* its origen; and hereto its remarkable

motions

motions of *flux* and *reflux*. This again directs us to the *Moon*, and the rest of the Celestial *phaseis*. The moisture that comes from the *Clouds* is drawn up in *vapours* : To the Scientifical difcernment of which, we must know the *nature* and *manner* of that action, their fufpenfe in the *middle region*, the qualities of that *place*, and the *caufes* and *manner* of their precipitating thence again : and fo the reafon of the *Sphærical* figure of the *drops* ; the caufes of *Windes*, *Hail*, *Snow*, *Thunder*, *Lightning*, with all other igneous appearances, with the whole *Phyfiology* of *Meteors* muft be enquired into. And again (3.) in our difquifition into the *formal Caufes* , the knowledge of the nature of *colours*, is neceffary to compleat the Science. To be inform'd of this, we muft know what *light* is ; and *light* being effected by a motion on the Organs of *fenfe*, 'twill be a neceffary requifite, to underftand the nature of our *fenfitive* faculties, and to them the effence of the *foul*, and other fpiritual fubfiftences. The manner how it is *materially* united, and how it is aware of corporeal *motion*. The feat of *fenfe*, and the place where 'tis *principally* affected : which cannot be known but by the *Anatomy* of our parts, and the knowledge of their Mechanical ftructure. And if further (4.) we contemplate the *end* of the *effect* we inftanc't in, its *principal final* Caufe, being the *glory* of its *Maker*, leads us into *Divinity* ; and for its *fubordinate*, as 'tis defign'd for *alimental* fuftenance to living creatures, and *medicinal* ufes to man, we are conducted into *Zoography*, and the

the whole body of *Phyſick*. Thus then, to the *know-ledge* of the moſt contemptible *effeƐt* in nature, 'tis neceſſary to know the whole *Syntax* of Cauſes, and their particular *circumſtances*, and *modes* of aƐtion. Nay, we *know nothing*, till we *know our ſelves*, which are the ſummary of all the world without us, and the *Index* of the Creation. Nor can we know our ſelves without the *Phyſiology* of corporeal Nature, and the *Me-taphyſicks* of Souls and Angels. So then, every Science borrows from all the reſt; and we cannot attain any ſingle one, without the *Encyclopædy*. I have been the more diffuſe and particular upon this head, becauſe it affordes a catalogue of the Inſtances of our *Ignorance*; and there-fore though it may ſeem too largely ſpoken to in relation to the particular I am treating of, yet 'tis not improper in a more general reference to the ſubjeƐt.

CHAP.

CHAP. XXVI.

All our Science *comes in at our* senses. *Their* infallibility *inquired into.* The Authors design in this last particular.

(5.) THE *knowledge* we have comes from our *senses,* and the *Dogmatist* can go on higher for the original of his certainty. Now let the *Sciolist* tell me, why things must needs be *so,* as his individual *senses* represent them. Is he sure, that objects are not otherwise *sensed* by others, then they are by him? and why must his *sense* be the infallible *Criterion?* It may be, what is *white* to us, is *black* to *Negroes,* and our *Angels* to them are *Fiends.* Diversity of *constitution,* or other circumstances varies the *sensation,* and to them of *Java* Pepper is *cold.* And though we agree in a common name, yet it may be, I have the same representation from *yellow,* that another hath from *green.* Thus two look upon an *Alabaster* Statue; he call's it *white,* and I assent to the appellation: but how can I discover, that his inward *sense* on't is the same that mine is? It may be *Alabaster* is represented to him, as *Jet* is to me, and yet it is *white* to us both. We accord in the *name:* but

it's

it's beyond our knowledge, whether we do fo in the *conception* anfwering it. Yea, the contrary is not without its probability. For though the *Images*, *Motions*, or whatever elfe is the caufe of *fenfe*, may be alike as from the object; yet may the reprefentations be varyed according to the nature and quality of the Recipient. That's one thing to us looking through a *tube*, which is another to our naked *eyes*. The fame things feem otherwife through a *green* glafs, then they do through a *red.* Thus objects have a different appearance, when the *eye* is violently any way *diftorted*, from that they have, when our Organs are in their proper *fite* and *figure*, aud fome extraordinary alterations in the Brain duplicate that which is but a fingle object to our undiftemper'd *Sentient.* Thus, that's of one *colour* to us ftanding in *one place*, which hath a contrary afpect in *another* : as in thofe verfatile reprefentations in the neck of a *Dove*, and folds of *Scarlet*. And as great diverfity might have been exemplified in the other *fenfes*, but for brevity I omit them. Now then, fince fo many various circumftances concurre to every *individual* conftitution, and every mans *fenfes*, differing as much from others in its *figure*, *colour*, *fite*, and infinite other *particularities* in the *Organization*, as any one mans can from it felf, through divers *accidental* variations : it cannot well be fuppos'd otherwife, but that the

Y

con=

conceptions convey'd by them muſt be as *diverſe*. Thus, one mans *eyes* are more *protuberant*, and ſwelling out; anothers more *ſunk* and *depreſſed*. One mans *bright*, and ſparkling, and as it were ſwimming in a *ſubtile*, lucid moiſture; anothers more *dull* and heavy, and deſtitute of that *ſpirituous* humidity. The *colour* of mens *eyes* is various, nor is there leſs diverſity in their bigneſs. And if we look further into the more *inward* conſtitution, there's more variety in the internal *configurations*, then in the *viſible* outſide. For let us conſider the different qualities of the *Optick* nerves, *humours*, *tumours* and ſpirits; the divers *figurings* of the brain; the *ſtrings*, or *filaments* thereof; their difference in tenuity and aptneſs for motion: and as many other circumſtances, as there are individuals in *humane nature*; all theſe are diverſified according to the difference of each *Craſis*, and are as unlike, as our *faces*. From theſe diverſities in all likelyhood will ariſe as much difference in the manner of the recep:ion of the *Images*, and conſequently as various *ſenſations*. So then, how objects are repreſented to my *ſelf*, I cannot be ignorant, being conſcious to mine own *cogitations*; but in what manner they are received, and what impreſſes they make upon the ſo differing *organs* of another, he only *knows*, that *feels* them.

There

'There is an obvious, an eafie objection, which I
have fufficiently caveated againft; and with the confiderate it will fignifie no more then the inadvertency
of the Objectors. 'Twill be thought by flight difcerners a ridiculous *Paradox*, that all men fhould not
conceive of the objects of *fenfe* alike; fince their agreement in the *appellation* feems fo ftrong an argument of
the identity of the *fentiment*. All, for inftance, fay, that
Snow is *white*, and that Jet is *black*, is doubted by none.
But yet 'tis more then any man can determine, whether his *conceit* of what he cals *white*, be the fame
with anothers; or whether, the notion he hath of
one *colour* be not the fame another hath of a very
diverfe one. So then, to direct all againft the *knowing
Ignorant*, what he hath of fenfible evidence, the very
ground work of his *demonftration*, is but the knowledge of his own *refentment* : but how the fame things
appear to others, they only *know*, that are *confcious*
to them; and how they are in *themfelves*, only he that
made them.

Thus have I in this laft particular play'd with the
Dogmatift in a perfonated *Scepticifm* : and would not
have the defign of the whole *difcourfe* meafur'd by the
feeming tendency of this part on't. The *Sciolift* may
here fee, that what he counts of all things moft abfurd and irrational, hath yet confiderable fhew of
probability to plead its caufe, and it may be more

then fome of his prefumed *demonftrations.* 'Tis irreprehenfible in *Phyfitians* to cure their Patient of one difeafe, by cafting him into another, lefs defperate.
And I hope, I fhall not deferve the frown of the
Ingenuous for my innocent intentions ; having in this
only imitated the practice of bending a *crooked* ftick
as much the other way, to ftraighten it.   And if
by this verge to the other extream, I can bring
the *opinionative Confident* but half the way, *viz.* that
difcreet modeft æquipoize of Judgment, that becomes the fons of *Adam*; I have compaft what I.
aim at.

CHAP.

CHAP. XXVII.

Conſiderations againſt Dogmatizing. (1) *'Tis the effect of* Ignorance. (2.) *It inhabits with untamed* paſſions, *and an ungovern'd* Spirit. (3.) *It is the great* Diſturber *of the World.* (4.) *It is* ill manners, *and immodeſty.* (5.) *It holds men captive in* Error. (6.) *It betrayes a* narrowneſs *of* Spirit.

I Expect but little ſucceſs of all this upon the *Dogmatiſt*; his opinion'd aſſurance is paramont to Argument, and 'tis almoſt as eaſie to reaſon him out of a *Feaver*, as out of this *diſeaſe* of the mind. I hope for better fruit from the more generous *Vertuoſi*, to ſuch I appeal againſt *Dogmatizing*, in the following conſiderations; that's well ſpent upon impartial ingenuity, which is loſt upon reſolved prejudice.

(1.) *Opinionative confidence* is the effect of *Ignorance*, and were the *Scioliſt* perſwaded *ſo*, I might ſpare my further reaſons againſt it: 'tis affectation of *knowledge*, that makes

him

him confident he hath *it* ; and his confidence is counter evidence to his pretensions to *knowledge*. He is the
greatest *ignorant*, that knows not that he is *so* : for 'tis a
good degree of *Science*, to be sensible that we *want it*.
He that knows most of himself, knows least of his
knowledge, and the exercised understanding is conscious
of its disability.   Now he that is so, will not lean too
assuredly on that, which hath so frequently deceived
him, nor build the *Castle* of his intellectual security,
in the Air of Opinions. But for the shallow passive intellects, that were never engag'd in a through search of
verity, 'tis such are the *confidents* that engage their irrepealable assents to every slight appearance. Thus meer
sensible conceivers, make every thing they hold a *Sacrament*, and the silly vulgar are *sure* of all things. There
was no Theoreme in the *Mathematicks* more certain to
Archimedes, then the *Earth's* immoveable *quiescence* seems
to the multitude : nor then did the impossibility of
Antipodes, to antique ages. And if great *Philosophers* doubt
of many things, which popular dijudicants hold as certain as their *Creeds*, I suppose *Ignorance* it self will not
say, it is because they are more *ignorant*. Superficial
pedants will swear their controversal uncertainties, while
wiser heads stand *in bivio.* Opinions are the *Rattles*
of immature intellects, but the advanced Reasons have
out-grown them. True knowledge is modest and
wary; 'tis ignorance that is so bold, and presuming.
Thus those that never travail'd beyond one *Horizon*,
                                                                          will

will not be perſwaded that the world hath any Countrey better then their own : while they that have had
a view of other Regions, are not ſo confidently perſwaded of the precedency of that they were bred in,
but ſpeak more indifferently of the *laws*, *manners*,
commodities, and *cuſtoms* of their native ſoil : So they
that never peep't beyond the common belief in which
their eaſie underſtandings were at firſt indoctrinated ,
are ſtrongly aſſured of the Truth, and comparative excellency of their receptions, while the larger Souls, that
have travelled the divers *Climates* of *Opinions*, are more
cautious in their *reſolves*, and more ſparing to determine.
And let the moſt confirm'd *Dogmatiſt* profound far into
his indeared opinions, and I'le warrant him 'twill be an
effectual cure of *confidence.*

(2.) *Confidence in Opinions* evermore dwells with
untamed *paſſions,* and is maintained upon the depraved *obſtinacy* of an ungovern'd *ſpirit.* He's but a novice
in the Art of *Autocraſy,* that cannot caſtigate his *paſſions* in reference to thoſe *preſumptions,* and will come as
far ſhort of *wiſdom* as *ſcience* : for the Judgement being
the leading power, and director of *action*, if It be
ſwaid by the *over-bearings* of *paſſion*, and ſtor'd with
lubricous opinions in ſtead of clearly conceived *truths,*
and be peremptorily reſolved in them, the *practice* will
be as irregular, as the *conceptions* erroneous. *Opinions* hold
the ſtirrup, while *vice* mount into the ſaddle.

(3.) *Dog-*

(3.) *Dogmatizing* is the great disturber both of our *selves* and the *world* without us : for while we wed an *opinion*, we resolvedly engage against every one that opposeth it. Thus *every man*, being in some of his *opinionative* apprehensions *singular*, must be at variance with *all men*. Now every opposition of our espous'd opinions furrows the *sea* within us, and discomposeth the minds *serenity*. And what happiness is there in a *storm* of passions ? On this account the *Scepticks* affected an indifferent æquipondious *neutrality* as the only means to their *Ataraxia*, and freedom from *passionate* disturbances. Nor were they altogether mistaken in the way, to their design'd felicity, but came *short* on't, by going *beyond* it : for if there be a repose naturally attainable this side the *Stars*, there is no way we can more hopefully seek it in. We can never be at rest, while our quiet can be taken from us by every thwarting our opinions : nor is that content an happiness, which every one can rob us of. There is no *felicity*, but in a *fixed stability*. Nor can genuine *constancy* be built upon *rowling* foundations. 'Tis true staidness of mind, to look with an equal regard on all things ; and this unmoved *apathy* in opinionative uncertainties, is a warrantable piece of *Stoicism*. Besides, this *immodest obstinacy* in opinions, hath made the world a *Babel*; and given birth to disorders, like those of the *Chaos*. The primitive fight of *Elements* doth fitly embleme that of *Opinions*, and those *proverbial contrarieties* may be reconcil'd, as soon as peremptory

con-

contenders. That hence grow *Schisms*, *Heresies*, and *anomalies* beyond *Arithmetick*, I could wish were more difficult to be proved. 'Twere happy for a distemper'd *Church*, if evidence were not so near us. 'Tis zeal for *opinions* that hath filled our *Hemisphear* with smoke and darkness, and by a dear experience we know the fury of those *flames* it hath kindled. 'Tis lamentable that *Homo homini Dæmon*, should be a *Proverb* among the Professors of the *Cross*; and yet I fear it is as verifiable among them, as of those without the pale of visible *Christianity*. I doubt we have lost S. *John's* sign of *regeneration*: *By this we know that we are past from death to life, that we love one another*, is I fear, to few a sign of their spiritual *resurrection*. If our Returning Lord, shall scarce find *faith* on earth, where will he look for *Charity*? It is a stranger this side the Region of *love*, and *blessedness*; bitter zeal for *opinions* hath consum'd it. Mutual agreement and indearments was the badge of *Primitive* Believers, but we may be known by the contrary *criterion*. The union of a Sect within it self, is a pitiful *charity*: it's no concord of *Christians*, but a conspiracy against *Christ*; and they that love one another, for their *opinionative concurrences*, love for their *own sakes*, not their *Lords*: not because they have his *image*, but because they bear one *anothers*. What a stir is there for *Mint*, *Anise*, and *Cummin controversies*, while the great practical *fundamentals* are unstudyed, unobserved? What eagerness in the prosecution of *disciplinarian* uncertainties, when the *love* of God and our

Z *neighbour*,

*neighbour,*thofe Evangelical *unqueftionables,* are neglected ?
'Tis this hath confum'd the nutriment of the great and
more neceffary Verities, and bred differences that are
paft any accommodation, but that of the *laft dayes* decifi-
ons. The fight of that day will refolve us, and make us
afham'd of our petty quarrels.

Thus *Opinions* have rent the world afunder, and divided it almoft into *indivifibles.* Had *Heraclitus* liv'd now,
he had wept himfelf into *marble,* and *Democritus* would
have broke his *fpleen.* Who can fpeak of fuch fooleries
without a *Satyr,* to fee aged Infants fo quarrel at *put-
pin,* and the *doating* world grown child *again* ? How fond
are men of a bundle of *opinions,* which are no better then
a bagge of *Cherry-ftones* ? How do they *fcramble* for their
Nuts, and *Apples,* and how zealous for their petty Victories ? Methinks thofe grave contenders about *opinionative
trifles,* look like aged *Socrates* upon his boyes *Hobby-horfe,*
or like fomething more *ludicrous* : fince they make things
their *feria,* which are fcarce tolerable in their fportful *intervals,*

(4.) To be *confident in Opinions* is *ill manners* and *im-
modefty* ; and while we are peremptory in our perfwafi-
ons, we accufe all of *Ignorance* and *Error,* that fubfcribe
not our affertions. The *Dogmatift* gives the *lye* to all dif-
fenting apprehenders, and proclaims his judgement fitteft, to be the *Intellectual Standard.* This is that fpirit of
immorality, that faith unto diffenters, *Stand off,* I am
                                                        more

more *Orthodox then thou art* : a vanity more capital then Error. And he that affirms that things muſt needs be as he apprehends them, implies that none can be right till they ſubmit to his *opinions*, and take him for their director.

(5.) *Obſtinacy in Opinions* holds the Dogmatiſt in the chains of *Error*, without hope of emancipation. While we are confident of *all* things, we are fatally deceiv'd in *moſt*. He that aſſures himſelf he never *erres*, will alwayes *erre* ; and his preſumptions will render all attempts to inform him, ineffective. We uſe not to ſeek further for what we think we are poſſeſt of ; and when falſhood is without ſuſpicion embrac't in the ſtead of truth, and with confidence retained : *Verity* will be rejected as a ſuppoſed Error, and irreconcileably be hated, becauſe it oppoſeth what is truly ſo.

(6.) It betrayes a *poverty* and *narrowneſs* of *ſpirit*, in the Dogmatical aſſertors. There are a ſet of Pedants that are born to ſlavery. But the more generous ſpirit preſerves the liberty of his judgement, and will not pen it up in an *Opinionative Dungeon*; with an equal reſpect he examins all things, and judgeth as impartially as *Rhadamanth* : When as the Pedant can hear nothing but in favour of the conceits he is amorous of; and cannot *ſee*, but out of the grates of his *priſon*. The determinations of the nobler Mind, are but *temporary*, and he holds them,

Z 2

but

but till better evidence repeal his former apprehenfions. He won't defile his affent by proftituting it to every conjecture, or ftuff his belief, with the luggage of uncertainties. The modefty of his expreffion renders him *infallible*; and while he only faith, he *Thinks fo*, he cannot be deceiv'd, or ever affert a *falfhood*. But the wife Monfeur *Charron* hath fully difcourft of this *Univerfal liberty*, and fav'd me the labour of enlarging. Upon the Review of my former confiderations, I cannot quarrel with his *Motto* : in a fenfe *Je ne fcay*, is a juftifiable *Scepticifm*, and not mif-becoming a Candidate of *wifdom*. *Socrates* in the judgement of the *Oracle* knew more then *All men*, who in his own knew the leaft of *any*.

A N

AN
APOLOGY
FOR
Philoſophy.

I T is the glory of *Philoſophy*, that *Ignorance* and *Phrenſie* are it's Enemies; and it may ſeem leſs needful to defend *It* againſt *ſtupid* and *Enthuſiaſtick Ignorants*. However, leaſt my diſcourſe ſhould be an advantage iu the hands of *phancy* and *folly*; or, which is the greater miſchief, leſt it ſhould diſcourage any of the more enlarged ſpirits from modeſt enquiries into Nature; I'le ſubjoyn this brief *Apology*.

If *Philoſophy* be *uncertain*, the former will confidently conclude it *vain*; and the later may be in danger of pronouncing the ſame on their pains, who

ſeek

seek it ; if after all their labour they muſt reap the wind,
meer opinion and conjecture.

But there's a part of Philoſophy, that owes no anſwer to
the charge. The *Scepticks*, ΠΑΝΤΑ ΕΣΤΙΝ ΑΟΡΙΣΤΑ,
muſt have the qualificarion of an exception ; and at leaſt
the *Mathematicks* muſt be priviledg'd from the endictment. Neither yet are we at ſo deplorable a loſs,
in the other parts of what we call *Science*; but that we
may meet with what will content ingenuity, at this diſtance from perfection, though all things will not compleatly ſatisfie ſtrict and rigid *enquiry*. *Philoſophy* indeed
cannot immortalize us, or free us from the inſeparable
attendants on this ſtate, *Ignorance*, and *Error*. But ſhall
we malign it, becauſe it entitles us not to an *Omniſcience* ?
Is it juſt to condemn the *Phyſitian*, becauſe *Hepheſtion*
dyed ? Compleat knowledge is reſerved to gratifie our
glorified faculties. We are ignorant of ſome things from
our *ſpecifical* incapacity ; of more from our *contracted* depravities : and 'tis no fault in the *ſpectacles*, that the *blind
man* ſees not. Shall we, like ſullen children, becauſe we
have not what we would ; contemn what the benignity of Heaven offers us ? Do what we can, we ſhall be
imperfect in all our attainments ; and ſhall we ſcornfully
neglect what we may reach, becauſe ſome things are denyed us ? 'Tis madneſs, to refute the Largeſſes of divine
bounty on *Earth*, becauſe there is not an *Heaven* in them.
Shall we not rejoyce at the gladſome approach of day,
becauſe it's overcaſt with a cloud, and follow'd by the
obſcurity

obscurity of night ? and sublunary vouchsafements have their allay of a contrary ; and uncertainty, in another kind, is the annex of all things this side the *Sun*. Even Crowns and Diadems, the most splendid parts of terrene attains, are akin to that, which *to day is in the field*, and *to morrow is cut down*, and *wither'd* : He that enjoy'd them, and knew their worth, excepted them not out of the charge of *Universal Vanity*. And yet the Politician thinks they deserve his pains ; and is not discourag'd at the *inconstancy* of humane affairs, and the *lubricity* of his subject.

He that looks perfection, must seek it above the *Empyreum* ; it is reserv'd for *Glory*. It's that alone, which needs not the advantage of a foyl : Defects seem as necessary to our now-happiness, as their Opposites. The most refulgent colours are the result of light and shadows. *Venus* was never the less beautiful for her Mole. And 'tis for the Majesty of Nature, like the *Persian Kings*, sometimes to cover, and not alway to prostrate her beauties to the *naked view* : yea, they contract a kind of splendour from the seemingly obscuring veil ; which adds to the enravishments of her transported admirers. He alone sees all things with an unshadowed comprehensive *Vision*, who eminently *is All* : Only the God of *Nature* perfectly knows her ; and light without darkness is the incommunicable claim of him, that dwells in *Light inaccessible*. 'Tis no disparagement to *Philosophy*, that it cannot *Deifie* us, or make good the impossible promise of the *Primitive Deceiver*. It
is

is that, which he owns above her, that muſt perfectly remake us after the Image of our Maker.

And yet thoſe raiſed contemplations of God and Nature, wherewith *Philoſophy* doth acquaint us; enlarge and
ennoble the ſpirit, and infinitely advance it above an ordinary level. The ſoul is alway like the objects of its delight and converſe. A *Prince* is as much above a *Peaſant*
in *ſpirit*, as *condition* : And Man as far tranſcends the
Beaſts in largeneſs of deſire, as dignity of Nature and
employment. While we only converſe with *Earth*, we
are *like* it ; that is, unlike our ſelves : But when engag'd
in more refin'd and intellectual entertainments ; we are
ſomewhat more, then this narrow circumference of fleſh
ſpeaks us. And, me thinks, thoſe generous *Vertuoſi*, who
dwell in an higher Region then other Mortals, ſhould
make a middle ſpecies between the *Platonical* ΘΕΟΙ,
and *common Humanity.* Even our Age in variety of glorious examples, can confute the conceit, that *Souls* are
equal : And the only inſtance of that *Conſtellation* of
Illuſtrious Worthies, which compoſe *The* ℝ O Y A L
S O C I E T Y, is enough to ſtrike dead the opinion of the
Worlds decay, and conclude it in it's Prime. Reflecting
upon which great perſons, me thinks I could eaſily believe, that Men may differ from one another, as much as
Angels do from *unbodyed Souls.* And perhaps more can
be pleaded for ſuch a *Metaphyſical Innovation*, then can
for a *ſpecifical* diverſity among the *Beaſts.* Such as theſe,
being in good part freed from the intanglements of

ſence

sense and *body*, are imployed like the spirits above ; in contemplating the divine Artifice and wisdom in the works of Nature ; a kind of anticipation of the *Æthereal* happiness and imployment. This is one part of the *Life* of *Souls*.

While we indulge to the *Sensitive* or *Plantal* Life, our delights are common to us with the creatures *below us* : and 'tis likely, they exceed us as much in them, as in the senses their subjects ; and that's a poor happiness for Man to aim at, in which Beasts are his Superiours. But those *Mecurial* spirits which were only lent the Earth to shew Men their folly in admiring it ; possess delights of a nobler make and nature, which as it were antedate *Immortality* ; and, at at humble distance, resemb'e the joyes of the world of *Light* and *Glory*. The *Sun* and *Stars*, are not the worlds *Eyes*, but *These* : The *Celestial Argus* cannot glory in such an universal view. These out-travel theirs, and their *Monarchs* beams : passing into *Vortexes* beyond their Light and Influence ; and with an easie twinkle of an Intellectual Eye look into the *Centre*, which is obscur'd from the upper Luminaries. This is somewhat like the Image of *Omnipresence* : And what the *Hermetical Philosophy* saith of *God*, is in a sense verifiable of the thus *ennobled soul*, That *its Centre is every where, but its circumference no where*. This is the ΑΛΗΘΙΝΟΣ ΑΝΘΡΩΠΟΣ; and what *Plotinus* calls so, the *divine life*, is somewhat more. Those that live but to the lower *concupiscible*, and relish no delights but *sensual* ;

Aa   it's

it's by the favour of a *Metaphor*, that we call them *Men*. As *Aristotle* saith of Brutes, they have but the Μιμήματα ἀνθρωπίνης ζωῆς, only some shews and *Apish imitations* of *Humane*; and have little more to justifie their Title to Rationality, then those *Mimick Animals*, the supposed *Posterity* of *Cham*: who, had they retain'd the priviledge of Speech, which some of the *Fathers* say they own'd before the *Fall*; it may be they would plead their cause with them, and have laid strong claim to a Parity. Such, as these, are *Philosophies* Maligners, who computing the usefulness of all things, by what they bring to their *Barns*, and *Treasures*; stick not to pronounce the most generous contemplations, needless unprofitable subtilties: and they might with as good reason say, that the *light* of their Eyes was a superfluous provision of Nature, because it fills not their *Bellies*.

Thus the greatest part of miserable Humanity is lost in *Earth*: and, if Man be an *inversed Plant*; these are *inversed Men*; who forgetting that *Sursum*, which Nature writ in their Foreheads, take their Roots in this sordid Element. But the *Philosophical soul* is an *inverted Pyramid*; Earth hath but a point of this *Æthereal Cone*. *Aquila non captat muscas*, The Royal Eagle flies not but at noble Game; and a young *Alexander* will not play but with Monarchs. He that hath bren cradled in Majesty, and used to Crowns and Scepters; will not leave the Throne to play with Beggars at *Put-pin*, or be fond of of *Tops* and *Cherry-ftones* : neither will a Spirit that dwells with Stars, dabble in this impurer Mud ; or ftoop to be a Play-fellow and Copartner in delights with the Creatures, that have nought but *Animal.* And though it be neceffitated by its relation to flefh to a Terreftrial converfe ; yet 'tis like the *Sun,* without contaminating its Beams. For, though the body by a kind of *Magne-tifm* be drawn down to this *fediment* of univerfal dreggs ; yet the thus impregnate fpirit contracts a *Verticity* to ob-jects above the *Pole* : And, like as in a falling Torch, though the groffer Materials haften to their Element ; yet the flame afpires, and, could it mafter the dulnefs of its load, would carry it off from the ftupid Earth it tends to. Thus do thofe enobled fouls juftifie *Ariftotles* Νᾶς διεςΘεν ἡ Θεῖθ μόνον ; and in allayed fenfe that title, which the Stoicks give it, of ἀπόσπασμα Θεᾶ. If we fay, they are not in their bodies, but their bodies in them ; we have the Authority of the divine *Plato* to vouch us : And by the favour of an eafie fimile we may affirm them to be to the body, as the light of a Candle to the grofs, and fæculent fnuff ; which, as it is not pent up in it, fo nei-ther doth it partake of its ftench and impurity. Thus, as the *Roman* Orator elegantly defcants, *Erigimur, & la-tiores fieri videmur* ; *humana ·defpicimus, contemplantefq; fupera & cœleftia, hæc noftra, ut exigua, & minima, contem-nimus.*

And yet ther's an higher degree, to which *Philofophy* fublimes us. For, as it teacheth a generous contempt of

what

what the grovelling defires of *creeping* Mortals Idolize
and dote on; fo it raifeth us to love and admire an Object, that is as much above terreftrial, as *Infinite* can
make it. If *Plutarch* may have credit, the obfervation of
Natures Harmony in the *celeftial motions* was one of the
firft inducements to the belief of *a God* : And a greater
then he affirms, that the vifible things of the Creation
declare him, that made them. What knowledge we have
of them, we have in a fenfe of their Authour. His face
cannot be beheld by Creature-Opticks, without the allay
of a reflexion; and Nature is one of thofe mirrors, that
reprefents him to us. And now the more we know of
him, the more we love him, the more we are like him,
the more we admire him. 'Tis here, that *knowledge wonders*; and there's an *Admiration*, that's not the *Daughter*
of *Ignorance.* This indeed ftupidly gazeth at the unwonted *effect* : But the Philofophick paffion truly admires
and adores the fupreme *Efficient.* The *wonders* of the Almighty are not feen, but by thofe that go *down into the
deep.* The *Heavens* declare their *Makers Glory*; and *Philofophy theirs*, which by a grateful rebound returns to its
Original fource. The twinkling fpangles, the Ornaments
of the upper world; lofe their beauty and magnificence;
while they are but the objects of our narrow'd fenfes :
By them the *half* is not *told us*; and vulgar fpectators
fee them, but as a confufed huddle of petty *Illuminants.*
But *Philofophy* doth right to thofe *immenfe fphears*, and
advantagioufly reprefents their Glories, both in the vaft-
ness

ness of their *proportions*, and regularity of their *motions*. If we would see the wonders of the *Globe* we dwell in; *Philosophy* must rear us above it. The works of God speak forth his mighty praise: A speech not understood, but by those that *know them*. The most Artful melody receives but little tribute of Honour from the *gazing beasts*; it requires skill to relish *it*. The most delicate musical accents of the *Indians*, to us are but *inarticulate hummings*; as questionless are ours to their otherwise *tuned Organs*. Ignorance of the Notes and Proportions, renders all *Harmony* unaffecting. A gay Puppet pleaseth children more, then the exactest piece of *unaffected Art*: it requires some degrees of *Perfection*, to admire what is truly *perfect*, as it's said to be an advance in Oratory to relish *Cicero*. Indeed the unobservant Multitude, may have some general confus'd apprehensions of a kind of *beauty*, that guilds the outside frame of the Universe: But they are Natures courser *wares*, that lye on the *stall*, exposed to the transient view of every *common Eye*; her choicer *Riches* are lock't up only for the sight of *them*, that will buy at the expence of *sweat* and *Oyl*. Yea, and the visible Creation is far otherwise apprehended by the *Philosophical Inquirer*, then the *unintelligent Vulgar*. Thus the *Physitian* looks with another Eye on the *Medicinal hearb*, then the *grazing Oxe*, which swoops it in with the common *grass*: and the swine may see the *Pearl*, which yet he values but with the *ordinary muck*; it's otherwise pris'd by the skilful *Jeweller*.

And from this laſt Article, I think, I may conclude
the charge, which hot-brain'd folly layes in againſt
Philoſophy; that it leads to *Irreligion*, frivolous and vain.
I dare ſay, next after the *divine Word*, it's one of the beſt
friends to *Piety*. Neither is it any more juſtly accountable for the impious irregularities of ſome, that have
paid an homage to its ſhrine; then *Religion* it ſelf for
the extravagances both *opinionative* and *practick* of high
pretenders to it. It is a vulgar conceit, that *Philoſophy* holds a confederacy with *Atheiſm* it ſelf, but moſt
injurious: for nothing can better antidote us againſt it:
and they may as well ſay, that *Phyſitians* are the only
murtherers. A *Philoſophick Atheiſt*, is as good ſenſe as a
Divine one: and I dare ſay the Proverb, *Ubi tres Medici, duo Athei*, is a Scandal. I think the Original of
this conceit might be, That the Students of Nature,
conſcious to her more *cryptick* wayes of working, reſolve many ſtrange effects into the nearer efficiency of
ſecond cauſes; which common *Ignorance* and *Superſtiti-
on* attribute to the Immediate cauſality of the *firſt*: thinking it to derogate from the Divine Power, that any thing
which is above their apprehenſions, ſhould not be
reckon'd above *Natures* activity; though it be but his
Inſtrument, and works nothing but as impower'd from
him. Hence they violently declaim againſt all, that
will not acknowledge a *Miracle* in every extraordinary
effect, as ſetting Nature in the Throne of *God*; and ſo
it's an eaſie ſtep to ſay, they deny him. When as indeed,

deed, Nature is but the chain of second causes; and to suppose second causes without a first, is beneath the *Logick* of *Gotham*. Neither can they (who, to make their reproach of Philosophy more *anthentick*, alledge the Authority of an *Apostle* to conclude it *vain*) upon any whit more reasonable terms make good their charge; since this allegation stands in force but against its *abuse*, *corrupt sophistry*, or *traditionary impositions*, which lurk'd under the mask of so serious a name: at the worst, the Text will never warrant an universal conclusion any more; then that other, where the Apostle speaks of *silly women*, (who yet are the most rigid urgers of this) can justly blot the *sex* with an unexceptionable note of *infamy*.

Now, what I have said here in this short *Apology* for *Philosophy*, is not so strictly verifiable of any that I know, as the *Cartesian*. The entertainment of which among truly ingenuous unpossest *Spirits*, renders an after-commendation superfluous and impertinent. It would require a *wit* like its Authors, to do it right in an *Encomium*. The strict Rationality of the *Hypothesis* in the main, and the *critical* coherence of its parts, I doubt not but will bear it down to Posterity with a *Glory*, that shall know no *term*, but the *Universal ruines*. Neither can the *Pedantry*, or prejudice of the present Age, any more obstruct its motion in that *supreme sphear*, wherein its desert hath plac'd it; then can the howling Wolves pluck *Cynthia* from her *Orb*; who regardless of their

noise,

noiſe, ſecurely glides through the undiſturbed *Æther.*
Cenſure here will diſparage *it* ſelf, not *it.* He that accuſeth the *Sun* of *darkneſs,* ſhames his own *blind eyes;*
not its *light.* The barking of *Cynicks* at that *Hero's*
Chariot-wheels, will not ſully the glory of his *Triumphs.*
But I ſhall ſuperſede this *endleſs* attempt : *Sun-beams* beſt
commend themſelves.

F I N I S.

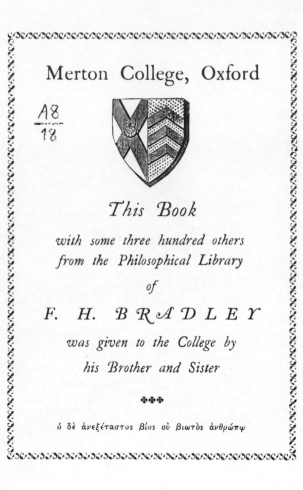

ESSAYS

ON SEVERAL

Important Subjects

IN

PHILOSOPHY

AND

RELIGION.

By JOSEPH GLANVILL,
Chaplain in Ordinary to His Majesty, and
Fellow of the *R. S.*

Imprimatur,
Martii 27.1675. *Thomas Tomkins.*

LONDON,
Printed by *J. D.* for *John Baker,* at the Three Pid-
geons, and *Henry Mortlock,* at the Phœnix in
St. *Pauls* Church-Yard, 1676.

ESSAYS.

VIZ.

I. Againſt CONFIDENCE in PHI-
LOSOPHY.

II. Of SCEPTICISM, and CERTAINTY.

III. MODERN IMPROVEMENTS
of Knowledg.

IV. The USEFULNESS of PHI-
LOSOPHY to THEOLOGY.

V. The Agreement of REASON, and
RELIGION.

VI. Againſt SADDUCISM in the matter of WITCHCRAFT.

VII. ANTIFANATICK *Theologie*, and
FREE *Philoſophy*.

To the most Honourable

HENRY

Lord Marquess, and Earl of *Worcester*, Earl of *Glamorgan*;

Lord *HERBERT*

Of *Chepstow*, *Ragland*, and *Goure*,

Lord President of *Wales*,

Lord Lieutenant of the Counties of *Glocester*, *Hereford*, *Monmouth*, and *Bristol*;

Knight of the most Noble Order of the *Garter*,

And one of the Lords of His Majesties most Honourable Privy Council, *&c.*

MY LORD,

ALthough perhaps in strictness of judging there is somewhat of Impertinency in such Addresses, yet Custome hath obtain'd licence for us Writers *thus* to express our acknowledgments of favours, and to give publick testimonies to the Deserts of excellent Persons: Your Lordship affords me plenty of subject for both these, and I humbly crave your leave to use the Liberty that is

granted

granted without cenſure on ſuch occaſions, to declare part of my reſentments of them.

There is nothing more ſubſtantial, or valuable in Greatneſs, than the power it gives to oblige ; for by doing benefits we in ſome meaſure are like to *Him*, who is the Lover of Men, and cauſeth his Sun to ſhine upon the good, and upon the evil : Nor doth God Himſelf glory in the abſoluteneſs of his Power, and uncontroulableneſs of his Soveraign Will, as he doth in the diſplays of his Goodneſs : This, my Lord, is the right, and honourable uſe of that Greatneſs he is pleaſed to vouchſafe unto Men ; and this is that which makes it amiable, and truly illuſtrious : Your Lordſhip knows *this*, and are as much by Nature as by Judgment, formed to live according to ſuch meaſures : And I think there was never Perſon of your Lordſhip's rank, whoſe general faſhion, and converſation was more ſuited to the ſweeteſt and moſt obliging Rules of living : For beſides that your natural Genius hath nothing haughty, or rough in it, nothing but what is *modeſt*, *gentle*, and *agreeable*, your Lordſhips whole deportment is ſo *affable*, and *condeſcending*, that the benignity of your temper ſeems to ſtrive for ſuperiority over the greatneſs of your quality , which yet it no

way

way *lessens*, but *illustrates*. This is that which highly deserves, and commands the love, and venerations of all that have the honour, and happiness to know you : And you may justly challenge their devotion, and highest esteem upon all other accounts that can give a great Person any title to them. For your immediate descent is from a long masculine line of great Nobles, and you are a Remainder of the illustrious Blood of the PLANTAGENETS. What your Family hath deserv'd from the *Crown*, the vast supplies afforded his late Majesty by that *Loyal Marquess*, your Grand-Father, and the sufferings of your House for Him, do sufficiently declare to the World : But your Lordship hath no need that Arguments of Honour, and respect should be fetcht from your Progenitors ; the highest are due to your personal Vertues, and that *way* of *living* whereby you give example to Men of quality, and shew, how Honour, and Interest is to be upheld. For you spend not your time, and Estate in the Vanities and Vices of the Town, but live *to* your Country, and *in* it, after a splendid, and most honourable Fashion, observing the *Magnificence* and *Charity* of the ancient Nobility, with all the *Decency*, and *Improvements* of latter Times. And perhaps your

Lord-

Lordſhip's *way* is one of the beſt patterns the Age yields, of a *Regular greatneſs*, in which *grandeur* is without *vanity* ; and *Nobleneſs* without *Luxury*, or *Intemperance* : Where we ſee a *vaſt* Family without *noiſe*, or *confuſion* ; and the greateſt *plenty*, and *freedom*, without provocations to any *Debauchery*, or *Diſorder*. So that your Lordſhip's cares, and thoughts are not taken up with the little deſigns that uſually entertain idle, or vainly imployed Men, but in the Service of your King, and Country, and conduct of your Affairs, with prudence and generoſity ; in which you not only ſerve the preſent Age, but provide for the future. And, my Lord, among the acknowledgments that are due to your Vertues, I cannot but obſerve the care you take for the conſtant, daily Worſhip of God in your Family, according to the *Proteſtant* Religion, profeſt by the *Church of England*, and the example your Lordſhip gives by your own attendance on it. This is the ſureſt Foundation of greatneſs, yea 'tis the Crown, and luſtre of it : And when all other magnificence is in the duſt, and is ſhrivel'd into nothing, or at the beſt, into a cold, and faint remembrance, the effects of this will ſtay by us, and be our happineſs for ever ; And all other ſplendors, in compariſon, are but like,

like the ſhining of rotten wood to the Glorys of the Sun, and Stars. This alſo is the beſt fence and ſecurity to our preſent comforts and injoyments, both in reſpect of that temperance and ſobriety it produceth, and chiefly on the account of the bleſſing of the Supream *Donor*, who hath made it the promiſes of *this* Life, as well as of *that which is to come* : And therefore the wickedneſs of thoſe that take Liberty from their Riches and worldly greatneſs, to defie God, and deſpiſe Religion, is as fooliſh and improvident, as 'tis monſtrous and unreaſonable: and thoſe brutiſh Men do not render themſelves more hateful for their impiety, than they are deſpicable for their folly. But I need not ſay this to your Lordſhip, who are ſenſible of the abſurdities, and malignity of this vice, and give not the leaſt countenance, or incouragement to it by your practice; being cautious to abſtain from all expreſſions, that grate on the Honour of God, as you are free from any that can give juſt offence unto Men : For your Lordſhip is none of thoſe that ſhoot the *arrows of bitter words*, and *ſet* their *mouths againſt the Heavens*; but your diſcourſe and converſation is adorn'd with that *modeſty* and *decency* that becomes a great Nobleman, and a good Chriſtian.

a   My

My Lord, I have not given you theſe few juſt acknowledgments, with deſign to gratifie or pleaſe your Lordſhip, I know I need your pardon for the trouble your modeſty receives from them ; but I have done it for the ſake of *others*, becauſe we live in an Age wherein there is ſcarcity of ſuch examples. I know 'tis uſually *indecent* to commend Perſons to themſelves ; but the cuſtome of Dedications will excuſe this, which even *ſeverity* and ill nature cannot impeach of flattery, or extravagance.

And as I owe this Teſtimony to the merits whereby you ſerve and oblige the Age, ſo I ſhould acknowledg the Obligations your Lordſhip hath conferr'd on my ſelf : but this will be a great duty, and buſineſs of my Life ; for ſuch empty expreſſions as theſe verbal ones, are very unſuitable returns for real and great favours ; and if ever better acknowledgments are in my power, I ſhall ſtill remember what I owe your Lordſhip.

I now moſt humbly preſent you with a *Collection* of ſome *Eſſays* upon ſubjects of importance. The deſign of them is to lay a foundation for a good habit of thoughts, both in *Philoſophy*, and *Theology*. They were ſome of them written ſeveral years ago, and had trial

of

of the World in divers Editions: Now they come abroad together (with some things that are *new*) reduced to such an Order, as is most agreeable to my present judgment. I could have added much upon such fertile, and useful Arguments; but I am willing to believe, I have said enough for the capable and ingenious, and I doubt too much for others. If your Lordship shall pardon their imperfections, and accept of the devotion where-with they are offer'd you, it will be the greatest honour, and satisfaction to,

My Lord,

Your Lordships most humble,

Most obliged, and most intirely

devoted Servant,

JOSEPH GLANVILL.

The

The PREFACE.

I Shall not trouble the Reader with much formality, or tediousness of Prefacing, but only give a brief account of the following Discourses. I know it will be no plausible excuse for any of their Imperfections to alledg, that some of them were written when I was very young; since they came abroad again in an Age, wherein more maturity of judgment is expected: But the truth is, I am not grown so much wiser yet, as to have alter'd any thing in the main of those conceptions. If I had thought it worth the while, I might have been more exact in new modelling, and could perhaps have given them a turn that would have been more agreeable to some phancies, but my Laziness, or my Judgment made me think there was no need of that trouble.

The FIRST *Essay against* Confidence in Philosophy, *is quite changed in the way of Writing, and in the Order. Methought I was somewhat fetter'd and tied in doing it, and could not express my self with that ease, freedom, and fulness which possibly I might have commanded amid fresh thoughts: Yet 'tis so alter'd as to be in a manner new.*

The SECOND *of* Scepticism, and Certainty, *was written when I was warm in the Consideration of those matters, for the satisfaction of a particular Friend; what I say was enough for his use, though the Subject is capable of much more; and I had inlarged on it, but that I am loth to ingage further in Philosophical Arguments. I have annext some of the things I said to Mr.* White, *but the main of this Essay was never extant before.*

The THIRD *of* Modern Improvements, *was first a Controversie: I have here given it another shape. As I never begun a Quarrel, so I never will continue any, when I can fairly let it fall. The Discourse was written violently against by one, who was wholly unconcern'd. The interest he pretended, was the defence of his Faculty against a Passage, wherein he would have me say, That the ancient Physicians could not cure a Cut-finger; which I never affirm'd, or thought. But that Person is now so well known, that I need say no more of him, or of that Contest. His long studied, and triumphant Animadversions have given me no reason, or occasion to alter any thing in the Treatise, except some few* Errors
of

of the Press, *over which he most insulted. He hath written divers things against me since, but I have kept the promise I publickly made, and have never read them.*

Besides this Antagonist, *the learned Dr.* Meric Casaubon, *writ* Reflections on this Essay *in a Letter to Dr.* Peter Du Moulin, *who it seems had presented it to him. They were Printed in the year* 1669, *and my Answers soon after ready: But considering that the Doctor allow'd all that which was my main design, and only oppos'd his own mistakes, and suspicions, I thought fit to suppress my Reply; and was the rather silent because not willing to appear in a Controversie with a Person of Fame and Learning, who had treated me with so much Civility, and in a way so different from that of my other Assailants.*

I have further to advertise concerning this Essay, *That whereas I mention several Discourses of Mr.* Boyl's, *as intended for the Publick, 'tis likely that some of them by this may be extant, though my privacy and retirement hath not afforded me the notice of their publication.*

The Fourth Essay *of the* Usefulness *of* Philosophy *to* Theology, *was Printed under the Title of* Philosophia Pia. *I was commanded to reprint it by a Person of* Honour, *and great Fame, for whose Learning and universal Accomplishments I have high and just venerations. This put into my thoughts the design of revising of some of my other Writings, and bringing them together into a small Collection, which I have here done.*

The Fifth *of the* Agreement *of* Reason *and* Religion, *was at first a* Visitation Sermon, *twice Printed before; I have now only cast it into the form of a Discourse. It contains the substance of many thoughts and anxieties about that important matter, in a little compass. My chief care was to state, and represent the whole affair clearly; which I think I have done. The subject hath been written on by divers since, who some of them have perplext the matter again; others have added no one thought. They have written a great deal, I wish I could say, to purpose. I know this freedom is capable of a wrong interpretation, but I am urged to it by a little vexation that the pretenders to such a subject should afford me no advantage for the improving my conceptions on it.*

The Sixth Essay *was one of the first written, and printed four times already. It stands in this place because it shews a particular*

The Preface.

lar *service Philosophy doth, in securing one of the out-works of Religion. The* Dæmon of Tedworth *that was annext, is ready to be* Printed *by it self, with a further Confirmation of that certain, though much opposed Relation. Since the publishing of these* Considerations *there hath a thing been put out, of the* Question of Witchcraft, *denying there are* Witches, *upon some of the weakest pretences I have urged, and disabled. Who ever reads this Essay will see that that Writer was answer'd before he gave himself the trouble to be an Author on that Subject.*

The SEVENTH *is entirely new. 'Tis a description of such a Genius in* Theology *and* Philosophy, *as I confess I my self like; and I believe some others may. But I blame no Mans different sentiment, who allows the liberty of judging that himself takes. I have borrowed the countenance, and colour of my Lord* Bacons *story; of which I have given the brief contents. The Essay is a mixture of an* Idæa, *and a disguised History.*

Reader, *I have done now: But I make thee no promise that I will not write again; for I perceive that those promises are hardly kept. To appear often in the* Press *I know is censur'd; but I see not why that should be a fault, whilst the* Books *themselves have not greater. If a Man write well, he may deserve excuse at least; if otherwise, by use he may mend; or if there be no hopes of that, his writing often is not worth objecting. Nor hath any one need to complain, since no one is concern'd about what another Prints, further than himself pleaseth: And since Men have the liberty to read our* Books, *or not: Methinks they might give us leave to write, or forbear. This I say, because I know this ill-natur'd humour, puts restraint upon the Pens of some great Men; and tempts others to make promises, and excuses, which I think do not become them. For my part I have as little leasure to write Books as other Men, for I have that to do which may be reckoned an Imployment; but every Man hath some vacancies, and I love now and then in this manner to imploy mine. 'Tis an innocent way of entertaining a Mans self, to paint the image of his thoughts, and no better a Writer than my self may happen to divert, if not to instruct, some others by it.*

ERRATA.

ERRATA.

The Reader is defired to take notice of the following *Errours* of the *Prefs*, fome of which are fo near, in found, to the words of the Author, that they may eafily be miftaken for his.

ESSAY. I.

For.	Read.	Page.	Line.
BEft compactnefs	*Feaft* compactnefs,	13	2
The herb, and the flower	Herb, and flower,	16	2
Before *us.* our difcoveries	Before *us,* our difcoveries,	25	34
All opinions	All *their* opinions,	26	21
Old Law,	Old *Saw,*	28	29
Heavens above, &c.	Heavens above *it,*	28	32
Other opinions	Opinions,	30	11
His *faying*	His *fayings*	31	24

ESSAY. II.

For.	Read.	Page.	Line.
Revile againft	*Rail* againft.	43	4
Boafts of ;	Boafts ;	47	16
Ifellus	*Pfellus*	53	19
Are *certain*	*Contain*, and are	62	13

ESSAY. III.

For.	Read.	Page.	Line.
I take 'twas	I take *it* 'twas,	4	10
Virulam	*Verulam*	34	14
Self-*abfurd*	Self-*affur'd*	52	12

ESSAY. IV.

For.	Read.	Page.	Line.
Since *then*	Since *them*	17	16
Difference	*Deference*	26	25
Jumblings, intermixtures	Jumblings *and* intermix-tures	32	13, 14
Flighted	*Slighted*	34	7

ESSAY. V.

For.	Read.	Page.	Line.
Their *own* intereft	Their interefts	28	8

ESSAY.

ESSAY. VI.

For	Read.	Page.	Line.
Streams	*Steams*	14	22
From whatever	What ever	56	17
She apprending	She *apprehended*	56	22

ESSAY. VII.

For	Read.	Page.	Line.
To them. All	To them, All	6	13, 14
From *the* World	From *your* World	6	37
Such of them *that*	Such of them *as*	7	1
They that made	*That* they made	11	6
Main *works*	Main *marks*	30	33
(1.)	(2.)	43	31

Note, that the Sum of my Lord *Bacons Atlantis*, being the brief contents of his Story, printed in the beginning of the 7*th* Essay, was intended as a Preface to it, and should have been in the *Italick* Character; but the Printer hath not done that; nor made a sufficient Break to distinguish my Lord *Bacons* Contents (ending *Page* 2. *Line* 12.) from the Authors Story.

Essay.

Essay I.

Against Confidence *in* Philosophy,

And Matters of Speculation.

ONE of the first things to be done in order to the enlargement, and encrease of Knowledg, is to make Men sensible, how *imperfect* their *Understandings* are in the present state, and how *lyable* to *deception* : For hereby we are disposed to more *wariness* in our Enquiries, and taken off from *bold* and *peremptory* Conclusions, which are some of the greatest hinderances of *Intellectual* improvements in the World. Therefore, by way of *Introduction* to *Philosophy* and grounded Science, we must endeavour first to destroy the *confidence* of *Assertions*, and to establish a *prudent reservedness* and *modesty* in Opinions. In order to *this*, I shall here set down some thoughts I have had on this Subject. And in doing it, I shall

1. Offer some considerable *Instances* of Humane *Ignorance* and *Deficiency*, even in the main, and most usual things in Nature. 2. I shall enquire into the *Causes* of our *imperfection* in Knowledg, which will afford *further evidence* and *proof* of it : and 3. Add some *Strictures* against *Dogmatizing* in *Philosophy*, and all matters of *uncertain* Speculation.

My Instances shall be drawn, 1. From the *Nature* of our *Souls* ; and 2. from the *Constitution* of our *own*, and *other Bodies*.

About the *former* I consider, That if Certainty were *any where* to be expected, one would think it should be had in the Notices of *our Souls*, which are our *true* selves, and whose Sentiments we most inwardly know : In things *without us*,

B   our

our *shallowness* and *ignorance* need not be matter of much wonder, since we cannot pry into the hidden things of Nature, nor observe the first Springs and Wheels that set the rest in motion. We see but little parcels of the Works of God, and want *Phænomena* to make entire and secure *Hypotheses* : But if *that* whereby we know *other* things, know not *it self* ; If our *Souls* are strangers to things *within them*, which they have *more* advantage to understand than they have in matters of *external Nature* ; I think then, that this *first* will be a *considerable Instance* of the *scantness* and *imperfection* of our *Knowledg*.

(1.) I take notice therefore, That the Learned have ever been at great odds and uncertainty about the *Nature* of the *Soul* ; concerning which *every* Philosopher (almost) had a *distinct* Opinion : The *Chaldæans* held it a *Vertue without form* ; *Xenocrates*, and the *Ægyptians*, a *moving Number* ; *Parmenides*, a compound of *Light* and *Darkness* ; *Hesiod* and *Anaximander*, a consistence of *Earth* and *Water* : *Thales* call'd it a *Nature without rest* ; *Heraclides* supposed it to be *Light* ; *Empedocles* to be *Blood* ; *Zeno*, the *Quintessence* of the *Elements*. *Galen* would have it to be an *hot Complexion* ; *Hippocrates*, a *Spirit diffused through the Body* ; *Plato*, a *self-moving Substance* ; *Aristotle*, an *Entelechy*, or no body knows what ; and *Varro*, an *heated* and *dispersed Air*.

Thus have some of the greatest Men of antient times *differ'd* in one of the *first Theories* of *Humane Nature*, which may well be reckon'd an Argument of *uncertainty* and imperfection : And yet I account not the difficulties about *this*, to be so *hopeless*, as they are in *less noted Mysteries*. The great occasion of this diversity, and these mistakes, is, That Men would *form* some *Image* of the Soul in their *Fancies*, as they do in the contemplation of *corporeal* Objects : But this is a wrong way of speculating *Immaterials*, which may be seen in their *effects* and *attributes*, by way of reflection ; but if, like Children, we run behind the Glass to look for them, we shall meet nothing there but disappointment.

2. There hath been as much trouble and diversity in enquiring into the *Origine* of the *Soul*, as in searching into the nature of it : In the opinion of some learned Men, It was from the beginning of the World, created with the Heavens and
Light :

Light: others have thought it an extract from the *Universal Soul:* Some fancied, it descended from the Moon; others from the Stars, or vast spaces of the *Æther* above the Planets; some teach, That God is the immediate Author of it; some that it was made by Angels; and some by the Parents. Whether it be *Created* or *Traduced,* hath been the great Ball of contention to the *latter* Ages, and after all the stir about it, 'tis still as much a question as ever, and perhaps may so continue till the great Day, that will put an end to all Differences and Disputes. The Patrons of *Traduction* accuse their Adversaries of affronting the *Attributes* of God; and the Assertors of *Immediate Creation* impeach them of violence to the *nature of things:* And while each of the Opinions strongly opposeth the other, and feebly defends it self; some take occasion thence to say, That both are right in their Oppositions, but both mistaken in their Assertions. I shall not stir in the Waters that have been troubled with so much contention: The Famous St. *Austin,* and others of the celebrated Antients, have been content to sit down here in a profest Neutrality, and I will not endeavour to urge Confessions in things that will be acknowledged; but shall note some Difficulties, that are not so usually observed, which perhaps have more darkness in them, than *these* so much controverted Doctrines.

1. I begin with the *Union* of the *Soul* and *Body:* In the *Unions* that we *understand,* there is still, either some *suitableness* and likeness of Nature in the things united, or some *middle, participating* Being by which they are joyn'd; but in this there is neither. The natures of Soul and Body, are at the most extream distance; and their essential Attributes most opposite: To be *impenetrable, discerpible* and *unactive,* is the nature of all *Body* and *Matter,* as such: And the properties of a *Spirit* are the direct contrary, to be *penetrable, indiscerpible,* and *self-motive:* Yea, so different they are in all things, that they seem to have nothing but *Being,* and the *Transcendental* Attributes of *that,* in common: Nor is there any appearance of *likeness* between them: For what hath *Rarefaction, Condensation, Division,* and the other properties and modes of Matter, to do with *Apprehension, Judgment,* and *Discourse,* which are the proper acts of a Spiritual Being? We cannot

then

then perceive any *congruity*, by which they are united : **Nor** can there be any *middle* ſort of Nature that partakes of each, (as 'tis in ſome Unions) their Attributes being ſuch *extreams :* or, if there is any ſuch Being, or any ſuch poſſible, we know nothing of it, and 'tis utterly unconceivable. So that, what the *Cement* ſhould be that unites *Heaven* and *Earth*, *Light* and *Darkneſs*, *viz.* Natures of ſo diverſe a make, and ſuch diſagreeing Attributes, is beyond the reach of any of our Faculties : We can as eaſily conceive how a thought ſhould be united to a Statue, or a Sun-beam to a piece of Clay : how words ſhould be frozen in the Air, (as ſome ſay they are in the remote North : or how Light ſhould be kept in a Box ; as we can apprehend the *manner* of this *ſtrange Union.*

2. And we can give no better account how the *Soul moves the Body.* For whether we conceive it under the notion of a *Pure Mind,* and *Knowledg,* with Sir *K. Digby;* or of a *Thinking Subſtance,* with *Des-Cartes;* or of a *penetrable, indiſcerpible, ſelf-motive* Being, with the *Platoniſts;* It will in all theſe ways be unconceivable how it gives motion to unactive matter : For how that ſhould *move a Body,* whoſe nature it is to *paſs through* all Bodies without the leaſt *jog* or *obſtruction,* would require ſomething more than we know, to help us to conceive. Nor will it avail to ſay, that it moves the Body by its *vehicle* of corporeal Spirits ; for ſtill the difficulty will be the ſame, *viz. How it moves them ?*

3. We know as little, How the *Soul ſo regularly directs the Animal Spirits,* and Inſtruments of Motion which are in the Body ; as to ſtir any we have a will to move : For the paſſages through which the Spirits are convey'd, being ſo numerous, and there being ſo many others that croſs and branch from each of them, 'tis wonderful they ſhould not loſe their way in ſuch a Wilderneſs : and I think the wit of Man cannot yet tell how they are directed. That they are conducted by ſome *knowing* Guide, is evident from the *ſteadineſs* and *regularity* of their motion : But *what* that ſhould be, and *how* it doth it, we are yet to ſeek : That all the motions within us are not directed by the meer mechanick frame of our Bodies, is clear from experience, by which we are aſſured, that thoſe we call *Spontaneous* ones, are under the *Government* of the *Will :* at leaſt

the

the *determination* of the Spirits into *such* or such paſſages, is from the *Soul*, whatever we hold of the conveyances after; and *theſe*, I think, all the Philoſophy in the World cannot make out to be *purely mechanical*. But though this be gain'd, that the *Soul* is the *principle* of *Direction*, yet the difficulty is no leſs than it was before: For unleſs we allow it a kind of inward ſight of every Vein, Muſcle, Artery, and other Paſſage of its own Body; of the exact ſite and poſition of them, with their ſeveral Windings, and ſecret Chanels, it will ſtill be as unconceivable, how it ſhould direct ſuch intricate Motions, as that one that was born blind ſhould manage a Game at Cheſs, or marſhal an Army: And if the *Soul* have any ſuch knowledg, we are not aware of it; nor do our minds attend it: Yea, we are ſo far from this, That many times we obſerve not any method in the outward performance, even in the greateſt variety of interchangable motions, in which a ſteady Direction is difficult, and a Miſcarriage eaſie: As we ſee an Artiſt will play on an Inſtrument of Muſick without minding it; and the Tongue will nimbly run diviſions in a Tune without miſſing, when the Thoughts are engaged elſewhere: which effects are to be aſcribed to ſome *ſecret Art* of the Soul (if *that* direct) to which we are altogether ſtrangers.

4. But beſides the Difficulties that lie more deep; we are at a loſs even in the knowledg of our *Senſes*, that ſeem the moſt *plain* and *obvious* of our Faculties. Our eyes that ſee other things, ſee not themſelves; and the *Inſtruments* of *Knowledg* are *unknown*. That the *Soul* is the *percipient*, which alone hath *animadverſion* and *ſenſe*, properly ſo call'd; and that the *Body* is only the *receiver*, and *conveyer* of corporeal *Motions*, is as certain as Philoſophy can make it. *Ariſtotle* himſelf teacheth it in that Maxim, Νῶς ὁρᾷ ὴ νῶς ἀκύει: And *Plato* affirms, That the Soul hath life and ſenſe; but that the *Body* in ſtrictneſs of ſpeaking, hath neither the one nor other: Upon which poſition all the Philoſophy of *Des Cartes* ſtands: And it is ſo clear, and ſo acknowledg'd a Truth, among all conſidering Men, that I need not ſtay to prove it: But yet, what are the *Inſtruments* of ſenſitive Perception, and *particular convers* of outward Motions to the ſeat of Senſe, is difficult to find; and

and how the *pure Mind* can receive information from things
that are not like it felf, nor the objects they reprefent, is, I
think, not to be explain'd.   Whether *Senfation* be made by
corporeal Emiffions, and *material Images* ; or by *Motions* that
are convey'd to the common fenfe, I fhall not difpute : the
latter having fo generally obtain'd among the Philofophers:
But, How the Soul by *mutation*, and *motion* in *matter*, a fubftance of an *other* kind, fhould be excited to action ; and how
thefe fhould concern it, that is of fo divers a nature, is hardly
to be conceiv'd.   For *Body* cannot act on any thing, but by
Motion ; *Motion* cannot be receiv'd but by *Matter*, the *Soul* is
altogether *immaterial* ; and therefore, how fhall we apprehend it to be fubject to *fuch Impreffions ?* and yet *Pain*, and
the *unavoidablenefs* of our Senfations evidently prove, That it
is fubject to them.

Befides, How is it, and by what *Art* doth the Soul read,
That *fuch* an *Image*, or Motion in matter, (whether that of
her Vehicle, or of the Brain, the cafe is the fame) *fignifies
fuch an Object ?* If there be any fuch Art, we conceive it not :
and 'tis ftrange we fhould have a Knowledg that we do *not
know.*   That by diverfity of *Motions* we fhould fpell out *Figures, Diftances, Magnitudes, Colours* ; things not *refembled*
by them, we muft afcribe to fome *implicit inference*, and deduction ; but *what* it *fhould be* ; and by what *Mediums* that
Knowledg is advanced, is altogether *unintelligible.*   For
though the Soul may perceive *Motions* and *Images* by fimple
fenfe, yet it feems unconceivable it fhould apprehend what
they *fignifie*, and reprefent, but by fome fecret Art and way
of inference : An illiterate Perfon may fee the Letters, as well
as the moft Learned, but he knows not what they mean ; and
an Infant hears the founds, and fees the motion of the Lips,
but hath no conception convey'd to him, for want of knowing the fignification of them : fuch would be our cafe, notwithftanding all the motions and impreffions made by external things, if the Soul had not fome unknown way of learning by them the quality of the Objects.   For inftance, *Images* and *Motions* have but very *fmall* room in the Brain, where
they are receiv'd, and yet they reprefent the *greateft* Magnitudes ;   The Image, Figure, (or what-ever elfe it may be
call'd)

call'd) of an Hemisphere of the Heavens, cannot have a Subject larger than the pulp of a Walnut ; and how can such petty Impressions, make known a Body of so vast a wideness, without some kind of *Mathematicks* in the Soul : And except this be suppos'd, I cannot apprehend how *Distances* should be perceiv'd ; but all Objects would appear in a cluster. Nor will the Philosophy of *Des-Cartes* help us here ; For the moving *divers Filaments* in the Brain, cannot make us perceive such modes as Distances are, unless some such Art and Inference be allow'd, of which we understand nothing.

5. The *Memory* is a Faculty in us as *obscure*, and perhaps as unaccountable as any thing in Nature. It seems to be an *Organical* Power, because Diseases do often blot out its Ideas, and cause Oblivion : But what the marks and impressions are by which the Soul *remembers*, is a question that hath not yet been very well resolv'd. There are four principal Hypotheses by which an account hath been attempted ; The *Peripatetick*, the *Cartesian*, the *Dighæan* and the *Hobbian*.

1. According to the *Peripatetick* Schools, *Objects* are conserv'd in the memory by certain *Intentional Species* (as they call them) a sort of Beings, that have a necessary dependance upon their Subjects ; but are not material in their formal Constitution and Nature. I need not say much against these arbitrary precarious Creatures, that have no foundation in any of our Faculties : Or be that how it will, They are utterly *unintelligible* ; neither *bodily*, nor *spiritual* ; neither produc'd out of *any* thing, as the *matter* of their production ; nor out of *nothing*, which were *Creation*, and not to be allow'd to be in the power of every, or any finite Being. And though there were no such contradictious contrivance in the framing these Species, yet they could not serve any purpose, as to the Memory, since 'tis against the nature of *emanative* Effects, such as these are, to subsist but by the continual influence of their Causes ; and so, if this were the true Solution, we could remember nothing longer than the Object was in presence.

2. The account of *Des-Cartes* is to this purpose ; The Spirits are sent about the Brain, to find the *tracks* of the Objects we would call to mind ; which Tracks consist in *this, viz, That the Pores through which the Spirits that came from*
the

the Objects past, are more easily open'd, and afford a more ready passage to those others that seek to enter; whence ariseth a *special motion* in the *Glandule,* which signifies *this* to be that we would remember.

But if our *Remembrance* arise from the *easie motion* of the *Spirits* through the *opened* passages (according to this Hypothesis); How then do we so distinctly remember such a variety of Objects, whose Images pass the *same* way? And how the *Distances* of Bodies that *lie in a Line?* Why should not the impell'd Spirits find *other* open passages, besides those made by the thing we would remember? When there are such continual motions through the Brain from numerous other Objects? Yea, in such a pervious substance as that is, why should not those subtile Bodies meet, every where an easie passage? It seems to me that one might conceive as well, how every Grain of Corn in a Sieve should be often shaken through the same holes, as how the Spirits in the repeated acts of Memory should still go through the same Pores: Nor can I well apprehend but that those supposed open'd passages, would in a short time be stopt up, either by the natural gravity of the parts, or the making new ones near those; or other alterations in the Brain.

3. The *Hypothesis* of Sir *Kenelm Digby,* is next, *viz.* That things are preserv'd in the Memory by *material Images* that flow from them, which having imping'd on the common sense, rebound thence into some vacant Cells of the Brain, where they keep their ranks, and postures, as they entred, till again they are stirr'd, and then they appear to the Fancy as they were first presented.

But how is it conceiveable, That those active Particles which have nothing to unite them, or to keep them in any order, yea which are continually justled by the occursion of other minute Bodies, (of which there must needs be great store in this Repository) should so long remain in the same state and posture? And how is it that when we turn over those Idæa's that are in our memory, to look for any thing we would call to mind, we do not put all the Images into a disorderly floating, and so make a Chaos of confusion there, where the exactest Order is required: And indeed according

to

to this account, I cannot ſee but that our Memories would be more confuſed than our Dreams : and I can as eaſily conceive how an heap of Ants can be kept to regular and uniform Motions.

4. Mr. *Hobbs* attempts another way ; there is nothing in us, according to this Philoſopher, but *Matter* and *Motion*: All *Senſe* is *Reaction* in *Matter* [*Leviath.* Chap. 1.] the *decay* of that *Motion*, and *Reaction*, is *Imagination* ; [Chap. 2.] And *Memory* is the ſame thing, *expreſſing that decay.* [*Ib.*] So that according to *M. H.* all our *Perceptions* are *Motions*, and ſo is *Memory* : Concerning which, I obſerve but two things ;

1. Neither the *Brain*, nor *Spirits*, nor any other *material* Subſtance within the Head, can for any conſiderable time conſerve Motion. The *Brain* is ſuch a *clammy* Conſiſtence, that it can no more retain it than a *Quagmire*, The *Spirits* are more *liquid* than the Air, which receives every Motion, and loſeth it as ſoon : And if there were any *other corporeal* part in us, as fitly temper'd to keep Motion as could be wiſht ; yet (2.)the *Motions* made in it would be quickly *deadned* by *Counter-Motions*;and ſo we ſhould never remember any thing,longer than till the next Impreſſion : and it is utterly impoſſible that ſo many Motions ſhould orderly ſucceed one another,as things do in our Memories ; For they muſt needs, ever and anon, thwart, interfere, and obſtruct one another, and ſo there would be nothing in our Memories, but Confuſion and Diſcord.

Upon the whole we ſee, that this ſeemingly plain Faculty, the *Memory*, is a Riddle alſo which we have not yet found the way to reſolve.

I might now add many other difficulties, concerning the *Underſtanding, Fancy, Will*, and *Affections* : But the Controverſies that concern *theſe*, are ſo hotly managed by the divided Schools, and ſo voluminouſly handled by diſputing Men, that I ſhall not need inſiſt on them : The only Difficulties about the *Will*, its *nature* and *manner* of *following* the *Underſtanding*, &c. have confounded thoſe that have enquired into it ; and ſhewn us little elſe, but that our Minds are as *blind*, as that *Faculty* is ſaid to be by moſt Philoſophers. Theſe Controverſies, like ſome Rivers, the further they run, the

C   more

more they are hid : And perhaps after all our Speculations and
Difputes, we conceive lefs of them now, than did the more
plain, and fimple Underftandings of former times. But whether we comprehend or not, is not my prefent bufinefs to enquire, fince I have confined my felf to an Account of fome
great Myfteries, that do not make fuch a noife in the World :
And having fpoken of fome that relate to our *Souls* ; I come
now to fome others that concern

II. *BODIES :* I begin with our *Own* ; which though
we *fee*, and *feel*, and have them *neareft* to us, yet their inward
Conftitution and Frame, is hitherto an undifcovered Region :
And the faying of the Kingly Prophet, that *we are wonderfully
made*, may well be underftood of that *admiration*, that is
the Daughter of Ignorance.

For, 1. There hath no good account been yet given, how
our *Bodies* are *formed :* That there is *Art* in the contrivance of
them, cannot be denied, even by thofe that are leaft beholden
to Nature : and fo elegant is their compofure, that this very
Confideration faved *Galen* from being an *Atheift :* And I cannot think that the branded *Epicurus*, *Lucretius* and their Fellows were in earneft, when they refolv'd this Compofition into a *fortuitous range of Atoms :* 'Twere much lefs abfurd to
fuppofe, or fay, that a Watch, or other curious *Automaton* ;
did perform divers *exact* and *regular* Motions, by *chance* ; than
'tis to affirm, or think, that this admirable *Engine*, an *Humane
Body*, which hath fo many Parts, and Motions, that *orderly*
cooperate for the good of the whole, was framed without the
Art of fome knowing Agent : But who the fkilful, particular
Archeus fhould be ; and by *what* Inftruments, and *Art* this Fabrick is erected, is ftill unknown. That God hath *made us*,
and *fafhion'd* our Bodies in *the nethermoft parts of the Earth*,
is undoubted ; But he is the *firft* and *univerfal* Caufe, who
tranfacts things in Nature by *fecondary* Agents, and not by
his own *immediate hand :* (The fuppofal of *this* would deftroy
all Philofophy, and enquiry after Caufes) So that *He* is ftill
fuppofed ; but the Query is of the *next*, and *particular Agent*,
that forms the Body in fo exquifite a manner ; a Queftion that
hath not yet been anfwered. Indeed by fome 'tis thought
enough to fay, That it is done by the *Plaftick Faculty* ; and by
others

others 'tis believ'd that the *Soul* is that that forms it. For the *Plastick Faculty*, 'tis a *big word*, but it conveys nothing to the Mind : For it signifies but *this*, that the Body is *formed* by a *formative Power*; that is, 'tis *done*, by a *power of doing it*. But the doubt remains still, what the *Agent* is that hath *this power* ? The other Opinion of the *Platonists*, hath two Branches : some will have it to be the particular Soul, that fashions its own Body ; others suppose it to be the general Soul of the World : If the former be true, By what *knowledg* doth it do it ? and *how* ? The *means*, and *manner* are still *occult*, though that were granted. And for the *other* way, by a *general Soul* ; That is an *obscure* Principle, of which we can know but little ; and how that acts (if we allow such a being) whether *by knowledg*, or *without*, the Assertors of it may find difficulty to determine. The former makes it little less than *God* himself ; and the *latter* brings us back to *Chance*, or a *Plastick Faculty*. There remains now but one account more, and that is the *Mechanical* ; *viz.* That it is done by *meer Matter* moved after *such*, or *such* a manner. Be that so : It will yet be said, that *Matter* cannot move *it self* ; the question is still of the *Mover* ; The Motions are *orderly*, and *regular* ; Query, *Who guides ?* *Blind Matter* may produce an elegant effect for once, by a great Chance ; as the Painter accidentally gave the Grace to his Picture, by throwing his Pencil in rage, and disorder upon it ; But then *constant* Uniformities, and Determinations to a *kind*, can be *no Results* of *unguided Motions*. There is indeed a *Mechanical Hypothesis* to this purpose ; That the Bodies of *Animals* and *Vegitables* are formed out of *such* particles of Matter, as by reason of their Figures will not lie together, but in the order that is necessary to make *such* a Body ; and in *that* they naturally concur, and rest ; which seems to be confirm'd by the *artificial Resurrection* of *Plants*, of which *Chymists* speak, and by the regular Figures of Salts, and *Minerals* ; the *hexagonal* of *Chrystal*, the *Hemi-spherical* of the *Fairy-Stone*, and divers such like. And there is an experiment mentioned by approved Authors, that looks the same way ; It is, That after a decoction of Herbs in a frosty Night, the shape of the Plants will appear under the Ice in the Morning : which Images are supposed to be made by the congregated *Effluvia* of the

Plants

Plants themselves, which loosly wandring up and down in
the Water, at last settle in their natural place and order, and
so make up an appearance of the Herbs from whence they were
emitted.   This account I confess hath something ingenious in
it; But it is no solution of the Doubt.   For how those *hete-*
rogenous Atoms should hit into their proper places, in the
midst of such various and tumultuary Motions, will still remain a question : Let the *aptness* of their *Figures* be granted,
we shall be yet to seek for something to *guide* their *Motions* :
And let their *natural Motion* be what it will, *gravity* or *levity*,
direct or *oblique*, we cannot conceive how *that* should carry
them into every particular place where they are to lie ; especially considering they must needs be sometimes diverted from
their course by the occursion of many other Particles.   And
as for the *Regular Figures* of many *inaminate* Bodies, that consideration doth but *multiply* the doubt.

2. The *union* of the *parts* of *Matter*, is a thing as difficult
as any of the former :   There is no account that I know, hath
yet appear'd worth considering, but *that* of *Des-Cartes* ; *viz.*
That they are *united* by *juxta-position*, and *rest*.   And if this
be all, Why should not a bag of Dust be of as firm a Consistence, as Marble or Adamant ?   Why may not a Bar of Iron
be as easily broken as a pipe of Glass ; and the Ægyptians *Py-*
ramids blown away, as soon as those *inverst ones* of smoke.
The only reason of difference pretended by some, is, that the
Parts of *solid* Bodies are held together by natural *Hooks* ; and
strong ones, by *such* Hooks as are more *tough* and *firm :* But
how do the parts of these *Hooks* stick together ?   Either we
must suppose *infinite* of them *holding each other* ; or come at
last to parts united by *meer juxta-position*, and *rest*.   The former is very absurd, for it will be necessary, That there should
be *some*, upon which the *Cohesion* of *all the rest* should *de-*
pend ; otherwise, all will be an heap of Dust.   But in favour
of the Hypothesis of *Des-Cartes*, it may be said, That the
closeness and *compactness* of the parts resting together, makes
the *strength* of the *Union :* For, (as that *Philosopher* saith)
Every thing continues in the state wherein it is, except something
more powerful alter it ; and therefore the Parts that rest close together will so continue, till they are parted by some other stron-

ger

ger Body : Now the *more* parts are pent together, the *more* able they will be for *resistance* ; and what hath best *compactness*, and by consequence *fewer parts*, will not be able to make any alteration in a Body that hath *more*. According to this Doctrine, what is *most dense*, and *least porous*, will be *most* coherent,. and *least* discerpible ; which yet is contrary to experience. For we find the most *porous*, *spongy* Bodies, to be ofttimes the most *tough* of Consistence. We easily break a Tube of Glass or Chrystal ; when one of Elm, or Ash, will hardly be torn in pieces : and yet as the *parts* of the *former* are *more*, so are they more at *rest* ; since the *liquid* Juice diffused through the Wood is in continual agitation, which in *Des-Cartes* his *Philosophy* Is the cause of *fluidity* ; so that according to his Principles, the *dryest* Bodies should be the most *firm* ; when on the contrary, we find that a *proportionate humidity* contributes much to the *strength* of the *Union*. (Sir *K. Digby* makes it the *Cement* it self) and the *driness* of many Bodies is the cause of their *fragility*, as we see 'tis in *Wood*, and *Glass*, and divers other Things.

3. We are as much at a loss about the *composition* of *Bodies*, whether it be out of *Indivisibles*, or out of parts always divisible : For though this question hath been attempted by the subtilest Wits of all Philosophick Ages ; yet after all their *distinctions*, and *shifts*, their new-invented words, and *modes*, their *niceties* and tricks of *subtilty*, the Matter stands yet unresolv'd. For do what they can, *Actual*, *Infinite extension every where* ; *Equality* of all *Bodies*, *Impossibility* of *Motion*, and a world more of the most palpable Absurdities, will press the Assertors of *Infinite Divisibility* : Nor on the other side, can it be avoided, but that all *Motions* would be equal in *velocity* : That the *Lines* drawn from side to side in a *Pyramid*, would have *more Parts* than the *Basis* : That *all Bodies* would be *swallowed* up in a *Point* ; and many other Inconsistencies will follow the Opinion of *Indivisibles*. But because I have confined my self to the Difficulties that are not so usually noted; I shall not insist on *these*, but refer the Reader, that hath the humour, and leisure, to inquire into such Speculations, to *Oviedo*, *Pontius*, *Ariaga*, *Carelton*, and other Jesuites, whose management of this Controversie, with equal force on either side,

ſide, is a conſiderable Argument of the unaccountableneſs of this Theory, and of the weakneſs of our preſent Under-ſtandings.

I might now take into conſideration the Myſteries of *Moti-on*, *Gravity*, *Light*, *Colours*, *Viſion*, *Sounds*, and infinite ſuch like, (things *obvious*, yet *unknown*) but I inſiſt no further on Inſtances, but deſcend to the ſecond thing I propounded to treat of, *viz.*

II. The *C A U S E S* of our *Ignorance*, and Miſtakes; And in them we ſhall find further evidence of the imperfection of our Knowledg. The Cauſes to be conſider'd, are either, 1. The *Difficulties* and *Depth* of *Science* : Or, 2. The *pre-ſent temper of our Faculties.* Science is the *Knowledg* of things in their *Cauſes* ; and ſo 'tis defined by the Pretenders to it. Let us now enquire a little into the difficulties of attain-ing ſuch Knowledg.

1. We know no Cauſes by *Simple Intuition*, but by *Conſe-quence* and *Deduction* ; and there is nothing we ſo uſually in-fer from, as *Concomitancy* ; for inſtance, We *always* feel *heat* when we come near the *Fire*, and *ſtill* perceive *Light* when we ſee the *Sun* ; and thence we conclude, that theſe are the Cauſes reſpectively of *Heat*, and *Light* ; and ſo in other things. But now in this way of inference there lies great uncertainty : For if we had never ſeen more Sun, or Stars, than we do in cloudy weather, and if the Day had always broke with a Wind, which had increaſt and abated with the Light ; we ſhould have believed firmly that one of them had been the cauſe of the other; and ſo Smoke had been undoubtedly thought the efficient of the Heat, if nothing elſe had appeared with it. But the Philoſophy of *Des-Cartes* furniſheth us with a better Inſtance ; All the World takes the Sun to be the Cauſe of Day, from this Principle of Concomitance : But that Philoſopher teacheth, That Light is cauſed by the *Conamen*, or endeavour of the Matter of the Vortex to recede from the Centre of its Motion ; ſo that were there *none* of *that fluid Æther* in the midſt of our World, that makes up the *Sun*, yet the *preſſure* of the *Globuli* (as he calls thoſe Particles) upon our Eyes, would not be conſiderably leſs : and ſo according to this Hy-potheſis, there would be *Light* though there were no *Sun*, or

Stars ;

Stars; and *Evening*, and *Morning* might *naturally* be *before*, and *without the Sun.* Now I say not that this Opinion is true and certain; but 'tis *possible*, and I know no absurdity in it; and consequently, our concluding a *Causality* from *Concomitancy*, *here*, and in *other* Instances may deceive us.

2. Our *best natural* Knowledg is *imperfect*, in that, after all our confidence, *Things still are possible to be otherwise* : *Our Demonstrations* are raised upon *Principles* of our *own*, not of *Universal* Nature; And, as my Lord *Bacon* notes, we judg from the *analogy* of our *selves*, *not the Universe* : Now many things are *certain*, according to the *Principles* of one Man, that are *absurd* in the apprehensions of many others : and some appear *impossible* to the *vulgar*, that are *easie* to Men of more improved Understandings. That is extravagant in one Philosophy, which is a plain truth in another : and perhaps what is most impossible in the apprehensions of Men; may be otherwise in the *Metaphysicks*, and *Physiology* of Angels. The sum is, We conclude *this* to be *certain*, and *that* to be *impossible* from our own narrow Principles, and little Scheams of Opinion. And the *best Principles* of *natural* Knowledg in the World, are but *Hypotheses*, which *may be*, and *may be otherwise* : So that though we may *conclude* many things upon such and such Suppositions, yet still our Knowledg will be but fair, and hopeful *Conjecture* : And therefore we may affirm that things are *this* way, or *that*, according to the Philosophy that we have espoused; but we strangely forget our selves when we plead a *necessity* of their being so in Nature, and an *impossibility* of their being otherwise. The *ways* of God in *Nature* (as *in Providence*) are not as *ours* are : Nor are the Models that we frame any way commensurate to the vastness and profundity of his Works; which have a *depth* in them greater than the *Well* of *Democritus*.

3. We cannot properly and perfectly know any thing in Nature without the knowledg of its *first Causes*, and the Springs of Natural Motions : And who hath any pretence to *this?* Who can say he hath seen Nature in its *beginnings?* We know nothing but *Effects*, nor can we judg at their immediate Causes, but by proportion to the things that do appear; which no doubt are very *unlike* the *Rudiments* of Nature.

ture. We see there is no resemblance between the *Seed*, and the *Herb*, and the *Flowre*; between the *Sperm*, and the *Animal*; The *Egg*, and the *Bird* that is hatcht of it; And since there is so much *dissimilitude* between *Cause* and *Effect* in these *apparent* things, we cannot think there is *less* between them and their *first*, and *invisible* Efficients : Now had not our Senses assured us of it, we should never have suspected that *Plants*, or *Animals* did proceed from such *unlikely Originals*; never have imagined, that *such Effects* should have come from *such Causes*, and we can conceive as little now of the nature and quality of the Causes that are beyond the prospect of our Senses : We may frame Fancies and Conjectures of them, but to say that the *Principles* of Nature are *just* as *our Philosophy* makes them, is to set bounds to Omnipotence, and to circumscribe infinite Power, and Wisdom, by our narrow Thoughts and Opinions.

4. Every thing in Nature hath *relation* to divers others; so that no one Being can be perfectly known without the knowledg of many more : Yea, every thing almost hath relation to all things; and therefore he that talks of *strict Science*, pretends to a kind of *Omniscience*. All things are linkt together; and every Motion depends upon many prerequired Motors; so that no one can be perfectly known singly. We cannot (for instance) comprehend the cause of any Motion in a Watch, unless we are acquainted with other dependent Motions; and have insight into the whole mechanical contexture of it; and we know not the most contemptible Plant that grows in any perfection, and exactness, until we understand those other things that have relation to it; that is, almost every thing in Nature. So that each Science borrows from all the rest, and we attain not any single one, without comprehending the whole Circle of Knowledg.

I might say much more on this Subject, but I may have further occasion of speaking to it, under the *second* General, *viz.* The Consideration

II. Of the Imperfection of our present Faculties; and the malign Influence our *Senses* and *Affections* have upon our Minds. I begin with the *S E N S E S*; and shall take no-
notice,

tice, 1. Of their *Dulneſs* ; and 2. of their *liableneſs* to Errour and *Miſtake*.

1. Our *Senſes* are very *ſcant* and *limited* ; and the *Operations* of Nature *ſubtil*, and *various*. They are only its *groſſer* Inſtruments, and ways of working that are *ſenſible* ; the *finer* Threads, and *immediate* Actions are out of reach ; Yea, it's *greateſt* works are perform'd by *inviſible, inſenſible* Agents.

Now moſt of our *Conceptions* are taken from the *Senſes*, and we can ſcarce judg of any thing but by the help of *material* Images, that are *thence* convey'd to us. The *Senſes* are the *Fountain* of *natural* Knowledg ; and the *ſureſt* and *beſt Philoſophy* is to be raiſed from the *Phænomena*, as *they* preſent them to us : when we leave *theſe*, and retire to the *abſtracted notions* of our minds, we build Caſtles in the Air, and form *Chymerical Worlds*, that have *nothing real* in them. And yet when we take our accounts from thoſe *beſt* Informers, we can learn but very little from their Diſcoveries. For we ſee but the *ſhadows*, and *outſides* of things ; like the men in *Plato's* Den, who ſaw but the *Images* of external Objects, and but *ſo many* as came in through the narrow entrance of their Cave. The *World* of *God*, no doubt, is an other thing, than the *World* of *Senſe* is ; and we can judg but little of its *amplitude* and *glory* by the imperfect Idea we have of it. From this narrowneſs of our Senſes it is, that we have been ſo long ignorant of a World of Animals that are with us, and about us, which now at laſt the *Glaſſes*, that in part cure this imperfection, have diſcover'd ; and no doubt, there is yet a great variety of living Creatures that our *beſt* Inſtruments are *too groſs* to diſcloſe : There is *Prodigious fineneſs*, and *ſubtilty* in the *works* of *Nature*, which are too *thin* for our *Senſes*, with all the advantages Art can lend them : And many, the greateſt, and the beſt of its Objects are ſo *remot* that our Senſes reach them not by any *Natural* or *Artificial* helps : So that we cannot have *other* than *ſhort* and *confuſed* apprehenſions of thoſe works of Nature : And I ſometimes fear, that we ſcarce yet ſee any thing as it is. But this belongs to an other conſideration, *viz.*

2. Our *Senſes* extremely *deceive us* in their *reports*, and informations ; I mean, they give occaſion to our minds to deceive themſelves. *They* indeed repreſent things *truely* as they *appear*

D

to

to *them*, and in *that* there is *no deception*; but then, we *judge* the
exterior *Realities* to be *according* to thofe *appearances*, and *here*
is the Error and Miftake.   But becaufe the *Senfes* afford the
ground and *occafion*, and we naturally judg according to *their*
impreffions, therefore the *Fallacies* and *Deceits* are imputed to
their mifinformations.   This I premife, to prevent a Philofophical miftake, but fhall retain the common way of fpeaking,
and call *thofe* the *errors* of the *Senfes.*   That *thefe* very frequently mifreport things to us, we are affured even from themfelves : a *ftraight* ftick feems *crooked* in the *Water*, and a *fquare*
Towre *round* at a *diftance* ; All things are *Yellow* to thofe that
have the *Jaundice*, and all Meats are *bitter* to the *difaffected*
Palate : To which vulgar Inftances it will prefently be anfwer'd, that the Senfes in thofe cafes, are not in their *juft circumftances* ; but want the fit *medium*, due *diftance*, and *found
difpofition :* which we know very well, and learn there was
fomewhat amifs ; becaufe our Senfes reprefent thofe things o-
therwife at othertimes : we fee the ftick is *ftraight* when it is
out of the Water ; and the Tower is *fquare* when we are *near*
it. Objects have *other Colours*, and Meats *other taftes*, when the
Body, and its Senfes are in their ufual temper.   In fuch cafes,
Senfe rectifies its own miftakes, and many times one the errors
of another ; but if it did not do fo, we fhould have been *alwayes deceived even* in *thofe* Inftances : and there is no doubt,
but that there are many other *like deceptions*, in which we have
no contrary evidence from them to difabufe us; not in the matters of common Life, but in things of *remoter fpeculation*, which
this ftate feems not to be made for.   The Senfes muft have their
due *medium*, and *diftance*, and *temper* ; if any of *thefe* are a-
mifs, they reprefent their Objects *otherwife* to us than they
are : Now *thefe*, we may fuppofe. they generally have, in the
neceffary matters of Life, if not to report things to us as they
are in themfelves, yet to give them us *fo*, as may be for our
accommodation, and advantage : But how are we affur'd,
that they are *thus rightly difpofed*, in reference to things of
Speculative Knowledg ? What *medium*, what *diftance*, what
temper is neceffary to convey Objects to us juft *fo*, as they are
in the *realities* of Nature ? I obferv'd before that our Senfes
are *fhort, imperfect*, and uncommenfurate to the vaftnefs and

pro-

profundity of things, and therefore cannot receive the *just* I-mages of them : and yet we judg all things according to those *confused,* and *imperfect Ideas,* which must needs lead us into infinite errors, and mistakes.

If I would play the *Sceptick* here, I might add, That no one can be sure that any Objects appear in the same manner to the Senses of other men, as they do to his: Yea, it may seem probable, that they *do not ?* For though the I*mages, Motions,* (or whatever else is the cause of Sence) may be *alike* as from them; yet the *representations* may be much varied according to the *nature* and *quality* of the *recipient* : we find things look otherwise to us through an *Optick* Tube, then they do when we view them at a distance with our *naked* eyes : the same Object appears *red,* when we look at it through a Glass of *that* Colour, but *green* when we behold it through one of *such* a Tincture. Things seem *otherwise* when the Eye is *distorted,* then they do, when it is in its *natural, ordinary,* posture; and some *extraordinary alterations* in the Brain *double that* to us, which is but a *single* Object : Colours are *different,* according to different *Lights,* and *Positions* ; as 'tis in the necks of *Doves,* and folds of Scarlet : Thus *difference* in *circumstances alters* the *sensation;* and why may we not suppose as *much diversity* in the Senses of *several* men, as there is in those *accidents,* in the perceptions of *one ?* There is *difference* in the *Organs* of Sense, and *more* in the *temper* and *configuration* of the *inward* parts of the Brain, by which motions are convey'd to the seat of Sense; in the *Nerves, Humours* and *Spirits,* in respect of *tenuity, liquidity, aptitude* for *motion,* and divers other circumstances of their nature ; from which it seems that great diversity doth arise in the manner of receiving the *Images,* and consequently in the perceptions of their Objects. So then, though every man knows, *how* things appear to *himself,* yet *what* impressions they make upon the so *different* Senses of another, *he only knows* certainly, that is *conscious* to them. And though all men agree to call the *impression* they feel from *such,* or *such* an Object, by the *same* name; yet no one can assuredly tell but that the *Sentiment* may be *different* ; It may be one man hath the impression of *Green* from *that,* which in another begets the Sense of *Yellow* ; and yet they both call it *Green,* because from their infancy they were wont to join *that* word to *that* Sentiment, which fuch an Object produc'd in their *particular* Senfe ; though in *feveral* men it were a very divers one.   *This* I know fome will think hard to be underftood ; but I cannot help that : Thofe that *Confider* will find it to be very plain; and therefore I fhall fpend no more words about it.

The Sum is, Our Senfes are good Judges of *Appearances*, as they concern us : but how things *are* in themfelves, and how they *are* to others, it fhould feem, we cannot *certainly* learn from them : And therefore when we determine that they *are*, and *muft* be according to the reprefentations of our *individual* Senfes, we are very often grofly deceiv'd in fuch fentences ; to which yet we are exceeding prone ; and few but the moft exer-cifed minds, can avoid them. Of this I'le give a *great* Inftance or two.

1. It is almoft *univerfally* believ'd (at leaft by the vulgar,) that the *Earth refts* on the *Centre* of the World ; and thofe an-cient Philofophers have been extreamly hooted at, and derided, that have taught the contrary doctrine: For my part, I fhall af-firm nothing of the main queftion; but this I fay, That the com-mon inducement to believe it ftands ftill, viz. the *Teftimony* of *Senfe*, is no argument of it: And whether the opinion of *Pytha-goras*, *Copernicus*, *Des-Cartes*, *Galilæo*, and almoft all late Philofo-phers, of the *motion* of the *Earth*, be *true*, or *falfe* ; the belief of its *Reft*, as far as it arifeth from the *prefum'd evidence* of *Sence*, is an error.

That there is fome common motion that makes the day, and night and the varieties of feafons, is very plain and fenfible; but whether the *Earth*, or the *Sun* be the Body mov'd, none of our Senfes can determine; To *Senfe* the *Sun ftands ftill* alfo; and *no* Eye can perceive its *Actual* motion. For though we find that in a little time it hath *chang'd* its *Pofition*, and *refpect* to us ; yet whether *that change* be cauf'd by *its tranflation* from *us*, or *ours* from *it*, the *Senfe* can never tell : and yet from *this*, and *this* only, the greateft part of mankind believes its motion. On the other fide, The ftanding ftill of the *Earth* is concluded the *fame* way ; and yet, though it did move, it would appear *fixt* to us as *now* it doth, fince we are carried with it, in a *regular* and moft *even* courfe, in which cafe *motion* is not *perceiv'd* ; as

we

we find fometimes in failing in a Ship, when the *Shores* feem to *move*, and not *that* ; —— *Littus, Campiq; recedunt.*

But I give another Inftance of a like deception; It is, 2. The *tranflation of our own paffions* to *things without us* : as we judg *Light* and *Heat*, and *Cold*, to be *formally* in the *Sun, Fire,* and *Air* ; when as indeed they are but *our own perceptions.* As they are in thofe external Subjects, they are nothing, but *fuch* or *fuch configurations and motions* in matter;but when they *work* on *us*, they produce different *fentiments*, which we call *Heat*, and *Light*,&c. This will appear to be true to any one that can *freely* and *attentively* confider it ; and yet it will be thought fo ftrange and abfurd by the generality of men, that they will affoon believe with *Anaxagoras*, that *Snow is black*, as him that affirms, that the *Fire* is not *formally hot* ; that is, that the *very thing* we *feel*, and call *Heat* in our felves, is not *fo* in *that body:* when as *there*, it is but a *violent agitation* of the *fubtile*, and *divided* parts of matter, that in it felf is nothing *like* what we perceive from it, and call *Heat* : That we are *hot* our felves, we *feel* ; but that the *Fire* hath any fuch *formal* quality as is in our Senfe, *no Senfe* can inform us ; and yet from its fuppofed evidence men generally *fo* conclude. Which is an other confiderable Inftance of the *falfe* judgments we make on the occafion of our Senfes.

And now, It is not only *common* underftandings that are abufed,and deceiv'd by their Senfes; but even the moft advanc'd Reafons are many times mifled by them : And fince we live the Life of *Beafts* before we grow up to Men, and our minds are *Paffive* to the impreffions of Senfe, it cannot be, that our firft knowledg fhould be other, than heaps of Errour, and mifconception ; which might be rectified by our *after-judgments*, but that 'tis another unhappinefs of our natures, that thofe early impreffions ftick by us, and we are exceedingly apt pertinacioufly to adhere to them : And though our improving underftandings do in part undeceive us, and deftroy fome *groffer* errours ; yet *others* are fo faftned, that they are never after remov'd, or diffetled. So that we are not quite weaned from our *Child-hood* till we return to our *fecond Infancy*; and even our Grey-Heads out-grow not thofe errors, which we learnt before the Alphabet. And therefore fince we contracted fo

many

many prejudices in our tender years, and thoſe Errors have as plauſible an appearance, as the moſt genuine truths, the beſt way to attain true Knowledg is to *ſuſpend* the giving our confirm'd aſſent to thoſe Receptions, till we have looked them over by an impartial inquiry; To reckon of them all as falſe, or uncertain, till we have examin'd them by a *free*, and *unpoſ-ſeſt* Reaſon; and to admit nothing but what we *clearly*, and *diſtinctly perceive*. This is the great *Rule*, in the excellent Method of *Des-Cartes*; but the practiſe of it requires ſuch a *clear*, *ſedate* and *intent* mind, as is to be found but in a very few rare tempers; and even in *them*, *prejudices* will creep in, and ſpoil the *perfection* of their *Knowledg*.

I might diſcourſe next of thoſe Errors that do ariſe from the *fallacies* of our *Imaginations*, whoſe unwarrantable com-poſitions and *applications*, do very frequently abuſe us: and in-deed, the *Reaſon* of the greateſt part of mankind is nothing elſe but *various Imagination*; Yea, 'tis a hard matter for the *beſt* and *freeſt* minds to deliver themſelves from the *Prejudices*, of Phancy; which, beſides the numerous leſſer Errors they betray us into, are great occaſions (particularly) of thoſe many miſtakes we are guilty of in ſpeculating *Immaterial* Natures, & inquiring into the *Attributes* of God; and we are much entangled, and puzled by them, in all things we think, or ſay about *Infinity*, *Eternity* and *Immenſity*, and moſt other of the ſublime Theorics both of *Philoſophy*, or *Theology*. But *theſe* all ariſe, either from the *falſe Images* of *Senſe*, and the undue compoſitions, and wrong inferences that we raiſe from them; and therefore I ſhall not need make *this* a diſtinct head from the other, of which I have juſt treated.

I come now, II. To conſider the evil Influence our *Affe-ctions* have over our Underſtandings, by which they are great Reaſons of our *Ignorance*, and *Miſtakes*. *Periit Judicium ubi res tranſiit in affectum*. That *Jupiter* himſelf can-not be *Wiſe*, and in *Love*, was a ſaying of the Ancients, and may be underſtood in a larger Senſe then They meant. *That* under-ſtanding *only* is capable of paſſing a juſt Sentence, that is, as *Ariſtotle* ſaith of the *Law*, Νᾶς ἄνευ ὀρέξεως; but where the *Will* and *Paſſions* have the caſting voice, the cauſe of Truth is deſ-perate.

perate.   Now this is the prefent unhappy ftate of Man; our *lower* powers are gotten *uppermoſt*, and we fee like Men *on their Heads*, as *Plato* obferv'd of old, *That on the right hand, which indeed is on the left.*   The *Woman* in us ftill profecutes a deceipt like *that* begun in the Garden; and we are wedded to an *Eve*, as fatal as the Mother of our Miferies.   The *Deceiver* foon found this foft place in *Adam*, and Innocency it felf did not fecure him from *this* way of feduction : We now fcarce fee any thing but through our paſſions, that are wholly blind, and incapable: So that the Monſters that ſtory relates to have their *Eyes* in their *Breaſts*, are pictures of us in our *inviſible ſelves*.

And now, all things being double-handed, and having *appearances* both of *Truth*, and *Falſhood*, the ingaged affection *magniſieth* the *ſhews of Truth*, and makes the belov'd opinion appear as *certain*; while the *conſiderations* on the *otherſide* being *leſſened* and neglected, feem as nothing, though they are never fo *weighty* and confiderable.   But I fhall be more particular in the account of thefe Deceptions.

Our Affections ingage us, by our *love* to *our ſelves*, or *others*; the former in the Inſtance of, 1. *Natural diſpoſition,* 2. *Cuſtom* and *Education*, and 3. *Intereſt* : the *latter*, in our over-fond *Reverence* to 4. *Antiquity* and *Authority.*

1. There is a certain *congruity* of *ſome* opinions to the particular tempers of fome men : For there is a *complexion*, and *temperament* in the *mind*, as well as in the *body* : And the doctrines that are fuited to the genius, and fpecial difpoſition of the underſtanding, find eaſy welcom, and entertainment : whereas, *thoſe* that are *oppoſite* to it, are rejected with an invincible contempt and hatred.   On this account we find men taking in fome particular Opinions with ſtrange pleaſure and fatisfaction, upon their firſt propoſals ; when they are incurably barred up againſt others, that have the advantage of more reafon to recommend them.   And I have obſerv'd often, that even fome Theories in Philofophy will not lie in fome minds, that are otherwife very capable and ingenious : of which I take this to be a conſiderable Inſtance, That divers learned men profefs, They cannot conceive a *Spirit* (or any being) without *extenſion*; where as others fay, They cannot conceive, but that whatever is *extended* is *impenetrable*,

and

and confequently *corporeal* ; which diverfity I think, I have reafon to afcribe to fome difference in the natural temper of the mind.

2. But another very fatal occafion of our miftakes, is the great prejudice of *Cuftom* and *Education* : which is fo unhappily prevalent, that though the Soul were never fo truly ἄγϱαφον γϱαμμαΤεῖον (as the Philofopher call'd it) an unwritten table in it felf; yet this doth very often fo fcribble on it, as to render it incapable of other impreffions: we judg all things by thofe *Anticipations*; and condemn, or applaud them, as they differ, or agree, with our firft Opinions. 'Tis on this account that almoft every Country cenfures the *Laws, Cuftoms,* and *Doctrines* of *every other,* as *abfurd,* and *unreafonable,* and are confirm'd in their *own* follies beyond poffibility of conviction. Our firft Age is like the melted wax to the prepared Seal, that receives any impreffion ; and we fuck in the opinions of our Clime and Country, as we do the common Air, without thought, or choice ; and which is worfe, we ufually fit down under thofe Prejudices of Education and Cuftom all our Lives after: For either we are loth to trouble our felves to examine the Doctrines we have long taken for granted, or we are fcar'd from inquiring into the things that Cuftom and common Belief have made Venerable and Sacred. We are taught to think, with the *Hermit,* that the *Sun* fhines no were but in our Cells, and that *Truth* and *Certainty* are confin'd within that Belief, in which we were firft inftructed. From whence we contract an obftinate adherence to the conceits in which we were bred, and a refolv'd contempt of all other Doctrines : So that what *Aftrologers* fay of our *Fortunes,* and the events of common life, may as well be faid of the opinions of the moft, that they are written in their Stars, having as little freedom in them as the effects of Deftiny. And fince the *Infufions* of *Education* have fuch intereft in us, are fo often appeal'd to as the dictates of *Truth,* and *impartial* Reafon ; 'tis no wonder we are fo frequently deceiv'd, and are fo imperfect in our Knowledg. Another caufe of which is,

3. The power that *Intereft* hath over our Affections, and by them over our *Judgments.* When men are ingag'd by *this,* they can find Truth *any where*; and what is *thought conve-*
nient

nient to be true, will at laft be *believed* to *be fo. Facilè credimus quod volumus.* So that I do not think, that the learned Affertors of vain, and falfe Religions, and Opinions, do always profefs againft their Confciences ; rather their Intereft brings their Confciences to their Profeffion ; for this doth not only corrupt Mens Practife, but very often pervert their Minds alfo, and infenfibly miflead them into Errours.

4. But our *Affections* mifguide us by the refpect we have to *others*, as well as by that we bear to our felves : I mentioned The Inftances of *Antiquity*, and *Authority*. We look with a fuperftitious Reverence upon the accounts of paft Ages, and with a fuperciliousSeverity on the more deferving products of our own : a vanity that hath poffeft all times as well as ours ; and the *golden* Age was *never prefent*. For as an inconfiderableWeight by vertue of it's diftance from theCentre of the Ballance will out-weigh much heavier bodies that are nearer to it ; fo the moft light, and vain things that are far off from the prefent Age, have more Efteem, and Veneration then the moft confiderable, and fubftantial that bear a modern date : and we account *that* nothing worth, that is not fetcht from a far off ; in which we very often deceive our felves as that Mariner did, that brought home his Ship Fraught with common Pebbles from the Indies. We adhere to the Determinations of our Fathers as if their Opinions were *entail'd* on us ; and our Conceptions were *ex Traduce*.

And thus while every Age is but an *other fhew* of the *former*, 'tis no wonder that humane fcience is *no more* advanced above it's *ancient* Stature: For while we look on fome admired Authors as the Oracles of all Knowledg, and fpend that time, and thofe pains in the Study and Defence of their Doctrines, which fhould have been imploy'd in the fearch of Truth, and Nature ; we muft needs ftint our own Improvements and hinder the Advancement of Science ; Since while we are Slaves to the Opinions of thofe before us. Our Difcoveries, like water will not rife higher then their Fountains ; and while we think it fuch Prefumption to endeavour beyond the *Ancients*, we fall fhort of *Genuine Antiquity*, Truth: unlefs we fuppofe them to have reach't perfection of Knowledg in fpight of their own acknowledgments of Ignorance.

E   And

And now whereas it is obferv'd, that the *Mathematicks* and *Mechanick* Arts have confiderably advanc'd, and got the ftart of other Sciences; this may be confidered as a chief caufe of it, That their Progrefs hath not been retarded by this reverential awe of former Difcoveries: 'Twas never an Herefie to out-limn *Apelles*, or to out-work the *Obelisks*: *Galilæus*, without a Crime, out-faw all Antiquity, and was not afraid to believe his Eyes, in reverence to *Ariftotle* and *Ptolomy*. 'Tis no difparagement to thofe famous Optick Glaffes that the Ancients never us'd them; nor are we *fhy* of their Informations, becaufe they were *hid from Ages*. We believe the *polar* vertue of the *Loadftone*, without a *Certificate* from the *dayes* of old, and do not confine our felves to the *fole* conduct of the *Stars*, for fear of being *wifer* than our *Fathers*. Had *Authority* prevail'd *here*, the *fourth* part of the Earth had been yet *unknown*, and *Hercules Pillars* had ftill been the Worlds *Ne ultra*: *Seneca's Prophefie* had been an *unfulfil'd* Prediction, and one Moity of our Globes an *empty Hemifphere*.

'Tis true, we owe much reverence to the Ancients, and many thanks to them for their Helps and Difcoveries; but *implicitly* and *fervilely* to fubmit our Judgments to all Opinions, is inconfiftent with that refpect that we *may*, and *ought* to have to the *freedom* of our our own *Minds*, and the *dignity* of *Humane Nature*. And indeed (as the great Lord *Bacon* hath obferv'd) we have a wrong apprehenfion of *Antiquity*, which in the common acception is but the *nonage* of the World. *Antiquitas feculi eft juventus Mundi*: So that in thofe Appeals, we fetch our Knowledg from the Cradle, and the comparative infancy of days. Upon a true account, the *prefent* Age is the *greateft Antiquity*; and if *that* muft govern and fway our Judgments, *let multitude of days fpeak*. If we would reverence the Ancients as we ought, we fhould do it by imitating their Example, which was not *fupinely* and *fuperftitioufly* to fit down in fond admiration of the Learning of thofe that were before them, but to examine their Writings, to avo d their Miftakes, and to ufe their Difcoveries, in order to the further improvement of Knowledg: This they did; efpecially the Philofopher *Ariftotle* ufed the moft freedom in cenfuring and reproving the fuppofed Errors and Miftakes of the

elder

elder Philosophers, of any that ever had that Name : And therefore there is the less reason why Men should make his Writing *Textuary*, and as it were *infallible*, without daring to use the liberty that he taught by his practice.

It was from this servile humour of idolizing some fortunate and fam'd Authors, that arose that silly vanity of *impertinent Citations*, and alledging *Authorities* in things, that neither require nor deserve them. The Man, no doubt, thought the saying to be Learning, and an Elegancy, *That Men have Beards, and that Women have none* ; when he had quoted *Beza* for it : and that other aim'd to be accounted no mean Clerk, that could say, *Pax res bona est*, saith St. *Austin* : This folly, as ridiculous as it is, was once very common among those that courted the reputation of being Learned ; and it is not quite worn out of use yet among the Vulgar of Scholars, though all the wiser have outgrown, and do despise it ; And the rest will do the same, when they come to consider, how vain and inglorious it is, to have our Heads and Books laden, as Cardinal *Campeius* his Mules were, with old and useless Luggage. And if the magnificence of many Pretenders to Knowledg were laid open, it would amount to no more, than the old Boots and Shooes of that proud and expos'd Ambassadour. Methinks it is but a poor easie Knowledg that can be learnt from an Index ; and a mean ambition to be rich in the Inventory of an others Treasure. *Authorities* alone make no *number*, unless evidence of Reason stand before them, and all the *Ciphers* of *Arithmetick*, are no better than a *single nothing*.

But I return to the consideration of *Antiquity* : If we impartially look into the *Remains* of *ancient* days, we shall find but little to justifie our so slavish a veneration of them : For if we take an account of the state of Science from the beginning, and follow the History of it through the most famous Times, we shall find, that though it hath often changed its Channel, removing from one Nation to another ; yet it hath been neither much *improved*, nor *altred*, but as Rivers are in passing through different Countries, viz. in *Name*, and *Method* : For the succeding Times subscribing to, and copying out those that went before them, with little more than verbal

E 2 Diver-

Diverfity, Knowledg hath ftill been *really* the fame poor and
mean Thing, though it hath appeared in pompous Cloathing,
and been dignified by the fervices of many great and renowned
Names.   The *Grecian* Learning was but a Tranfcript of the
Chaldean and *Ægyptian*; and the *Roman* of the *Grecian* : And
though thofe former Days had, no doubt, many great Wits,
and *thofe* that made noble Difcoveries ; yet we have reafon to
think that the moft confiderable and moft worthy of them,
have perifht and are forgotten.   For as the forementioned
great Man, the Lord *Bacon* hath obferv'd, *Time*, as a *River*,
brings down to us what is more *light* and *fuperficial*, while
the Things that are more *folid* and *fubftantial* are funk and
loft.

And now after *all this*, it will be requifite for me to add,
That I intend not thefe Remarques in favour of any *new* Con-
ccits in *Theology*, to gain credit to *fuch* by difparaging Chriftian Antiquity : No, *Here* the *old* Paths are undoubtedly *beft*,
quod verum id prius : And I put as much difference between
the pretended *New Lights*, and *Old Truths*, as I do between
the *Sun* and an evanid *Meteor* : Though I confefs in *Philofophy* I am a *Seeker*.   *Divine Truths* were moft pure in their
Beginnings ; they were born in the *fulnefs* of time ; and, (as
fome fay the Sun was Created) in their *Meridian* Strength
and Luftre :   But the *Beginnings* of *Philofophy* were in a very
obfcure Dawn, and perhaps 'tis yet fcarce *Morning* with it.
And therefore what we cannot find among former Inquirers,
we are to feek in the Attempts of more *Modern Men*, and in
the Improvements of nearer Ages :   And not be difcouraged
by the Old Law, *Nil dictum quod non dictum prius*.   For as
to *Knowledg*, there is no doubt but there are many things *new*
under the *Sun*, and *this* Age hath fhewn many *Novelties* even
in the Heavens above, *&c.*

I have thus fhewn thee How our *Senfes* and *Affections* miflead our Underftandings; and fo are great occafions of our Ignorance and Errors ; to which I may add,

III. That the *Underftanding* more immediately contributes
to *its own* Deceptions, through its *Precipitancy*, and *haft* in
concluding. *Truth* is not to be attained, without much *clofe*
                                                          and

and *severe* inquiry : It is not a *wide Superficies*, easie to be
seen, but like a *Point* or *Line* that requires *Acutness* and *Intention* to discover it ; which is the more difficult, because it
is so mingled with *Appearances* and *specious* Errors, like the
Silver in *Hiero's* Crown of Gold ; or rather like the Grains
of *Gold* in a *Mass* of *baser* Mettals ; It requires much *Care,*
and *nice Observation* to extract and separate the *precious Oar*
from so much *vile Mixture* ; so that the *Understanding* must
be *patient,* and *wary,* and *thoughtful* in seeking Truth ; It
must go step by step, and look every way, and regard many
Things : It must distrust Appearances, and be shy of Assent,
and consider again and again before it fixeth. This Method
is necessary to the attainment of Knowledg ; but the *Mind* is
generally indisposed to so much Labour and Caution. It is
impatient of *suspence,* and *precipitant* in concluding ; *averse* to
deep Meditation, and ready to *catch* at every *Appearance :*
And hence also it is that we embrace Shadows of Fancy and
Opinion, and miss of true and substantial Knowledg.

Having now given *Instances* of the *Imperfection* of our present Knowledg, and shewn some of its Causes, which are further evidence of it ; I come to offer a few Considerations on
the whole, against *Dogmatizing,* and *Confidence* in uncertain
Opinions. As,

1- *Confidence* in *Philosophy,* and Matters of *Doubtful Speculation* betrays a grosser, and more stupid sort of *Ignorance* ;
For 'tis the first step of Knowledg to be sensible that we want
it : The most exercised Understandings are most conscious to
their Imperfections ; and he that is sensible of the frequent
failings of his Judgment, will not lean with much trust, and
assurance on that which hath so often deceived him, nor build
the Castle of his *intellectual* Security in the Air of Opinions :
But on the other side, the shallow, unthinking Vulgar, are
sure of all things, and bestow their *peremtory, full* assent on
every slight appearance. *Knowledg* is always *modest* and *wary* ;
but *Ignorance* is *bold* and *presuming,* as *Aristotle* hath observ'd
of the *confidence* and *forwardness* of Youth. Thus those that
have always liv'd at home, and have never seen any *other*
Country, are confidently perswaded that their *own* is the *best* ;
whereas

whereas they that have travel'd, and obſerv'd other Places,
ſpeak more coldly and indifferently of their native Soils; and
ſo thoſe confined Underſtandings that never looked beyond the
Opinions in which they were bred, are exceedingly aſſur'd of
the Truth, and comparative excellency of their own Te-
nants; when as the *larger* Minds that have travail'd the divers
Climates of Opinions, and conſider'd the various Sentiments
of inquiring Men, are more *cautious* in their *Concluſions,* and
more *ſparing* in *poſitive* Affirmations. And if the Dogmatiſt could be perſwaded to weigh the *Appearances* of Truth
and Reaſon, that are in many other Opinions that he counts
unreaſonable and *abſurd,* this would be a means to *allay,* if not
to *cure* his Confidence.

2. *Dogmatizing* in things uncertain, doth commonly inha-
bit with *untamed Paſſions,* and is uſually maintain'd upon the
obſtinacy of an *ungover'd* Spirit. For one of the firſt Rules in
the *Art* of *Self-Government,* is, to be *modeſt* in Opinions:
And *this Wiſdom* makes Men *conſiderate* and *wary,* diſtruſtful
of their own Powers, and jealous of their Thoughts: He
that would *rule* himſelf, muſt be *circumſpect* in his Actions;
and he that would be *ſo.* muſt not be *haſty,* and over-*confident*
in his Concluſions. 'Tis *Pride,* and *Preſumption* of ones ſelf
that cauſeth ſuch forwardneſs and aſſurance; and where thoſe
reign, there is neither *Vertue* nor *Reaſon*; No *regular Government,* but a miſerable *Tyranny* of *Paſſion* and *Self-will.*

3. *Confidence* in Opinions, is the great diſturber both of
our *own Peace,* and of the *quiet* of other Men. He that *affirms* any thing *boldly,* is thereby ingaged againſt every one
that oppoſeth it; He is *concern'd,* and *undertakes* for his Te-
nent, and muſt *fight* his way: He confronts every different
Judgment, and quarrels all Diſſenters; He is angry that others
do not ſee *that,* which he preſumes is ſo clear; he clamours
and reviles; He is ſtill *diſputing,* and ſtill in a ſtorm: He cannot bear a *Contraction,* nor ſcarce a *Suſpence* of Judgment. So
that his Peace is at every ones Mercy, and whoever will croſs
his ſaying, throws him into the Fire, and deſtroys his Quiet:
And ſuch a Man need not be more miſerable. On this account
the *Stoicks* affected an *indifferency* and *neutrality* in all Things,
as the only means to that *freedom* from *Paſſion* and *Diſturbance,*
                                                        which

which they fought : and if there be any repofe attainable by
the Methods of Reafon, there is nothing fo like to afford it,
as *unconcernment* in doubtful Opinions.   The *contrary* Zeal
and affurance, as it robs every Man of his *private* happinefs,
fo hath it deftroyed the *Peace* of *Mankind :* It hath made the
World an *Aceldama*, and a *Babel*.   For *this* is the ground of
all the *Schifms*, and *ftrivings* of Sects, that have fill'd our
Air with Smoke and Darknefs ; yea, and kindled the fierce
Flames that have confumed us.   Every vain *Opiniator* is as
much *affured* as if he were infallible ; His Opinions are
Truths, certain *Truths*, *Fundamental* Ones ; and the *contrary*
Doctrines *Heretical* and *Abominable*.   Hence arife *Difputes*,
Hatreds, *Separations*, *Wars*, of which we have feen, and yet
fee very much ; and God knows how much more we may :
Of all which Mifchiefs here is the Gronnd, *viz.* Mens *pre-*
fumptions of the *certainty* of their *own Conceits* and *Ways :*
and could they but be induced to be *modeft* in them, and to
look on them with the eye of lefs affurance, it would abate
their *Heats* and *Animofities*, and make way for Peace, and
charitable Agreement in the things that are *undoubtedly True*,
and *Good*.

4. *Confidence* in *Opinions* is *ill Manners*, and an affront to
all that differ from us ; For the Dogmatift chargeth every one
with *Ignorance* and *Error*, that fubfcribes not his Saying.   In
effect, he gives the lie to whofoever dares diffent from him ;
and declares that his Judgment is fitteft to be the *Intellectual*
Standard.   This is that Spirit of *Pride* and *Rudenefs*, that
faith to every different Apprehender, *Stand off*, I am more
Orthodox than thou art ; a Vanity that is worfe than any fimple
Error.

5. *Dogmatizing*, and Confidence in doubtful Tenents, holds
the Opiniator faft in his Mifconceits and Errors.   For he that
is confident of all things, is unavoidably deceiv'd in moft ;
and he that *affures* himfelf he *never* errs, will always err : His
Prefumptions will defeat all attempts of better Information.
We never feek for *that* which we think we *have already*, but
reject thofe Aids that make promife and offer of it.   And he
that huggs *Vanity* and *Falfhood*, in the confidence of undoubted *Truth* and *Science*, is commonly intractable to the Methods

thods that should rectifie his Judgment.   *Ignorance* is far sooner cured, than *false conceit* of *Knowledg* : and he was a very wise Man that said, *There is more hope of a Fool, than of him that is wise in his own Eyes.*

6. Dogmatizing shews *Poverty*, and *narrowness* of Spirit : There is no greater *Vassallage*, than that of being enslaved to Opinions.   The *Dogmatist* is pent up in his Prison, and sees no Light but what comes in at those Grates.   He hath no *liberty* of *Thoughts*, no *prospect* of various *Objects* : while the *considerate* and *modest* Inquirer, hath a *large* Sphere of Motion, and the satisfaction of more *open* Light ; He sees *far*, and injoys the pleasure of surveying the *divers* Images of the Mind. But the *Opiniator* hath a *poor shrivel'd* Soul, that will but just hold his little Set of Thoughts : His Appetite after Knowledg, is satisfied with his few *Mushromes*, and neither knows nor thinks of any thing beyond his Cottage and his Rags.

I might say a great deal more to the shame of this folly, but what I have writ will be *enough* for the Capable and Ingenious ; and much *less* would have been *too much* for others.

And now when I look back upon the main Subject of these Papers, it appears so *vast* to my Thoughts, that me-thinks I have drawn but a *Cockle-shell* of Water from the *Ocean* : Whatever I look upon, within the *Amplitude* of *Heaven* and *Earth*, is evidence of Humane *Ignorance* : For all things are a *great Darkness* to us, and we are *so* to our selves : The *plainest* things are as *obscure*, as the most *confessedly mysterious* ; and the *Plants* we tread on are as much *above* us, as the *Stars* and *Heavens* : The things that *touch* us, are as *distant* from us as the *Poles*, and we are as much *Strangers* to *our selves*, as to the People of the *Indies*.   On review of which, me-thinks I could begin anew to represent the *imperfection* of our *Knowledg*, and the *vanity* of *bold Opinions*, which the Dogmatists themselves *demonstrate*, while each Disputer is *confident*, that the *others confidence* is vain, from which a third, with more reason, may conclude the *same* of the confidence of *both* : And one would think there should need no more to bring those assured Men to modest Acknowledgments, and more becomming Temper than *this*, That there is nothing about which the

Reason

Reason of Man is capable of being employed, but hath been the Subject of *Dispute*, and *diverse* apprehension : So that the Lord *Montaigne* hath observ'd, *Mankind is agreed in nothing, no not in this, That the Heavens are over us ;* Every Man almost differs from another, yea and every Man from himself; and yet every one is assured of his own *Schemes* of conjecture, though he cannot hold that Assurance but by this *proud* Absurdity, That *he alone is in the right, and all the rest of the World mistaken.* I say then, there being so much to be produced both from the *natural* and *moral* World, to the *shame* of *boasting Ignorance* ; I cannot reckon of what I have said but as an *imperfect* Offer at a Subject, to which I could not do right, without discoursing all Things : On which account I had resolv'd once to suffer this Trifle to pass out of Print and Memory : But then considering, that the *Instances* I had given of humane *Ignorance* were not only *clear* ones, but *such* also as are not *ordinarily* suspected ; from whence to our shortness in other things, 'tis an easie Inference ; I was thence induced to think it might be useful to promote that temper of Mind that is necessary to true Philosophy and right Knowledg.

F   OF

Notes to the introduction

1. M. Nicolson, "The Real Scholar Gypsy", *Yale Review,* New Series, XVIII, 1928, pp. 347–63.
2. *Plus Ultra,* London: 1668, pp. 142–43.
3. Traherne, *Centuries,* III: 36; *Centuries, Poems and Thanksgivings,* ed. H. M. Margoliouth. 2 vols., Oxford: 1958, I, p. 132.
4. Wood, *Athenae Oxonienses,* ed. Bliss, London: 1817, III, 1244.
5. Sextus Empiricus, *Outlines of Pyrrhonism,* I, 181: ed. with an English trans. Rev. R. G. Bury, 3 vols., London and New York: 1933–6, I, p. 103.
6. R. H. Popkin, *The History of Scepticism from Erasmus to Descartes,* rev. ed., Assen: 1964, p. 146.
7. Boyle, *The Works of the Honourable Robert Boyle,* ed. Thomas Birch, new ed., 6 vols., London: 1772, I, p. 303.
8. op. cit., IV, p. 42.
9. cf. *Boswell's Life of Johnson,* ed. G. B. Hill and L. F. Powell, 6 vols., Oxford: 1934, I, p. 205.
10. Hume, *Enquiries concerning the Human understanding,* etc. ed. L. A. Selby-Bigge, second ed., Oxford: 1902, p. 76.
11. *The Diary and Correspondence of Dr. John Worthington,* ed. J. Crossley, Chetham Society: 1847, I, p. 301.
12. White, *Exclusion,* London: 1665, p. 75.
13. J. I. Cope, *Joseph Glanvill, Anglican Apologist,* St. Louis: 1956, p. 108, n. 14.
14. White, *Exclusion,* sig. A2r.
15. *Conway Letters,* ed. M. Nicolson, New Haven: 1930, p. 194.
16. Thomas Birch, *History of the Royal Society*, London: I, 1756, pp. 500–1.
17. Birch, *History,* II, 1757, p. 197 n.

18. R. Parr, op. cit., p. 49: cf. W. F. Mitchell, *English Pulpit Oratory from Andrewes to Tillotson,* London: 1932, p. 229.
19. Bodleian Ms. Notebook. Locke f. 14, p. 139.
20. Locke, *An Essay concerning Human Understanding* (London: 1689), IV: 6: 11, ed. A. C. Fraser, 2 vols., Oxford: 1894, II, p. 262: cf. J. Gibson, *Locke's Theory of Knowledge,* London: 1917, pp. 257 f.
21. Locke, op. cit., III: 6: 9, ed. Fraser, II, p. 64.
22. Locke, op. cit., II: 32: 14–16: ed. Fraser, II, p. 521.
23. Locke, op. cit., II: 8: 7: ed. Fraser, I, p. 168.
24. Locke, op. cit., *Epistle to the Reader,* ed. Fraser, I, pp. 22–3.
25. Locke, op. cit., II: 13: 18: ed. Fraser, I, p. 229.
26. Locke, op. cit., *Epistle to the Reader,* ed. Fraser, I, p. 22.
27. Birch, *History,* I, p. 499.
28. Birch, op. cit., II, p. 7.
29. Sprat, *The History of the Royal Society,* London: 1667, p. 113.
30. Glanvill, *Plus Ultra,* London: 1668, pp. 84–5.
31. Glanvill, *An Essay Concerning Preaching,* London:1678, p.48. .
32. Descartes, *Works,* trans. Elizabeth S. Haldane and G. R. T. Ross, 2 vols., Cambridge: 1911–12, *passim.*
33. op. cit., I, pp. 239–40.
34. op. cit., I, p. 246.
35. op. cit., I, p. 247.
36. op. cit., I, p. 248.
37. 20 November 1629: *Oeuvres de Descartes,* ed. C. A. and P. Tannery, 12 vols., Paris: 1897–1913, I, pp. 80–82.
38. Locke, *An Essay concerning Human Understanding,* III: 4: 11, ed. A. C. Fraser, 2 vols., Oxford: 1894, II, p. 38.
39. op. cit., IV: 18: 3, ed. Fraser, II, pp. 416–7.
40. op. cit., III: 10: 34, ed. Fraser, II, p. 146.
41. op. cit., IV: 17: 4, ed. Fraser, II, p. 397.
42. Bacon, *Of the Advancement of Learning, Philosophical Works,* ed. J. M. Robertson, London and New York: 1905, pp. 90–91.

43. Coleridge, *Biographia Literaria,* ch. xiii, second edition, 2 vols., London: 1847, p. 298.
44. Locke, op. cit., II: 25: 8, ed. Fraser, I, p. 430.
45. Cope, *Joseph Glanvill,* p. 159.
46. D. Davie, *Articulate Energy,* London: 1955, pp. 97 ff.
47. J. Toland, *Christianity not Mysterious,* London: 1696, pp. 16– 17: cit. J. W. Yolton, *John Locke and the Way of Ideas,* London 1956, p. 120.
48. E. Gilson, *The Christian Philosophy of St. Thomas Aquinas,* trans. L. K. Shook, London: 1957, p. 227.
49. Hobbes, *Leviathan,* ed. A. R. Waller, Oxford: 1904, p. 1.
50. Glanvill, *Essays on several important subjects,* etc., London: 1676, Essay V, p. 5.
51. A. N. Whitehead, *Symbolism,* Cambridge: 1928, *passim.*
52. C. S. Lewis, *The Screwtape Letters,* new ed., London: 1961, p. 13.
53. Traherne, *Centuries,* III, 36–7; *Centuries, Poems and Thanksgivings,* ed. H. Margoliouth, 2 vols., Oxford: 1958, I, p. 132.

Bibliography

1. Manuscript sources:
   Locke, John. Bodleian Ms. Notebook. Locke f. 14.

2. Primary sources:
   Bacon, Francis. *The Proficience and Advancement of Learning,* London: 1605.
   Bacon, Francis. *The Philosophical Works of Francis Bacon,* ed. with an introduction by John M. Robertson, London and New York: 1905.
   Birch, Thomas. *The History of the Royal Society,* 4 vols., London: 1756–7.
   Boswell. *Boswell's Life of Johnson,* ed. G. B. Hill and L. F. Powell, 6 vols., Oxford: 1934.
   Boyle, Robert. *The Works of the Honourable Robert Boyle,* ed., with the life of Boyle, by Thomas Birch, new ed. 6 vols., London: 1772.
   Browne, Sir Thomas. *Pseudodoxia Epidemica.* London: 1646.
   Browne, Sir Thomas. *The Works of Sir Thomas Browne,* ed. Sir Geoffrey Keynes, 6 vols., London: 1928–31.
   Burton, Robert. *The Anatomy of Melancholy,* London: 1621.
   Descartes, Rene. *Oeuvres de Descartes,* ed. Charles Adam and Paul Tannery, 12 vols., Paris: 1897–1913.
   Descartes, Rene. *The Philosophical Works of Descartes,* trans. Elizabeth S. Haldane and G. R. T. Ross, Cambridge: 1911–12.
   Sextus Empiricus. *Sextus Empiricus,* ed. with an English trans. by Rev. R. G. Bury, Loeb Classical Library, 3 vols., London and New York: 1933–6, *Outlines of Pyrrhonism,* Vol. I.
   Glanvill, Joseph. *The Vanity of Dogmatizing*: or, Confidence in Opinions, London: 1661.

Glanvill, Joseph. *Lux Orientalis*, or An Enquiry into the Opinion of the Eastern Sages, concerning the Praeexistence of Souls, London: 1662.

Glanvill, Joseph. *Scepsis Scientifica*: or, Confest Ignorance, the Way to Science, London: 1665.

Glanvill, Joseph. *Plus Ultra*: or, The Progress and Advancement of Knowledge since the Days of Aristotle, London: 1668.

ΛΟΓΟΥ ΘΡΗΣΚΕΙΑ: or, A Seasonable Recommendation and Defence of Reason; in the Affairs of Religion, London: 1670.

Glanvill, Joseph. *Essays on Several Important Subjects in Philosophy and Religion,* London: 1676.

Glanvill, Joseph. *An Essay concerning Preaching*: written for the direction of a young divine, London: 1678.

Glanvill, Joseph. *Sadducismus Triumphatus,* London: 1681.

Glanvill, Joseph. *The Vanity of Dogmatizing,* reprinted in facsimile with a bibliographical note by Moody E. Prior, New York, Facsimile Text Society: 1931. Series 3, vol. 6.

Glanvill, Joseph. *Scepsis Scientifica,* reprinted with an introductory essay on the life and works of Glanvill by John Owen, London: 1885.

Hobbes, Thomas. *Leviathan,* or the Matter, Form, and Power of a Commonwealth, Ecclesiastical and Civil, London: 1651.

Hobbes, Thomas. *Leviathan,* ed. A. R. Waller, Oxford: 1904.

Hume, David. *Enquiries Concerning the Human Understanding & Concerning the Principles of Morals,* ed. with introduction by L. A. Selby-Bigge, second ed., Oxford: 1902.

Locke, John. *An Essay Concerning Human Understanding,* London: 1689.

Locke, John. *An Essay Concerning Human Understanding,* ed. A. C. Fraser, 2 vols., Oxford: 1894.

Sprat, Thomas. *The History of the Royal Society,* with verses addressed to the Society by A. Cowley, London: 1667.

Sprat, Thomas. *The History of the Royal Society,* ed. J. I. Cope and H. W. Jones, London and St. Louis: 1959.

Toland, John. *Christianity not Mysterious*, London: 1696

Traherne, Thomas. *Centuries, Poems and Thanksgivings*, 2 vols., ed. H. M. Margoliouth, Oxford: 1958.

White, Thomas. *Sciri*, sive Sceptices et scepticorum a iure disputationis exclusio, London: 1663.

White, Thomas. *Exclusion of Scepticks from all Title to Dispute*, London: 1665.

Wilkins, John. *An Essay towards a Real Character and a Philosophical Language*, London: 1668.

Wood, Anthony à. *Athenae Oxonienses*, 2 vols., London: 1691—2,

Wood, Anthony à. *Athenae Oxonienses*, ed. Philip Bliss, third edition, with additions and continuation, 4 vols., London: 1817—20.

Worthington, Dr. John. *The Diary and Correspondence of Dr. John Worthington*, 2 vols., ed. James Crossley, Chetham Society, Manchester: 1847, 1886.

3. Secondary sources:

Bennett, Joan. "An Aspect of the Evolution of Seventeenth-Century Prose", *Review of English Studies*, vol. XVII, no. 67, July 1941, pp. 281—92.

Bredvold, Louis. *The Intellectual Milieu of John Dryden*, Studies in Some Aspects of Seventeenth-century thought, University of Michigan Press, Language & Literature, vol. 12: 1957.

Brooks, Cleanth and Wimsatt, William K. *Literary Criticism, A Short History*, New York: 1957.

Burtt, E. A. *The Metaphysical Foundations of Modern Physical Science*, etc., with a bibliography, second ed., London: 1932.

Cohen, J. "On the Project of a Universal Character", *Mind*, N.S. LXIII, January, 1954, pp. 49—63.

Coleridge, S. T. C. *Biographia Literaria*, 2 vols., second ed., London: 1847.

Coleridge, S. T. C. *Biographia Literaria*, ed. George Watson, Everyman's Library, London and New York: 1956.

Cope, J. I. *Joseph Glanvill, Anglican Apologist*, St. Louis: 1956. Washington University Studies.

Croll, M. W. "The Baroque Style in Prose", pp. 456 ff. in *Studies in English Philology. A Miscellany in honor of Frederick Klaeber*, edited by Kemp Malone and Martin B. Ruud, Minneapolis: 1929.

Davie, Donald. *Articulate Energy*, An Inquiry Into the Syntax of English Poetry, London: 1955.

Gibson, J. *Locke's Theory of Knowledge and its Historical Relations*, Cambridge: 1917.

Gilson, Etienne. *The Christian Philosophy of St. Thomas Aquinas*, trans. L. K. Shook, London: 1957.

Greenslet, Ferris. *Joseph Glanvill*, A Study in English Thought and Letters of the Seventeenth Century, New York: 1900. Columbia University Studies in English.

Jones, R. F. *The Seventeenth Century*, Studies in the History of English Thought and Literature from Bacon to Pope by R. F. Jones, and others writing in his honor, Stanford: 1951.

Lewis, C. S. *The Screwtape Letters*, and Screwtape Proposes a Toast, new ed., with a new preface, London: 1961.

Mitchell, W. F. *English Pulpit Oratory from Andrewes to Tillotson*, A Study of its literary aspects, London: 1932.

Nicolson, Marjorie Hope. "The Real Scholar Gypsy", *Yale Review*, New Series, XVIII, 1928, pp. 347–63.

Nicolson, Marjorie Hope. ed., *Conway Letters*, The Correspondence of Anne, Viscountess Conway, Henry More, and their friends, 1642–1684, collected from ms. sources, with a biographical account, New Haven: 1930.

Popkin, R. H. "Joseph Glanvill: A Precursor of David Hume", *Journal of the History of Ideas*, vol. XIV, January 1955, pp. 292–297.

Popkin, R. H. *The History of Scepticism from Erasmus to Descartes*, rev. ed., Assen: 1964.

Whitehead, A. N. *Symbolism*: Its meaning and effect, Barbour-Page Lectures, University of Virginia, 1927, Cambridge: 1928.

Wiley, Margaret. *The Subtle Knot,* Creative Scepticism in seventeenth century England, London: 1952.

Willey, Basil. *The Seventeenth Century Background,* Studies in the thought of the age in relation to poetry and religion, London: 1934.

Williamson, George. *The Senecan Amble,* a Study in prose from Bacon to Collier, London: 1951.

Yolton, John W. *John Locke and the Way of Ideas,* London: 1956.

SOCIETY & THE VICTORIANS

General Editors: John Spiers
and Cecil Ballantine

This series makes available again important works by and about
the Victorians. Each of the titles chosen has been either out of
print and difficult to find, or exceedingly rare for many years.
A few titles, although available in the secondhand market, are
needed in modern, critical editions and the series attempts to
meet this demand. It is a subsidiary intention to call attention
to some books less well known and unjustly neglected.

Acknowledged authorities in their respective fields normally
provide new introductions, textual and bibliographical notes.
Texts will be reprinted by photolithography from first editions,
or from later editions where these have special significance.
Each book will be reproduced in its original size.

Available now:

GEORGE GISSING: *Isabel Clarendon* (London, 1886,
2 volumes). Edited by Dr. Pierre Coustillas, University of
Lille. With a new introduction of 18,000 words, textual
and bibliographical notes and Gissing's own unpublished
revisions. 2 vols. £5. 5. 0, $12.60. SBN 901759 00 7.

Series prospectus available free.